Standards, Schooling and Education

Standards, Schooling and Education

A Reader edited by Alex Finch and
Peter Scrimshaw for the Contemporary
Issues in Education Course
at The Open University

HODDER AND STOUGHTON

in association with
The Open University Press

British Library Cataloguing in Publication Data

Standards, schooling and education.
1. Education – Addresses, essays, lectures
I. Finch, Alex   II. Scrimshaw, Peter
III. Open University
370′.8   LB41

ISBN 0 340 25757 1

Printed and bound in Great Britain for
Hodder and Stoughton Educational,
a division of Hodder and Stoughton Ltd,
Mill Road, Dunton Green, Sevenoaks, Kent, by
Richard Clay (The Chaucer Press) Ltd, Bungay, Suffolk

Contents

Contents

Preface

This Reader is one of two collections of papers published in connection with the Open University course E200, entitled 'Contemporary Issues in Education'. The course is primarily intended for all those interested in education, including parents, school governors and administrators.

Because this Reader is only part of a total learning package, it does not claim to offer a complete picture of the issues with which it deals. Nevertheless, we believe that there are many connections between the papers included, and our introductory papers are designed to bring these connections into prominence.

It is not necessary to become an undergraduate of the Open University in order to take E200. Further information about the course may be obtained by writing to: The Admissions Office, The Open University, P.O. Box 48, Walton Hall, Milton Keynes, MK7 6AB.

General Introduction

Standards and values in education

Controversy over standards in education has been a feature of political and academic debate throughout the post-war period in Britain. Like most educational controversies this one involves far more complex issues than might appear at first sight.

On one level the debate appears to be fairly straightforward, centring around the question of how the educational efficiency of schools can be improved and monitored. Given agreed aims for education, it might be argued, the question of how to maintain standards is a purely technical one. But it is clear that in contemporary Britain any reasonably detailed statement of aims of education (or at least of their relative importance) is itself going to be controversial. Thus the debate is in part not simply about how to improve standards, but about which changes constitute real improvement and what priorities should be given to various categories of aims, given that not all of them can be fully achieved in practice.

One way of approaching this question of priorities is to ask what it is worthwhile for an individual in our culture to learn.

A common view is that an educated person is one who has reached a certain basic level of competence in each of a variety of areas. Although the precise specification of these areas is itself controversial, it is sufficient for our present purposes to identify the promotion of intellectual, social, artistic and physical development as at least some of the general aims of education for which a strong case might be made. But to say that there might be agreement on that much hardly resolves the controversies involved.

To begin with, there is the matter of deciding upon the best balance between these categories of aims. It is often said that a good education is one which develops the individual's potential to the full. This assertion is, if you think about it, no more than a comforting vacuity. Any individual, except possibly someone with severe brain-damage, has the potential to learn a tremendous amount. He or she can, for instance, master any one of the 3,000 languages in use in the world today, develop any of a vast range of physical skills and capacities, and reach an above average level of attainment in some selection from a wide variety of practical, scientific, or artistic competences. What limits the actual learning of anyone is not their learning potential but the basic fact of human mortality. Quite apart from any other external restrictions created by societal factors, death intervenes before any of us gets beyond even the most basic exploitation of our real capacities. It is because this is so that we are faced with the perplexing problem of choosing (for ourselves or others) a limited range of things to learn. The problem is not identifying what someone can learn, but selecting out what it is most important to learn. It is partly because there is significant disagreement on what is important that there is controversy about what the detailed aims of education should be.

Even if we stick to the crude distinctions drawn earlier between intellectual, social, artistic and physical development, it is clear that there is no current consensus on what constitutes the right balance between these. Furthermore, within each of these categories there is ample room for dispute over the relative importance of different sub-groups of aims. Should scientific understanding, for instance, be given greater emphasis today, when this necessarily creates a pressure to downgrade the relative importance of, say, historical or religious understanding? Even within a single area such as science, what is the right balance between, for instance, theoretical and applied science, or different disciplines?

If the argument about helping individuals to fulfil their potential cannot resolve these questions for us, what about an appeal to the social nature of man? Given that we are social beings, may not the best education be that which prepares us to live in and contribute to society?

Like the argument about individual potential, this claim gains most of its initial attraction from its vacuity. We may all safely agree with it, provided that we do not go on to ask what sort of living, what sort of contribution and what sort of society we are in favour of. Yet it is precisely these more detailed questions which need to be answered before we can establish specific educational priorities. Do we, for instance, want to prepare people to maintain our present society, or to change it, in whole or in part? If partial change is favoured, what needs changing and why?

Once we ponder these questions the appeal of the societal argument fades. What constitutes improving society is as controversial a matter as the educational priorities it is intended to justify. To mention only some dimensions, in our culture different people might favour a society which moved towards being more cooperative *or* competitive, community-minded *or* individualistic, culturally homogeneous *or* culturally differentiated, socially mobile *or* socially immobile, economically stable *or* economically expanding.

To sum up, we are suggesting that decisions on educational priorities rest in turn on a complex set of moral and social preferences and beliefs about what is best for individuals and society as a whole. Thus, because these questions are controversial, educational priorities will also be continually open to debate.

How then is this relevant to the controversy over standards in schools?

Firstly it may be that sometimes what appear to be debates about *falling* standards in schools are really about *changing* standards in schools. For instance, the call to maintain standards in basic skills in secondary schools can be read as at least partly an implicit rejection of moves to give aesthetic and emotional developments a higher priority. Secondly, we must note that the particular role of the schools in the total education of individuals is also controversial. It is, for example, quite possible for someone to argue that sex education should not be provided in schools precisely because they believe it to be too important for parents to leave it to teachers.

Having said all this, it remains the case that the standards debate is not only about what to teach but also about how to do it effectively.

In the post-war period the controversy over standards within the schooling system has been conducted at three interrelated levels. First, it has involved changes at the national and local levels of the system. A notable development here has been the extension of the scope of public examinations to include a greater and greater proportion of school leavers, together with the creation of new forms of examination, organization and techniques through the development of the CSE boards. On the other hand the phasing out of the eleven-plus examination during the 1970s marked a countervailing trend which was not without its effects upon the primary schools. However, this movement away from 'examinations' at primary level appears (1980) to be going into reverse, with various kinds of nationally and locally sponsored forms of monitoring of pupil progress making a noticeable reappearance.

Secondly, there has been the almost continual ebb and flow of public and educational opinion concerning the best way of organizing the local provision of schooling. Something of the complexity of these changes may be seen by noting the move from selective to comprehensive patterns, the emergence in some areas of various kinds of middle schools and the debate over the merits of neighbourhood schools as against the availability of genuine parental choice. Superimposed upon these discussions have been related debates over what size of school is best and over the role (if any) to be allocated to private schools within the overall system.

Thirdly, there have been many changes made at the classroom level, too. These also have been drawn into the general controversy over standards. The relative merits of streaming, setting, banding and mixed ability teaching have all been much argued. So too have the effects upon pupils of what are crudely labelled the traditional and progressive methods of teaching and learning, together with other developments such as vertical grouping and various systems of pastoral and counselling provision in the schools.

In part, difference of view concerning the desirability of these organizational and structural changes can be explained in terms of the points already made about the central role of discrepancies in values in the standards debate. Apparently purely organizational decisions in education have a way of influencing, often rather unexpectedly, what is learned as well as how and when. But values enter into these matters in another way. For decisions about school and classroom organization will also have consequences for who learns, how much, as well as what it is they learn. In a society divided upon the desirability of aiming if necessary to promote the excellence of the best at some cost to the standards achieved by the rest, organizational patterns at every level are likely to be politically contentious. It is here that we find the confused ideological interface between the issues of standards, equality and social justice. Nor is this aspect of educational controversy a clearcut conflict between élitists and egalitarians, each struggling to promote educational policies which will create or sustain the distribution of power status and cultural opportunities within society that they favour. For one thing, many intermediate positions on the relative importance that should be given to different social values can be (and are) held, creating political groups whose commitments span the divide between the two extremes. Furthermore, the empirical evidence on the societal effects of education is complex and incomplete, creating ample opportunities for divergences in policy proposals, even amongst those sharing broadly similar social values.

So far we have assumed that the relevance of schooling to a person's later life is a function of what he or she actually learns. Knowledge, as the saying goes, is power, and its possession is also a legitimate source of prestige and respect from others. But this view is itself simplistic. In our society (as in any other) different kinds of knowledge provide different kinds and degrees of power, and are accorded different levels of respect. Indeed to speak of 'society' as an homogeneous entity in this way is itself too simple, for the sort of knowledge one group values another may not.

Furthermore, we cannot assume that what is learned is always what others believe to have been learned. The whole apparatus of marking, examining and certification is interposed between learning and public recognition of that learning. Yet this apparatus itself is always liable to provide only a distorted and selective picture of what a learner really knows. If it is solely by the results of this assessment that others judge the learner's capacities then (at best) a degree of error is unavoidable. In addition the existence of some sort of assessment system (which is arguably unavoidable in a highly bureaucratized society) may itself partially displace the attention of both learners and teachers, directing them towards pursuing the paper shadow of education rather than its real substance. It is at least arguable that the increasing role of formalized assessment in schooling is as likely to corrupt educational standards as it is to sustain them.

Finally, we should look briefly at the ways in which these issues link up with the emerging debate over educational control and accountability. The obvious linkage can be simply stated: the purpose of systems of accountability and control is to check upon and thus in some way improve educational standards. But as we might expect in the light of the earlier discussion, there is more to it all than this.

To begin with, different patterns of control distribute power over the educational system in different ways. Given that various groups involved have more or less extensively divergent educational priorities, this sucks the accountability issue into the political debate too. It also raises in an acute form the question of the relative rights and competences of parents, elected representatives, professional educators and that enigmatic entity 'society' to make decisions on educational matters.

The issues raised in this introduction, together with others interrelated with them are explored in more depth in the remainder of this collection. Philosophical analysis, empirical studies of various kinds, reasoned statements of political and educational preferences are all relevant to the debate, and all are represented (albeit necessarily in selection only) in the pages that follow. Even a careful reading of such a selection as this cannot enable the reader to reach unassailable conclusions on these matters. However, we believe that the collection will have fulfilled a useful purpose if it reveals something of the issues involved, and enables readers to see more clearly the nature of the further evidence and arguments needed to move towards a reasoned position.

Part One

Education and values

In the title of this collection we have assumed that schooling (by which we mean those activities which go on in educational institutions at all levels) is not necessarily equivalent to education. In the opening paper in this part of the collection R. S. Peters provides a philosophical analysis which helps to explicate this distinction.

Peters suggests that to think of someone as being educated is usually to accept that his form of life is a desirable one, showing him as having a widely based knowledge and an understanding of the general principles that lie behind this knowledge. In the case of the educated man, this knowledge and understanding, Peters suggests, must also be something which directs and informs his actions, giving them some overall shape and coherence.

If we accept this account as accurately representing our own conception of education then, Peters argues, we can identify certain ways of systematically promoting a person's education each having distinctive strengths and limitations. While noting that many things are simply picked up from teachers by learners, without either being fully aware of the fact, he argues that the teacher's efforts should be directed towards the conscious promotion of education through training, instruction, the teaching of principles, the transmission of critical thought, and ordered but non-authoritarian discussion.

A formal analysis of this sort must, of course, leave many questions open. It does not, for example, prescribe in any close sense what specific sorts of values and ways of life an educated person will be committed to. On the other hand, such an analysis can provide us with a helpful framework within which to compare and criticize more substantive educational recommendations. It also immediately makes clear that schooling may not, in practice, promote education in the full sense, or indeed always be intended so to do. Much schooling, for instance, is limited in the contribution it makes to promoting critical thought or a coherent overall view of life, as we shall see more fully in Part Two.

However, the remaining contributors to this part of the collection very largely accept the broad ideal of education that Peters' analysis identifies. Where they differ is in the kinds of values and world views that they seek to promote, and in the role they see for schooling in contributing to educational development. Some of them in addition also point out the importance of education in promoting societal purposes, as distinct from contributing to the individual's own development considered in isolation.

But what things, we must then ask, are valuable to learn? And who can (and should) be expected to learn them? And which of these things should be learned in schools?

A social democratic answer is (very obliquely) embodied in Crosland's views on comprehensives. He argues that these are valuable institutions because, compared to the selective system,

- they are more socially just;
- they are efficient, both for increasing achievement levels of individuals and (by so doing) benefiting our society economically;
- they need not lower the level of achievement of the bright;
- they promote social cohesion and weaken class barriers by increasing social mobility.

Maude's objections to this position are that it 'levels down' achievement and creates the illusion that this has not been done by pretending that standards in institutions are the same when they are not, and by replacing academic learning by social education as a soft option.

Like the others, Freire agrees that education cannot be neutral. But he would see Crosland's position as only reformist, protecting the infrastructure of our unjust and élitist society by surface reforms. The basic choices are between educating for domestication (to fit into the society) or to develop critical thought. The first choice is implied in Crosland's acceptance of the importance of selecting and preparing pupils for roles in society and of an objective of creating social cohesion between what Freire sees as totally incompatible social classes. Maude, while supporting a meritocratic competition approach, assumes a 'banking' concept of knowledge which Freire rejects.

For Freire, knowledge is both discovered and created by the learner. It is the teacher's role to engage in open debate (dialectic) with him, not to assume that it is the teacher's right to set the learner's aims.

Freire's experience has been in South American societies in which class divisions are much more rigid and oppressive than in Britain; thus his ideological position is a very definite one. Against this, he (like the young Marx) saw a change in individual awareness (or the growth of critical consciousness) as a major priority. But many Marxists see this emphasis as at least partially incorrect, because it ignores both the constraints placed upon the individual by the power structure of society, and the fact that this power structure remains the same even if there has been some change in the awareness of individuals within the society concerned.

Simon's position is an intermediate one here. He argues that for Marxists (at least those of his own persuasion) the crucial issue in education is to ensure a general education for all pupils, based upon discipline and structured but active learning. This requires resisting claims that some pupils are incapable of such learning, and the attempts of some radicals to divert their efforts into community curricula, child-centred learning, or anarchist-inspired dreams of deschooling society. Thus, like Maude, he favours hard learning and disciplined teachers, but believes *all* pupils are capable of real intellectual achievement.

Finally, the paper by Barnett which concludes Part One presents a uitable counterpoint to that by Peters from which we began. Barnett sees he major role of education as being the development in individuals of a apability to tackle the practical situations of life. In his paper he is entrally concerned with the technological capabilities (or lack of them) of he British, and the impact of this lack upon our chances of increased conomic growth.

In an historical survey of British educational attitudes stretching back nto the nineteenth century Barnett sees the root of the problem to lie in a commitment to a conception of the educated man that saw the development of the cultural, moral and religious virtues of the Victorian public school as the ideal at which to aim. This commitment is still, he argues, too much with us, in a period when he believes we need to adjust the basic values of our society and education to give a greater emphasis to industrial success.

1.1 What is an educational process?

R. S. Peters

Introduction

In exploring the concept of education a territory is being entered where there are few signposts. To use Ryle's phrase, the 'logical geography' of concepts in the area of education has not yet been mapped.* This feature of the field of education was vividly brought home to me in the autumn of 1963 when I was working on my Inaugural Lecture on *Education as Initiation*, and was unable to unearth any previous explicit attempt to demarcate the concept of 'education'. It is not surprising, therefore, that in presenting at the start what amounts to a bird's eye view of the contours of this territory, I have to rely mainly on my own previous attempt to map it.

1 The task-achievement analysis of 'education'

Any such survey must start with the observation that 'education' is a concept which is not very close to the ground. By this I mean that it is not a concept like 'red' which picks out a simple quality, like 'horse' which picks out an object, or like 'running' or 'smiling' which pick out observable occurrences. We do not ask, 'Are you instructing him in algebra or are you educating him in algebra?' as if these were two alternative processes. But we might ask, 'Are you educating him by instructing him in algebra?' 'Education', in other words refers to no particular process; rather it encapsulates criteria to which any one of a family of processes must conform. In this respect it is rather like 'reform'. 'Reform' picks out no particular process. People can be reformed, perhaps, by preventive detention, by reading the Bible, or by the devotion of a loving wife. In a similar way people can be educated by reading books, by exploring their environment, by travel and conversation – even by talk and chalk in a classroom. The concepts of 'reform' and 'education' have proper application if these processes satisfy certain criteria. 'Education' and 'reform' are not part of the furniture of the earth or mind; they are more like stamps of approval issued by *Good Housekeeping* proclaiming that furniture has come up to certain standards.

How then are we to conceive of processes by means of which such standards are to be achieved? In my Inaugural Lecture I attacked mis-

* Editors' Note: This was written in 1967; R. S. Peters may not think this to be true in the 1980s.

Source: PETERS, R. S. (ed) (1967) *The Concept of Education*. London: Routledge and Kegan Paul, pp. 1–23.

ading models which provide pictures of what goes on in terms of shaping
aterial according to a specification, or of allowing children to 'grow'. I
entioned in a footnote, which I did not have time to develop, that a much
ore adequate way of conceiving what goes on, which provides a *rationale*
r my notion of education as initiation, is to regard processes of education
, tasks relative to achievements. This accounts for the feature of educa-
on which I rather laboured: that its standards are intrinsic not extrinsic
it. This task-achievement analysis I now propose to explain.

Aristotle made the point long ago in relation to performances such as
earning' and 'inferring', that the end is built into the concepts. Ryle has
ade it more recently in relation to activities such as 'looking' and
unning'. When a man finds something that he has lost or wins a race, he
oes not indulge in something different from looking or running, neither
oes he produce something or reach an end which is extrinsic to the
ctivity in which he is engaged. He merely succeeds in it. He achieves the
andard or attains the end which is internal to the activity and which
ives it point. In a similar way a man who is educated is a man who has
ucceeded in relation to certain tasks on which he and his teacher have
een engaged for a considerable period of time. Just as 'finding' is the
chievement relative to 'looking', so 'being educated' is the achievement
elative to a family of tasks which we call processes of education.

'Education' is, of course, different in certain respects from the examples
f achievements that Ryle gives. To start with 'education' like 'teaching'
an be used as both a task and an achievement verb.[1] Teachers can work
way at teaching without success, and still be teaching; but there is a
ense, also, in which teaching someone something implies success. 'I
aught the boy the ablative absolute construction' implies that I was
uccessful in my task. But I can also say 'I taught him Latin for years, but
e learnt nothing.' Similarly I can work away at educating people, with-
ut the implication that I or they achieve success in the various tasks
vhich are engaged in; but if I talk of them as 'educated' there is an
mplication of success.

But whose success are we talking about? That of the teacher or of the
earner? This is tantamount to asking to whose tasks the achievements
vhich constitute 'being educated' are relative, those of the teacher or those
of the learner. Obviously both are usually involved, but it is important to
ealize that the tasks of the teacher could not be characterized unless we
ad a notion of the tasks of the learner. For whereas 'learning' could be
characterized without introducing the notion of 'teaching', 'teaching'
could not be characterized without the notion of 'learning'. The tasks of
he teacher consist in the employment of various methods to get learning
processes going. These processes of learning in their turn cannot be
characterized without reference to the achievements in which they culmi-
nate. For to learn something *is* to come up to some standard, to succeed in
some respect. So the achievement must be that of the learner in the end.
The teacher's success, in other words, can only be defined in terms of that

of the learner. This presumably is the logical truth dormant in the saying that all education is self-education. This is what makes the notion of 'initiation' an appropriate one to characterize an educational situation; for a learner is 'initiated' by another into something which he has to master, know, or remember. 'Education' picks out processes by means of which people get started on the road to such achievements.

2 The moral requirements of 'education'

The second way in which 'education' is different from ordinary cases of tasks and achievements is that it is inseparable from judgments of value. It is, as I have pointed out, a logical truth that any method of education employed by a teacher must put the pupil in a situation where he is learning, where some sort of task is presented to him. But a teacher might try to condition children to 'pick up' certain things without their realizing that they were picking anything up. In saying that this is not a process of education we would be implying that this was morally bad, because conditions of wittingness and voluntariness on the part of the pupil were missing; for we regard it as morally unjustifiable to treat others in this way. To say that we are educating people commits us, in other words, to morally legitimate procedures. Often such minimal moral demands, which are connected with respect for persons, are further extended to exclude procedures such as giving children orders, which is thought by some to involve some sort of moral indignity. Discouragement of individual choice would be another procedure which many might condemn as being morally reprehensible. They might express their disapproval by saying that this was not 'education'.

The way in which moral considerations enter into the achievement aspects of education is clearer than the way in which they enter into the task aspect. For it is obvious enough that the achievements or states of mind that give content to the notion of an educated man must be regarded as valuable. Finding a thimble that has been hidden is a Rylean type of achievement: but it is a trivial one. The achievements involved in education cannot be of this type. For if something is to count as 'education', what is learnt must be regarded as worth-while just as the manner in which it is learnt must be regarded as morally unobjectionable; for not all learning is 'educational' in relation to the content of what is learnt. If it were we might have periods on the timetable devoted to astrology and to Bingo and homilies by headmasters on the art of torture.

In this respect, also, 'education' is like 'reform'; for it would be as much of a contradiction to say 'My son has been educated but has learnt nothing of value' as it would be to say 'My son has been reformed but has changed in no way for the better.' This, by the way, is a purely conceptual point. The connexion between 'education' and what is valuable can be made

.plicit without commitment to content. It is a *further question* what the ᵣrticular standards are in virtue of which achievements are thought to be ῾value and what grounds there might be for claiming that these are the ⱦrrect ones. It may well be that arguments can be produced to show why .tional men should value some standards rather than others; but at the .oment there is no such established harmony. So when people speak of ᵈducation' it is essential to know what their standards of valuation are in ᵗder to ascertain the aspect under which some process or state of mind is ᵉing commended.

This connexion with commendation does not, of course, prevent us ᵒm speaking of 'poor' education when a worth-while job has been ⱦotched or of 'bad education' when we think that much of what people are ῾orking at is not worth-while, though it is a nice question to determine at ῾hat point we pass from saying that something is 'bad education' to ᵤᵧing that it is not education at all. Neither does it prevent us from using ᵤe word in a purely external descriptive way when we speak of an ᵈducational system' just as we can use the term 'moral' of someone else's ᵓde without committing ourselves to the judgments of value of those ⱦhose code it is. Anthropologists can talk of the moral system of a tribe; so ᵘlso can we talk as sociologists or economists of the educational system of a ᵓmmunity. In employing the concept in this derivative sense we need not ᵗhink that what is going on is worth-while, but members of the society, ᵥhose system it is, must think it is.

Talk of 'education', then, from the inside of a form of life, is inseparable ⱦrom talk of what is worth-while, but with the additional notion written ᵢnto it that what is worth-while has been or is being transmitted in a ᵐorally unobjectionable manner. But under this general aegis of desira-ᵇility 'education' picks out no one type of task or achievement. People ᵈiffer in their estimates of desirability. They therefore differ in the ᵉmphasis which they place on achievement and states of mind that can be ᵗhought of as desirable. This diversity is what makes talk of 'aims of ᵈducation' apposite; for people who talk in this way are not suggesting ᵤims extrinsic to education: they are enunciating their priorities in giving ᵓontent to the notion of an 'educated man'.

To take a parallel: it might be said that the aim of reform was to make ᵐen better. This is harmless enough provided that it is realized that 'make ᵐen better' is built into the concept of 'reform'. But something more ᵖspecific might be said such as: the aim of reform is to encourage a sense of ʳesponsibility. This might be countered by saying that the aim of reform is ᵗo get people to have respect for persons. Such a dispute would be an ᵃttempt to give precise content to the general notion of 'making a man ᵇetter'. Similarly discussions about the aims of education are attempts to ᵍive more precise content to the notion of the 'educated man' or of a man ᵂho has achieved some desirable state of mind. Is moral education more ᵢmportant, for instance, than the development of scientific understanding? This might have particular point when talking about some of the children

referred to in the Newsom Report. Or perhaps we talk about 'wholenes
in order to emphasize all-round excellence and sensitivity. Or we ma
want to stress the importance of cutting the coat of what is worth-whi
according to the cloth of individual aptitude. Talk of developing th
potentialities of the individual is then appropriate. Such 'aims' point ou
specific achievements and states of mind which give content to the forma
notion of 'the educated man' which is a shorthand for summarizing ou
notion of a form of life which is worth-while enough to deserve bein
handed on from generation to generation.[2]

So much, then, for the moral aspect of 'education' as a family of task
and achievements which make it rather different from the simpler case
used by Ryle to illustrate this way of conceiving certain classes of inten
tional activities. I want now to consider other criteria of 'being educate
as an achievement which have to do with knowledge and understanding.
shall then deal with the tasks which lead up to achievements falling unde
these criteria.

3 The achievement aspect of 'education'

We do not call a person educated who has simply mastered a skill ever
though the skill may be very worth-while, like that of moulding clay. For a
man to be educated it is insufficient that he should possess a 'know-how' o
knack. He must also know that certain things are the case. He must have
developed some sort of conceptual scheme at least in the area in which he
is skilled and must have organized a fair amount of information by means
of it.

But even this is not enough; for we would be disinclined to call a man
who was merely well-informed an educated man. To be educated requires
also some understanding of principles, of the 'reason why' of things. The
Spartans, for instance, were militarily and morally trained. They knew
how to fight; they knew what was right and wrong; they were possessed of
a certain kind of lore, which stood them in good stead in stock situations.
They were thus able to comb their hair with aplomb when the Persians
were approaching at Thermopylæ. But we could not say that they had
received a military or moral education; for they had never been encouraged to understand the principles underlying their code. They had
mastered the content of forms of thought and behaviour without ever
grasping or being able to operate with the principles that could enable
them to manage on their own. They were notorious for falling victims to
potentates, priests, and profligates on leaving their natural habitat where
their code was part of the order of things. Failure to grasp underlying
principles leads to unintelligent rule of thumb application of rules, to the
inability to make exceptions on relevant grounds and to bewilderment
when confronted with novel situations.

Given, then, that being educated implies the possession of knowledge,

ut rules out *mere* knowledge, in that it also requires understanding of
rinciples, could a man be educated whose knowledge and understanding
confined to one sphere – mathematics, for instance? There is a strong
iclination to deny that we could call a man 'educated' who had only
eveloped his awareness and understanding in such a limited way; for our
otion of an educated man suggests a more all-round type of development.
Vhen we say that people go to a university to become educated and not
ist to become scientists, from what does this antithesis derive? Does it
erive from the concept of 'education' or from our underlying valuations
bout the constituents of the good life which ought to be passed on which
icludes e.g. aesthetic and moral awareness as well as scientific under-
:anding? Certainly 'training' always suggests confinement. People are
·ained *for* jobs, *as* mechanics, and *in* science. No one can be trained in a
eneral sort of way. But this lack of specificity is just what is suggested by
:ducation'. It is not clear to me where this is due to the concept of
:ducation' itself or to our refusal to grant that what is worth-while could
e confined to one form of awareness. To pose the problem succinctly: is
1e saying 'Education is of the whole man' a conceptual truth in that
:ducation' rules out onesided development? Or is it an expression of our
1oral valuations about what is worth-while?

There is no necessity, for the purposes of this article, to decide between
hese two alternatives, as it has no particular implications for what is to
ount as an educational process. There is, however, another aspect of the
nowledge requirement built into 'education' which has implications.
This is its attitudinal aspect. By this I mean that the knowledge which a
nan must possess to qualify as being educated must be built into his way
·f looking at things. It cannot be merely inert. It is possible for a man to
now a lot of history, in the sense that he can give correct answers to
uestions in classrooms and in examinations, without ever developing a
iistorical sense. For instance he might fail to connect his knowledge of the
ndustrial Revolution with what he sees when visiting Manchester or the
Velsh Valleys. We might describe such a man as 'knowledgeable' but we
vould never describe him as 'educated'; for 'education' implies that a
nan's outlook is transformed by what he knows.

It is this requirement built into 'education' that makes the usual con-
rast between 'education' and 'life' rather ridiculous. Those who make it
isually have in mind a contrast between the activities that go on in
:lassrooms and studies and those that go on in industry, politics, agricul-
:ure, and rearing a family. The curriculum of schools and universities is
:hen criticized because, as the knowledge passed on is not instrumental in
iny obvious sense to 'living', it is assumed that it is 'academic' or relevant
·nly to the classroom, cloister, study, and library. What is forgotten is that
activities like history, literary appreciation, and philosophy, unlike Bingo
ind billiards, involve forms of thought and awareness that can and should
ipill over into things that go on outside, and transform them. For they are
:oncerned with the explanation, evaluation and imaginative exploration

of forms of life. As a result of them what is called 'life' develops differen dimensions. In schools and universities there is concentration on th development of this determinant of our form of life. The problem of th educator is to pass on this knowledge and understanding in such a wa that they develop a life of their own in the minds of others and transforn how they see the world, and hence how they feel about it.

There is another element in what I have called the 'attitudinal aspect' the sort of knowledge which is built into the concept of 'being educatec [. . .]. Such knowledge must not be 'inert' in another sense; it must involv the kind of commitment which comes through being on the inside of a forr of thought and awareness. A man cannot really understand what it is t think scientifically unless he not only knows that evidence must be foun for assumptions, but cares that it should be found; in forms of though where proof is possible, cogency, simplicity, and elegance must be felt t matter. And what would historical or philosophical thought amount to there was no concern about relevance or coherence? All forms of though and awareness have their own internal standards of appraisal. To be o the inside of them is both to understand this and to care. Indeed th understanding is difficult to distinguish from the caring; for without suc care the activities lose their point. I do not think that we would call person 'educated' whose knowledge of such forms of thought and aware ness was purely external and 'inert' in this way. There can be no End of th Affair where The Heart of the Matter is lacking. And, of course, ther never *is* an End of the Affair. For to be educated is not to have arrived; it to travel with a different view.

The achievement aspect of 'education' connected with knowledge ha now been sketched. Before passing to the task aspect, under which educa tional processes have to be considered, it will be as well to pause and summarize the main criteria of 'education' under this aspect which are to be satisfied by an 'educated' man.

(i) An educated man is one whose form of life – as exhibited in his conduct, the activities to which he is committed, his judgments and feelings – is thought to be desirable.

(ii) Whatever he is trained to do he must have knowledge, not jus knack, and an understanding of principles. His form of life must also exhibit some mastery of forms of thought and awareness which are no harnessed purely to utilitarian or vocational purposes or completely confined to one mode.

(iii) His knowledge and understanding must not be inert either in the sense that they make no difference to his general view of the world, his actions within it and reactions to it *or* in the sense that they involve no concern for the standards immanent in forms of thought and awareness, as well as the ability to attain them.

Criteria involved in the task aspect of 'education'

Educational processes are related to these various activities and modes of thought and conduct characterizing an 'educated man' as task is related to achievement. They are those in which people are initiated into or got going on activities and forms of thought and conduct which they eventually come to master. I have argued already that, apart from the requirement that processes belonging to this family be morally unobjectionable, they must also be considered from the point of view of the learner whose achievements give content to the concept of an 'educated man'. They must therefore approximate to tasks in which the learner knows what he is doing and gradually develops towards those standards of excellence which constitute the relevant achievement. In this family obviously are included processes such as training, instruction, learning by experience, teaching, and so on.

If we look at such processes from the teacher's point of view he is intentionally trying to get learning processes going by exhibiting, drawing attention to, emphasizing, or explicating some feature of what has to be learnt and putting the learner in a position where his experience is likely to become structured along desirable lines. From the learner's point of view such processes must be ones in which he knows what he is doing. Things may happen to him while asleep or under hypnosis which bring about modifications of his consciousness; but we would not call them processes of education. The learner must know what he is doing, must be conscious of something that he is trying to master, understand, or remember. Such processes, therefore, must involve attention on his part and some type of action, activity, or performance by means of which he begins to structure his movements and consciousness according to the public standards immanent in what has to be learnt.

It is necessary, however, to distinguish educational processes proper from other processes bordering on them which do not satisfy one or other of these criteria. There are first of all what I will call extrinsic aids and secondly what I will call rather loosely processes of 'picking things up'. Let us consider them briefly in this order.

(a) Extrinsic aids

There are all sorts of things done by teachers in classrooms which help children to learn things which are really aids to education rather than processes of education. I mean conditions such as praise and reward which help children to learn things. These are not processes of education; for their connexion with what is learnt is purely extrinsic. They may facilitate the learning of anything; but what is involved in learning anything can be explicated without reference to them. To take a parallel; it is an empirical fact that children learn things better if they are nice and

warm rather than shivering with cold. So a sensible teacher will make sure
that the radiators in the classrooms are turned on. It may also be the case
that children learn things better if the teacher smiles approvingly when
the child gets things right. This is, perhaps, another empirical fact which
is relevant to education. But neither turning on the radiators nor smiling
at children are educational processes, whatever their status as aids to
education. [...]

(b) Picking things up

I used the word 'picked up' rather than 'learnt' advisedly to characterize a
way of acquiring an attitude that borders on education, without being a
process of education in a strict sense.[3] Obviously enough this attitude is
implicit in the practice of the teacher who employs such a method and is
passed on partly by identification. All sorts of things are picked up in this
way – desirable things such as a passion for poetry, nuances of style and
argument, objectivity towards facts, respect for persons; undesirable
things such as partisan allegiances, contempt for people of different per-
suasions, bad manners, and class-consciousness; and trivial things such as
mannerisms, a tone of voice, gestures.

My reluctance to call such goings-on processes of education is not just due
to the fact that what is passed on may be trivial or undesirable, but to the
difficulty of conceiving them as tasks either on the part of the teacher or of
the learner. [...] They are not 'learning' processes in a full sense; for they are
different from explicit imitation or copying, where something is explicitly
attended to for assimilation. They happen to people; they are not
achievements. Nevertheless this kind of contagion only actually spreads if
both teacher and learner are actively engaged on something. It does not
happen if the teacher is just fiddling about or the children are staring out of
the window. The attention of both has to be focused on some task; then these
subsidiary processes may get going. If the teacher gets too self-conscious
about them, the business gets blurred. He has to have his mind on what
Lawrence called 'the holy ground' between teacher and taught. His dedica-
tion to it may then become incorporated in the consciousness of his pupils,
and many other nuances may be imparted. [...]

5 Educational processes

I have now, as it were, got out of the way what I called aids to education
and processes of picking things up, both of which border on being processes
of education. I want now to pass on to processes of education proper which
can be viewed as a family of tasks leading up to the achievement of being
educated. The achievement of being 'educated', as I have set it out, is
complex. It involves mastery of some skills, knowledge, and understand-

ing of principles. For such an ideal to be realized many different sorts of things have to be learnt. In view of this it is improbable that there can be just one educational process. Too many educational theories are extrapolations from one type of learning situation which is taken as a paradigm for all. I propose therefore to isolate the different aspects of 'being educated' and consider briefly which educational processes are of particular relevance to each of them.

(a) Training

Consider, first of all, the learning of skills. This presents itself pre-eminently as a task to the learner. He is usually presented with a paradigm of a skilled performance and, by a mixture of constant practice and imitation, he may eventually come to master it. A skill is not by its very nature something that could be learnt for all time in a flash of insight. Neither can it be learnt by reading books or by instruction alone. This helps of course, but only because it provides a guide for practice. Constant practice is absolutely essential, especially under the eye of a skilled performer who both corrects and provides a paradigm of the performance. Skills are difficult to master; so extrinsic forms of motivation usually have to supplement the intrinsic motivation provided by the desire to achieve or get something right.

To a teacher 'skills' usually denote reading, writing, and computation which have to be mastered before education can proceed very far. Because of the difficulties they present to a child, all kinds of attempts are made to harness the learning of these skills to other things that the child wants to do. But this is merely an intelligent way of providing an incentive to learning; it is nothing to do with the type of learning process required to master the skill. A child may be brought to the task of reading by the incentive of advertisements or by the necessity of reading instructions if he wants to cook. But when the actual reading begins there is no escape from practice, instruction, correction and example.

The general name we have for this type of learning process is 'training'. The concept of 'training' has application when (i) there is some specifiable type of performance that has to be mastered, (ii) practice is required for the mastery of it, (iii) little emphasis is placed on the underlying *rationale*. Example and instruction by another are a great help in the realm of skill, but they are not absolutely essential. A person might learn to type, for instance, without either, though it would be a lengthy business. But he could never learn to do this without practice. 'Training' has application, however, in a wider realm than that of skill; for roughly speaking the concept of 'training' also has application whenever anything coming up to a clear-cut specification has to be learnt. Military training includes not only arms drill and training skills such as shooting; it also includes the inculcation of habits such as punctuality and tidiness. Such habits cannot be learnt by practice and imitation alone as might a skill like swimming or swinging a golf club, because of the lack of close connexion with bodily movements. It is conceivable that something like swimming could be just picked up or 'caught' by practice and imitation without a word being said. But a habit like that of honesty, which is not just a kind of 'know-how' or knack, could never be picked up just like this.

Consider, for instance, what a child has got to know before he can develop a habit like that of stealing. He must be able to distinguish between himself and others and must have developed the notion of property; he must also grasp that people have a right to things and that these things must not be appropriated without permission. A child, strictly speaking, cannot 'steal' who has not a range of concepts such as these. He cannot learn what 'stealing' is just by watching others. For he cannot tell what an action is just from the outside; he has also to know how the agent conceives what he is doing. To realize that something is a case of theft he must, therefore, have developed the conceptual scheme without which 'theft' is an unintelligible notion. The notion of theft cannot be tied down, either, to any specifiable range of bodily movements. For all sorts of things can count as property and there are an infinite number of ways of appropriating them. A child cannot therefore learn to steal or not to steal without instruction and correction as well as practice and imitation. The notion of 'moral training' as distinct from that of 'moral education' suggests the learning of a moral code which is tied down to specifiable rules such as 'Thou shalt not steal'. Moral education suggests, in addition, the passing on of the underlying rationale, the understanding of principles. But even training in this sphere, as well as in many others, involves much more than the mere mastery of a 'know-how' or 'knack'. The child has also to know that certain classes of action are wrong. Such knowledge could never just be 'caught'. The learning of skills is thus only one particular case of 'training'.

(b) Instruction and learning by experience

Knowing what things are and that certain things are the case is a matter of developing a conceptual scheme that has to be fitted to phenomena. This can only be learnt by a process which involves the meaningful use of language by a teacher to structure relevant experience by the learner. In acquiring a body of knowledge of this sort instruction and explanation are as essential as first-hand experience. There is prevalent at the moment a widespread horror of instruction because this is associated with sitting children down in rows and telling them things which may be beyond their ken and which they may not be interested in learning about anyway. It is argued in reaction to this that children have at certain ages spontaneous curiosity in what things are and why they happen; they also have a natural desire to master things, provided they are not too difficult. A wise teacher will therefore be thoroughly cognizant of the stage of conceptual development which each child has reached. She will often take the children out of the classroom where they can be confronted with the relevant experiences and will fill the classroom itself with things which are carefully related to these stages of conceptual development. She will be at hand always when the child's natural curiosity impels him to ask questions which are almost inevitable, given the confrontation between intriguing objects and a conceptual scheme which is ripe for the next increment. In this way there can be no danger of knowledge being inert. For what is learnt is always what the child is ready to absorb and eager to discover. In this way information from adults and from books can be built firmly into the developing cognitive structure of the child in relation to first-hand experience.

This is admirable provided that the teachers attempting to practise such a method are intelligent enough to understand what they are meant to be doing and skilful enough to make provision for children to whom they cannot be attending,[4] and provided that classroom conditions and the teacher-pupil ratio do not make it a pipe dream. But it should be realized that it is really just a more intelligent method of instruction. Rather a lot of nonsense is talked in this context about children 'discovering' things which is rather reminiscent of Socrates' demonstration in *The Meno* that even a slave can make a geometrical 'discovery' if he is given the chance. The point is that a child may find out what others know, but he does not, if he is not asked the right sort of questions at the appropriate time, and if his experience is not guided in certain directions. A certain amount of practice is required for the child to learn to use necessary concepts; but nothing like the same amount as in the case of skills. For once the rule has been grasped governing the use of the concept, further instances are easily recognized. Of course knowledge acquired in this or any other way must be used fairly often or else it may be forgotten. But the supposition is that if it is acquired spontaneously in relation to first-hand experience forgetting is less likely.

(c) Teaching and the learning of principles

If the knowledge of the human race had ended with Aristotle this account of knowledge and of the methods necessary to acquire it might be sufficient. It is indeed significant that those who advocate educational methods which stress the importance of first-hand experience have in mind mainly children of 7–12 who are at what Piaget calls the stage of concrete operational thought when the world of things presented through the senses is being ordered and structured. What is required at this stage is plenty of experience together with classificatory schemes to structure it. The classroom thus becomes a Lyceum in miniature.

But what of the grasp of principles necessary for understanding rather than low-level knowledge? What of the 'rape of the senses' necessary for principles like the law of inertia to emerge? What of the reliance on one typical and crucial instance so central to the hypothetico-deductive method of Galileo which Piaget postulates as developing almost naturally from the previous stage? Of what importance at this stage is all this dashing around and first-hand experience? As Hobbes put it, under the spell of Galileo: 'For when we calculate the magnitude and motions of heaven or earth, we do not ascend into heaven that we may divide it into parts, or measure the motions thereof, but we do it sitting still in our closets, or in the dark.'[5] Understanding principles does not depend upon the accumulation of extra items of knowledge. Rather it requires reflection on what we already know, so that a principle can be found to illuminate the facts. This often involves the postulation of what is unobservable to explain what is observed. So it could never be lighted upon by 'experience'.

What then is there to be said about the learning of principles? The basic requisite is that people should first acquire in some way or other the low-level rules or assumptions which the principles illuminate. It is both logically absurd and educationally unsound to suppose that people could attain the necessary understanding of principles without first having acquired quite a lot of knowledge; for principles provide backing to rules or assumptions at a lower level of generality. In science, for instance, there could be no appeal to principles unless there were a mass of empirical generalizations which could be seen to fall under them; in morals there could be no appeal to principles without rules to justify by means of them. The grasp of principles, therefore, is inseparable from the acquisition of knowledge of a more mundane sort. This logical truth is often neglected by rationalistic educators who think that people can grasp scientific concepts, or pass them on to children, without knowing any science, or who believe that moral principles can be grasped by children who have not had a basic training in moral rules.

There is, of course, nothing absolute about what constitutes a principle. It is merely a higher-level assumption or rule that can be appealed to in order to substantiate and give unity to lower order ones. The one is thus immanent in the many. Evidence that the principle has been grasped is provided if a person knows how to go and deal with new situations in the light of it. People are brought to a grasp of principles by a mixture of explanation and a selective survey of the many. Words like 'insight' are used in connexion with the grasp of principles. It is difficult to state precisely what is meant by such words, but once people have it very little in the way of further practice is necessary as in the case of skills. Neither are principles quickly forgotten like the lower-level information which they unify. The typical term for the educational process by means of which people are brought to understand principles is 'teaching'; for 'teach', unlike 'train' or 'instruct', suggests that a *rationale* is to be grasped behind the skill or body of knowledge.

(d) The transmission of critical thought

Societies can persist in which bodies of knowledge with principles imma-nent in them can be handed on without any systematic attempt to explain and justify them or to deal honestly with phenomena that do not fit. Fixed beliefs are thus perpetuated. When this is done we are presumably con-fronted with what is called indoctrination rather than teaching; for indoc-trination is incompatible with the development of critical thought. Critical thought, however, is a rationalistic abstraction without a body of knowledge to be critical about. The problem of the teacher is to pass on a body of knowledge in such a way that a critical attitude towards it can also develop. If too much emphasis is placed on critical thought the danger is that all processes of education will be conceived too much in terms of what is necessary for a critical attitude to emerge. This is one of the dangers immanent in Dewey's system in which the concept of being 'educated' is more or less co-extensive with that of being critical.

There is no innate tendency to think critically, neither is it easy to acquire. Indeed as Bacon argued, it goes against the inveterate tendency of the human race which is to believe what we want to believe and to accept on trust things that we are told. The clue to how such an inveterate tendency can be overcome was provided by Plato when he described thought as the soul's dialogue with itself. It is a pity that this clue was not followed up. For the notion might not then have developed that reason is a sort of mental gadget that can be used by the individual if it is not too clogged up with passion or, as Hume described it, 'a wonderful and unintelligible instinct in our souls'. Given that critical thought about the assumptions in which we are nurtured rather goes against the grain, it will only develop if we keep critical company so that a critic is incorporated within our own consciousness. The dialogue within is a reflection of the dialogue without. This is a paradigm of an educational situation; for educational processes are those by means of which public modes of thought and awareness, which are mainly enshrined in language, take root in the consciousness of the individual and provide avenues of access to a public world.

The best way of making sure of such a living organic structure of thought is probably to employ the *ad hominem* method of question and answer used by Socrates. This brings the learner very quickly to probe into his presuppositions and to make explicit principles which were pre-viously only dimly apprehended. If the learner is constantly prodded into doing this he gradually begins to think in a more clear, coherent, and structured way; for there is a sense in which we do not really know what we think about anything until we have had to state it explicitly and defend it. If this process continues for quite a time the learner gradually takes the questioner into his own mind and begins to develop the form of thought himself. He can come to formulate objections to his assumptions himself and keep on reformulating what he thinks or proposes to do until he hits on something to which he can find no objections.

It is important to realize that such a critical clarification of principles is a very different exercise from applying them in concrete circumstances. This seems to be the burden of Oakeshott's attack on rationalism and the starting point of his conception of political education.[6] He is not much interested in the discussion and justification of principles. What fascinates him is the judgment required to apply them in particular circumstances. He sees clearly that such judgment cannot be acquired in salons, studies, or seminars. It comes through practical experience in the presence of those who already have it.

It does not follow either that a person who has mastered a form of thought such as history, or one of the sciences, is skilled in testing the hypothesis that may emerge from reflection or discussion. He must, of course, be familiar from the inside with how experiments can be designed, or how records and manuscripts are interpreted. But many of the great theoretical scientists have been poor experimentalists just as some of the great historians have arranged the facts in a new pattern rather than discovered a lot of new ones by ingenious techniques of research. From the point of view of education what is essential is the grasp of a conceptual scheme for ordering facts rather than skill in research.[7] The various forms of thought – historical, moral, scientific, aesthetic – all have their own such schemes and thus provide different perspectives for the interpretation of experience. They can, however, only have such a transforming effect on a person's outlook if they are passed on in the right way at the right time and if they are informed by that passion for truth which lies at the heart of all of them. Without this, critical discussion can degenerate into verbal legerdemain, and a parade of principles can be equivalent to name-dropping. Whether such a passion is due to fostering the natural curiosity of the child, is caught from those who are already possessed by it, or develops because an individual is confronted by conflicting opinions, is difficult to determine.

(e) Conversation and 'the whole man'

What then of the processes which lead to the development of an educated man in the full sense of a man whose knowledge and understanding is not confined to one form of thought or awareness? Nowadays all sorts of educational experiments are being contrived to 'liberalize' vocational training and to ensure that premature specialization does not distort a man's view of the world. No doubt formalized correctives to specialization are necessary, though it is arguable that the proper place for them is at school rather than at university. But the question is whether explicit learning situations are sufficient to bring about this integrated outlook.

he classical way of ensuring this, surely, has been not courses but
onversation.

Conversation is not structured like a discussion group in terms of one
orm of thought, or towards the solution of a problem. In a conversation
ecturing to others is bad form; so is using the remarks of others as
pringboards for self-display. The point is to create a common world to
vhich all bring their distinctive contributions. By participating in such a
hared experience much is learnt, though no one sets out to teach anyone
nything. And one of the things that is learnt is to see the world from the
iewpoint of another whose perspective is very different. To be able to take
n active part in a real conversation is, of course, an achievement. It is not
ossible without knowledge, understanding, objectivity, and sensitivity to
thers. But it is also a learning situation of an informal sort. A vast amount
f learning all through life takes place in such informal situations. Are we
osing faith in the likelihood of anything emerging if it is not carefully
ontrived? Or are we just the victims of shortage of space, pressure of
umbers, and the bureaucratization of our educational system?

This is the point of mentioning conversation as the culmination of a
ecture on educational processes which has been concerned mainly with
what goes on in formal situations. For just as educational processes are not
confined to classrooms, so also for an educated man the distinction
between formal and informal situations of learning is only one of degree.
His experience is not only transformed by all that he has mastered, learnt,
and understood, but is always exemplifying the processes by means of
which such mastery, knowledge, and understanding have been acquired.
The achievements constantly generate new tasks. Even in his middle age
he can really listen to what people say irrespective of the use he can make
of it or them. This is a considerable achievement. But then as Spinoza said
of the state of human blessedness: 'all excellent things are as difficult as
they are rare'.

Notes

1 See SCHEFFLER, I. (1960) *The Language of Education*. Springfield, Ill.: Thomas
  (chapter IV).
2 It should be stressed that what has been said relates only to thinking of
  something as a form of *education*. It is only under this aspect that we are implying
  that there is something worth-while immanent in scientific activity, for instance,
  and that there is no discontinuity between the tasks and the achievements. But
  we can train people to do 'science' for purely utilitarian or vocational purposes if
  we wish. The same applies to carpentry or cooking. We *can* look at such activities
  in a purely instrumental way. Whether we should do so or not is a further
  question. In discussing this we are not engaged in a debate about the aims of
  education, but in a debate about whether we ought to educate people rather
  than train them, or whether something like science or carpentry has the intrinsic
  value which many would ascribe to it. It may well be too that there are many
  tasks and achievements engaged in at school, such as reading and computation,

which, like boarding a bus or doing five-finger exercises, have a value which is almost entirely instrumental in relation to our educational aims. This may well be so. It does not contradict my thesis; rather it draws attention to the necessity of looking at what goes on in schools in a wider context. Schools are obviously concerned with things other than education – with health, for instance, with selection, and with vocational training.

3 The concept of education, could, perhaps, be extended to include such border-line processes. What exactly one calls 'education' in this twilight area does not much matter provided that the similarities and differences are recognized.

4 See SARASON, S. B., DAVIDSON, K. S. and BLATT, B. (1962). *The Preparation of Teachers*. New York: John Wiley.

5 HOBBES, T. (1650) *De Corpore* (Molesworth edn, 1839), English Works (chapter 7).

6 See OAKESHOTT, M. (1962) *Rationalism in Politics*. London: Methuen.

7 It is important to make this point at a time when there is a growing demand that universities should fulfil two functions which are not altogether compatible – develop research not so much for its own sake but in order to solve the practical problems of the nation, and provide a 'liberal' education for a larger percentage of the population than heretofore.

1.2 Comprehensive education

Anthony Crosland

Speech delivered at the North of England Education Conference on 7 January 1966

I want to talk about comprehensive reorganization[...] It is a subject which arouses intense discussion, and now absorbs much time and effort on the part of local education authorities. I think it only right, therefore, to try and put the basic issue in perspective, and to report to you on the progress so far made.

In doing so, I must warn you that I shall talk also about social and even political values. A few people still think that social and political aspirations can, and should, somehow be kept out of education. But of course they cannot and should not. Education and society interact on each other at every point. The structure of education must have a profound effect on the social structure – on the degree of equality, of equity, of opportunity, of social mobility; similarly, the content and character of education must profoundly influence the values and standards of adult society. Conversely, the social-class structure will affect the demand for education and the pool of ability available; likewise, the values and character of the society must affect what is taught in the schools and generally, indeed, the national attitude to education. And I hesitate to mention the further mundane but crucial fact that only elected politicians (and not, dare I say, even the wisest Royal Commission) can and should decide how much shall be spent on education as compared with other claims on our resources – health, housing, pensions, roads, defence, or personal consumption.

It is for these reasons (obvious enough in all conscience) that in every society decisions about education – about priorities in spending or the organization of the school system – must have a social dimension and reflect value-judgments about justice, class, equality, ethics, or economic growth. It is for this reason that every educational philosophy, from Plato through Arnold to Dewey, has articulated the social and moral values of its time and of its author. And it is for this reason that every educational system in recorded history – whether of Athens or Sparta, of New Guinea or the Pueblo Indians, of Russia or America today – has mirrored the needs and aspirations of the community which created it. And as these needs and aspirations change, so the system must be changed if dangerous tensions are to be avoided.

It is against this background that we must see the movement towards comprehensive education. For I believe this represents a strong and

Source: CROSLAND, ANTHONY (1974) *Socialism Now and Other Essays*. London: Jonathan Cape, pp. 193–210.

irresistible pressure in British society to extend the rights of citizenship. Over the past three hundred years these rights have been extended first to personal liberty, then to political democracy, and later to social welfare. Now they must be further extended to educational equality. For until recently our schools have been essentially middle-class institutions, and our educational system essentially geared to educating the middle class, plus a few from below who aspired to be middle class or looked like desirable recruits to the middle class. The remainder were given cheaper teachers and inferior buildings and were segregated in separate schools. But today the pressure of democracy, under either political party, insists on full civil rights and full incorporation in the educational as in other fields.

However, let me now try to make the more specific case for comprehensive education and against the tripartite or bipartite system of schools which we have had since 1944. In summary, I believe this system to be educationally and socially unjust, inefficient, wasteful and divisive. I doubt if any indictment could be more wide-ranging than that.

First, and to me most important, I assert that separatism is socially unjust. Now to demonstrate this, I must ask you to consider what it is that we are measuring when, at eleven-plus, (and however careful our selection procedures) we get out our labels and ticket our children, or most of them, for life: when, in Sir Frederick Clarke's phrase, we divide them up between the unselected goats and the carefully selected sheep.

Fifty years ago everyone, and even twenty years ago most people, would have answered that we were testing something, whether we called it measured intelligence, ability or aptitude, which was biologically inherited and fixed in a child for life. That was the philosophy which underlay the Hadow and Norwood Reports and the 1944 Act – that we were faced with children who differed from each other genetically and permanently, and who therefore needed to be educated in separate schools. By a further divine dispensation, fortunate indeed for the educational administrator, the differences fell into a precise numerical pattern – 25 per cent academic and 75 per cent non-academic – which most conveniently fitted the existing pattern of schools.

Today we see matters quite differently. The researches of sociology and psychology have taught us, what only a few pioneers like Burt proclaimed in the past, that measured intelligence, unlike specific gravity, is not a fixed and innate quantity. It is not something given in limited measure in the genetic make-up of the new-born child. What is given is a bundle of assorted potentials, and what happens to them is a matter of nurture, of stimulus and response. The intelligence quotient is a function partly, of course, of inheritance, but also of environment and background.

Moreover, the environmental factors which exert the strongest influence on measured intelligence and hence on educational performance – the factors of home and neighbourhood, of size of family and parental aspirations – are all strongly linked to social class. [. . .]

What then are we doing when, at the age of eleven, we divide our children into 25 per cent grammar and 75 per cent secondary modern? It is not, I suppose, in dispute that the grammar school offers more in terms of life-chances. The grammar school child – and I am talking now of children of the same level of attainment and the same potential when they start at secondary school – has a statistically much greater chance than the secondary modern child of going on to higher education, and of commanding, therefore, a wide choice of occupations. He is four or five times as likely to be prepared by subject specialists for the examinations which lead to higher education. He will generally be taught in smaller classes: the pupil–teacher ratio in January 1964 was 17.5, compared with 20.3 in the secondary modern schools. The latest salary analysis shows that over 70 per cent of grammar school staff are paid salaries above the basic scale, compared with 45 per cent in secondary modern schools. John Vaizey suggested in 1958 that the average grammar school child received 170 per cent more a year in terms of resources than the average secondary modern school child; and there is no reason to think that the differential has been narrowed since then.

This is in no way to minimize the remarkable efforts of the secondary modern schools in recent years. It is to their enormous credit that without the stimulus of the top 20 per cent of ability they have nevertheless helped able youngsters to get good GCE results and to go on to higher education. But this has been in spite of the odds being loaded against them. Given, then, that the grammar school offers more ample chances and opportunities in after-life, and given that IQ at eleven reflects home background as well as innate intelligence, what the eleven-plus is doing is this: it penalizes the working-class boy not necessarily for innate stupidity but partly for his social background, for his less educated parents, his larger family, his crowded home, his slum neighbourhood, his generally less favourable environment. And at the same time we diminish his opportunities for improving his ability by continued education. [...]

Now of course we cannot wholly correct an unfavourable background by a change in school organization. The argument goes far wider than educational policy. To make equal opportunity in education a reality, we shall have not only to eliminate bad housing and inadequate incomes, but steadily to make good the educational deficiencies of parents who cannot give their children the encouragement they need. True equality of opportunity cannot be accomplished in one generation, or by education alone; it needs a wider social revolution.

But as soon as we concede that measured intelligence is not a quantity fixed for life, and that it depends, moreover, partly on the child's environment, we must surely think it indefensible to segregate children into different schools at the age of eleven. It is, of course, in the nature of things that as we grow to manhood we go different ways. Life itself is a selective process. But we must allow that process to work fairly; we must allow time for the beneficial influence of education to compensate for the deficiencies of upbringing and early circumstance. Segregation as early as eleven-plus is indefensible. We must keep the choices open, and defer as long as possible the irrevocable selection. Amid all the shifting contours of educational planning I am certain of this: that the system must allow the individual to pick up, to make good, to try again. You do not feed a child less because it grows slowly or has some initial handicap to overcome.

To me, then, the central and irresistible argument against the eleven-plus lies in the denial of social justice and equal opportunity which it implies. [...]

However, perhaps arguments based on social justice will seem too remote to hard-headed educational administrators – though I have never noticed, happily, that such people in England are lacking in principle or idealism; far from it. But lest we still have left a nucleus of conscienceless bureaucrats, I turn now to my second argument against separatism. This is based on the inefficiency implicit in it. I refer especially to the extreme fallibility, the hit-and-miss nature, of the process of selection. Wherever you draw the line, there will be people on either side of it with very little between them, quite apart from the fact that from one test to another a child's IQ performance can and does vary considerably.

In the early 'fifties, as you know, intensive research was carried out which showed that while the procedures applied by local authorities – using standardized tests and teachers' assessments – were in one sense highly efficient, there were still about 10–12 per cent of 'wrong' allocations made each year. That is to say, for every hundred children, some five or six were allocated to secondary modern schools who, had they been sent to grammar schools, might have been more successful than another five or six who were in fact sent to grammar school. And if we allow for the fact that children actually allocated to grammar schools would be expected to show up better than those who were not, the results suggest that the number of really 'wrong' allocations may have been much larger. I may add that subsequent transfers enabled only one or two children per hundred to move into grammar schools from secondary modern. This shows the acute danger of miscalculation at the age of eleven; it also shows how hard it is to correct the miscalculation if you segregate children into different schools.

But there is also – and this is my third argument – a wider social waste involved. If ever there was a country which needed to make the most of its resources, it is Britain in the second half of the twentieth century; and the chief resource of a crowded island is its people. Moreover, the proportion of relatively inexpert and unskilled jobs to be done declines from year to year. To behave in these circumstances as though there were a fixed 25 per cent of top ability at eleven not only flies in the face of the evidence which I have quoted; it amounts to feckless prodigality.

The extent to which we are wasting good educational talent, for what are in part social causes, was fully and horrifyingly documented in the Crowther and Robbins Reports. Not all the waste, of course, is linked with the eleven-plus; some is due to early leaving or poor performance in grammar school. Yet it is also clear that, despite all that has been done in the secondary modern schools by able and devoted teachers to minimize the damage, there has been a frightful waste of latent talent through the sheer fact of segregation, through the discouragement put upon a large group of the population by the label of failure. The proof lies in the subsequent upgrading in comprehensive schools of the eleven-plus failures, and indeed in the award of some of our highest academic honours to those who at eleven had fallen on the wrong side of the line.

There are, I believe, two ways in which a fully comprehensive system will minimize this waste. One relates to the element of self-fulfilling prophecy in the educational system. We know from researches how vital are the expectations of parents and teachers to the performance of the children. Children expected to do well, on the whole, do well; children marked with the brand of failure on the whole will fail.

Failure in the eleven-plus – the only exam, as has recently been pointed out, in which three-quarters of those concerned know they must fail – is conspicuously such a brand. If anyone doubts this they have only to see the effect of failing the eleven-plus on the morale of both parents and children.

But if, by eliminating early selection, we could also lessen the early sense of failure, we might not only avoid a lot of unnecessary human misery; we might also find a sharp increase in the performance of many of the 75 per cent who now so often fulfil the gloomy prophecy made about them at the cruelly early age of eleven.

In addition, the truly comprehensive school is given an enormous impetus and inspiration by having within it the full range of ability. The secondary modern schools have, to their credit, introduced GCE courses for the benefit of those who could profit by them; but without the example of the top range of ability as pace-setters, it is all too easy for children not to make the effort, to accept society's verdict and let it go at that.

For we all know how much students learn informally rather than formally, from each other rather than from their elders. We know that standards in a school are partly set by what sociologists call 'the student culture', by the young taste-makers and opinion-moulders. If these are hostile to brains, hostile to school and the teacher, then intellectual standards will be low. But to the extent that an academic stream exists, setting at least one model and acting as intellectual pacemaker, to that extent the standard will improve. It must, surely, be the experience of many of you here, as it is the finding of studies on both sides of the Atlantic, that the achievement of those who would otherwise be in a secondary modern school, and notably those in the middle ranges of ability, where the greatest waste is now, is markedly higher in a comprehensive school – due to the extra stimulus, [...] the upgrading imparted by the academic stream.

But what of the bright boy? Will he not suffer? And, more generally, is not an élitist system, a Platonic meritocracy, essential to efficiency and survival in a competitive and scientific world? As to the latter point, I have little anxiety. We have long combined almost the most élitist educational system with almost the slowest rate of economic growth of any advanced industrial nation. Both America and Sweden with their comprehensive systems have outstripped us in efficiency. I should suppose that what we most need from this point of view is a huge widening of educational opportunity. There is no evidence at all that we need to preserve selection at eleven-plus.

And why should the bright boy or girl suffer by attending a comprehensive rather than a selective grammar school? Exact comparison is difficult in Britain, because most comprehensive schools operate in areas where the grammar schools still cream off a large proportion of the brighter pupils. But there is some evidence, from a large-scale international research project not yet published, that in mathematics, at least, the bright pre-university pupils in countries with a comprehensive system do just as well as similar pupils in countries with a highly selective system such as our own. Moreover, to support the point which I have just made, the mathematics performance of pupils of lower ability is much higher in the comprehensive countries than in selective countries. This would suggest both that 'more' does not necessarily mean 'worse' for brighter pupils, and that the total 'yield' may be greater in a comprehensive system.

In Britain, indeed, the comprehensive schools may be so concerned to do as well academically as the grammar schools that the danger may be the opposite one – too much concentration on the bright pupils. But this danger will no doubt be counteracted as the need to compete narrowly with the grammar schools disappears.

A particular fear is also expressed, which one must again respect, that the grammar or direct grant schools provide the only opportunity for bright working-class boys to rise out of their class and obtain an academic education. I think the point I have just made largely answers this. And there is this further point. One must not disregard the wastage of working-class children which already occurs from the grammar schools, where they are much less likely than boys from better homes – even when they have gained admission – to stay on and do well. This may be bound up with one of the weaknesses which the grammar schools have developed under the selective system – namely, a comparative neglect (sometimes an almost callous neglect) of their lower streams who are thought not to be up to the GCE.

I pass now from social waste to my fourth argument – a more controversial one, though I personally feel it deeply: that separate schools exacerbate social division. It cannot be denied that the eleven-plus divides overwhelmingly according to social class: indeed, because of streaming in the primary school, social-class division in schools begins to operate at the

ge of eight. What we euphemistically describe as educational selection is
or the most part social selection; and our educational division is largely a
lass division.

This is so partly for the perhaps natural reason that schools and
eachers react to social as well as to educational factors. As Dr Douglas
eminds us, 'Children who come from well-kept homes and who are
hemselves clean, well clothed and shod, stand a greater chance of being
ut in the upper streams than their measured ability would seem to
ustify.' But of course the more fundamental cause is the one which I have
lready stressed: that measured intelligence at eleven is partly a function
f environment, and that environment is closely linked with social class.
Vhat we are testing at eleven, therefore, is to a large extent social-class
ackground.

Now by selecting for a superior school children who are already well-
avoured by environment, we are not merely confirming, we are hardening
nd sharpening, an existing social division. This can surely not be thought
lesirable. I will not argue the point in terms of equality. But I will argue it
n terms of a sense of community, of social cohesion, of a nation composed
f people who understand each other because they can communicate. If
he only time we can, as a society, achieve this common language is when
ve go to war, then we are at a much less advanced stage than many
ocieties which the anthropologists describe as primitive. We have only to
onsider our industrial relations, and the lack of communication and
nutual understanding reflected in them, to see the depth of social division
n Britain today. Of course, education alone cannot solve this problem.
But so long as we choose to educate our children in separate camps,
reinforcing and seeming to validate existing differences in accent,
language and values, for so long will our schools exacerbate rather than
diminish our class divisions.

Of course the elimination of separatism at eleven-plus is only a necessary, and not a sufficient, condition of reducing the divisive effect of our
school system. We should not much improve matters if selection gave way
merely to rigid streaming within a strictly neighbourhood pattern of
schools. This would re-create many of the old evils within a comprehensive system.

When I speak of streaming, I naturally do not mean to imply that it can
or should be avoided, totally and at every age. I refer to unnecessarily
early and rigid streaming. Here of course there must be an improvement
as a result of comprehensive reorganization, and in the place that matters
most – the primary schools. We all know what strains and rigidities the
eleven-plus has imposed on the primary schools – the over-emphasis on
tracking and streaming and cramming. But the case for early streaming
will disappear as the eleven-plus disappears. There will, indeed, be much
wider scope in the primary schools for innovation and experiment and the
release of creative ability – from teachers and pupils alike. The newer and
better methods of teaching, in mathematics, in English and in French, are

more likely to be tried and more likely to bring good results; and subjec[
like music are less likely to get crowded out of the curriculum.

And as far as the comprehensives themselves are concerned, I am mo[
interested, as I go round the country, to find how strong is the reactio[
against some of the early practices of rigid and premature streaming[
There seems to be a general loosening-up and a greater willingness t[
experiment.

The problem of the one-class neighbourhood school is more intractabl[
It is not, of course, a problem created by going comprehensive: four out c[
five secondary modern schools are neighbourhood schools, and mos[
grammar and direct grant schools are predominantly middle class – the[
do not become classless merely by having a small working-class stratum[
any more than the House of Commons became truly representative o[
British society sixty years ago merely because Keir Hardie was elected t[
it. The problem is the result of gross social inequality combined with ba[
town-planning. In the long term the mere fact of wider educationa[
opportunity will gradually improve matters. In the short term it is for th[
local authorities to give close attention to the boundaries of catchmen[
areas; and [...] I have urged them to make such schools as socially an[
intellectually comprehensive as is practicable, perhaps by linking togethe[
two districts of a different character. This is very much the kind of problem[
on which further light will, I hope, be thrown by the special programme o[
research that the Government has launched.

Even with rigid streaming and neighbourhood schools, it would be har[
to maintain that a comprehensive system could produce as sharp a socia[
cleavage as the present division into separate schools. But with the elimination of streaming in primary schools, the movement against prematur[
streaming in the comprehensive schools, and the growing realization by[
local education authorities of the need to make their new comprehensives[
socially heterogeneous, I think I may reasonably claim that the new[
system will reduce the sense of social division and increase the sense o[
social cohesion in contemporary British society.

It was, I think, these various considerations – of equity, efficiency,
avoidance of waste and social cohesion – which produced over the last
decade an increasing revulsion against the eleven-plus, and a gathering
movement towards comprehensives. And it was they which caused this
Government to set the seal of national approval on this movement. [...]

Any new organization must give the majority of children more opportunities than did the old. I believe that the old social and intellectual
stratification of the school system is no longer acceptable to democratic
opinion in the 1960s. We must therefore set ourselves a new objective,
which is not to deprive the minority of their present educational standards, but to give all our children a more ample opportunity.

1.3 The egalitarian threat

Angus Maude

Taking a long view, one must conclude that the most serious danger facing Britain is the threat to the *quality* of education at all levels. The motive force behind this threat is the ideology of egalitarianism.

It is this that drives nearly all the people who seek to 'reform' education – its organization, its institutions, its curricula and its teaching methods. The element of envy, conscious or repressed, can for the most part be ignored. It is the reformers who cherish the highest ideals, who are emotionally committed to the concept of equality, that are the most dangerous. In the name of 'fairness' and 'social justice', sentimentality has gone far to weaken the essential toughness on which quality depends.

In theory, the egalitarian only wants all children to have equal opportunities to secure a good education. In the event, his emotions take him a good deal further than this. He instinctively dislikes any process which enables some children to emerge markedly ahead of their fellows. Since it is difficult to disguise this, in practical terms, as anything but a recipe for disaster, he is forced to rationalize his emotional prejudices in a variety of ways.

In the name of 'equality of opportunity', the egalitarian seeks to destroy or transmogrify those schools which make special efforts to bring out the best in talented children. It is a long, slow and expensive business to raise the standards of all institutions to those of the best; in his impatience, the egalitarian takes the alternative course of levelling down the higher standards towards a uniform mediocrity. Since it is 'unfair' that two children of equal ability should receive schooling of unequal quality, he seeks the easier way of trying to prevent parents from buying a better schooling for their children than the taxpayers and ratepayers are prepared to pay for in the maintained system. Since this would result in some boys and girls being worse educated than at present, it is in fact a recipe for social *in*justice.

The egalitarian does not, however, stop there. He complains bitterly of the excessive 'competitiveness' of the conventional system of education, and claims that his reforms would remove the 'stresses' from which children are alleged to suffer. Not only does he dislike class marks and competitive examinations, he has a horror of any test which some children might fail. This leads him on to decry the importance of academic standards and discipline – and indeed of learning itself. He will advocate a variety of 'new teaching methods', which in fact absolve anyone from teaching and anyone from having to learn.

Source: COX, C. B. and DYSON, A. E. (eds) (1969) *Fight for Education: A Black Paper*. Critical Quarterly Society.

The egalitarian rationalizes his dislike of academic disciplines by talking of 'education for social living'. He prefers this to real learning, because it is impossible for any recognizable élite to emerge from anything so woolly and unmeasurable. The idea is to remove from the educational process anything which calls for effort and incites children to excel. Some children must be held back, in order to avoid 'discouraging' the rest.

No system of education based on this philosophy of emotional prejudice can possibly provide a useful preparation for life as it actually has to be lived. When the adolescent who has been coddled along in this way finally has to face the realities of life, he is liable to disappointments, frustrations and resentments far more searing than those which the educational reformers claim to have spared him at school. Perhaps the most ridiculous pretence is the claim – strongly urged by the Provost of King's College, Cambridge, in his notorious Reith Lectures of 1967 – that removing competitiveness from education will result in a less competitive society. And even if it were possible to remove all the difficulties and challenges from life, would life really be worth living?

Of course, no system of education that purports to treat all children in the same way can possibly perform its essential functions. Either it will fail to bring out the best in the cleverer children, or it will end by discouraging those who are less gifted. *Pace* the egalitarians, the object of the exercise is *not* to 'give every child an equal chance'; it is to give every child the *best possible* chance to develop and make the most of his own special talents. If we could achieve this, even for the dullest child, then it could not possibly be a source of disquiet to anyone but an emotional chucklehead that some children will excel in their attainments. Indeed, God help us if they do not.

Genuine quality, in learning as in everything else, cannot be achieved by continually taking easy short cuts. One must strive, and strive hard, to achieve it. Moreover, when quality *has* been achieved, it must be recognized, respected, and rewarded. The appreciation of quality – which it should be one of the prime objects of education itself to inculcate – demands a certain humility in the observer. And if the educational system is to inculcate a respect for quality, then those who are responsible for education must have a proper respect for quality in education.

All kinds of education are *not*, as the egalitarians pretend, of equal worth and importance, nor can anything but harm come of claiming equal status for all kinds of educational institution. Whatever you may *call* a technical college – and even if you install a department of social sciences in it – it is *not* the same as a university. Nor is a course of further education, designed to provide a ticket for a job, of the same worth as a degree course designed to widen the mental horizon and deepen perception. (Although, obviously, a well grounded course in pure science or technology, studied in depth, is likely to be of more educational value than a composite smattering of 'liberal arts' or 'social sciences'.)

Equality of opportunity is a worthy ideal, but there is no method of achieving it *quickly* which will not inflict fresh injustices and damage the total quality of our society. A century ago, Bagehot wrote of the menace of philanthropists who have 'inherited from their barbarous forefathers a wild passion for instant action'. The menace is with us still, and the egalitarian philanthropist is the worst. If he is allowed to have his way, he will produce an even more inefficient society than we have already. Worse still, he will destroy our culture, with his pretence that intellect and its cultivation do not matter.

The attempt to impose uniformity by eliminating the effects of accident will fail in the end, but it may do great harm before the reaction comes. It is only through variety that progress is achieved. The pursuit of quality will mean that some will excel, and if they do not, there will be no excellence. To try forcibly to prevent the emergence of an élite will produce more frustration than it averts, and will produce a mediocrity of thought more dangerous even than the mediocrity of attainments. There are certain standards of quality which are essential to the survival of civilization, and they cannot be achieved and preserved except by rigorous and applied effort. The utmost toughness is required, somewhere at least in the educational system, if standards are to be maintained.

No society can abandon all toughness in its educational system without, in the end, becoming soft itself. If it becomes soft, it will not survive. There is no hope for a people, none of whom has been taught to do anything properly or to think any problem through, with rigour, to its essence.

The pendulum has already swung too far. It is necessary now to get very tough with the egalitarians, who would abolish or lower standards out of 'sympathy' with those who fail to measure up to them. We must reject the chimera of equality and proclaim the ideal of quality. The egalitarians, whose ideas of 'social justice' are prescriptions for mediocrity and anarchy, must be prevented from having any control over the education of the young. It is the business of politicians to fight this battle in Parliament and council chamber, and the wise citizen and parent will support those who do fight it. But it is the business of dons and schoolteachers, if they value the quality of the learning which it is their professional privilege to advance and communicate, to do battle against the enemies within their own gates. The Trojan horse of egalitarianism has already been dragged deep into their citadel.

1.4 Education: domestication or liberation?

Paulo Freire

I am convinced that the so-called commonplace is not always just the cliché suggested in its verbal expression. The commonplace on the contrary is very often found only in the formal expression of the language, and is therefore merely apparent. When language is 'bureaucratized' into conventional formulae, it satisfies the need we sometimes experience of concealing in the cliché the importance of some theme which is awaiting its critical perception.

On other occasions there is not even the formal expression of the language – the verbal expression describing the fact becomes a commonplace from the very obviousness of the fact. Whichever the case, our principal task is to transcend the naïveté which allows itself to be deceived by appearances; we thus acquire the critical attitude which breaks through the obscurity of the commonplace or of the apparent commonplace and brings us face to face with the fact until now concealed. This is the attitude of this essay – that of seeking to apprehend the deeper meaning of facts and at the same time to strip them of their disguises.

Thus, the first apparent commonplace, on the critical analysis of which will depend the understanding of this essay, can be expressed thus: education cannot be neutral.[1]

If we claim to go beyond the naïve, formal interpretations of the human task of education, this must be the starting point of a critical or dialectical reflection. Lacking this critical spirit, either because we are alienated to thinking statically and not dynamically, or because we already have ideological interests, we are incapable of perceiving the true role of education, or if we do perceive it, we disguise it. We tend to ignore or to obscure the role of education, which, in that it is a social 'praxis' will always be in the service either of the 'domestication' of men or of their liberation. Thus we almost always lose ourselves in verbalistic considerations on the subject of what is termed 'the educational crisis'; or on the subject of the need for reforms in the didactic processes; in the face of the fundamental problems of structure, with which the educational process is concerned, we indulge ourselves in these amusements.

At other moments, alarmed by the inevitable choice we have to make between education as a domesticating praxis and education as a liberating praxis, we seek a third way – which is non-existent *per se*. We declare

---

Source: United Nations Educational, Scientific and Cultural Organization (1972). *Prospects: Quarterly Review of Education*, Vol II, No. 2, Summer 1972 © UNESCO 1972. pp. 173–181. Reproduced by permission of UNESCO.

education to be neutral, as if it were not a human obligation, as if men were not beings in history, as if the teleological character of the educational praxis were not the factor which determined the nonviability of its neutrality. Furthermore, all we do in affirming this neutrality is to opt for domestication which we simply proceed to disguise.

Neutral education cannot, in fact, exist. It is fundamental for us to know that, when we work on the content of the educational curriculum, when we discuss methods and processes, when we plan, when we draw up educational policies, we are engaged in political acts which imply an ideological choice; whether it is obscure or clear is not important. To recognize that neutral education is not viable involves a critical form of thinking and of perceiving reality, and demands an ever-growing practice of that manner of thinking which continually revises itself, seeking always to overcome its opposite, which is the naïve manner of thinking. It is this requirement, stemming from critical thinking, which imposes on us the need of taking our earlier affirmation that education is not neutral, as a problem to be 'unveiled' as a problem, and not seeing it as a set phrase or as a mere 'slogan'. It is this critical manner of thinking which always desires to go beyond the deceptive appearances, to seek the *raison d'être* of facts, and the relationships between different facts, within the totality of which they are a part. However, for the critical mind, the simple affirmation that 'neutral education' is not viable should not stop at the level of merely being aware of the fact. The mere awareness of the fact does not constitute a full knowledge of it.[2] What is necessary is a penetration into the reality of which the fact is a dimension, so that mere opinion about it can be transcended by the precise knowledge of it through the apprehension of the 'reason for its being'.

For example, at the moment in which we see the educational act as the object of our critical reflection, and not as something we are merely aware of, we perceive that this act, temporally and spatially, does not restrict itself to the limitations of the description which the naïve consciousness sometimes makes of it. That is to say, it is not constituted solely by the effort which societies make for its cultural preservation. If one considers the case of the dependent societies, education is on the one hand the expression of their alienation, and on the other the instrument of a further alienation which is an obstacle to its being genuine. Thus the expression 'cultural preservation', for the critical consciousness, is vague and obscure, and conceals something which needs to be clarified. In fact, the vagueness of the expression 'cultural preservation' can be explained with exactness as the perpetuation of the values of the dominating classes who organize education and determine its aims. In that it constitutes a superstructure, systematic education functions as an instrument to maintain the infrastructure in which it is generated. Hence the nonviability of its neutrality. When education is oriented towards this preservation – and educators are not always aware of this – it is obvious that its task is to adapt new generations to the social system it serves, which can and must be reformed and modernized, but which will never be radically transformed.

It is impossible for the power-élites to organize, plan or reform education with the aim of laying open to question the essence of the social system in which precisely they are élites. Their real desire, on the contrary, must be, let us repeat, to 'recuperate' the educatees, which is as much as to say, to adapt them to the system. Their ideas and values, their way of being, are announced as if they were – or should be – the ideas, values and way of being of all society, even though the popular classes cannot share them, perhaps because of their ontological inferiority.

It is without question that the concretizing of these aims requires at one and the same time the 'domesticating' character of this education and the explanation of it. As the social order is 'sacralized', systematic education must necessarily become a powerful instrument of social control.[3]

The point of departure of this domesticating education (which requires the de-dialectization of thought) must be, paradoxically enough, in the very dialectization which exists between the consciousness and the world, or in other words, in the relationship between man and the world. It is curious to observe that the act of de-dialectization, of reducing thought to a state of naïveté, must have the same radical origin as the dialectizing and critical-making force of thought which is at the base of education as the praxis of liberty. None of these antagonistic forms of education or of cultural action can escape the consciousness-world dialectization, even though their practices are diametrically opposed with regard to this dialectization. Thus, education or cultural action for domestication is bound to divide the consciousness from the world, and to consider the consciousness as an empty space within man which is to be filled with contents.[4] This separation, which results in the consciousness and the world being taken as statically opposed separate entities, implies the negation of the power of reflection of the consciousness, which is transformed into the empty space referred to. In fact, 'world and consciousness are not statically opposed to each other, they are related to each other dialectically, within their original and radical unity. For this reason the truth of one is to be gained through the other; truth is not given, it conquers itself and makes itself. It is, at once, discovery and invention.'[5]

This is precisely what education, or cultural action for domestication cannot claim. Instead, as an ideologizing instrument it imposes the mythification of the world instead of its truth, through the truth of the consciousness which critically 'unveils' this world. Thus, the mythification of the world – the world of the consciousness – means the mythification of the consciousness: consciousness of the world.

It would then be an unpardonable contradiction on the part of the power-élites if they consented to the kind of cultural action on a large scale which considered social reality (which mediates men) as the object of their truly critical analysis.

This is because this type of cultural action implies an epistemological practice which would be the contradiction of the one which characterizes cultural action for domestication.

The epistemological practice of cultural action or education for domestication divides teaching and learning, knowing and working, thinking and doing, informing and forming, re-knowing existing knowledge and creating new knowledge. In this kind of action, knowing is receiving information, or stocking 'deposits' made by others.[6]

Hence the form of action has the characteristic – which it never loses – of being a mere act of transferring knowledge. In this act, the educator – he who knows – transfers existing knowledge to the educatee: he who does not know. In this practice, knowledge is a mere given fact and not a permanent process which entails the praxis of men on the world. In this strange epistemology, there is no knowable object, but complete knowledge which the educator possesses. Thus it is incumbent on him to transfer, bring, extend, give and hand over to the 'ignorant' educatee, the 'knowledge' he possesses. In this way, the active character of the consciousness, when it is 'intentionality' towards the world, becomes passive; it is this active character which on the one hand explains man's ability for 're-knowing' existing knowledge, and on the other his ability for creating new knowledge. This practice of 'anaesthetizing', of de-dialectizing thought can also be seen in the emphasis laid on the 'focalist' rather than the totalizing perception of reality. This twisted view of the facts, which is not only unable to apprehend the relationships existing between them, but not even the relationships existing between the parts which constitute the totality of each of them either, is profoundly alienating. This way of seeking knowledge, which implies a conception of an immobile reality, can only lead us to a distorted view of things, which thus 'empty themselves' of their unquestionable temporality. Thus, we never get beyond the superficiality of the phenomena which we do not manage to understand in all their complexity and dynamism.

This way of acting is both alienating and 'domesticating', no matter whether the educators are or are not conscious of this.

It is not difficult to come on the practice of 'domestication' which we are analysing in systematic education, whatever its level. In the primary and secondary schools, in the university (and also in adult-education campaigns) we are witness to the transfer of knowledge, and not the search for knowledge, to knowledge as a process, to knowledge as something without conditions, taken as chaste and universal, to the split between teaching and learning, to the understanding of reality as something immobile, where reality is seen as a given fact and not as a process or a state of 'becoming' in order to be able to 'be'.

We could add to all this the myth that science is neutral, that the scientist is impartial, the myth of what must necessarily come out of his lack of preoccupation with the aims laid on the results of his activity as a scientist.

Let us see, in more concrete terms, although not extensively, how, and in what areas, education figures as the practice of 'domestication'.

First of all, since the school is an instrument of social control,[7] it cannot be a theoretical context, dialectically related to a concrete or objective context in which facts occur. Instead of permanently seeking the reason for the existence of the objective facts, in order to theorize them, the school becomes an agency specialized in the formal enunciation of them. Its false point of departure implies the epistemological distortion we have already spoken of, in which to know is reduced to a mechanical dualism expressed in the transference-reception of given facts.

Thus the relations between educator and educatee are the relations of a subject to an object, which means that the latter is the mere recipient of the contents of the knowledge of the former. The educator, he who knows, he who separates the act of teaching from the act of learning, is therefore always the educator of the educatee, while the latter is always the educatee of the educator. This explains the antidialogical character of this form of education. This situation of antidialogue is not only present in the epistemological relationship already referred to, but is also present in the disciplinary relationship. The educator is the one who thinks, who says his word, who knows; the educatee has the illusion that he is thinking, through the thinking of the educator; he has the illusion that he is saying his word, in repeating what the educator says; he has the illusion that he knows, because the educator knows.[8] Inasmuch as the school cannot be a genuinely theoretical context; inasmuch as the educator is the transmitter of a knowledge which merely describes reality as a given fact; inasmuch as the educator declares that he knows what ought to be taught, and does not recognize that he learns as he teaches, it seems obvious to him that it is incumbent on him to choose the content of the educational curriculum. The educatee can do nothing but let himself docilely be filled with this content. 'Because of this, in general, the good educatee is neither restive, nor indocile; he does not show doubt, he does not wish to know the reason for facts, he does not go beyond set models, he does not denounce "mediocratizing" bureaucracy, he does not refuse to be an object. The good educatee, in this type of education, on the contrary, is he who repeats, who refuses to think critically, who adapts to models, who finds it nice to be a rhinoceros.'[9] (See Ionesco: Rhinoceros.)

Before all this force of domestication, stands one really important question: Why is it possible for man, in spite of everything, to emerge critically, denouncing the ways of domestication? The answer to this basic question sends us back again to the problem of the consciousness, of its reflective character (and not only its reflective character), of its intentionality.

If all this attempt at alienating, at de-dialectizing thought 'domesticates' the capacity of the consciousness for reflection and criticism, or of man to be a conscious being, it cannot however make this capacity disappear. Sooner or later, the power of reflection and criticism reconstitutes itself in the very process of its 'domestication'. This is why we are able to talk about the liberation of man, even when we have to say that this does not stem from the mere recognition that it is necessary, but rather from the praxis which transforms the world in which we are not free. Contrary to education for domestication, education for liberation is an eminently Utopian praxis. This does not mean that it cannot be carried out. The Utopian nature of this type of education is expressed in the permanent state of unity which exists between the acts of denouncing and announcing, which give it life. In fact, domesticating education, which satisfies the interests of the dominating élites and corresponds to their ideology, can never be Utopian in the sense discussed here.

What denunciation can those who dominate make, unless it is the denunciation of those who denounce them? What can they announce except their own myths? What does their future as dominators consist of but the preservation of their present as privileged beings? Only education for liberation can be Utopian, and because it is Utopian, prophetic and hopeful. I cannot be prophetic or hopeful if my future is to be the repetition of a 'well-conducted' present, or of this present simply 'reformed' in some of its secondary aspects. Only those who are dominated can truly denounce and announce – denounce the world in which they exist but are forbidden to be, and announce the world in which they are able to be, and which demands their historical commitment in order for it to be brought into being. It is only they who have a future different from the present, an aspiration to be created and re-created. In their present as dominated beings can be found the plan of their liberation, which can be identified with the future which they must build.[10]

Contrary to education for domestication, education for liberation, Utopian, prophetic and hopeful, is an act of knowing and a means of action for transforming the reality which is to be known.

The epistemological focus of attention changes radically from one to another of the opposing forms of education or cultural action.

While in education for domestication one cannot speak of a knowable object but only of knowledge which is complete, which the educator possesses and transfers to the educatee, in education for liberation there is no complete knowledge possessed by the educator, but a knowable object which mediates educator and educatee as subjects in the knowing process. Dialogue is established as the seal of the epistemological relationship between subjects in the knowing process. There is not an 'I think' which transfers its thought, but rather a 'we think' which makes possible the existence of an 'I think'. The educator is not he who knows, but he who knows how little he knows, and because of this seeks to know more, together with the educatee, who in turn knows that starting from his little knowledge he can come to know more. Here there is no split between knowing and doing; there is no room for the separate existence of a world of those who know, and a world for those who work.

While in the domesticating practice the educator is always the educator of the educatee, in the liberating practice the educator must 'die' as exclusive educator of the educatee in order to be 'born' again as educatee of the educatee. At the same time, he must propose to the educatee that he 'die' as exclusive educatee of the educator in order to be 'born' again as educator of the educator.[11] This is a continual passage back and forth, a humble, creative movement, which both have to make.

Because educator-educatee accept in communion with each other the role of subjects in the educational act which is a permanent process, the educator no longer has the right to establish the curriculum-content of education, which does not belong exclusively to him. The organization of the curriculum, which must be regarded as a 'knowable object' by both educator-educatee and educatee-educator, requires the investigation of what we usually term the 'thematic universe'[12] of the educatees. Taken as the point of departure of the process, the investigation of the 'thematic universe' not only reveals to us the preoccupations of the educatees, but also their state of perception of their world.

When the curriculum whose structure is based on the themes investigated, becomes for the educatees a series of problems to be 'unveiled' as such, education for liberation takes the form of the permanent unity existing between the investigation of the thematic and its presentation as a problem. If, in the moment of our investigation – which is already cultural action – we come on the themes and the levels of perception of reality, in the moment when the problematization of these themes is presented as a knowable object, the perception of reality undergoes a change, and a new set of themes emerges, through a new vision of old themes or through a perception of themes hitherto not perceived.

Thus, education (or cultural action for liberation, which it cannot fail to be) reproduces the dynamism which characterizes the historical-social process. Its mobility depends on the mobility of the facts which must genuinely be known in the practice of education. It is only through an education which does not separate action from reflection, theory from practice, consciousness from the world, that it is possible to develop a dialectic form of thinking which contributes to the insertion of men as subjects in their historical reality.

In that it is Utopian and demythologizing, education or cultural action for liberation implies a constant risk which we do not always want to run, since we are tempted by the stability we fear to lose. In the long run, in preferring stability, immobility, self-censure, conspiratorial silence, all we do is renounce liberty because we are afraid of it. We shall thus not be able critically to have 'unusual ideas about education', since thinking in this way is to be committed, and requires of us a greater risk: that of putting into practice some of the unusual ideas.

Notes and References

1 I have insisted on this point in various different studies. See FREIRE, PAULO (1970) *Pedagogy of the Oppressed*. New York: Herder and Herder; and (1970) 'Cultural Action for Freedom', *Harvard Educational Review* and The Center for the Study of Development and Social Change, *Monograph Series*, No. 1.

2 For this see NICOL, EDUARDO (1965) *Los Principios de la Ciencia*. Mexico: Fondo de Cultura Económica; and FREIRE, PAULO (1969) *Extension o Comunicación?* Santiago: ICIRA, and (1971) Montevideo: Tierra Nueva.

3 See the essays of ILLICH, IVAN and REIMER, EVERETT (n.d.) *An Essay on Alternatives in Education*. Mexico: CIDOC (Cuaderno No. 1005).

4 FREIRE, PAULO, *Pedagogy of the Oppressed*, op. cit.; and (1971) 'Education as Cultural Action', in COLONNESE, LOUIS M. (ed.) *Conscientization for Liberation*. Washington, D.C.: Division for Latin America United States Catholic Conference.

5 FIORI, ERNANI (1971) 'Education and Conscientization', *Conscientization for Liberation*, op. cit., pp. 126–7.

6 We ironically term this type of action 'banking education': *Pedagogy of the Oppressed*, op. cit.

7 Again I suggest the reading of the essays of Ivan Illich, op. cit.: the best expression of denunciation today of the myth of schooling.

8 FREIRE, PAULO, *Pedagogy of the Oppressed*, op. cit.

9 FREIRE, PAULO (1970) 'Notes on Humanisation and its Educational Implications'. Mimeographed for the Seminar of Educ-International: Tomorrow began yesterday, Rome, November 1970.

10 For this theme, see FREIRE, PAULO, 'Cultural Action for Freedom', op. cit.

11 See FREIRE, PAULO (1970) 'Politische Alphabetisierun. Einführung ins Konzept einer humanisierenden Bildung', *Lutherische Monatshefte*, November 1970.

12 In *Pedagogy of the Oppressed*, I give a whole chapter to this question. In addition, as Unesco Consultant in the Instituto de Capacitación e Investigación en Reforma Agraria, ICIRA, Santiago, Chile, I coordinated a team to carry out an investigation of this type in one of the rural areas of Chile. The final report was recently published under the title: *Investigación de la Tematica Cultural de los Campesinos de 'El Recurso'*, edited by Maria Edy Ferreira and José Luis Fiori.

1.5 Problems in contemporary educational theory: a Marxist approach[1]

Brian Simon

There is today a proliferation of approaches, particularly in the social sciences, which claim to be Marxist, neo-Marxist, or in some way based on Marxism. Some of these seem to take a stance far removed from the basic principles of Marxism. Reviewing a book reflecting some of these trends recently, Eugene Kamenka writes that 'For those who have no prior independent logic, body of knowledge or discipline of thought, the Fichteanized or Hegelianized, phenomenologicalized Marx, shorn of his constant empirical reference to history and society, can be very bad medicine indeed', promoting 'muddle and confusion' rather than 'clear and detailed logical and historical thinking'.[2]

I intend to steer clear of the forms of 'Marxism' Kamenka here refers to, though such thinking has penetrated into education; nor will I attempt a systematic exposition of Marxism and its application to education; this would be impossible in a short paper. All that I can hope to do is to illuminate the nature of the Marxist approach, as I understand it, through an analysis of some contemporary problems in the field of education. Though Marx himself wrote little bearing directly on education in its institutionalized form, it is my contention that an approach based on Marxism is relevant to a wide range of educational issues – issues which are necessarily related to social evolution as a whole, whether in its concrete material aspect, or in the realm of ideas. Further, there are today many controversial questions – both theoretical and practical – that require attention, but have been neglected by Marxists. There is an urgent need to clarify such issues, both to assist those working in the field in the 'here and now', and to contribute to the formulation of long-term objectives. This paper is an exploratory study towards these ends.

First, as background, a few words on the vexed question of the relation between education and the state, since this underlies any assessment of the social function of education. At a risk of considerable oversimplification it is possible to identify two views held by Marxists. The first maintains that education – institutionalized education in particular – is an integral aspect of the state apparatus (in Lenin's sense); that its function is to ensure (1) the reproduction of social relations, and (2) assimilation of the new generation into the existing social order (Althusser defines education as an Ideological State Apparatus – ISA). In this sense, then, education is seen as imposed and controlled by the dominant forces in society as one of the means of maintaining and reproducing the existing social order. This is clearly a highly determinist view as to its role.

Source: *Journal of Philosophy of Education*, Vol. 12, 1978, pp. 29–39.

The second view differs in that it interprets institutionalized education primarily as an area of struggle; as an arena where opposing (or at least differing) objectives meet – objectives reflecting the interests of different social classes, strata or groups. In this view education is not seen primarily as part of the oppressive apparatus of the state (in the sense that the armed forces, police, judicature, etc., may be), nor even as an ISA in the Althusserian sense, though it is recognized that the structure and content of the system may be preponderantly influenced by the dominant social class (or classes). Historical analysis, it is claimed, confirms that struggles over the nature of education are characteristic of a divided society, and that the net outcome is often a compromise where a new situation is reached embodying opposed objectives (the 1870 Education Act, supported by working class elements, as well as both the industrial bourgeoisie and the landed interest, each for different reasons, is a case in point). Hence conflicts necessarily arise in education, and indeed always have done. Such conflicts, reflecting opposed interests (and perspectives), express themselves in different forms; for instance, in terms of the structure of the system, of its content, or of the nature of the educational process. This latter view seems the more illuminating of the two, and that closest to the traditional Marxist approach, with its stress on historical analysis. Further, it seems particularly appropriate to the situation in Britain, where direct central government control over education has always met with strong resistance, based on specific historical conditions and practices.

If the first view can be described as doctrinaire, certainly it allows little scope for effective initiative 'from below' (as it were) to change the system. The second, on the other hand, does provide a theoretical basis for such action, and so for direct involvement, by Marxists and others of course, in the contemporary controversial issues I wish to discuss.

The great perennial questions in education seem to me to be three, and these can be briefly put: What should be taught? To whom? How?

In Britain today these questions are posed against the background of the move to comprehensive secondary education. This is, and has been, a complex process. From the standpoint of the Labour Movement (with which Marxism must be primarily concerned) this transition contains positive features, specifically because it represent a move to an organizational form which *potentially* (or *theoretically*) allows the whole population, without distinction of class, race or sex, to experience a common, basic education which (again potentially) can impart a humanist, formative culture, embracing also the fundamentals of science and technology, relevant to the education of all in the mid-late twentieth century.[3] In this sense the transition implies the demise of the functionally organized school system which, through formalized systems of streaming and selection (with 'appropriately' differentiated content) docketed and programmed each child to a preconceived goal.

The degree to which these potential objectives have so far been achieved, however, should not be exaggerated. The social context in which the transition is taking place is one marked by sharp antagonisms, and these are reflected in the schools in many ways. Nevertheless, overall, from the standpoint of the Labour Movement, which has worked to achieve this objective from the turn of the century and before, the transition has been marked by positive effects.

But it should also be recognized that, in some senses at least, this transition has also been necessary for the maintenance and smooth functioning of the existing social order. This for two main reasons: first, because the new system seemed likely to reduce the wastage of human abilities urgently required as a direct result of economic and technological advance (as documented, for instance, in the Crowther report of 1958); and second, because it appeared likely to reduce friction between social classes and promote harmony (the social engineering aspect of comprehensive education as defined, for instance, by Anthony Crosland and others).

The comprehensive school, then, as a movement, itself embodies opposing objectives in the sense defined earlier. This is one reason why there is so much controversy as to the objectives of these schools, as well as to their internal organization and procedures – in the circumstances this is hardly surprising. If we add to this the more general context in which schooling operates today – which expresses itself in terms of the so-called urban crisis, the economic and fiscal crisis relating to the financing of education, and even the administrative crisis arising from local government reorganization and the sudden switch to corporate management techniques – it becomes evident that the new system is coming into being in conditions which are exceptionally unstable. It is, then, easy to understand why there is and has been a certain confusion as to educational objectives and means, sharply focused by the Tyndale enquiry but reflected also at the secondary stage. This is the context in which controversial issues have arisen in education.

First let me state, quite briefly, what I take to be the Marxist perspective in education, at least in terms of the possibilities and requirements of advanced industrial societies, whatever their social system. This is, through primary and secondary education, to impart a general, formative, humanist culture to be followed by professional (or vocational) education – and to *all*. How? By grasping and utilizing all the resources of modern pedagogy; and I suggest, with Comenius in the seventeenth century and with Bruner and Luria today, that this is a theoretically feasible objective (if the necessary conditions are provided). The rationale for this standpoint will be elaborated later, but these are the general objectives in relation to which ideological (or theoretical) issues arise which Marxists see as important. In general these are those standpoints which oppose these objectives on the grounds either that they are undesirable in themselves, or, more usually perhaps, that they are impossible of achievement.

First, there are those theories regarding human potential derived from intelligence testing. In Britain we are now just beginning to emerge from an educational system that was dominated by what can best be described as 'mental testing ideology' to a quite remarkable degree. This is a question to which Marxists have devoted a good deal of attention; it is clearly central to the formulation both of short- and long-term perspectives.

Intelligence-testing theorists claimed to have discovered laws about the distribution of Intelligence holding good for all societies, and to which, it was suggested, school systems should correspond. These theories, therefore, provided a rational justification for the establishment of hierarchical school systems. In Britain in particular intelligence testing was used both as the theoretical justification of the system and as the instrumental means by which the system operated (through streaming and selection).

For these reasons any attempt to open up the system required as a first condition a thoroughly critical look at the theories derived from testing, and at its technology. Marxists, I suggest, were in a good position to undertake this, partly because the theories underlying mental testing approached the analysis of mind and of the development of mental abilities in ways which were suspect, both in terms of dialectics and of materialism. Perhaps a few examples will help to indicate the difficulties, for Marxists, in assenting to propositions derived from this field.

First, then, the concept of 'Intelligence' itself as formulated by psychometrists, conceived as a unitary 'factor of the mind' derived from statistical analysis of the results of mass testing, raises the question as to its status or nature. Such a factor appears as a statistical artefact, one applicable, perhaps, to 'man in general', but hardly so to the mind of any given individual, and certainly not derived from study and observation of any given individual in his growth and development.

Second, the theory that is basic to intelligence testing – that individual mental development is the resultant of the 'interaction' of the two factors, heredity and environment. The problem here is that Marxism does not see the child as the passive product of external circumstances.

Third, the assumption as to the stability of 'Intelligence', said to have been proved by mass testing over time (though later somewhat modified); the assumption that there is something in each individual's brain and higher nervous system which is *unaffected by* education and experience (as Burt used to claim). Marxism, which stresses movement and change, the interconnection and interrelation of phenomena, finds this concept static and metaphysical.

Fourth, the assumption that Intelligence must always be 'normally' distributed in any representative population; a theory that Marxist concepts of social evolution would appear to contradict.

Fifth, the kind of evidence adduced by psychometrists (for instance, Cyril Burt) as confirmatory of this point regarding differences in brain structure (or substance); evidence which appears to be contradicted by modern researches into the physiology of the higher nervous system which tend to stress the flexibility, mutability, potentiality for change of this system.

Sixth, the evident and clear cultural bias of early intelligence tests which thereby 'proved' (or provided confirmatory evidence in support of the theory of the intellectual superiority of the middle (or upper middle and professional) class over the working class; a finding which seemed to Marxists possibly more a comment on the nature of the test items – or of the concept of Intelligence embodied in these – than scientific and unequivocal statements about differential levels of Intelligence among social classes.

Finally, to descend from the sublime to the ridiculous, the kind of historical evidence (based on Dick Whittington and his ilk) adduced, for instance, by Burt as to how it came about that those endowed genetically with high levels of Intelligence land up at Hampstead, and those with low levels at West Ham.

There is no space here to argue these points – that has been done elsewhere – but perhaps enough has been said to indicate why those adopting a Marxist standpoint were among the first to carry through a critique of intelligence-testing theories and practices in this country. The fact is that the initial assumptions built into testing theory – and specifically into its technology and procedures – are in themselves alien to the approach Marxists make to these questions. In addition, Marxists understood that such a critique was necessary if teachers, parents, administrators and others were to be brought to believe that the system, which found its rational justification in these theories, was not, in fact, based on an accurate understanding of the nature of the child's mind – or of its potentialities. To achieve this was *one* condition for changing the system (there were, of course, others).

Nor is this all. These ideas, as we have seen, have recently been revived, in a *racial* context in the United States and in a class context in Britain (see the articles by Burt, Eysenck and Lynn in the series of Black Papers on Education). Indeed I am tempted to say that, so long as the conditions exist where such ideas are useful to particular social groups or classes, so long will they constantly reappear. In any case it is clear that this is still a contemporary issue, and one important for education. That is why Marxists (and others, of course) must continue to express their standpoint on this question.

Basically, Marxists reject views regarding the primacy of genetic determination of human intellectual development; as explained later, they place their main emphasis on the process of education (conceived of in its widest sense) as the main determinant of intellectual as well as other aspects of development.

This does not imply, incidentally, that every child is born equal, or of equal potential (whatever that may mean); only that, as mentioned above, the main determinant of development lies in the nature of the child's life experiences, of which organized and systematic education forms an important part.

While taking a highly critical attitude, then, to placing the major emphasis on hereditary determination, Marxists also reject the parallel but seemingly opposite claim that it is not hereditary, but *environmental disadvantage* which sets sharp limits to, or determines, educability.

This standpoint holds, in effect, that the mass of working class children are so disadvantaged by the nature of their family life and circumstances as to be incapable of abstract, conceptual thought, and therefore of profiting from a systematic education.

It may be worth pointing to the speculative nature of this theory – originally derived, in part at least, from the late Professor Luria's pioneering work on the relation between language and mental development (although Luria himself would hardly have gone along with the theory as elaborated).

Linguistic deprivation is advanced as the reason why working class children 'fail' when confronted with the demands and rigours of an academic education. This analysis, then, seeks the reason for failure within the children themselves, or their families, rather than in the circumstances of a divided society with its attendant housing, health and recreative problems which themselves require social action on a massive scale.

Environmental determinism of this type, it is argued, can be as vicious as hereditarian determinism, and is equally unacceptable on rational grounds, in particular perhaps, to Marxists. As mentioned earlier, both these forms of determinism are based on the concept that the child's development is the simple *product* of the interaction of the two 'factors' – heredity and a supposed unchanging environment. The latter, in the schema, is conceived as a kind of global entity which is external to the child and operates on him from outside.

This concept is really the simplest mechanical materialism brought to a fine pitch by David Hartley in the eighteenth century – it seems scarcely adequate as an interpretation of human development today, yet it seems this is the sense in which the concept of the 'environment' is used by Burt and Jensen when they claim that variance in 'Intelligence' is due 80 per cent to heredity and 20 per cent to 'environment'.

The matter is far more complex than this, and I will return to it later. But it is relevant at this stage to note that the Marxist approach to child development places the main emphasis on the child's active relationship with adults, other children, the school and other phenomena, both natural and artificial, surrounding him or her. It is through this process of *activity* that the child's specific abilities, skills and habits, his speech and behaviour are generally formed.

It is, perhaps worth noting that Burt used to claim that the theory of the primacy of 'Intelligence' as a factor of the mind lent support to the idealist philosophic outlook, and he is right. In the same way the environmentalist approach, which reaches its apotheosis in Skinnerian behaviourism, seems to be the modern expression of what Marxists refer to as mechanical materialism which sees man essentially as the passive product of external circumstances. Marx always contended that these two philosophic standpoints are opposite sides to the same coin; and pointed out that what both ignore, or fail to grasp, is *dialectics* – the very possibility of movement and change, the interconnection, or interpenetration of subject and object which, incidentally, surely lies at the very heart of the educational process (conceived as a *process*).

How does the argument concerning linguistic deprivation proceed, and why is it important?

Children who are linguistically, or educationally, deprived, it is argued (in their best interests of course), require a special *differentiated* educational content, or forms of activity.

Here we meet a wide variety of ideological standpoints which deny the desirability, or even the possibility, of providing common basic educational experiences for all children; a position which leads, objectively, to differentiation and back to divisive practices in education.

A wide variety of ingenious theories are utilized to support this position, some dressed up as radical, even revolutionary, nostrums.

These range from the (no doubt well intentioned) plea for special 'community based' curricula for EPA [Educational Priority Area] children (on the grounds that the very deprivation these children suffer necessitates a specific approach) to, at the other end of the spectrum, the overtly sophisticated relativism of 'new direction' sociology.

This latter standpoint advances an unbelievably a-historical (and entirely speculative) theory as to how 'high status' curriculum and subject matter become so defined, and enshrined in the school curriculum – as a result, apparently of battles for status and 'legitimacy' between competing groups. This argument then 'legitimizes' (to use their term) the conclusion that any curriculum is 'as good as' another. The more radical expression of this view claims that the knowledge man has accumulated over the last two or three thousand years is 'bourgeois knowledge' and therefore by definition alienating to the working class – more particularly if 'transmitted' by teachers who are themselves, again by definition, middle class.

No-one who has made any kind of serious study of Marxism could conceivably claim the authority of Marx, Engels or Lenin for so extreme a relativist position relating to knowledge. Marxism, of course, fully accepts that in any specific historical circumstances, there is bound to be an 'ideological' component to knowledge – indeed this concept is fundamental to Marxism – but Marxism certainly accepts the concept of objective knowledge, and of man's capacity consistently to approximate to it. The whole question of the validity of the relativist view of knowledge was argued out in detail by Lenin in *Materialism and Empirio-Criticism* 70 years ago, and it is ironic that it should be left to Professor Flew to draw this work to the attention of the 'new sociologists' who claim to take their stand on Marxism.

The devaluation of knowledge consequent on extreme relativist positions has clear dangers when applied to education. We have seen in recent years how some young teachers, accepting this standpoint, and in their sentimental generosity identifying with their working class pupils, come to see their role as shielding them from the demands of formal schooling, and consequently act more as social workers than as teachers with the specific function of inducting pupils into knowledge and of developing the skills and abilities that derive from the objectives of an all-round humanist education appropriate to the mid–late twentieth century.

It is self-evident that Marxism must reject this approach which, in the last resort, leads to solipsism – a blind alley if ever there was one – and which, from a Marxist standpoint, simply provides a new ideological means of denying to the working class access to knowledge, science and culture.

Marxists also, not surprisingly perhaps, take a critical attitude to libertarian or anarchist positions which, fundamentally, deny the need for structure, purpose, direction or any kind of authority in education.

These approaches usually base themselves on an idealist position (philosophically) as to the nature of the child and the potentialities of his inner, spontaneous, 'natural' development.

Unfortunately no serious criticism of this approach has yet been made from a Marxist standpoint, so far as I am aware. It is clear enough how such a critique would proceed, however, if we take Froebel as an example. The main principle here, it seems, is that the child contains within himself all potentialities for development which will unfurl naturally, provided that the child has opportunity for spontaneous activity in rich environment, the function of the kindergarten, covering the first seven years of life, being to 'make the inner outer'. (Froebel's insistence that, thereafter, the school's function is to 'make the outer inner' seems totally ignored by Froebelians; yet this sharp dichotomy in the school's function surely reflects a rather fundamental philosophic weakness.)

Froebel's ideas on early childhood education have penetrated deeply into the so-called progressive movement. They are important in our context since they deny the possibility of common educational experiences, stressing what is unique and so what differentiates every individual rather than what human beings have in common.

A Marxist critique of, for instance, A. S. Neill, Paul Goodman and other modern anarcholibertarians is highly desirable. This should not ignore the positive aspects of these thinkers (and practitioners), and that is that they brought back into the picture the importance of the child's activity – or self-activity, as Froebel puts it; an aspect of teaching and learning that traditional approaches, seeing the child as the passive assimilator of transmitted knowledge, tended to obscure.

Another position linked closely with these is that of the de-schoolers. It is clear that, so far as Illich's educational analysis is concerned, he bases himself very fully on the work of the American anarchist Paul Goodman.

There can be no question that the Marxist approach leads to rejection of Illich's main thesis which, in education, appears to be that, if the educational system could be destroyed, this would bring down with it the whole technocratic, monopoly-dominated, consumer-orientated society (as he defines it), and open the way to the joyous and convivial Utopia he envisages.

There has been no serious Marxist critique of Illich's outlook (if we except that by Gintis in the *Harvard Educational Review*); but the main thrust of such a critique is clear enough. On the one hand, much of Illich's criticism of the nature of the existing educational system could be accepted; Illich focuses on the deadening effect of schooling under capitalism, its separation from life, its concentration on examinations and certification, and so on. But in the Marxist view, this criticism does not lead to the conclusion that the system must be destroyed – rather that it should be transformed so that it meets more directly the interest of the mass of the people, even if the struggle for the transformation of education can only be effective if integrally linked with the wider political struggle for social change.

Marxists could not conceivably accept the naïve view that the way to transform society in any fundamental sense is to destroy the educational system, even if that were a practical objective. The transformation of society to bring about a new social-economic formation is only possible through the achievement of political power – that is, by the transformation of the state. The means to achieve this objective involve a broad (political, economic and social) movement – not the destruction of peripheral institutions such as schools and universities.

Objectively it may be that Illich is reflecting current trends – the increasingly obvious lack of concern by the ruling forces in society for educational advance; even for implementing compulsory education. In the United States, for instance, state legislation on this issue is certainly not being enforced with any energy, while much heart-searching is going on among historians as to why compulsory education was originally introduced.

I have touched on some of the contemporary ideological issues in education, and given an idea of what I conceive to be a Marxist approach to these. Each should be subjected to a full analysis, and hopefully will be in the not too distant future.

I want to outline what I conceive to be a Marxist approach to some related questions concerning education, teaching and learning.

First, then, there is the general question of what to teach – the content of education. Here the Marxist approach leads to a rejection of pluralistic notions, for instance the idea (or basic principle) that different sorts of curricula should be provided for different groups or classes (or sexes). Marxists certainly reject the notion that education for the working class must be based on, or derived from, some kind of specifically working class or proletarian culture (with the concomitant view that the knowledge now taught in schools and colleges is necessarily some kind of bourgeois knowledge that must be rejected).

In my view Lenin put the Marxist position on these questions very clearly when criticizing the so-called 'proletcult' movement in the USSR in the early 1920s – a movement which also rejected science and culture as bourgeois, and supported the concept of an independent proletarian culture. On this issue Lenin said, first, that it was right to reject the methods and ethos of the 'old school', with its stress on rote learning, its aridity and isolation from life. But, second, Lenin stressed again and again (in his speech to the Youth Leagues)[4] what he saw as the crucial issue: that to be a Communist (and the schools should educate Communists) the student must acquire human knowledge as it had been accumulated in the past. Marx himself, he pointed out, took his stand on the firm foundation of human knowledge gained under capitalism.

Students, said Lenin, must assimilate this knowledge, but assimilate it *critically*; 'One can become a communist,' he said, 'only when one enriches one's mind with a knowledge of all the wealth created by mankind', and when one knows how to apply it. In his draft resolution to the Proletcult conference he carried on the battle:

Marxism won for itself its world-historical significance as the ideology of the revolutionary proletariat by the fact that it did not cast aside the valuable gains of the bourgeois epoch, but, on the contrary assimilated and digested all that was valuable in the more than 2000 years of development of human thought and culture.

It was this that needed to be taken further under socialism as the means of developing 'a really proletarian culture'. The draft resolution goes on to reject 'as theoretically wrong and practically harmful all attempts to invent a special culture' and to use it as the basis of development and education.

This view of Lenin's is in line with the Marxist outlook which accepts the independent existence of the external world (as a 'reality', independent of man), and the view that, through social productive labour and the consequent (or concomitant) development of language and consciousness, man has gained an increasing understanding, and so control, of nature; that is, has accumulated *knowledge*. Marxism sees human beings as the product of labour on the one hand, and of knowledge on the other.

In the process of social evolution man's specifically human abilities are both formed and *objectified* (as it were) in the products of labour; so man is surrounded with a humanized world.

The knowledge (and abilities) so gained are specific to man; that which makes men human. Through the emergence of language, which allows abstraction and generalization, man's cultural heritage can be, and is, handed on from generation to generation through what may be called 'social inheritance'. In this process education is clearly central – indeed education can be seen as *the mode of development of human beings*. It is in this respect that man differs from the rest of the animal world – and it is for this reason that different laws apply to man's development than the purely biological. To allow the growth of a full humanity, it is precisely this knowledge that must be made available to men – to all men (as I suggested earlier). This is what needs to be taken into account in considering the content of education.

In his speech to the Youth Leagues, Lenin said that knowledge gained under bourgeois rule must be assimilated – but *critically*. What is meant by this?

Lenin meant simply that knowledge is affected by (or, better, embodies) ideological preconceptions resulting from the nature of the class society in which this knowledge is gained; and that these preconceptions distort that knowledge to a greater or lesser extent. To assimilate this knowledge 'critically' is to attempt to identify this component – to adopt a critical stance to it so that true knowledge is cleansed (as it were) from this adulteration; or more correctly (exactly) reflects reality – or approximates more closely to objective truth.

This point has been referred to already when discussing the difference between the Marxist and the 'relativist' position of 'new direction' sociology, which denies any possibility, as I see it, of approximating to objective truth since it does not accept this as a worthwhile concept. The Marxist position relates to the overall ideological framework (and set of concepts) by which a given society (or, better, a given class in a dominant position in society) explicates, or rationalizes, its form and character, and its position in the universe.

On the whole, Marxists hold that ideological components of this kind enter most directly into what we now call the social sciences, for instance, into such fields as economic theory or, indeed, psychometry. Such components, which reflect or justify the existing social order, have as their objective function the assimilation of the population into existing norms so preserving the status quo. Hence Lenin's insistence on the *critical* assimilation of knowledge gained under capitalism as a function of the school in socialist society. But such, also, must be the objective of Marxist educators in a capitalist society. This implies that the function of the school is to make available to all access to the main areas of knowledge and culture accumulated in the past, together with the ability to apply that knowledge in practice.

So much for the content of education. We may turn now to methodological (or pedagogic) issues. And here attention may first be given to the Italian Communist, Gramsci, who applied Marxist ideas to education in his prison notebooks, written in the 1920s (and under very adverse conditions).[5] His ideas are very relevant to contemporary concerns. Gramsci saw the function of the school system generally to prepare the student to function as an autonomous, creative, responsible individual. His objective is what he calls the 'creative school', organized as a collective, and developing 'the capacity for intellectual and practical creativity, and of autonomy of orientation and initiative'.

Gramsci saw education as a participatory process; in some senses as a *transaction* between teacher and taught. He refers to the need for 'the truly active participation' of the pupil in school. The relation between teacher and pupil is seen as active and reciprocal so that every teacher is also a pupil and vice versa.

While stressing the importance of activity in education, Gramsci took issue with some of the 'progressive' theorists of his day. Criticizing one of the exponents of the theory that teachers cannot pre-determine 'from outside' the development of the 'spiritual activity' of the child, Gramsci wrote:

It is believed that a child's mind is like a ball of string which the teacher helps to unwind. In reality each generation educates the new generation, i.e. forms it, and education is a struggle against instincts linked to the elementary biological functions, a struggle against nature, to dominate it and create the 'contemporary' man of the epoch.

Again, stressing the active nature of the common school, Gramsci wrote, 'The entire common school is an active school, though it is necessary to place certain limits on libertarian ideologies in this field and to stress with some energy the duty of adult generations to "mould" the new generations' (unfashionable perhaps, but surely correct).

In a perceptive paragraph, Gramsci states, 'The active school is still in its romantic phase, in which elements of struggle against the mechanical and Jesuitical school have become unhealthily exaggerated – through a desire to distinguish themselves sharply from the latter, and for political reasons. It is necessary,' he adds, 'to enter the "classical", rational phase, and to find in the ends to be attained the natural source for developing appropriate methods and forms' (a phrase worth pondering by Marxists – and others).

What is the basis for this stress on *activity* in the Marxist position? In my view it is central to the Marxist outlook on education, and is derived essentially from Marx's Theses on Feuerbach, where he struggled to express, and formulate, his fusion of dialectics on the one hand and contemporary materialism (which had already shown its inadequacy) on the other.

The mechanistic materialism of the late eighteenth century, the psychological expression of which lay in associationism (as developed by David Hartley and applied to education systematically by Joseph Priestley) led to the conclusion that man is, to all intents and purposes, the passive product of external circumstances. Its explanation of human formation lay in the impact of external stimuli through the senses, the building up of trains of associations, and so the formation of knowledge, character, and habits. This system allowed no scope for what Marx later called 'self-activity'. This outlook was crystallized in Marx's day in Robert Owen's great slogan 'Circumstances make Man'.

This was certainly a liberating concept at the time. Change men's circumstances, said Owen, and you change man – and this is what he set out to do at New Lanark. But such an explanation of social and human change allows no scope for human activity, or self-change, and, as Marx pointed out, it is logically defective, since it leads to the necessity of dividing society into two parts, one of which is superior to society. Put simply, it implies that certain men (Robert Owen, for example) are not themselves formed by circumstances in so far as they are able, as it were, to rise above them and form the circumstances of others – become their 'educators'. Indeed this theory or outlook cannot explain how men's circumstances may be changed – and yet they palpably are!

'The materialist doctrine that men are products of circumstances and upbringing,' wrote Marx in one of his Theses, 'and that, therefore, changed men are products of other circumstances and changed upbringing, forgets that *it is men that change circumstances* and that the educator must himself be educated' (my italics).

The defect of this materialism, in Marx's view, was its failure to account for (or subsume) the *active* side of human development. This failure resulted from conceiving of reality only in the form of an object, for contemplation, 'but not as human sensuous activity, practice, not subjectively, which was also a reality'. (Marx is referring here to the fact that man creates his own circumstances, lives in a *humanized* world – as referred to earlier.) This failure, according to Marx, left the way open to idealist interpretations which could only be abstract, since idealism 'does not know real, sensuous activity as such'.

As is well known, Marx expressed his synthesis, or seized the contradiction, thus:

The coincidence of the changing of circumstances and of human activity can be conceived and rationally understood only as *revolutionizing practice*.

Man, through his own activity – *in the process of his activity* – both changes his external circumstances and changes himself. Man's consciousness and his activity are, then, a unity; activity implies both changing consciousness and a changed external world.

Marxists hold that this concept – that of the unity of consciousness and activity – is fundamental to education. It clearly profoundly influenced Gramsci. Its implications have been most fully developed in the work of Soviet psychologists, particularly Vigotski, Luria, Leontiev, Galperin, Elkonin and others.

This approach leads to the concept of abilities as historically formed in the process of the child's education (rather than given); and has led now to a widely accepted theory relating to necessary stages in the development of specific abilities in children – stages involving physical actions of various kinds (including external speech, internal speech, thought) are seen as central to the development of specific mental abilities (Galperin).

Of key importance for human formation, in the Marxist view, is the role of language with its powers not only of abstraction and generalization, but also as the means by which the child organizes his own behaviour. Through language, in the child's communication with adults in the process of education, what Luria calls 'complex functional systems' are built up in the brain and higher nervous system which underlie the specific abilities and skills developed in the child in the process of education. This process differs qualitatively from the way learning takes place in animals.

From this it may be concluded that the child requires opportunity for activity in education; but that activity must allow the child to 'meet' situations necessary for the development of specific abilities. That is to say that, when the desired outcome is the development of specific abilities (linguistic, mathematical, scientific) careful structuring of the child's activity is required. This does not imply, however, that all educational time, as it were, needs to be of this type; only that this is relevant to certain fields of cognitive development.

There is no space to develop the implication of these ideas or findings in terms of pedagogic means, but enough has been said to make it clear that Marxists find it difficult to enter into current discussions relating to teaching styles based on crude parameters such as the formal/informal or progressive/traditional dichotomies. Briefly, Marxists tend to be critical of 'formal' styles for underrating the importance of the child's activity, and of 'informal' styles for lack of a clear rationale and psychological underpinning (as also for lack of 'structure', but by 'structure' Marxists understand something very different from its normal meaning). In my view the specific contribution of Marxism to the understanding of child development has much to offer to current thinking and practice in education, whether in socialist or capitalist countries.

The main conclusion, however, relevant to the concerns of this paper, is the stress laid by Marxists, arising from this analysis, on human educability and potentialities, and on the consequent need to provide effective and systematic educational opportunities for all. Of course, in any realistic view, Marxists must accept that many obstacles of very various nature exist to stultify or prevent the realization of human potentialities today. The sharp social and political conflicts that characterize society are certainly reflected in the schools, as we see all too clearly. I have not attempted in this paper to deal with these; only to try to set out, as clearly as I can, the Marxist orientation to certain major theoretical issues in education today.

Notes and References

1 This paper is a revised version of an article with a similar title published in *Marxism Today*, June 1976.
2 *Times Literary Supplement*, 19 November 1976.
3 The continued existence of the private (independent) sector qualifies this statement, except in so far as the concept of the comprehensive school implies its eventual absorption into a single system.
4 *Selected Works*, 9, pp. 467–83.
5 HOARE, Q. and NOWELL-SMITH, E. (eds) (1971) *Selections from the Prison Notebooks of Antonio Gramsci*. London: Lawrence and Wishart, pp. 26–43.

1.6 Technology, education and industrial and economic strength

Correlli Barnett

Let me begin my main argument by offering a definition of 'capability'. I mean it in the normal English sense by which we refer to someone as a 'capable' person; that is, an ability successfully to tackle the practical situations of life. This also means possessing the specialized skills and knowledge necessary successfully to tackle the operational problems of a particular professional sphere – as when we speak of 'a capable engineer' or 'a capable general'.

[In the present context] I am specially talking about capability in the process of designing, making and marketing products that people will wish to buy in preference to rival ones. In other words, for a country like Great Britain, individual and collective capability at the business of being an advanced industrial economy.

There are of course the neo-Puginites or neo-Morrisites who like to think of Britain as leading the world into a post-industrial phase where this form of capability will be obsolete, and who despise so material a matter as GNP as unethical or – the trendy version – unecological. Yet these high-minded escapists are among the first to howl about the need for more resources to be invested in hospitals, schools, good works, prison improvement, subsidies for the arts and what not. A country of static or declining GNP will not be an 'Erewhon' but a pinched and increasingly bitter place. Poverty may be noble as a concept; it is rarely so in the flesh.

I therefore take it as a given fact that the 56 million people of this country can only prosper on the basis of competitive success in the business of designing, making and marketing products and services in very large quantities. I take it that this audience does not think that our mass urban population can all live by opening craft pottery shops or pseudo-provençal bistros, or starting agricultural communes.

First question to answer: are we at present capable as an advanced industrial nation, or not? The figures speak for themselves: our GNP is only three times larger than that of Sweden, though our population is *eight* times larger. West Germany's GNP is twice ours, though her population is only half as much again. France, with a smaller population than ours, enjoys a GNP half as much again. The evidence of our incapability fills our newspapers and journals week after week. The present distresses of the British motor industry bear out the analysis of the Central Policy Review Staff two years ago that in every respect, from product design through production and marketing, the British motor industry is less capable than

Source: *Journal of the Royal Society of Arts*, No. 5271, Vol. CXXVII, February 1979, pp. 118–127.

its rivals; in terms of productivity less capable by half. And the car industry is no Victorian heavy, like steel, but a relatively new industry; one which in other countries is a pacemaker.

Take another modern industry: oil-refining. Do you remember the much-trumpeted productivity deal at Esso's Fawley refinery in 1960? It was to be the prototype of management–union agreements on ending restrictive practices. In 1975 it was found to be bottom in terms of productivity out of twelve Esso refineries from Hamburg to California. The labour editor of the *Sunday Times* in reporting this story concluded that 'The lesson of Fawley is that inefficiency is so deeply imbedded in our industrial life style that it cannot be removed at a stroke...'. Inefficiency – i.e., lack of capability.

Even ICI, perhaps our most highly regarded company, gets greater productivity out of its European plants than its British ones.

But is our inferiority due not to incapability but to lack of investment, as the unions like to claim? Or to our bad luck in winning the war instead of losing it like the Germans? Bacon and Eltis found that while machine tools in British factories were newer than in American, US output was three times higher. They found no evidence that the average age and service life of manufacturing capital stock in the two countries can explain the productivity differences. An MTRA Report in 1966 showed that machine tools in the UK are utilized for only 40 per cent of the time available.[1] While some industries may have gone short of investment, the evidence appears to show that we fail to wring maximum production out of the plant we have – in other words, our problem really is incapability.

Nor can we comfortably argue that the Germans lost all their old plant in the war and re-equipped from scratch with Marshall Aid. Only 15–20 per cent of Germany's industrial equipment was damaged beyond repair in the war, while West Germany received only some two-thirds the amount of Marshall Aid that Great Britain did – 1.7 billion dollars as against 2.7 billion. In the five years after the Second World War Britain received in loans and grants from all sources some 8 billion dollars. That we could receive so much and yet end up so unsuccessful must be a further pointer that our real problem is indeed a pervasive incapability.

But how much has British education got to do with this incapability? Clearly the Prime Minister and his advisers thought it had much to do with it when he began the great education debate two years ago. Let me summarize some factual evidence.

At a time of unemployment around the one and a half million mark there is a persistent shortage of skilled workers. A Government survey in 1977 reported that in some areas there are too few sixteen-year-olds with adequate basic education to enable them to start skilled industrial training. The Advisory Council for Applied Industrial Research's report on *The Application of Semiconductor Technology* gave as one reason why we had already been overtaken by competitors in this field that we were suffering from a shortage of staff with the necessary combination of hardware and software abilities.[2]

Farther up the ladder, we find that in 1971 89 per cent of French chief executives had degrees, 78 per cent of West German, 77 per cent of Swedish and only 40 per cent of British. There is much recent research evidence to confirm the judgment in a Department of Industry study paper that:

Management generally, and technical jobs in particular have lower status than on the Continent ... Careers in industrial management have generally failed, in Britain, to attract the best-educated products of the most favoured social groups; they may also have attracted few of those with high general ability.

British management is by comparison with its rivals especially weak in engineers, while recent research has suggested that there is a strong correlation between a country's industrial performance and the number of highly-qualified engineers in management.

There is not [space here] to pile up the evidence now being accumulated by investigations by various research teams. It comes to this: at every level of British industry there is either a shortage of skilled and appropriately qualified personnel or, even if they have the paper technical qualifications, they tend in fact to be of lower personal calibre and of lower status within the firm than their European opposite numbers.

This reflects on our education in two ways. In the first place our education fails to provide the right quantities, and the right balance, of the appropriately skilled personnel we need for industrial capability. Secondly, the general ethos and thrust of British education are, if anything, hostile to industry and careers in industry. As a result too small a proportion of the national talent seeks a life in manufacture. The percentage of professional engineers employed in production actually fell from 9 per cent in 1966 to 6 per cent in 1975. The proportion of all graduates entering manufacturing fell from about 40 per cent in the years up to 1970 to only 26 per cent in 1973.[3] There are signs that very recently attitudes towards careers in industry may be changing, but it is too soon to say how permanent this will prove.

At present, therefore, we are *not* educating for capability, and we are paying the price for it in chronic industrial unsuccess.

Yet my main purpose is to show that there is nothing novel about this. Our comparative lack of capability as an industrial society is not a matter of the post-war era, but dates back before 1850, to the very moment when we lost our early technological monopoly and began to face rivals. And right from that time, too, the quality, quantity and values of British education have been a key factor in that lack of capability.

In the initial phase of industrialization between 1760 and 1840 formal education and training were not of decisive importance, because, of its nature, a primitive stage of machine-building and manufacturing operation required little more than the *native* capability of resourceful practical men; craftsmen turning old skills to new purposes; self-educated rule-of-thumb. Our entrepreneurs built their businesses by similar commercial methods, starting small as a local tradesman or craftsman, and expanding by grace of native *nous*. It is true that some early industrial figures were interested in the scientific developments of the time. Yet science itself in the late eighteenth century was, like industry, a matter of self-education and private experiment; a superior form of rule-of-thumb.

It therefore hardly mattered that in this period there was little basic education for the masses; that grammar schools and public schools were mostly in decay and anyway taught an irrelevant syllabus of Greek and Latin; that Oxbridge lay in gouty slumber.

There arose in British industry right from the start, therefore, a tradition of the resourceful amateur, the man who learned on the job and passed on his knowledge verbally to the next generation as a craft 'mystery' in the medieval style – rather than the man specially and systematically trained for his rôle, so that practical application was backed by theoretical understanding. This was true all the way from boardroom to workbench. From this derived a potent British myth – that of 'the practical man'. But this meant 'practicality' in a very primitive sense: not *educated* 'practicality'. The cult of the practical man carried with it, contrariwise, a positive mistrust of the application of intellectual study and scientific research to industrial operations; a deep suspicion of the very kind of highly trained and professionally educated man European and American industry looked for from the start. In 1850 *The Economist* was writing that 'the education which fits men to perform their duties in life is not to be got in school, but in the counting-houses and lawyer's office, in the shop or the factory'.

But in the course of the first half of the nineteenth century industrial products and processes were passing beyond the primitive stage of bolting on more plates when the boiler burst, or taking something out of the furnace when old Joe reckoned the colour was right. What was now needed was systematic formal training in basic scientific and engineering principles and in specialized applications like metallurgy, the chemical industry, machine design and manufacture, production methods; a need for intimate links between experimental science, technical education and the world of industry. As early as 1835 we find Richard Cobden warning after a visit to America that 'our only chance of national prosperity lies in the timely remodelling of our system, so as to put it as nearly as possible upon an equality with the improved management of the Americans.'[4] Just two years after the Great Exhibition of 1851 had seemed to consummate the triumph of British technology, Dr Lyon Playfair wrote in his book *Industrial Education on the Continent* that European industry was bound to overtake Britain if she failed to alter her outlook and methods.[5] Thus perceptive critics in Britain saw as early as this the connexion between education for capability and industrial success. Unfortunately it was not just critics but the State and public opinion in general that had seen the connexion abroad, and throughout the early nineteenth century European countries and America were creating institutions for technical education that would turn out '*educated* practical men'. Institutions, moreover, for technical education at the highest level. The French *Ecole Polytechnique*, with its still continuing enormous influence and prestige, was founded in 1794; the Polytechnische Institut of Vienna in 1815; the Technische Hochschule at Karlsruhe in 1825; at Dresden in 1828; Stuttgart in 1829. All the German technical high schools were advancing towards university rank, though it would be 1890 before they acquired the right to grant degrees. In 1855 the Zürich Polytechnikum was founded; the prototype for all the polytechnics that were to proliferate in Europe, especially in Germany. And although American society was so different from German, it was from the German model that America adapted her own education institutions in the nineteenth century. We may note that MIT was founded in 1865.

By around 1870 there were already some 3,500 students in German technical high schools, while the Royal Commission on Technical Instruction of 1884 wrote of the German polytechnic system:

To the multiplication of these Polytechnics ... may be ascribed the general diffusion of a high scientific knowledge in Germany, its appreciation by all classes of persons, and the adequate supply of men competent, so far as theory is concerned, to take the place of managers and superintendents of industrial works. In England, there is still a great want of this class of persons ...[6]

With special reference to the Paris International Exhibition of 1879, this Royal Commission reported:

Your commissioners cannot repeat too often that they have been impressed with the general intelligence and technical knowledge of the masters and managers of industrial establishments on the Continent.[7]

However, it was not simply technical education which our rivals were providing for their peoples, but complete and coherent national systems of education. By 1850 most European countries had followed the Prussian example of universal state primary education as the base of the educational pyramid, and widespread state secondary schools as the necessary foundation for technical and higher education.

In Britain by contrast no such educational advance had taken place by the 1850s. Primary education was still left to the churches, and in 1851 only about half the children between the ages of three and thirteen in England and Wales were getting any kind of education at all. Secondary education (outside the 'public' schools) consisted of a random patchwork of ancient grammar schools, many in decay, and private schools. With regard to technical education, there were merely local mechanics institutes and scientific societies, the Royal School of Mines and examining bodies like this Society. The new University of Durham had been founded to supply clergymen.

Yet there *had* been an educational revolution in Britain since the 1820s – the reform and expansion of the public schools which produced the British governing élite. And it is in the nature of the Victorian public school that we find the other key factor explaining why Britain was so slow and so inadequate in educating for industrial capability. The Victorian public school was inspired by the religious and moral idealism of the Romantic Movement. It turned away from the realities of the industrialized world of the era and from such topics as science and technology. Dr Arnold of Rugby, who did more than anyone to create the character of British public-school education, averred:

Rather than have it [science] the principal thing in my son's mind, I would gladly have him think the sun went round the earth, and that the stars were so many spangles set in the bright blue firmament. Surely the one thing needed for a Christian and Englishman to study is a Christian and moral and political philosophy.[8]

So the new or re-vamped public schools did not set out to equip their pupils to lead great industrial enterprises or a great industrial nation, but to turn them into Christian gentlemen able to govern the Empire and ornament the ancient professions like the Church and the Law. The eighteenth-century dissenting academy tradition of blending the arts and science into a practical preparation for a working life withered away. The prestige of the public schools as an avenue into gentility and the upper class seduced businessmen and engineers alike into sending their children to them. The public schools not only failed to educate a technical élite, they served to starve industry of the nation's highest available intellectual talent and the socially most prestigious groups. Industry and technology became what modern research confirms it still is in Britain – low in status, and hence, in a continual vicious circle, low in reward and low in human calibre compared with our rivals. By the 1850s an immense gulf had opened, from both sides, between industry and such education as there was – between the 'practical man' despising education on the one hand, and the public schools on the other concentrating on the classics, religion and games.

One must also take note here of the influence of liberal *laissez-faire* doctrine, with its condemnation of state intervention in such matters as education, which served to supplement industry's own complete lack of demand for technical education.

What were the effects by the 1860s of this virtual absence in Britain of all kinds of education for capability? Royal Commissions of the time tell us with vast thoroughness and a mass of evidence. The Schools Inquiry Commission of 1868 said this:

We are bound to add that our evidence appears to show that our industrial classes have not even the basis of sound general education on which alone technical education can rest . . . In fact our deficiency is not merely a deficiency in technical education, but . . . in general intelligence, and unless we remedy this want we shall gradually but surely find that our undeniable superiority in wealth and perhaps in energy will not save us from decline.[9]

Pretty prophetic, you may think! By way of contrast, the Royal Commission on Technical Education of 1884 wrote thus of Germany:

The one point in which Germany is overwhelmingly superior to England is in schools, and in the education of all classes of the people. The dense ignorance so common among workmen in England is unknown....[10]

So much then for the rank and file of British industry a hundred years ago. Of what we should call 'middle management' the House of Commons Select Committee on Scientific Instruction of 1867–8 observed:

Unfortunately this division may be disposed of in a very few words ... Its members have either risen from the rank of foreman or workmen, or they are an off-shoot from the class of smaller tradesmen, clerks, etc....[11]

And of top managers the same committee said that if they had risen from the ranks:

... any knowledge of scientific principles which they may have acquired is generally the result of solitary reading, and of observation of the facts with which their pursuits have made them familiar.[12]

However,

More generally the training of the capitalists and of the managers of their class had been that of the higher secondary schools...[13]

In other words, classics and Christianity. I will leave the last comment on education for capability in Britain around a hundred years ago with a German foreman in a chemical works who told visiting British Royal Commissioners:

There is a great lack of chemical knowledge even among foremen and managers of English dye-houses, and thus, in dealing with new colours and new effects, they are compelled to rely on 'rule of thumb' experience, which is often at fault.[14]

Now this gulf between such education as there was in Britain and her needs as an industrial nation did not go unremarked. The various Royal Commissions thundered away in great tomes of evidence and reports. In 1861 Herbert Spencer wrote, in words which might be Jim Callaghan's to-day, the following:

That which our school courses leave almost entirely out, we thus find to be what most nearly concerns the business of life. Our industries would cease, were it not for the information which men acquire, as best they may, after their education is said to be finished. The vital knowledge – and that by which we have grown as a nation to what we are, and which now underlies our whole existence – is a knowledge that has got itself taught in nooks and corners; while the ordained agencies for teaching have been mumbling little else but dead formulas.[15]

The cumulative evidence that we were already being surpassed technologically and that our want of education had much to do with this did have its effect between 1870 and the outbreak of the Great War. Reform did take place; new institutions *were* created. However, the improvements never came soon enough, nor on a large enough scale, nor on a sufficiently comprehensive plan. One may broadly say that in every field of education we continued to be some fifty years or more behind our rivals. Let me briefly summarize. Primary education, the basis of everything: the 1870 Education Act did *not* set up universal state primary education as Prussia had at the beginning of the century, but only provided funds out of the rates to set up new schools to supplement existing church schools. It wasn't until 1880 that there were enough school places for primary education to be made compulsory. By 1900 the 'Board Schools' were educating almost as many children as the church schools, and had become free. However, these schools offered education at rock bottom standards, drilling dirty and nit-ridden children through the three Rs. Compare a Royal Commission's comment on a Swiss primary school several years earlier: 'We were particularly struck by the clean and tidy appearance of the boys, and there was difficulty in realizing that the school consisted mainly of children of the lower classes.'[16] In 1894 the odds against an English elementary school child getting a scholarship to a secondary school were 270 to 1 against.

This was because despite reforms of the old grammar school and other piecemeal improvements it was not until the 1902 Education Act that Britain finally began to set up a coherent system of state secondary education. Even this reform fell short of expectations, because in 1913 transfers from elementary schools to secondary were only a quarter of the total hoped for. In 1909 three-quarters of English young people between fourteen and seventeen were under no kind of education at all.

So the base of the educational pyramid continued to be much too narrow. Reforms in technical and university education were no less piecemeal and inadequate. All the Royal Commission trumpetings in the 1880s resulted in the Technical Instruction Act by which local authorities were left to expand technical education on a penny rate, and, after 1890, on the proceeds from the duty on whisky. Instead of a complete and coherent system of technical education on the German model, all we had by 1902 according to one authority amounted 'with a few brilliant exceptions such as Owen's College, Manchester, to little more than congeries of technical and literary classes; a small number of polytechnics mainly in London; a rather large number of organized science schools and evening science and art classes ...'.[17]

And despite the 1902 Education Act, fewer than 20 first-class technical schools were built in Britain between 1902 and 1918. The Imperial College of Science and Technology was only founded in 1903. In 1908, when Germany possessed ten technical high schools of university rank, with some 14,000 students, Britain still had no such institutions, but instead 31 re-organized technical schools with a total of 2,768 students.

Development of traditional universities by no means made up the difference. Oxford and Cambridge, like the public schools, were very late and reluctant to introduce science and modern studies like languages, let alone what the Germans call 'Technik'. The first physics classes in the Clarendon Laboratory took place in 1870; next year the building of the Cavendish at Cambridge was begun. In the traditionally highly academic environment of Oxbridge, it was not so much 'Technik' – the industrial and operational aspects of science – that prospered as pure research. Another mandarinism thus took its place alongside the classics and mathematics; another form of intellectual snobbery to entice the gifted away from careers in manufacturing industry. In 1903 a private conference was held in Cambridge on – guess what – the gulf between Cambridge and industry. The Professor of Chemistry said at this meeting that he agreed 'with all the Vice-Chancellor had said as to the complaint of men engaged in business of various kinds that the University does not provide an education for their sons suited to their needs...'.[18]

In the same year the Professor of Mechanics and Mathematics at the Royal College of Science said of Oxford:

It is not only that Oxford keeps aloof from technical education, but she keeps aloof from the very much greater thing of which this movement is only a symptom, namely the phenomenon that trade and manufacture are no longer left to themselves as they used to be; they are being organized on scientific lines in all countries. She [Oxford] has always ostentatiously held herself aloof from manufactures and commerce. It is almost incomprehensible that a university aiming at breadth of culture should scorn those things which keep England in her high position....[19]

Not until 1908 did Oxford set up an engineering degree.

The years 1870 to 1900 saw the piecemeal founding of the first wave of 'red-brick' universities or university colleges – Birmingham, Aberystwyth, Cardiff, Bangor. In 1897 the British government expended £26,000 in grants to universities; the Germans nearly half a million. In 1902 Germany possessed 22 universities for a population of some 50 million; England seven for a population of 31 million. The second wave of red-brick universities only followed the 1902 Education Act.

Britain therefore entered the twentieth century an ill-educated, one might say ignorant, nation compared with its rivals; and particularly weak in those key areas of education on which industrial success depends. We see in these failures the combined baneful effects of liberal *laissez-faire*'s reluctance to embark on large-scale state education at all levels, the 'practical man's' scorn for technical education, and a public-school-educated governing élite's lack of comprehension that Britain stood or fell by her industrial capability. His Majesty's Inspectors of Education reported in 1908 that:

The slow growth of these technical institutions is, however, in the main to be ascribed to the small demand in this country for the services of young men well-trained in the theoretical side of industrial operations and in the service underlying them.[20]

The broader effects of our nineteenth-century failure to educate for capability in an industrial world were well summed up by Sir William Huggins, the President of the Royal Society, in 1903:

Expenditure by the Government on scientific research and scientific institutions, on which its commercial and industrial prosperity so largely depend, is wholly inadequate in view of the present state of international competition. I throw no blame on the individual members of the present or former Governments; they are necessarily the representatives of public opinion, and cannot go beyond it. The cause is deeper, it lies in the absence in the leaders of public opinion, and indeed throughout the more influential classes of society, of a sufficiently intelligent appreciation of the supreme importance of scientific knowledge and scientific methods in all industrial enterprises and indeed in all national undertakings . . . In my opinion the scientific deadness of the nation is mainly due to the too exclusively medieval and classical methods of our higher public schools. . . .[21]

And what by 1914 had been the cumulative penalty for our failure to educate for capability? A progressive defeat in the advanced technological markets of the world such as Europe and America and a retreat to the less demanding markets of backward regions; and – something which strikes a familiar note to-day – a progressive invasion of the British home market by foreign technology. When we embarked on industrial mobilization for munitions production during the Great War the extent of our own deficiencies and our dependence on foreign sources for advanced technology became painfully manifest to the Government. Britain produced only half the German quantity of steel and even then neither of the quality nor the specialized kinds produced in Germany. According to the official *History of the Ministry of Munitions*:

British manufacturers were behind other countries in research, plant and method. Many of the iron and steel firms were working on a small scale, old systems and uneconomical plant, their cost of production being so high that competition with the steel works of the United States and Germany was becoming impossible.[22]

The Iron and Steel Industrial Committee in 1917 found many ironmasters ignorant of the basic scientific principles underlying their own operations. It is a sombre fact that Britain only averted defeat in the Great War before 1916 by importing American steel and shells.

Lack of mass production light engineering factories that could be switched to shell-machining and fuse making, like the German clock and toy industries, forced Britain to create wartime factories for the purpose. This attempt immediately uncovered another deficiency – there was no modern machine-tool industry capable of supplying the advanced machinery. As the *History of the Ministry of Munitions* put it, 'The British machine-tool market was conservative both as regards novelty in design and quantity of output.'[23] Before the war, advanced machine tools had been imported from Germany and the United States. Since machine-tools are the key to many kinds of large-scale provision manufacture, it was only because of purchases of American, Swiss and Swedish machine-tools that the wartime munitions effort did not break down. But shortages continued to have a throttling effect in many fields.

Except for one factory, Britain had come to depend entirely on Germany for ball-bearings – an absolute essential of modern technology. In 1914 she was forced to turn to Swiss and Swedish sources until she could expand her own industry. As late as 1917 Swedish supplies were more than half those of home production, and in the last year of the war shortages of ball-bearings were another throttle on the production of internal combustion engines, tanks and aircraft. Yet another virtually total British lack in 1914 was a magneto industry. There was but one British firm with an annual production of just over a thousand of a simple type. Again Britain had come to depend on Germany. In any case British resources in internal-combustion manufacture were themselves small, as was the aircraft industry. Until 1916 we wholly relied on French aircraft engines and even by 1918 shortage of engines was a major brake on the creation of the independent bomber force. Likewise we relied on European or American sources for all kinds of instruments and gauges, for optical glass, for laboratory equipment, for glass bulbs and tubes for electric lights.

Perhaps the most conspicuous example of British dependence on German industry backed by German education for capability was in drugs and dyes. Whereas Germany was able to switch the largest chemical industry in the world from dyes to explosives and poison gases, Britain had to create a chemical industry almost from scratch in wartime, using confiscated German patents – essentially the birth of ICI. In the case of drugs, however, Britain had to go on covertly importing German products via Switzerland.

Under that most immediate of spurs, the danger of defeat in a great war, the British carried out a veritable industrial revolution to create the advanced industries she had lacked. One might say that the munitions drive of 1914–18 marks the first time that the nation had really accorded top priority to technological success, mobilizing and training its talent accordingly. But the coming of peace saw a swift return to the pre-war pattern. Education for capability continued to lag behind our needs and behind our rivals' efforts; and industry's competitiveness lagged with it.

By 1927 British exports had fallen to 73, taking 1913 as 100, while world trade as a whole had risen to 118. The 'practical man' – the *uneducated* practical man, that is – continued to exert his baneful influence on British industry, and on British education. The Balfour Report on Trade and Industry of 1929, the largest and most exhaustive of all the examinations of British industrial failings, quoted one progressive managing director as saying:

... the old-fashioned type of more or less self-made man, who had grown up as a practical man inside a factory, and reached a position of works manager, is now definitely out of date. His continuance in his position is, in my opinion, largely responsible for the parlous condition of many of our industries, particularly engineering and textiles....[24]

It is ironical that the new mass-production motor industry was by then dominated by a 'practical man' who was a complete throw-back to the early days of the Industrial Revolution – William Morris. Successful as a simple entrepreneur, he proved totally unable and unwilling to weld his shambles of disparate factories into an efficient large organization or to provide it with adequate product design facilities. Typically he refused to have graduates within his companies. Here, in the 1930s, lay one source of today's British Leyland disaster.

The Balfour Committee pointed out that although there was now state-aided scientific research, thanks to the founding of the National Physical Laboratory, as well as in university departments, the results were often neglected or wasted by industry.

Before British industries, taken as a whole, can hope to reap from scientific research the full advantage which it appears to yield to some of their most formidable trade rivals, nothing less than a revolution is needed in their general outlook on science; and in the case of some industries at least, this change of attitude is bound to be slow and difficult, in view of our old and deeply rooted industrial traditions.[25]

Lack of demand from industry continued to act as a major check on the expansion of technical education in Britain. The Balfour Committee reported:

The available information makes it clear that the present response of the leaders of industrial and commercial enterprises to the educational efforts made to train candidates for entry into the higher grades of these organizations is much less certain and widespread than in certain foreign countries, e.g., Germany or the United States.[26]

When this lack of interest was coupled with the lack of comprehension by British public opinion and by the governing élite of the need for huge investment in education, the result was a continued inadequacy of all those aspects of British education directed towards industrial and technological capability. Fundamental education continued to lag. In 1921 only 19 per cent of the population between 14 and 17 was in full-time education. In the 1920s generally only 12 per cent of elementary school children went on to secondary, technical or other full-time education. In 1918 Parliament agreed that compulsory part-time education would be introduced for children who left school before 18. This has still to come to pass. But in 1924 Germany did introduce such a system. In 1927 a private investigating committee reported on British technical education. It noted the fragmentary nature of the system; the dismally penny-pinched equipment compared with foreign institutions.[27] And in the universities, except for admittedly brilliant original research, science and technology made slow progress between the world wars. Whereas in 1922 there had been

9,852 students in these fields, in 1939 the number had crept up to 10,278. Germany had had 24,000 even before the Great War.

It is therefore not surprising that when we embarked on large-scale re-armament in 1936, the Government found, in the words of the Cabinet Defence Policy and Requirements Committee that 'the most serious factor in the completion of the proposed programme is the limited output of our existing resources'.[28]

The files of this Cabinet Committee fully bear out this gloomy judgment. The British steel industry, for example, remained so fragmented, so old-fashioned, so limited in total output that orders for the armour for the new cruisers and aircraft carriers had to be placed in Czechoslovakia. But the gravest bottle-neck lay in advanced machine-tools for various kinds of precision mass production. In 1933–7 Germany enjoyed nearly 50 per cent of the world's trade in machine-tools; our share was only 7 per cent. Britain therefore had to buy Swiss, German, Hungarian and American machine-tools to enable the re-armament and shadow-factory programme to go forward at all. We had to buy Swiss and American instrumentation for our new aircraft until such times as we could create our manufacture.

Nevertheless the principal bottleneck lay in a shortage of skilled manpower of all kinds, from tool-makers to production managers – which brings us straight back to the question of education for capability. Just as today, there was mass unemployment – and just as today, most of the unemployed were coolie labour useless in advanced technology. In May 1936 the Ministry of Labour reported that the total available unemployed in the engineering industry suitable for precision work numbered 2,000 in the whole country.[29] Time and again in the reports to the Defence Policy and Requirements Committee do we read of the inadequacy of the design departments of companies engaged on re-armament; the lack of production engineers; and the consequent heavy delays and immense muddles in production. That these difficulties were eventually overcome, and that British war production in the Second World War should prove a success story as in the Great War is owing, again as in the Great War, to the fact that under the spur of acute national danger we concentrated supreme effort and all our resources in talent on achieving technological success.

But we must not allow talismans like radar and the Spitfire to blind us to continued shortcomings in bread-and-butter production technology. Professor R. V. Jones writes in his *Most Secret War*:

They [the Germans] would take simple ideas, and put them straight into practice no matter what technical effort was involved, because they had a far greater command of precision engineering than we had (some notable exceptions such as Rolls Royce apart).[30]

So we come to the post-war era – as I'm sure you'll be glad to hear. I will not attempt to summarize our industrial performance since 1945 because it is now so well known; it follows the pattern set decades earlier, if not a century earlier, and delivers us into our present plight. I believe that antecedent shortcomings in education for capability have acted as one – I don't say the only – key factor in this. But I doubt – and this bears on the future – whether even today we have repaired our century-old backwardness in such education, whether in the primary schools, the secondary schools or in higher and technical education. Even more important, I doubt whether we have yet adjusted the basic values of our society and education in favour of industrial success as a major goal. Until we do this we shall never overcome that pervasive lack of capability, that inferiority of calibre at all levels compared with our rivals, that explain our present want of competitiveness.

Education for capability alone can keep Britain an advanced technological society and save her from becoming a Portugal, perhaps even an Egypt, of tomorrow.

References

1 Letter to *The Times* by KEITH LOCKYER, Professor of Operations Management, Management Centre, Bradford University, 10 October 1975.
2 HMSO, 1978.
3 *The Engineer in a Changing Society* by JOHN LYONS; address given to the IEE 10 March 1977.
4 Quoted in BARNETT, CORRELLI (1972) *The Collapse of British Power*. London: Methuen (p. 95).
5 Ibid.
6 Cmd. 3891, pp. 213–14.
7 Ibid., pp. 505–8.
8 BAMFORD, T. W. (1960) *Thomas Arnold*. London: Cambridge University Press (p. 120).
9 *Report of the Endowed Schools Commission* House of Commons, 1867–8, Vol. XXXVIII, Pt. I, p. 72.
10 Cmd. 3981, p. 337.
11 Report from the Select Committee on Scientific Instruction, House of Commons, 15 July 1868, Vol. XV, p. vi.
12 Ibid.
13 Ibid.
14 Cmd. 3981, p. 369.
15 SPENCER, HERBERT (1861) *Education: Intellectual, Moral and Physical*. London (p. 25).
16 Cmd. 3981, p. 20.
17 LOWNDES, G. A. N. (1937) *The Silent Social Revolution*. Oxford: Oxford University Press (p. 89).
18 SANDERSON, MICHAEL (1975) *Universities in the Nineteenth Century*. London: Routledge and Kegan Paul (p. 234).
19 Ibid., p. 235.
20 Cmd. 5130, p. 90.
21 Anniversary Address to the Royal Society, 1904.
22 *History of the Ministry of Munitions*, Vol. VII, Pt. II, pp. 1–2.

23 Op. cit., Vol. XII, Pt. I, p. 110.

24 Cmd. 3282, p. 213.

25 Ibid., p. 218.

26 Ibid., p. 213.

27 The Emmott Committee Report of an enquiry into the relationship of technical education to other forms of education and to industry and commerce.

28 CAB 16/112, DPR (DR), 9.

29 CAB 16/140, DPR 83.

30 JONES, R. V. (1978) *Most Secret War*. London: Hamish Hamilton (p. 230).

s the papers in Part One have indicated, the debate about standards is in art a matter of politico-ethical differences in value positions. But it is ually important to note that factual beliefs are also of great significance, terlocking and merging with our moral and political commitments. It is ese which form that complex interpretation of our social experiences om which we each develop our own opinions as to what educational olicies should be pursued. In Part Two we will be largely concerned with me of the factual aspects of the debate although, as you will see, the line etween facts and values is continually (and perhaps necessarily) blurred many of the papers in this part of the collection.

The standards debate centres largely around two kinds of chievements, namely what moral and social standards the schools are nd should be promoting and also what academic standards they are ncouraging. By and large, in the latter case, we can separate off the chool's role because it is the major source of academic learning for most eople. But in the moral and social area this is not so; for here the schools vork with or against other major influences on the learner and the shape of hese influences must be borne in mind when considering the role of chooling.

Kohlberg's paper provides an important opening perspective upon hese influences. In this and subsequent research, he and his associates aave developed the stage theory of moral development, identifying what is :laimed to be an invariant (and culture-independent) sequence in the ndividual's moral development. In this view, although social experience :an affect the rate of such development, it cannot alter this sequence.

These findings have several important consequences for the standards debate. Firstly, it suggests (as Piaget's earlier work in this and other areas of developmental psychology indicated) that effective schooling needs to be adjusted to the developmental level of the learner. In the case of moral and social development, this means that a raising of standards may require a systematic rethinking of schooling methods as thorough-going as those that Piaget's work set in train in other areas (e.g. Maths, Religious Education and History). The organizational implications of this are considerable, and so far very little explored.

Secondly, because adults differ in the level they reach, they will tend to view what constitutes achievement in moral education quite differently. The crucial distinction here is between the conventional and post-conventional perspectives. For people (probably the majority) at the conventional level, moral standards are conceived of in concrete terms, set by the reactions of others, or by some set of specific rules (such as the Ten Commandments). In the post-conventional stage, it is not what a

person's moral beliefs are that counts but the way in which he ho
them.

This enables us to see in retrospect that both Peters and Fre
although no doubt subscribing to very different political beliefs,
agreed in emphasizing the importance of autonomous critical thoug
Thus, by implication, they would see the achievement of po
conventional moral thinking as a crucial element in educational grow
But such aspirations are probably not shared by most adults in c
society, a fact of considerable significance to an understanding of t
whole standards controversy.

The social tensions implicit in life in a society containing adults at bc
the conventional and post-conventional stages of morality is clear
brought out in Hall's paper. Although it is written within a sociologic
framework, the post-war changes in social values that he describes can
some measure be seen as indicating a societal movement amongst sor
sections of the population away from a rule-conforming model of morali
towards a diversity of responses. These in part may represent pos
conventional responses and in part a reversion to the pre-convention
stage. Conversely, the reaction of the two social groups he identifies
which a conventional rule-following morality is strongest has been
appeal to commonsense morality and 'Englishness' to justify their mor
and social opposition to various kinds of liberalism in these matters.

Although these first two papers deal with moral standards in genera
their particular relevance to life in schools should not be overlooked. Son
aspects of this are taken up in Wright's paper. While you may feel that h
own value commitments emerge clearly enough, the evidence he assen
bles to support his view that standards of behaviour in schools have no
been falling dramatically needs to be faced up to, even by those whose ow
experience does not support his conclusions. Here, as elsewhere in th
standards debate, we need to ask what point in time we are taking as th
reference point against which current standards are being compared, an
quite what sorts of behaviour are under discussion. On this issue (as o
many others in education) the tendency towards simplistic formulation
of the problems makes it easier for all of us to retain comfortabl
stereotypes rather than face complicated realities.

A quite different aspect of these realities is represented by Campbell'
paper. Virtually all the earlier contributors have focused attention upor
the direct role of individuals and groups in affecting what is learned by
whom. Campbell's paper, however, illustrates the way in which adminis
trative decisions in education may be having significant and largely
unexpected effects upon learners. In the interests of continuity we have
removed many of the forty or so detailed research references he gives to
support his particular conclusions. Nevertheless what emerges from his
paper is the importance of carrying out systematic research before major
educational changes are made which may have quite unintended results.

This theme of unintended results is taken up in the paper by Hargreaves which follows. He is concerned to identify some of the ways in which the organization and conduct of schooling may have indirect influences upon pupil's attitudes and beliefs. His account provides a good introduction to an area of educational debate in which a systematic testing of the speculations of researchers against substantive evidence is arguably needed. While such research is not able to dissolve fundamental value conflicts it does at least have the important merit (if properly done) of providing something more resistant to our political preconceptions than mere opinion, and thus offers a focus around which such conflicts can be intelligently conducted.

But perhaps that point of view is itself naïve; after all, what even the most honest and careful researchers choose to look for will in part determine what they find. Furthermore, the kind of methodology used in a particular approach will itself have a subtle but significant influence upon what becomes visible to both the researcher and his audience, as the next two contributions to this collection make clear.

The first is an account by D. H. Lawrence of the experiences of a young teacher trying to establish herself in her first school. Despite being an imaginative piece of fiction (or perhaps because of its being so?), it presents a rich source for reflecting upon many of the issues that the other material in this collection raises. Here Lawrence (himself a school-teacher for a time) provides an insight into what it can feel like to be a teacher that few other approaches can offer. The tensions between the optimistic idealism of the heroine and the cynicism (or is it realism?) of the head are given concrete form in the narrative. The psychological impact of classroom pressures upon a teacher in difficulties are vividly presented, as are the real complexities of 'maintaining standards'. And what light do the encounters with Mrs Williams and the head throw upon more abstract debates about parents' rights and professional relationships?

However, we must remember that what we have here is a work of fiction – so how far does what we may personally feel to be plausible and illuminating in the narrative simply represent an externalizing of our own (limited) perceptions? Fiction may be seductively realistic without being true, simply because it tells us what we think we already know.

In contrast, the paper by Hargreaves that follows is fact. In it he presents an account of a single lesson in an urban middle school, identifying how the teacher copes with problems of discipline and control and the subtle interactions between the academic and disciplinary aspects of the lesson as it develops. Where Lawrence imagines, Hargreaves transcribes. Where Lawrence largely welds his interpretations into the narrative, Hargreaves largely separates out the two. But is it the case, nevertheless, that Hargreaves' narrative is, in the end, more true than Lawrence's? More precisely, in what ways is it more (and, maybe, in what ways less) true? That is a problem we leave with you.

One thing that does emerge from both the accounts, however, is the difficulty of clearly separating the effects of teaching upon the behaviour of learners from its effects upon their intellectual progress. How teachers control what goes on in a classroom and the kinds of interpersonal relationships they establish within it affect who learns how much of what. This point is taken up in a different way in the paper by Bennett which follows. His study of thirty-seven primary teachers and their pupils led to the conclusion that teaching style had a statistically significant effect upon a number of aspects of pupil attainment, and that these effects varied depending upon the personality type of the pupil. (You might like to consider how far this finding supports the general positions taken up by the various contributors to Part One: is it evidence for or against any of their claims, or not?)

The paper by Hoffmann which follows picks up another aspect of schooling, namely the role of assessment. Hoffmann looks critically at the difficulties involved in designing effective multiple choice questions for assessment purposes. This is, of course, a very specific aspect of assessment, but it represents the first obvious surface outcropping in this collection of a major underlying issue. One of the most important features of contemporary schooling is that it is increasingly carried on in large institutions to serve, in part, large-scale social and economic purposes. Thus there are considerable pressures upon teachers and administrators to conduct and monitor the learning of individuals in ways which ignore the latter's individuality. At the national and institutional levels a 'quality control' approach to education requires standardization of assessment procedures to enable accurate comparisons to be made. At the classroom level, control (pure and not-so-simple) requires standardization of the relationships between teachers and pupils and the establishment of classroom conventions and routine processes in ways illustrated in the earlier Lawrence and Hargreaves contributions. As we shall see, in Part Three it has been argued that these requirements are not without their links to structural features of certain kinds of societies. They also have effects upon teachers as a professional group, as will emerge in Part Four.

But if, to return to Hoffmann's paper in particular, the results obtained from such a common method of assessment as multiple choice questions are liable to misinterpretation, does not this raise doubts about the accuracy of current assessment methods, even viewed as devices to check that standards are being maintained? Just as the need for control in classrooms may militate against the creation of genuinely educative relationships between teacher and taught, so may a concern for maximizing test scores militate against the raising of the educational standards that those scores ostensibly record. On the other hand, if one takes this high line on these matters, what sort of evaluation *can* be made of these mysterious educational standards that cannot be captured in anything so vulgar as numbers?

In Rowntree's paper a number of further problems about assessment are raised. In particular, he points out some ways in which the mere existence of an assessment system itself reinforces the pressure upon teachers at the classroom level to view individual learners in stereotyped ways. The knowledge by the learner that he is an object of assessment may, Rowntree argues, also affect the learner's own conception of himself.

If so, we might speculate that the combined effects of rigid classroom assessment and control procedures might be to produce an alienation by the learner from the schooling process itself, a process which he might then (mistakenly?) identify with education. Alternatively, in accepting the simplified image of himself that these procedures embody, the learner may become, in Freire's sense, 'domesticated' and thereby remain as something less than an autonomous individual, locked instead into the localized conventions of the limited culture that is all that such a schooling can transmit.

The final paper by Woods begins to lead us out of the school once more into the wider world. The choice of subject options by secondary school pupils is something which obviously affects what sort of education they as individuals receive in those final years of compulsory schooling. But the problem of appropriately matching pupils' aptitudes and interests with the level of academic demand presented by particular courses also has relevance for society at large. It might be argued that getting this match right is an important contribution to raising academic standards overall. On the basis of a long term observation in a secondary modern school, Woods argues that subject choice decisions are in fact influenced by a variety of factors, not all of them directly related to any objective judgment by teachers, parents, or pupils of the aptitudes of the individual pupils whose subject choices are being considered. The social significance of this conclusion lies in the long term importance to individuals of passing examinations (and thus the importance of getting into examination classes in the first place). Furthermore, if, as Woods suggests, social class is one influential factor in subject choice, then the total effect of the many such individual decisions made in schools throughout the country would be to perpetuate class related inequalities in access to post-compulsory education and to occupations in which examination success is a prerequisite.

2.1 The child as moral philosopher

Lawrence Kohlberg

How can one study morality? Current trends in the fields of ethics, linguistics, anthropology, and cognitive psychology have suggested a new approach that seems to avoid the morass of semantical confusions, value bias and cultural relativity in which the psychoanalytic and semantic approaches to morality have foundered. New scholarship in all these fields is now focusing upon structures, forms, and relationships that seem to be common to all societies and all languages rather than upon the features that make particular languages or cultures different.

For twelve years, my colleagues and I studied the same group of seventy-five [American] boys, following their development at three-year intervals from early adolescence through young manhood. At the start of the study, the boys were aged ten to sixteen. We have now followed them through to ages twenty-two to twenty-eight. In addition, I have explored moral development in other cultures – Great Britain, Canada, Taiwan, Mexico, and Turkey.

Inspired by Jean Piaget's pioneering effort to apply a structural approach to moral development, I have gradually elaborated over the years of my study a typological scheme describing general structures and forms of moral thought that can be defined independently of the specific content of particular moral decisions or actions.

The typology contains three distinct levels of moral thinking, and within each of these levels distinguishes two related stages. These levels and stages may be considered separate moral philosophies, distinct views of the sociomoral world.

We can speak of the child as having his own morality or series of moralities. Adults seldom listen to children's moralizing. If a child throws back a few adult clichés and behaves himself, most parents – and many anthropologists and psychologists as well – think that the child has adopted or internalized the appropriate parental standards.

Actually, as soon as we talk with children about morality, we find that they have many ways of making judgments that are not 'internalized' from the outside, and that do not come in any direct and obvious way from parents, teachers, or even peers.

Moral levels

The *preconventional* level is the first of three levels of moral thinking; the second level is *conventional*, and the third *postconventional*, or autonomous.

Source: *Psychology Today*, September 1968.
Reprinted from *Psychology Today Magazine* copyright © 1968 Ziff-Davis Publishing Company.

While the preconventional child is often 'well behaved' and is responsive to cultural labels of good and bad, he interprets these labels in terms of their physical consequences (punishment, reward, exchange of favours) or in terms of the physical power of those who enunciate the rules and labels of good and bad.

This level is usually occupied by children aged four to ten, a fact long known to sensitive observers of children. The capacity of 'properly behaved' children of this age to engage in cruel behaviour when there are holes in the power structure is sometimes noted as tragic (*Lord of the Flies*, *High Wind in Jamaica*), sometimes as comic (Lucy in *Peanuts*).

The second, or conventional, level also can be described as conformist, but that is perhaps too smug a term. Maintaining the expectations and rules of the individual's family, group, or nation is perceived as valuable in its own right. There is a concern not only with *conforming* to the individual's social order but in *maintaining*, supporting, and justifying this order.

The postconventional level is characterized by a major thrust towards autonomous moral principles that have validity and application apart from authority of the groups or persons who hold them and apart from the individual's identification with those persons or groups.

Moral stages

Within each of these three levels there are two discernible stages. At the preconventional level we have:

Stage *1* Orientation toward punishment and unquestioning deference to superior power. The physical consequences of action, regardless of their human meaning or value, determine its goodness or badness.

Stage 2 Right action consists of that which instrumentally satisfies one's own needs and occasionally the needs of others. Human relations are viewed in terms like those of the marketplace. Elements of fairness, of reciprocity, and equal sharing are present, but they are always interpreted in a physical, pragmatic way. Reciprocity is a matter of 'you scratch my back and I'll scratch yours', not of loyalty, gratitude, or justice.

And at the conventional level we have:

Stage 3 Good-boy–good-girl orientation. Good behaviour is that which pleases or helps others and is approved by them. There is much conformity to stereotypical images of what is majority or 'natural' behaviour. Behaviour is often judged by intention; 'he means well' becomes important for the first time, and is overused, as by Charlie Brown in *Peanuts*. One seeks approval by being 'nice'.

Stage 4 Orientation towards authority, fixed rules, and the maintenance of the social order. Right behaviour consists of doing one's duty, showing respect for authority, and maintaining the given social order for its own sake. One earns respect by performing dutifully.

At the postconventional level, we have:

Stage 5 A social-contract orientation, generally with legalistic and utilitarian overtones. Right action tends to be defined in terms of general rights and in terms of standards that have been critically examined and agreed upon by the whole society. There is a clear awareness of the relativism of personal values and opinions and a corresponding emphasis upon procedural rules for reaching consensus. Aside from what is constitutionally and democratically agreed upon, right or wrong is a matter of personal 'values' and 'opinion'. The result is an emphasis upon the 'legal point of view', but with an emphasis upon the possibility of *changing* law in terms of rational considerations of social utility, rather than freezing it in the terms of Stage 4 'law and order'. Outside the legal realm, free agreement and contract are the binding elements of obligation. This is the 'official' morality of American government and finds its ground in the thought of the writers of the Constitution.

Stage 6 Orientation towards the decisions of conscience and towards self-chosen *ethical principles* appealing to logical comprehensiveness, universality, and consistency. These principles are abstract and ethical (the Golden Rule, the categorical imperative); they are not concrete moral rules like the Ten Commandments. Instead, they are universal principles of justice, of the reciprocity and equality of human rights, and of respect for the dignity of human beings as individual persons.

Up to now

In the past, when psychologists tried to answer the question asked of Socrates by Meno, 'Is virtue something that can be taught (by rational discussion), or does it come by practice, or is it a natural inborn attitude?' their answers usually have been dictated not by research findings on children's moral character but by their general theoretical convictions.

Behaviour theorists have said that virtue is behaviour acquired according to their favourite general principles of learning. Freudians have claimed that virtue is superego identification with parents, generated by a proper balance of love and authority in family relations.

The American psychologists who have actually studied children's morality have tried to start with a set of labels – the 'virtues' and 'vices', the 'traits' of good and bad character found in ordinary language. The earliest major psychological study of moral character, that of Hugh Hartshorne and Mark May in 1928–30, focused on a bag of virtues including honesty, service (altruism or generosity), and self-control. To their dismay, they found that there were *no* character traits, psychological dispositions, or entities that corresponded to words like honesty, service, or self-control.

Regarding honesty, for instance, they found that almost everyone cheats some of the time, and that if a person cheats in one situation, it does not mean that he *will* or *won't* in another. In other words, it is not an identifiable character trait, *dis*honesty, that makes a child cheat in a given situation. These early researchers also found that people who cheat express as much or even more moral disapproval of cheating as those who do not cheat.

What Hartshorne and May found out about their bag of virtues is equally upsetting to the somewhat more psychological-sounding names introduced by psychoanalytic psychology: 'superego strength', 'resistance to temptation', 'strength of conscience', and the like. When contemporary researchers have attempted to measure such traits in individuals, they have been forced to use Hartshorne and May's old tests of honesty and self-control, and they get exactly the same results – 'superego strength' in one situation predicts little about 'superego strength' in another. That is, virtue words like honesty (or superego strength) point to certain behaviours with approval but give us no guide to understanding them.

So far as one can extract some generalized personality factor from children's performance on tests of honesty or resistance to temptation, it is a factor of ego strength or ego control, which always involves nonmoral capacities like the capacity to maintain attention, intelligent-task performance, and the ability to delay response. 'Ego strength' (called 'will' in earlier days) has something to do with moral action, but it does not take us to the core of morality or to the definition of virtue. Obviously enough, many of the greatest evil-doers in history have been men of strong wills, men strongly pursuing immoral goals.

Moral reasons

In our research, we have found definite and universal levels of development in moral thought. In our study of seventy-five American boys from early adolescence on, these youths were presented with hypothetical moral dilemmas, all deliberately philosophical, some of them found in medieval works of casuistry.

On the basis of their reasoning about these dilemmas at a given age, each boy's stage of thought could be determined for each of twenty-five basic moral concepts or aspects. One such aspect, for instance, is 'motive given for rule obedience or moral action'. In this instance, the six stages look like this:

1 Obey rules to avoid punishment.
2 Conform to obtain rewards, have favours returned, and so on.
3 Conform to avoid disapproval, dislike by others.
4 Conform to avoid censure by legitimate authorities and resultant guilt.
5 Conform to maintain the respect of the impartial spectator judging in terms of community welfare.
6 Conform to avoid self-condemnation.

In another of these twenty-five moral aspects, 'the value of human life', the six stages can be defined thus:

1 The value of a human life is confused with the value of physical objects and is based on the social status or physical attributes of its possessor.
2 The value of a human life is seen as instrumental to the satisfaction of the needs of its possessor or of other persons.
3 The value of a human life is based on the empathy and affection of family members and others toward its possessor.
4 Life is conceived as sacred in terms of its place in a categorical moral or religious order of rights and duties.
5 Life is valued both in terms of its relation to community welfare and in terms of life being a universal human right.
6 Belief in the sacredness of human life as representing a universal human value of respect for the individual.

I have called this scheme a typology. This is because about 50 per cent of most people's thinking will be at a single stage, regardless of the moral dilemma involved. We call our types stages because they seem to represent an *invariant developmental sequence*. 'True' stages come one at a time and always in the same order.

All movement is forward in sequence, and does not skip steps. Children may move through these stages at varying speeds, of course, and may be found half in and half out of a particular stage. An individual may stop at any given stage and at any age, but if he continues to move, he must move in accord with these steps. Moral reasoning of the conventional, or Stage 3–4, kind never occurs before the preconventional Stage 1 and Stage 2 thought has taken place. No adult in Stage 4 has gone through Stage 6, but all Stage 6 adults have gone at least through 4.

While the evidence is not complete, my study suggests that moral change fits the stage pattern just described. (The major uncertainty is whether all people at Stage 6 go through Stage 5 or whether these are two alternate mature orientations.)

How values change

As a single example of our findings of stage sequence, take the progress of two boys on the aspect 'the value of human life'. The first boy, Tommy, is asked 'Is it better to save the life of one important person or a lot of unimportant people?' At age ten, he answers 'all the people that aren't important because one man just has one house, maybe a lot of furniture, but a whole bunch of people have an awful lot of furniture and some of these poor people might have a lot of money and it doesn't look it.'

Clearly Tommy is Stage 1 – he confuses the value of a human being with the value of the property he possesses. Three years later (age thirteen)

Tommy's conceptions of life's value are most clearly elicited by the question, 'Should the doctor "mercy kill" a fatally ill woman requesting death because of her pain?' He answers, 'Maybe it would be good to put her out of her pain, she'd be better off that way. But the husband wouldn't want it, it's not like an animal. If a pet dies you can get along without it – it isn't something you really need. Well, you can get a new wife, but it's not really the same.'

Here his answer is Stage 2 – the value of the woman's life is partly contingent on its hedonistic value to the wife herself but even more contingent on its instrumental value to her husband, who can't replace her as easily as he can a pet.

Three years later (age sixteen) Tommy's conception of life's value is elicited by the same question, to which he replies: 'It might be best for her, but her husband – it's a human life – not like an animal; it just doesn't have the same relationship that a human being does to a family. You can become attached to a dog, but nothing like a human you know.'

Now Tommy has moved from a Stage 2 instrumental view of the woman's value to a Stage 3 view based on the husband's distinctively human empathy and love for someone in his family. Equally clearly, it lacks any basis for a universal human value of the woman's life, which would hold if she had no husband or if her husband didn't love her. Tommy, then, has moved step by step through three stages during the ages ten through sixteen. Tommy, though bright (IQ 120), is a slow developer in moral judgment. Let us take another boy, Richard, to show us sequential movement through the remaining three steps.

At age thirteen, Richard said about the mercy killing, 'If she requests it, it's really up to her. She is in such terrible pain, just the same as people are always putting animals out of their pain', and in general showed a mixture of Stage 2 and Stage 3 responses concerning the value of life. At sixteen, he said:

I don't know. In one way, it's murder, it's not a right or privilege of man to decide who shall live and who should die. God put life into everybody on earth and you're taking away something from that person that came directly from God, and you're destroying something that is very sacred, it's in a way part of God and it's almost destroying a part of God when you kill a person. There's something of God in everyone.

Here Richard clearly displays a Stage 4 concept of life as sacred in terms of its place in a categorical moral or religious order. The value of human life is universal, it is true for all humans. It is still, however, dependent on something else, upon respect for God and God's authority; it is not an autonomous human value. Presumably if God told Richard to murder, as God commanded Abraham to murder Isaac, he would do so.

At age twenty, Richard said to the same question:

There are more and more people in the medical profession who think it is a hardship on everyone, the person, the family, when you know they are going to die.

When a person is kept alive by an artificial lung or kidney it's more like being a vegetable than being a human. If it's her own choice, I think there are certain rights and privileges that go along with being a human being. I am a human being and have certain desires for life and I think everybody else does too. You have a world of which you are the centre, and everybody else does too and in that sense we're all equal.

Richard's response is clearly Stage 5, in that the value of life is defined in terms of equal and universal human rights in a context of relativity ('You have a world of which you are the centre and in that sense we're all equal'), and of concern for utility or welfare consequences.

The final step

At twenty-four, Richard says:

A human life takes precedence over any other moral or legal value, whoever it is. A human life has inherent value whether or not it is valued by a particular individual. The worth of the individual human being is central where the principles of justice and love are normative for all human relationships.

This young man is at Stage 6 in seeing the value of human life as absolute in representing a universal and equal respect for the human as an individual. He has moved step by step through a sequence culminating in a definition of human life as centrally valuable rather than derived from or dependent on social or divine authority.

In a genuine and culturally universal sense, these steps lead toward an increased *morality* of value judgment, where morality is considered as a form of judging, as it has been in a philosophic tradition running from the analyses of Kant to those of the modern analytic or 'ordinary language' philosophers. The person at Stage 6 has disentangled his judgments of – or language about – human life from status and property values (Stage 1), from its uses to others (Stage 2), from interpersonal affection (Stage 3), and so on; he has a means of moral judgment that is universal and impersonal. The Stage 6 person's answers use moral words like 'duty' or 'morally right', and he uses them in a way implying universality, ideals, impersonality: he thinks and speaks in phrases like 'regardless of who it was', or 'I would do it in spite of punishment.'

Across cultures

When I first decided to explore moral development in other cultures, I was told by anthropologist friends that I would have to throw away my culture-bound moral concepts and stories and start from scratch learning a whole new set of values for each new culture. My first try consisted of a brace of villages, one Atayal (Malaysian aboriginal) and the other Taiwanese.

My guide was a young Chinese ethnographer who had written an account of the moral and religious patterns of the Atayal and Taiwanese villages. Taiwanese boys in the ten to thirteen age group were asked about a story involving theft of food. A man's wife is starving to death, but the store owner won't give the man any food unless he can pay, which he can't. Should he break in and steal some food? Why? Many of the boys said, 'He should steal the food for his wife because if she dies he'll have to pay for her funeral and that costs a lot.'

My guide was amused by these responses, but I was relieved: they were, of course 'classic' Stage 2 responses. In the Atayal village, funerals weren't such a big thing, so the Stage 2 boys would say, 'He should steal the food because he needs his wife to cook for him.'

This means that we need to consult our anthropologists to know what content a Stage 2 child will include in his instrumental exchange calculations, or what a Stage 4 adult will identify as the proper social order. But one certainly does not have to start from scratch. What made my guide laugh was the difference in form between the children's Stage 2 thought and his own, a difference definable independently of particular cultures.

Figure 1 indicates the cultural universality of the sequence of stages that we have found. Figure 1a presents the age trends for middle-class urban boys in the United States, Taiwan, and Mexico. At age ten in each country, the order of use of each stage is the same as the order of its difficulty or maturity.

In the United States, by age sixteen the order is the reverse, from the highest to the lowest, except that Stage 6 is still little used. At age thirteen, the good-boy, middle stage (Stage 3) is not used.

The results in Mexico and Taiwan are the same, except that development is a little slower. The most conspicuous feature is that at the age of sixteen, Stage 5 thinking is much more salient in the United States than in Mexico or Taiwan. Nevertheless, it *is* present in the other countries, so we know that this is not purely an American democratic construct.

Figure 1b shows strikingly similar results from two isolated villages, one in Yucatan, one in Turkey. While conventional moral thought increases steadily from ages ten to sixteen, it still has not achieved a clear ascendancy over preconventional thought.

Trends for lower-class urban groups are intermediate in the rate of development between those for the middle-class and those for the village boys. In the three divergent cultures that I studied, middle-class children were found to be more advanced in moral judgment than matched lower-class children. This was not due to the fact that the middle-class children heavily favoured some one type of thought that could be seen as corresponding to the prevailing middle-class pattern. Instead, middle-class and working-class children move through the same sequences, but the middle-class children move faster and further.

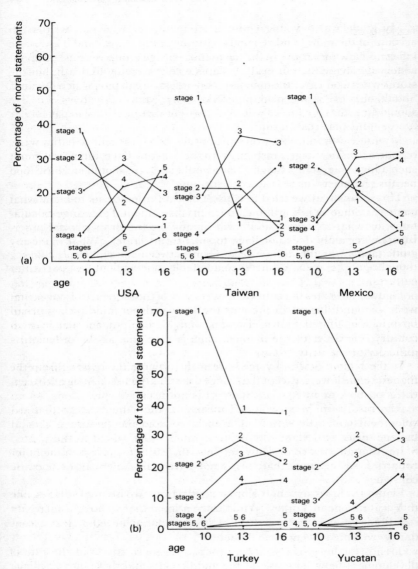

Figure 1   Cultural universality of the sequence of stages in moral development

This sequence is not dependent upon a particular religion, or any religion at all in the usual sense. I found no important differences in the development of moral thinking among Catholics, Protestants, Jews, Buddhists, Moslems, or atheists. Religious values seem to go through the same stages as all other values.

Trading up

In summary, the nature of our sequence is not significantly affected by widely varying social, cultural, or religious conditions. The only thing that is affected is the *rate* at which individuals progress through this sequence.

Why should there be such a universal invariant sequence of development? In answering this question, we need first to analyse these developing social concepts in terms of their internal logical structure. At each stage, the same basic moral concept or aspect is defined, but at each higher stage this definition is more differentiated, more integrated, and more general or universal. When one's concept of human life moves from Stage 1 to Stage 2, the value of life becomes more differentiated from the value of property, more integrated (the value of life enters an organizational hierarchy where it is 'higher' than property so that one steals property in order to save life), and more universalized (the life of any sentient being is valuable regardless of status or property). The same advance is true at each stage in the hierarchy. Each step of development, then, is a better cognitive organization than the one before it, one that takes account of everything present in the previous stage but makes new distinctions and organizes them into a more comprehensive or more equilibrated structure. The fact that this is the case has been demonstrated by a series of studies indicating that children and adolescents comprehend all stages up to their own, but not more than one stage beyond their own. And importantly, *they prefer this next stage*.

We have conducted experimental moral discussion classes that show that the child at an earlier stage of development tends to move forward when confronted by the views of a child one stage farther along. In an argument between a Stage 3 and a Stage 4 child, the child in the third stage tends to move toward or into Stage 4, while the Stage 4 child understands but does not accept the arguments of the Stage 3 child.

Moral thought, then, seems to behave like all other kinds of thought. Progress through the moral levels and stages is characterized by increasing differentiation and increasing integration, and hence is the same kind of progress that scientific theory represents. Like acceptable scientific theory – or like *any* theory or structure of knowledge – moral thought may be considered to partially generate its own data as it goes along, or at least to expand so as to contain in a balanced, self-consistent way a wider and wider experimental field. The raw data in the case of our ethical philosophies may be considered as conflicts between roles, or values, or as the social order in which men live.

The role of society

The social worlds of all men seem to contain the same basic structures. All the societies we have studied have the same basic institutions – family, economy, law, government. In addition, however, all societies are alike because they *are* societies – systems of defined complementary roles. In order to play a social role in the family, school, or society, the child must implicitly take the role of others towards himself and towards others in the group. These role-taking tendencies form the basis of all social institutions. They represent various patternings of shared or complementary expectations.

In the preconventional and conventional levels (Stages 1–4), moral content or value is largely accidental or culture bound. Anything from 'honesty' to 'courage in battle' can be the central value. But in the higher postconventional levels, Socrates, Lincoln, Thoreau, and Martin Luther King tend to speak without confusion of tongues, as it were. This is because the ideal principles of any social structure are basically alike, if only because there simply are not that many principles that are articulate, comprehensive, and integrated enough to be satisfying to the human intellect. And most of these principles have gone by the name of justice.

Behaviouristic psychology and psychoanalysis have always upheld the Philistine view that fine moral words are one thing and moral deeds another. Morally mature reasoning is quite a different matter, and does not really depend on 'fine words'. The man who understands justice is more likely to practise it.

In our studies, we have found that youths who understand justice act more justly, and the man who understands justice helps create a moral climate that goes far beyond his immediate and personal acts. The universal society is the beneficiary.

References

HARE, R. M. (1952) *The Language of Morals*. Oxford: Oxford University Press.

KOHLBERG, L. (1963) 'The development of children's orientations towards a moral order: 1 Sequence in the development of moral thought', *Vita Humana*, Vol. 6. Basle: S. Karger S. A. (pp. 11–33).

KOHLBERG, L. (1964) 'Development of moral character and ideology', in HOFFMAN, M. L. and HOFFMAN, L. W. (eds) *Reviews of Child Development Research*. New York: Russell Sage.

KOHLBERG, L. (1966) 'Moral education in the schools: a developmental view', in *School Review*, Vol. 74. Chicago: University of Chicago (pp. 1–30).

KOHLBERG, L. (in preparation) *Stages in the Development of Moral Thought and Action*. New York: Holt, Rinehart and Winston.

PECK, R. F. and HAVINGHURST, R. J. (1960) *The Psychology of Character Development*. New York: John Wiley.

WILSON, J. (1966) *Equality*. London: Hutchinson.

2.2 Social anxiety

Stuart Hall

The question is not why or how unscrupulous men work ... but why audiences respond.[1]

We have been traversing the terrain of traditional ideas and their historical roots. But now we must look at the way in which specific historical forces operated on this traditional ground-base to produce, in the 1960s and 1970s, a strong upsurge of conservative moral indignation about crime. Engels noted that 'in all ideological domains tradition forms a great conservative force. But the transformations which this material undergoes springs from class relations.'[2]

We have discussed some of the central images providing society with a degree of ideological unity around the traditional pole. Crucially, those images cohere in a vista of *stability* – of solid, bedrock and unchanging habits and virtues, presenting a sense of permanence even in 'bad times', a kind of base-line that, no matter what, remains 'forever England'. Here we are concerned to show how a set of specific social changes combined to undercut some of the crucial supports to this set of images of social order among sections of the population who have no alternative ideological structure which could perform a similar cohering function. This under-mining produces an effect in these class fractions which we have called 'social anxiety' – a product of both the dissolution of the material supports of that ideology, and the weakening of the broad social commitment to that ideology itself. We would suggest that one consequence of this 'state of flux' into which sections of the population are thrown in times of dislocation is the emergence of a predisposition to the use of 'scapegoats', into which *all* the disturbing experiences are condensed and then symbolically rejected or 'cast out'.[3] These scapegoats have attributed to them the role of *causing* the various elements of disorganization and dislocation which have produced 'social anxiety' in the first place. However, these scapegoats do not just 'happen', they are produced from specific conditions, by specific agencies, *as scapegoats*. First, however, we must pay attention to the erosion of 'traditionalism' as a particular cross-class alliance, and to the production of social anxiety. There seem to us to have been two distinct but related reasons for this.

In the post-war period we can identify two 'breaks' in the traditional ideologies, each of which produced a sense of the loss of familiar land-marks and thus provided the basis for growing 'social anxiety'. The first had to do with 'affluence'. The basis of 'affluence' was the post-war boom in production. But it was experienced as a particular kind of consumption

Source: HALL, S., CRITCHER, R., JEFFERSON, A., CLARKE, J. and ROBERTS, B. (1978) *Policing the Crisis* London: Macmillan, pp. 156–165.

– personal and domestic spending – and as a particular transformation of traditional values and standards. The association of 'affluence' with an attitude of 'unbridled materialism', hedonism and pleasure was seen as quickly leading on to 'permissiveness' – a state of the loosening of moral discipline, restraint and control. The 'new values' were distinctly at odds with the more traditional Protestant Ethic. And the groups or class fractions which most directly experienced the tension between the Protestant Ethic and the New Hedonism were those – the non-commercial middle classes, above all, the lower-middle classes – who had invested everything in the Protestant virtues of thrift, respectability and moral discipline.[4]

The second development tending to awaken and heighten 'social anxiety' arises in roughly the same period, but directly affected a rather different stratum. The scale of social change in the period was wildly exaggerated. But the adaptation of society to post-war conditions did indeed set in motion social changes which gradually eroded some of the traditional patterns of life, and thus the supports, of traditional working-class culture. Change *of a kind* was to be seen everywhere; and nowhere was it more concentrated in its effects than in the erosion of the 'traditional' working-class neighbourhood and community itself, and its 'hard core' – the respectable working class. By 'traditional' here, we mean, as Hobsbawm and Steadman-Jones have argued, that pattern of working-class life which established itself in the final decades of the nineteenth century – some aspects of which Steadman-Jones has dealt with under the title 'the re-making of the English working class'.[5] In a sense, the English working class was to a certain degree 'remade' once again, in the post-war years. Urban redevelopment, changes in the local economies, in the structure of skills and occupations, increased geographical and educational mobility, relative prosperity supported by the post-war recovery boom, and a spectacularized 'religion of affluence', though in one sense distinct processes, had a combined and decomposing effect, in the long-term sense, on the respectable working-class community.[6] The close interconnections between family and neighbourhood were loosened, its ties placed under pressure. Communal spaces and informal social controls, which had come to be customary in the classic traditional neighbourhoods, were weakened and exposed. The cultural and political response to these forces was considerably confused – a confusion which, there is little need to say, is most inadequately expressed in the familiar quasiexplanations of the period: 'embourgeoisement' and 'apathy'; but also in modifications within the traditional working-class ideologies of 'labourism'. In part, as we have argued elsewhere,[7] there was a strong tendency – the product of considerable ideological manipulation of reality – to reduce this complex and uneven process of change to the famous 'generation gap'. The distance – marked by the war – between the generations of the pre- and post-war eras exaggerated the 'sense of change'.

Middle-aged and older people clearly experienced these contradictory developments primarily as a 'sense of loss': the loss of a sense of family, of a sense of respect, the erosion of traditional loyalties to street, family, work, locality. In ways which are hard to locate precisely, that 'sense of loss' also had something to do with the experience of the war and the decline and loss of Empire – both of which had contributed, in their different ways, to the ideological 'unity' of the nation. Many familiar patterns of recreation and life were being reconstructed by the commercialization of leisure and the temporary onset of a conspicuous and privatized consumption: the transformation and decline of the English pub is, in this respect, as significant a sign as the more publicized exaggerations of teenage leisure and life. The 'springs of action' were unbent – but they did not immediately take another shape; instead there was a sort of hiatus, a degree of permanent unsettledness. Local integration was weakened - but not in favour of any alternative solidarities, outside the scope of the family circle, itself narrower, more nucleated. Poverty as a way of life was widely said and thought to be disappearing – though poverty itself refused to disappear; indeed, not long after it was, magically, redis covered.

One could begin to pinpoint this seed-bed of social anxiety at several points. One event which seems to bring all sorts of strands together, and to expose the reservoir of unfocused post-war social discontent in a particu larly sharp and visible form, is the Notting Hill race riots of 1958. Although overtly about 'race', it is clear that these events also served as a focus of social anxiety, touching many sources by no means all of which were, in any specific sense, racial.[8] Put another way, Notting Hill was complicated because there was a need to condemn both the violence of white youth, and yet point to the bad habits of immigrants which had caused the tension. There was, to use Stan Cohen's terminology, uncer tainty as to whether the 'folk-devils' were white working-class youth Teddy Boys or black immigrants. In time the racial issue was to be made clearer, but for the moment it was blurred.

No such general ambiguities surrounded the 'mods' and 'rockers' Cohen notes many sources of disquiet which came to be focused on groups of teenagers in conflict at seaside resorts:

The Mods and Rockers symbolized something far more important than what they actually did. They touched the delicate and ambivalent nerves through which post-war social change in Britain was experienced. No one wanted depressions or austerity, but messages about 'never having it so good' were ambivalent in that some people were having it too good and too quickly. . . . Resentment and jealousy were easily directed at the young, if only because of their increased spending power and sexual freedom. When this was combined with a too-open flouting of the work and leisure ethics, with violence and vandalism, and the (as yet) uncertain threats associated with drug-taking, something more than the image of a peaceful Bank Holiday at the sea was being shattered. One might suggest that ambiguity and strain was greatest at the beginning of the sixties. The lines had not yet been clearly drawn and indeed, the reaction was part of this drawing of the line.[9]

A genuine sense of cultural dislocation, then, came to focus not on structural causes but on symbolic expressions of social disorganization, e.g. the string of working-class youth sub-cultures. That these were themselves often 'magical solutions' to the same cultural or structural problems – attempts to resolve, without transcending, inherent contradictions of the class – was not the least of the ironies.[10]

What were in fact related but distinct developments were collapsed into three composite and overlapping images of unsettledness: youth, affluence and permissiveness. It was possible to perceive these challenges to the normal patterns in terms of a limited number of oppositions: undisciplined youth *versus* maturity; conspicuous consumption *versus* modest prosperity; permissiveness *versus* responsibility, decency and respectability. The residual resistance to these new ways thus first began to find articulation as a movement of moral reform and regeneration – whether rooted in the desire for a return to the concrete certainties of the traditional working-class respectability, or in the form of a campaign for the restoration of middle-class puritanism.

As these contradictory thrusts continued to afflict and challenge the dominant morality, and the axes of traditional working-class life continued to tilt at an alarming angle, so the general sense of dislocation increased. For those moral crusaders used to formulating their discontent in organized ways, there were the possibilities of joining movements – to clean up television, cleanse the streets of prostitutes, or eliminate pornography. But for those whose traditional forms of local articulation had never assumed these more public, campaigning postures, there was left only what one writer described as a nagging bitterness:

Most old people I met expressed resentment of the forces in society which have robbed them of the crushing certainty that all their neighbours shared the same poverty and the same philosophy, and were as uniformly helpless and resourceless as themselves. . . . But now they feel they were deceived. . . . The values and habits that grew out of their poverty have been abolished with the poverty itself. While they were still striving for social justice and economic improvement, they took no account of any accompanying change that would take place in their value-structure: they simply transposed themselves in imagination into the house of the rich, and it was assumed that they would take with them their neighbourliness and lack of ceremony, their pride in their work, their dialect and common sense. . . . Instead of imposing their own will upon changing conditions they allowed themselves to be manipulated by them, not preserving anything of their past, but surrendering it like the victims of a great natural disaster, who flee before the elements and abandon all that they have painstakingly accumulated. Perhaps, if they had understood what was happening, they would have preserved something of the old culture, but instead they raise their voices in wild threatening querulousness against the young, or the immigrants or any other fragment of a phenomenon that is only partially and fitfully available to them.[11]

Seabrook is at pains to emphasize that this hostility to outsiders is not simple prejudice; it is grounded in the social reality and material experience of those who have such fears:

The immigrants act as a perverse legitimation of inexpressible fear and anguish. What is taking place is only secondarily an expression of prejudice. It is first and foremost a therapeutic psychodrama, in which the emotional release of its protagonists takes precedence over what is actually being said.... It is an expression of their pain and powerlessness confronted by the decay and dereliction, not only of the familiar environment, but of their own lives, too – an expression for which our society provides no outlet. Certainly it is something more complex and deep-rooted than what the metropolitan liberal evasively and easily dismisses as prejudice.[12]

This 'expression of pain and powerlessness' is a root cause as well as an early symptom of social anxiety.

In the vocabulary of social anxiety blacks and Asians were ready-made symbols for, and symptoms of, a succession of dislocations: in housing, neighbourhood, family, sex, recreation, law and order. To communities beset by a 'sense of loss', their race and colour may well have mattered less than their simply *otherness* – their alienness. We say this in part because in this period social anxiety does not seem always to need to go outside its social and ethnic boundaries to discover the demons on which to feed. In some parts of the country, the language of race and the language used about travellers are interchangeable.[13] And, even closer to home, so far as the respectable poor are concerned, are always the *very* poor – the rough, the marginals, the lumpen-poor, the downwardly mobile, the disorganized outcaste and misfits. The lumpen-poor, being too close for the respectable working class to take much comfort from their suffering, have always been available as a negative reference point. Here, again, powered by pain and powerlessness, negative reference points become the source of an escalating sense of panic and social anxiety:

Those who emerge from the collapsed and dwindling matrix of traditional working class life often believe that their projection upwards is a great personal achievement. They tend to acquire the social attitudes of the groups they aspire to ... in a rather extravagant and extreme form. In their anxiety to identify themselves with the successful they often show great lack of charity and compassion with the poor and the weak. Those who are successful often seem pregnant with a sense of blame and indignation, which they lodge vociferously with a wide range of social deviants – the workshy, the young, the immigrants, the immoral.... People who are successful believe that success is a reflection of some moral superiority. They rate enterprise and initiative as the most worthwhile of all human characteristics, and what they rather vaguely call fecklessness or spinelessness as the most contemptible. But because their own success stems from virtue, its opposite must be true, that failure stems from vice. People at the bottom of the scale are felt to be a vaguely menacing influence, not in any obvious revolutionary way, but they do undermine the beliefs which legitimate those who are in positions of superiority. This is why the references to criminals, shirkers, drunks, are so venomous. The suspicion lingers that perhaps the ascription of total responsibility to the failures is no more justified than the arrogation of it by the successful.... It is not solicitude about social justice and order which prompts people to invoke the gallows and the birch and all the other agencies of punishment and repression. It is the knowledge that any attenuating concessions made to the failure and the wrong-doer would imply a consequent diminution of their own responsibility for their achievements. And this is a surrender they are not prepared to contemplate.[14]

The Folk Devil – on to whom all our most intense feelings about things going wrong, and all our fears about what might undermine our fragile securities are projected – is, as Jeremy Seabrook suggested above, a sort of alter ego for Virtue. In one sense, the Folk Devil comes up at us unexpectedly, out of the darkness, out of nowhere. In another sense, he is all too familiar; we know him already, before he appears. He is the reverse image, the alternative to all we know: *the negation*. He is the fear of failure that is secreted at the heart of success, the danger that lurks inside security, the profligate figure by whom Virtue is constantly tempted, the tiny, seductive voice inside inviting us to feed on sweets and honey cakes when we know we must restrict ourselves to iron rations. When things threaten to disintegrate, the Folk Devil not only becomes the bearer of all our social anxieties, but we turn against him the full wrath of our indignation.

The 'mugger' was such a Folk Devil; his form and shape accurately reflected the content of the fears and anxieties of those who first imagined, and then actually discovered him: young, black, bred in, or arising from the 'breakdown of social order' in the city; threatening the traditional peace of the streets, the security of movement of the ordinary respectable citizen; motivated by naked gain, a reward he would come by, if possible, without a day's honest toil; his crime, the outcome of a thousand occasions when adults and parents had failed to correct, civilize and tutor his wilder impulses; impelled by an even more frightening need for 'gratuitous violence', an inevitable result of the weakening of moral fibre in family and society, and the general collapse of respect for discipline and authority. In short, the very token of 'permissiveness', embodying in his every action and person, feelings and values that were the opposite of those decencies and restraints which make England what she is. He was a sort of personification of all the positive social images – only *in reverse*: black on white. It would be hard to construct a more appropriate Folk Devil.

The moment of his appearance is one of those moments in English culture when the suppressed, distorted or unexpressed responses to thirty years of unsettling social change, which failed to find political expression, nevertheless surfaced and took tangible shape and form in a particularly compelling symbolic way. The tangibility of the 'mugger' – like Teddy Boy, rocker and skinhead before him – his palpable shape, was a prompt catalyst: it precipitated anxieties, worries, concerns, discontents, which had previously found no constant or clarifying articulation, promoted no sustained or organized social movement. When the impulse to articulate, to grasp and organize 'needs' in a positive collective practice of struggle is thwarted, it does not just disappear. It turns back on itself, and provides the seed-bed of 'social movements' which are collectively powerful even as they are deeply irrational: irrational, to the point at least where any due measure is lost between actual threat perceived, the symbolic danger imagined, and the scale of punishment and control which is 'required'. These streams of social anxiety and eddies of moral indignation swirled and bubbled, in the 1960s and 1970s, at some level right beneath the surface ebb and flow of electoral politics and parliamentary gamesmanship. Seabrook remarked:

Most people I met who said they were socialists offered a ritual and mechanistic account of their convictions, which could not compete with the drama of the Right, which talks of the guts of the nation having been sapped by the Welfare State, and of a coddled and feather-bedded generation of shirkers and scroungers and loafers – words with an emotive power which the lexicon of the left has lost. The ascendancy of the Right is no less real for its relative failures to be collected in voting patterns: these have become institutionalized. Most people are not aware that there is any connection between their social beliefs and their voting habits.[15]

And that is precisely the gap, the opening into the mouth of Hell, from which the mugger was summoned.

However, this combining of the defence of the traditional world view with its appropriate scapegoats does not take place by magic. The necessary connexions have to be made, publicly forged and articulated – the 'sense of bitterness' described by Seabrook has to be worked on to come to identify its scapegoats. Ideological work is necessary to maintain the articulation of the subordinate class experience with the dominant ideology – 'universal' ideas do not become so or remain so without these connexions constantly being made and remade. The devils do, indeed, have to be *summoned*.

In the period with which we are concerned this leads us to a second source of the traditionalist view – to an altogether different and more powerful voice than that of the working class. It is a voice which takes both the dominant ideology and subordinate anxieties and moulds them together in a distinctive tone: that of moral indignation and public outrage. We have in mind here the 'appeal to common sense', to the 'experience of the majority' (often, nowadays, called the 'silent majority', just to enforce the point that it is not sufficiently heeded in the counsels of the experts and decision-makers), voiced by certain middle-class and, especially, lower-middle-class or 'petty-bourgeois' social groups. Their presence has increasingly been felt in public debates about moral and social problems; they have led the campaign against 'permissiveness', and are especially active in writing letters to the local press and airing views on 'phone-in' programmes. (We may think of this voice, collectively, as the *ideal audience* for the radio programme, *Any Questions*, or as the ideal correspondents of *Any Answers*.) Common sense – good stout common sense – is a powerful bastion for those groups which have made many sacrifices in exchange for a subaltern position 'in the sun', and who have seen this progressively eroded on three fronts: by what they think of as the 'rising materialism' of the working classes (too affluent for their own good); by the shiftless, work-shy layabouts who 'have never done an honest day's work in their lives' – the lumpen-bourgeoisie as well as the lumpen-proletariat; and by the high-spending style of consumption and progressive culture of the wealthier, more cosmopolitan, progressive upper-middle classes. These petty-bourgeois groups have been somewhat left behind in the pace of advancing social change; they have remained relatively static in jobs, position, attachments, places of residence, attitudes. They are still firmly in touch with the fixed points of reference in the moral universe: family, school, church, town, community life. These people have never had the upper-class rewards of wealth or the working-class rewards of solidarity to compensate them for the sacrifices they have made to compete and succeed. All the rewards they have ever had are 'moral' ones. They have maintained the traditional standards of moral and social conduct; they have identified – over-identified – with 'right thinking' in every sphere of life; and they have come to regard themselves as the backbone of the nation, the guardians of its traditional wisdoms. Whereas working people have had to make a life for themselves in the negotiated spaces of a dominant culture, this second petty-bourgeois group projects itself as the embodiment and last defence of public morality – as a social ideal. Although often similar to other middling groups in the society, the old middle classes and the old petty bourgeoisie – the 'locals' – find themselves opposed to the 'cosmopolitans', who have moved most and fastest in terms of jobs and attitudes in the last two decades, who feel themselves 'in touch' with less localized networks of influence, who therefore take 'larger', more progressive views on social questions – the *real* inheritors of that degree of post-war 'affluence' which Britain has enjoyed. As the tide of permissiveness and moral 'filth' has accumulated, and the middle and upper classes have lowered the barriers of moral vigilance and started to 'swing' a little with the permissive trends, this lower-middle-class voice has become more strident, more entrenched, more outraged, more wracked with social and moral envy, *and* more vigorous and organized in giving public expression to its moral beliefs. This is the spear-head of the moral backlash, the watchdogs of public morality, the articulators of moral indignation, the moral entrepreneurs, the crusaders. One of its principal characteristics is its tendency to speak, not on its own behalf or in its own interest, but to identify its sectional morality *with the whole nation* – to give voice on behalf of everybody. If subordinate class interests have come, increasingly, to be projected as a universal cry of moral shame, it is above all this petty-bourgeois voice which has endowed it with its universal appeal. The point, once again, is not that the two sources of traditionalism – working class and petty bourgeois – are the same, but that, through the active mediation of the moral entrepreneurs, the two sources have been welded together into a single common cause. This is the mechanism which is activated wherever the moral guardians assert that what *they* believe is also what the 'silent majority' believes.

The split within the middle class between its 'local' and 'cosmopolitan' fractions has produced two opposed 'climates of thought' about central social issues since the war. The split is to be found in the debate about 'permissiveness' and moral pollution, sexual behaviour, marriage, the family, pornography and censorship, drug-taking, dress, mores and manners, etc. The same polarization is evident also in the area of social welfare, crime, penal policy, the police and public order. In promoting some more liberal attitudes to crime and punishment, as well as in showing itself more tolerant towards deviant and sexual behaviour, 'progressive' opinion – as the traditionalists see it – has directly contributed to the speed at which moral values have been degraded, to the erosion of society's standards of public conduct. The 'progressives' have prepared the ground for the moral and political crisis which we are all now experiencing. It is easy to see why the lumpen should want to pollute respectable morality. But how have good, stalwart middle-class people been so bemused and misled? One explanation is that they have been misled by a conspiracy of intellectuals – the liberal establishment, united in a conspiracy against the old and tried ways of life, feeding on its vulnerable heart. This was the *trahison des clercs* which drove the Nixon administration into justifying to themselves the excesses of Watergate. But another, even more convenient explanation is that the 'progressives' have simply lost their way – because they have been consistently out of touch with what the great, silent majority think and feel (they feel, of course, conservatively). Thus liberals have been betrayed into talking and acting *against common sense*. In this scheme of things, the silent majority, common sense and conservative moral attitudes are one and the same, or mutually interchangeable. So the reference to 'common sense' as a final moral appeal also contracts quite complex affiliations with this larger debate. In this convergence, common sense is irrevocably harnessed to a traditionalist perspective on society, morality and the preservation of social order. The appeal to common sense thus forms the basis for the construction of traditionalist coalitions and alliances devoted to stoking up and giving public expression to moral indignation and rage.

What has been vital to this 'revivalist' movement in traditionalist ideology is its ability to use that thematic structure of 'Englishness' which we discussed earlier, to connect with and draw out the otherwise unarticulated anxieties and sense of unease of those sections of the working class who have felt 'the earth move under their feet'. And it is the potency of those themes and images (work, discipline, the family, and so on), rather than any detailed specification of their content, which has made those connexions possible.

By comparison, the 'liberalism' which has been the ethos of the cosmopolitan middle class has failed to touch those deep roots of experience. Identifying itself with 'progressive' developments of whatever nature, it has to all intents and purposes presented itself as the prime-mover and guardian of 'permissiveness', with all its attendant affronts to the traditional values and standards. Similarly, its liberal position on crime and social problems has been too distant, too academic to make connexions with everyday experience. It has argued its case in statistics, abstract analysis and in the 'quality' Sunday newspapers – and failed to offer anything comparable to the direct impact or pragmatic immediacy of the traditionalist world view.

It is of critical importance not to confuse these two sources of traditionalism in English culture in the debate about crime, not to treat their appearance inside common public forms as a 'natural' process. It is important to distinguish the 'rational core' of working-class traditionalism from that of its petty-bourgeois form. Two different class realities are expressed inside this apparently single stream of thought. We must remember the roots which both have in the real, concrete social and material experience of their subordination.

References

1 HARRIS, N. (1968) *Beliefs in Society*. London: Franklin Watts.
2 ENGELS, F. 'Ludwig Feuerbach and the End of Classical German Philosophy', in (1951) *Marx-Engels Selected Works*, Vol. 2. London: Lawrence and Wishart.
3 See HARRIS, *Beliefs in Society*; and GEERTZ, C. (1964) 'Ideology as a Cultural System', in APTER, D. (ed.) *Ideology and Discontent*. New York: Free Press.
4 See the eloquent portrait by A. Maude in *The English Middle Classes*, a seminal text, written in this period, and representing an important early moral *cri de coeur*.
5 STEADMAN-JONES, G. (1974) 'The Remaking of the English Working Class', *Journal of Social History*, Vol. 7, summer 1974.
6 See COHEN, S. (1972) *Folk Devils and Moral Panics: the creation of the Mods and Rockers*. London: MacGibbon and Kee; and CLARKE, J., HALL, S. M., JEFFERSON, T. and ROBERTS, B. (1976) 'Subcultures, Cultures and Class: a theoretical overview' in HALL, S. M. and JEFFERSON, T. (eds) *Resistance through Rituals*. London: Hutchinson.
7 CLARKE *et al.*, 'Subcultures, Cultures and Class'.
8 See GLASS, R. (1960) *Newcomers: the West Indians in London*. London: Allen and Unwin.
9 COHEN, S., *Folk Devils and Moral Panics*, p. 192.
10 See CLARKE *et al.*, 'Subcultures, Cultures and Class'; CLARKE, J. (1976) 'Style', in HALL, S. M. and JEFFERSON, T. (eds) *Resistance through Rituals;* and COHEN, P. (1972) 'Subcultural Conflict and Working Class Community', *Working Papers in Cultural Studies* No. 2, CCCS, University of Birmingham, Spring 1972.
11 SEABROOK, J. (1973) *City Close-up*. Harmondsworth: Penguin Books (p. 62).
12 Ibid., p. 57.
13 See CRITCHER, C. *et al.* (1975) 'Race and the Provincial Press', Report to Unesco; also available as CCCS Stencilled Paper No. 39.
14 SEABROOK, *City Close-up*, pp. 79–81.
15 Ibid., pp. 198–9.

2.3 Violence, indiscipline and truancy

Nigel Wright

Many people, it seems, feel certain that violence, indiscipline and truancy are now a common feature of our schools. As I write the *Daily Mirror* has a double-page spread about it, saying that the '3 Rs' have been joined by a fourth – 'Rebellion' – in the schools, and describing some sensational (if unattributed) examples: schools burnt to the ground, teachers chased screaming from the classroom. There are certainly plenty of such 'horror' stories about, and it is hard to avoid the impression that there has been a dramatic change for the worse in the last few years. I have searched for evidence on this matter: reliable evidence which would stand up to rigorous scrutiny (such as might be accepted in a court of law) and which would make it possible to judge how things have changed. Unfortunately, I have found none. Nor has Rhodes Boyson, who writes: '... it is very difficult to obtain comparative figures over a period of years. Accordingly, we have to rely on indications gleaned from speeches, reports and researches.'[1] Gleanings, speeches, reports and researches. Unfortunately, the speeches which suggest that things are getting worse are made by people like Boyson himself: people with an axe to grind who, although they say there is no evidence, manage to convince some sections of public opinion that schools are in chaos. The reports we get are very similar to those in the *Daily Mirror*: the objective is sensation, not the discovery of truth. As for research, there is very little to go on.

One teachers' union, the National Association of Schoolmasters, has been making an issue of violence in schools for a number of years. This is the union which represents the more 'discipline minded' teachers, and they have made several surveys in an attempt to gather hard evidence. In 1975 they published their most detailed study, *Violent and Disruptive Behaviour in Schools*. The foreword is by Dr L. F. Lowenstein, who writes:

It was hoped, when commencing this study, to show the public, and teachers and parents especially, the trends that violence and obstructive behaviour have taken over a period of time. It was especially hoped that some answer could be provided to the question 'Are violence and disruption, as well as vandalism, etc., on the increase or are they being contained or, even better, being successfully overcome?' I am sad to say that these questions have not been answered to my satisfaction and probably even less so to those of the critical and even sceptical reader. The reasons for this are the lack of objectivity and accuracy on the part of the teachers filling in the forms ...[2]

The NAS survey was indeed not very satisfactory, and it supplied no evidence that violence is on the increase. Above all else it illustrated how

Source: WRIGHT, NIGEL (1977) *Progress in Education*. London: Croom Helm, pp. 111–123.

difficult it is to get a *rough* idea of what's going on, never mind an objective and accurate picture. By comparison, an assessment of national reading standards is child's play.

Margaret Thatcher, when she was Secretary for Education in 1972, commissioned a survey of violence in schools. It took two years for the details to emerge and when they did they were of little help.[3] Only 100 (out of 162) Local Education Authorities supplied information. These reported that in the school year 1971/72 there were some 2,000 reported incidents of violence by pupil against pupil, 460 incidents of violence by pupil against teacher, and 74 of violence by parents against teachers. Less than 1 per cent of primary schools, and some 5 per cent of secondary schools, had reported any incident of violence during the year. But we do not know what proportion of incidents are reported by headteachers to the local authority, let alone how many headteachers know of every incident in their schools in the first place. We do not know whether these figures represent an increase or a decrease over earlier years. About 60 per cent of authorities thought there had been no significant increase in misbehaviour.[4] One might argue that local authorities are hopelessly out of touch with what is going on in their schools. Alternatively, one might contend that if things were really as bad as they are made out to be the local authority could not avoid knowing about it. Any conclusion is entirely speculative. The general impression of growing disorder is based entirely on anecdotes and the personal impressions of influential people. Sometimes these are reports by people who have left school, like this one:

... at break-time the junior boys ganged up ... and mobbed and mauled me horribly. But because I had to reappear in school, it was confined to ..., blood-chilling threats ... of what would happen ... at four o'clock. When school ended for the day we were spewed out of the classroom in a howling yelling crowd ... I was carried along to some waste ground and a concerted attack began on me. I was soon taking a bad bruising and I began bleeding profusely ... In this school and all its like there never was any code of school behaviour ... The only known criteria were bodily strength, lying, and low strategy ... In none of the lessons did I in the least understand what was supposed to be going on or have any inkling of what I was doing.[5]

Or there are letters to newspapers from influential people:

Another matter of the moment which is causing heart-searching is the weakening of authority. We are told that even the rank and file of the various unions are not prepared to follow their leaders. Is this surprising when we dismiss children from school without allowing them to ... understand the meaning of discipline?[6]

Then there are newspaper reports of incidents, like 'strikes' by pupils: 'The boys, being apprised of the presence of a large number of "strikers" outside, revolted. They banged the desks, and in a wild rush to get outside to join the other strikers they smashed the fittings. For a time the scene was one of great disorder.'[7] Sometimes clergymen regret the demise of Christian modes of behaviour: ' ... in these days particularly ... young

people are tempted to "order themselves" anything but "lowly and rever-
ently" to all their "betters", as well as to resent submission to their
"governors, teachers, spiritual pastors, and masters" ...."[8] Visitors to this
country are sometimes horrified: 'Commonwealth teachers, at a conference, expressed surprise at the bad discipline in English schools. ... Heads
and staffs should stand up to their children and restore order. Rowdyism
in class is a wasteful disgrace.'[9] Occasionally sociologists report on what
they have seen: 'Hostility is the key factor at———School. It is present
whenever a teacher deals with boys, but varies in intensity. At one extreme
... it can be almost ferocious, when for example an inexperienced teacher
wrestles with a lad for possession of a flick-knife, surrounded by cheering
boys. Or when a gang yell derisively at a teacher ...'[10] Occasionally, even
teachers reveal what's going on:

Are the boys generally well behaved? Do they work hard and take an interest in
their lessons? Do the boys in most classes reach an adequate standard of literacy?
Does the behaviour of the worst boys improve? Are the boys deterred from
misbehaviour? I think the answer to all these questions is a qualified 'no'. And yet
this is in spite of a rigorous system of corporal punishment. ... certain boys smoke,
steal, play truant or are wholly non-cooperative in class. The problems that face
any young teacher landed with such a class of third- and fourth-year boys are
enormous.[11]

Horrifying as some of these 'gleanings' are, there is a difficulty. Choose
any decade, since 1870, and it would be a straightforward task to fill a
hefty volume with reports and impressions of this kind.[12] Accounts of
pupil misbehaviour date from, at least, the Mimes of Herodas. As Professor J. W. Tibble put it in 1953:

Many schools today are very different from the schools attended thirty or forty
years ago by the older people among us. ... one frequently hears and reads sharp
criticisms in which the schools are blamed for a variety of defects which are
attributed to the young people of today. It is said that they lack discipline and
respect for their elders; their standards, whether in the basic skills or in behaviour,
are said to be lower; juvenile delinquency has increased. We must realize that
accusations of this kind are no new thing; we could produce examples for almost
any period as far back as written records go. In most cases the critics produce little
in the way of evidence of decline; they are aware that changes have taken place and
they feel strongly that things were better as they were.[13]

Professor Tibble was writing just as a period of widespread public alarm
about schools was drawing to a close. Many readers will remember the
'Blackboard Jungle' sensations in 1955 and 1956[14] when the press produced report after report very similar to those they are giving us today.
And now, in the 1970s we are experiencing another eruption of concern.
Anecdotes and impressions are a fickle guide to the truth, particularly
when the media decides to make them into an issue. Let me be quite clear:
I am *not* saying that all the anecdotes and impressions are false – though
some are and others are easily exaggerated.[15] I have not the slightest

doubt that every day there are very nasty incidents occurring in schools. My doubts are whether things are getting radically worse and, if they are, whether popular opinion is anywhere near locating the true causes. In *Roaring Boys* Edward Blishen wrote of his experiences as a young teacher in a secondary modern school in 1949/50. A colleague, 'Mr Boumphrey', had this to say: 'It's dreadful, dreadful. I hadn't realized there were schools like this.'[16] It may be that this is part of the story: we simply had not realized before that these things were going on. This does not mean that they were not going on: it is just that they were not given wide publicity, apart from outbreaks like the 'Blackboard Jungle' scare.

In Chapter 10 [not reprinted here] I offer a theory that this absence of publicity in normal times was partly a consequence of our divided education system. There are innumerable accounts of dreadful secondary modern schools in the past,[17] and of elementary schools before the war. But the public opinion makers – the journalists, broadcasters, politicians and, one might suggest, the middle classes generally – were not usually conscious of it, or worse, did not care. It is with the coming of comprehensive schools that these things have begun to 'crawl out of the woodwork'. Journalists, politicians and broadcasters now find that *their* children are going to schools alongside youngsters who would always in the past have been hidden from sight and sound in some back-street sink school. This is no consolation to those of us who are faced with having to send our child next September to the local school. But being aware of a problem is the first step towards doing something about it and in this sense the public concern is to be welcomed. I repeat that I have no doubt that some quarters of some schools are violent and distressing places. Furthermore it would be surprising if trends in society were not reflected in the schools, however hard schools try to insulate themselves. If this is true, attempts to reform schools will meet with limited success if we can not reform society. 'I'm sick of the smell of violence in this place,' says a teacher in Barry Reckord's play *Skyvers*.[18] So well he might be, but let us not pretend that there was a happy age in the past when it was otherwise.

Discipline is a more inscrutable matter than violence because there is no general agreement on how much of it is desirable or indeed on what it should consist of. What one person sees as indiscipline, another will see as a measure of freedom which they have deliberately introduced into the learning process. It seems certain that there is less discipline now in the military sense, but it is by no means clear that there is less order and commitment on the part of pupils to the tasks in hand. The fact – if it is a fact – that in the old days pupils *looked* as if they were working hard doesn't prove that they were learning more.[19] In fact, the evidence we have reviewed in earlier chapters suggests that they were not. I recorded a lady on the radio who said: 'Children aren't disciplined enough today. I think the child who has discipline and who knows what he should do and shouldn't do is a happier child and feels safer and more secure. The same as animals: a happy dog is a dog who feels secure when he's disciplined and knows what he must do and what he mustn't do. It's the same for children.' Fortunately, dogs resemble humans in only a limited number of ways, and going to school to learn is not one of them. My own feeling is that such facile views about discipline are a poor reflection of the educational experience of people who hold them. The question of discipline is a complex one, and thoughtful books have been written on the matter;[20] I do not intend to enter into the discussion here. As for *evidence* of declining discipline, there is none.

On truancy there is a little bit more evidence than on violence and indiscipline, but not much. And there are pitfalls. The matter is examined from several angles in *Truancy*, edited by Barry Turner, published in 1974.[21] An article by Paul Williams[22] describes the difficulties in defining truancy and collecting statistics. The figures most commonly quoted are attendance rates. But a 90 per cent attendance rate could mean that 10 per cent of the children were absent all of the time or that all of the children were absent 10 per cent of the time – or anything in between. And that's only the start of our troubles, for these figures do not tell us *why* children were absent. Finding out which children are truanting – with or without their parents' consent – and which have a reasonable excuse would involve checking out each individual case. This is an enormous task, and it simply has not been done on any large scale at different periods in time so that comparisons can be made. Maurice Tyerman, who has studied truancy for many years, writes in *Truancy*:

Reports that are available indicate that throughout the country the overall annual percentage of attendance is about 91%, and that there is no sign of a general decline in attendance though, of course, this may be occurring in certain schools and certain areas. In primary schools attendance is about 0.5 per cent higher than the overall average and about the same percentage lower for secondary schools. Attendance in the Autumn term tends to be a little higher than in the summer term and in both terms it is higher than in spring. Grammar schools tend to have better attendance figures than comprehensive schools and their attendance seems better than that of secondary modern schools. Attendance decreases as pupils become older, especially if they are in the lower sets or streams. Truancy appears to be responsible for about 2 per cent of absences overall and for much more than this in certain forms of certain schools in certain areas.[23]

This seems to be a fair summary of the available evidence.

One piece of evidence comes from the National Child Development Study which has followed some 16,000 children, born in one week of 1958, through their school careers. Major studies were conducted when the children were 7, 11 and 16. At the age of eleven (in 1969) it was found that 1 per cent of the children were truanting from school.[24] Truancy was strongly related to social class, was highest in North-West England and in Wales. There was little difference between streamed and non-streamed schools and within streamed schools there is disproportionately lower truancy in higher and middle streams and disproportionately higher truancy in lower streams. Truancy, not surprisingly, was (inversely) related to parents' enthusiasm for schooling. Truants were largely drawn from those children rated 'below average' in scholastic ability by their teachers. And there does seem to be an association between attendance rates and school attainment.[25] When the sample reached 16 years of age (in 1974) they were studied again.[26] Teachers felt that 20 per cent of the youngsters had truanted in the past year – 12 per cent somewhat, and 8 per cent certainly and quite frequently. Ten per cent of parents said their child had truanted occasionally and 3 per cent said they had done so at least once a week. But some parents had kept their child at home (most often to help out in one way or another) and did not count this as truancy. But most surprising of all, 52 per cent of children reported that they had stayed away from school in the past year when they should have been there. This figure must be taken with caution because the researchers did not clarify what was understood by 'should have been there'. By the time we subtract those who had some reasonable, or nearly reasonable, excuse and those who maybe took off one or two halfdays when life got on top of them, the number who could really be called truants would probably be much smaller. And it must be remembered that this group of sixteen-year-olds were the first to be affected by the raising of the school-leaving age to sixteen; comparable figures for earlier years do not exist. Worrying as some people may find these figures, they do not constitute evidence that truancy has increased.

In the autumn of 1973, D. Galloway studied persistent absenteeism (which is not necessarily truancy) from all the Sheffield comprehensive schools and their feeder primary schools over a seven-week period. He found that less than 1 per cent were persistently absent from primary schools, and that in comprehensive schools the percentage of persistent absentees ranged from 0.5 per cent in the first year to 4.4 per cent of fifth-year pupils.[27] A somewhat subjective assessment by Education Welfare Officers[28] suggested that 40 per cent of persistent absentees were absent with the knowledge of parents. Only 11 per cent of comprehensive absentees were definitely judged to be 'truants' (2.4 per cent in primary schools) though there were a further 28 per cent of the persistent absentees about whom there was a question mark (41 per cent in the primary schools). This would mean that a negligible proportion of first years were truanting, and at the most 1.7 per cent of fifth years. This gives quite a different picture from the National Child Development Study and it illustrates the difficulty in collecting truancy figures. The Sheffield study was done in the autumn term of 1973, while the NCDS survey was done in 1974. It may be that Sheffield, with its well-established and highly-regarded comprehensive system, is far better than the rest of the country. Or it may be that far more truancy is going on than head-teachers and education welfare officers know about. The Sheffield study took no account of pupils who turn up for morning or afternoon registration and *then* disappear. From the pupil's point of view this is the best technique for steering clear of trouble. It has been suggested that this mode of truancy –

registering as present and then slipping out for some or all of the lessons – is the 'growth sector' which there has been public concern about. There are no figures on this.[29] The Sheffield study also dispelled the myth that there is a connection between large schools and persistent absenteeism. Absenteeism was, however, strongly associated with social hardship.[30]

Galloway repeated his study in 1974 without finding significantly different results from those described above,[31] though shedding more light on the complex details of the matter. The survey was repeated in the subsequent year, so that in due course figures will become available for comparison. Galloway himself has concluded that '... truancy is a relatively minor cause of unjustified absence from school.'[32] The other reasons for prolonged absence which he lists are socio-medical reasons, 'school phobia', 'parents unable or unwilling to insist on return', psychosomatic illness and, most common of all, a mixture of these things. This brings us to an important point which has to be made about 'truancy'. Relatively few of the children who absent themselves from school can be labelled simply as 'naughty' or 'bloody-minded'. Most face other problems which may or may not be partly associated with the school. These problems will not be eliminated by stiffening punishments for absence or by tightening up school regimes. The whole question of absenteeism is a complex and sensitive one.

The Department of Education and Science decided to make its own survey of absenteeism in 1974 and on one day in January all schools in the country were asked to report details. It was found that about 10 per cent of all children in middle and secondary schools were absent. About 2 per cent of all children were absent without some legitimate reason.[33] This survey was criticized because it did not take into account pupils who slipped away after registration. Of course, some schools *do* look out for this; we do not know how many schools do not. And we have no figures at all for the extent of this method of truancy. But the striking thing about the DES figures was the consistency with all earlier information. For instance, in the late 1950s one investigator reported: '... it would be reasonable to assume that over the past few years secondary schools attain 91 per cent average annual attendance.'[34] This report suggested that 4 per cent of pupils were absent without explanation and perhaps 2 per cent of pupils were absent for 'unacceptable reasons'. The figure of a 90 per cent attendance rate (i.e. 10 per cent absenteeism) seems almost to be a magic figure. It recurs, give or take a percentage point, in all the literature of school absence.[35] The consistency of the figure casts grave doubt on claims that truancy is increasing. If it were true that post-registration truancy is increasing, one would also expect some increase in the number of pupils who are brazen enough to skip registration as well. And it is certainly not true that it is only in the last few years that pupils have 'discovered' that they can register and then skip lessons: pupils have known that trick since schools were invented. So there really is no evidence at all that truancy is greatly on the increase. The *Black Paper 1975* claims that '650,000 children play truant every day'.[36] No source is given for this figure,[37] and it is certainly wildly different from the figures suggested by any of the available evidence. Nor is there any evidence whatsoever for Rhodes Boyson's assertion that 'Where 25 years ago it was the badly-behaved boy who played truant, it may now be the good boy who stays at home for his own protection.'[38] As Tyerman points out in the passage quoted above (p. 107) there are certain schools in certain areas where the problem is more acute. Since there have always been schools in certain areas with acute problems, this seems to be something which needs tackling at local level. London has often been looked upon, recently, as a major problem area. But even here, overall, there seemed to be little change between 1950 and 1976. Thus 'during the 10 month period ending March 1950, the average percentage of attendance in London was 87.85 per cent'.[39] In 1976 the figure was 88–90 per cent.[40]

Even if we had conclusive evidence on truancy over a series of years, we would still have to face the question of what the figures mean. Why do children try to get out of school? Is it the school's fault, the parent's fault, the child's fault, society's fault – or is it wrong to talk in terms of 'faults' at all? These are the central questions; seeking answers to them is likely to be much more fruitful than a barren sifting and re-sifting of inadequate figures. Like so many other questions in education, they are too complex to be dealt with by polemic. Politicians with an axe to grind and journalists with a sensation to sell rarely make much contribution to answering the questions that matter.

Notes and References

1 BOYSON, RHODES (1975) *The Crisis in Education*. London: Woburn Press (p. 15).

2 NAS (1975) *Violent and Disruptive Behaviour in Schools*. National Association of Schoolmasters (p. 5).

3 Hansard, Vol. 877, 23 July 1974, col. 399/400.

4 DES (1974) *Education and Science in 1973*. Department of Education and Science (p. 4).

5 OWEN, HAROLD (1963) *Journey from Obscurity*, Vol. 1. Oxford: Oxford University Press. Owen is here writing about his schooldays in Shrewsbury in 1907.

6 Letter from the Dean of Norwich, *The Times*, 19 August 1911.

7 Report in the *Greenock Telegraph*, 16 September 1911, quoted in MARSON, D. (1973) *Children's Strikes in 1911*. Oxford: Ruskin College (p. 11). *History Workshop*.

8 Letter from W. H. Boyne Bunting, *The Times*, 19 May 1931.

9 Report in *The Times Educational Supplement*, 18 March 1960.

10 WEBB, JOHN (1962) 'The Sociology of a School', *British Journal of Sociology*, Vol. 13, p. 264. Webb goes on to describe further horrors. He notes that, 'The large number of secondary moderns which are of this type falls short, I hope, of a numerical majority.'

11 PARTRIDGE, JOHN : 1968) *Life in a Secondary Modern School*. Harmondsworth: Penguin Books (p. 127). The author is describing a secondary modern school in 1962.

12 I have accumulated, without any effort, a fat file full of quotations similar to those I have given. There is no space to include more here; in any case, even the most avid reader would soon tire of the constant refrain of the few age-old themes. As *The Times Educational Supplement* put it on 23 August 1941 (when, incidentally, there was an outcry about behaviour in schools and falling standards of literacy): 'Adult complaints as to the behaviour of children are not a new phenomenon. Delinquency among juveniles has ever been a satisfying topic for elderly critics . . .' For those who want really blood-curdling stuff, of course, there is nothing to beat the history of public schools – see, for example, OGILVIE, VIVIAN (1957) *The English Public School*. London: Batsford (pp. 106–29). All the best public schools seem to have been razed to the ground at least once in their time.

13 TIBBLE, J. W. (1953) Preface to WASHBURNE, CARLETON, *Schools Aren't What They Were*. London: Heinemann (p. 7).

14 See the popular press for those years. A brief account is given in TAYLOR, WILLIAM (1963) *The Secondary Modern School*. London: Faber (pp. 35–41).

15 In my own school an unfortunate little incident in which a white girl scratched a black girl in a quarrel outside the school gate was taken up by all the national press who carried amazing accounts of 'Race Riot at Comprehensive School' and so forth. If there was any danger of a race riot, it would have been fomented by the absurd reports in some newspapers.

16 BLISHEN, EDWARD (1955) *Roaring Boys*. London: Thames and Hudson (p. 125).

17 See MAYS, J. B. (1954) *Growing up in the City*. Liverpool: Liverpool University Press; BLISHEN, *Roaring Boys*; WEBB, 'The Sociology of a School'; PARTRIDGE, *Life in a Secondary Modern School*; HARGREAVES, DAVID H. (1967) *Social Relations in a Secondary School*. London: Routledge and Kegan Paul; TOWNSEND, JOHN (1958) *The Young Devils*. London: Chatto and Windus.

18 Not, unfortunately, published.

19 As any number of accounts testify. It is perhaps best put by Edward Blishen in *Roaring Boys* (p. 62): 'What I saw, for the most part, was the tedious orderliness of a class doing its normal work. It was often odd, this glimpse; the master orating, or bending over a book, or attending the blackboard, his mouth opening and shutting with that exaggeration that comes from distrust of one's audience; the boys fidgeting, nearly every one of them engaged in some private act of inattention that had to be prevented from breaking the general impression of alertness and relevance. Sometimes the teacher would be directing his remarks to one quarter of the room, and the rest would have collapsed into freedom; even, at times, I would see a hand raised with a pellet in it, a fist about to descend, the pages of a comic being secretly turned over.' Talking of comics, for how many of us does Bash Street School of the *Beano* come closer to the reality of our own school days than the picture of glorious order and contentment painted in some present-day reminiscences (e.g. by Mr Froome)? There is an extraordinary improbability about this account in *The Times* of 5 April 1921: 'The Croydon elementary schools re-opened yesterday after the Easter holidays, and the children came back as usual to find that the teachers had not. [The teachers had gone on strike over a pay dispute; only the headteachers had

come in to school.] Nevertheless, the school routine was not greatly affected. For the most part the children "carried on" by themselves ... even in these circumstances neither of the two education officers who made rounds of inspection during the day had a single case of disorder to report.... This spirit of self-discipline, it is claimed, is essentially a development of the careful handling of the children by the teachers. The tendency is more and more towards self-government by the children. They are trusted more than was the custom a few years ago, and encouraged to think more for themselves ... the present situation will provide a test of the justice of these claims...' A more common experience is described by Walter Greenwood in GREEN, GRAHAM (ed.) (1934) *The Old School.* London: Jonathan Cape (p. 77): 'Sometimes our teachers had cause to leave the room. Without exception each teacher of my knowledge set the class on its honour not to misbehave itself during his absence. He would depart and shut the door after him. A surge of restlessness would hiss round the room; fugitive strains from a mouth organ, thrummings of a jew's harp; the squashy smack of an ink sodden piece of blotting as it hit Claude ... on the neck ... Somebody would punch somebody else in the back or kick somebody's shin with the cool request to "Pass it on". So that while "it" was going the rounds chaos ensued. And when pandemonium was at its height the door would open ... The teachers' disgust for us was only equalled by our disgust for them, and for the School.... The handbell knelled us to imprisonment at 9 a.m. and 2 p.m. We were released at noon and 4.30 p.m.' Or, from the teacher's point of view: 'The astonishing thing about [the kids] is that they are alert and keen as needles for the knowledge that's not imposed, but the ear plugs are in as soon as you force any knowledge upon them. I am trying to find methods of unorganized education, informal lessons, with lots of facts dropped casually, so that they do not realize they are being taught. But, if they once suspect that you want them to learn, they resist.' (BOWIE, JANETTA (1975) *Penny Buff.* London: Constable (p. 64). The writer is remembering the period around 1930.)

20 A number of viewpoints are presented in TURNER, BARRY (ed.) (1973) *Discipline in Schools.* London: Ward Lock; there is an interesting discussion of the subject in WILSON, P. S. (1971) *Interest and Discipline in Education.* London: Routledge and Kegan Paul.

21 TURNER, BARRY (ed.) (1974) *Truancy.* London: Ward Lock.

22 Ibid., pp. 20–8.

23 Ibid., pp. 11–12.

24 FOGELMAN, K. R. and RICHARDSON, K. (1974) 'An Anatomy of Truancy', *The Teacher*, 27 September 1974.

25 Ibid.

26 FOGELMAN, KEN (ed.) (1976) *Britain's Sixteen-Year-Olds.* London: National Children's Bureau.

27 GALLOWAY, D. (1976) 'Size of School, Socio-Economic Hardship, Suspension Rates and Persistent Absence from School', *British Journal of Educational Psychology*, Vol. 46.

28 The Education Welfare Service is run by local authorities. The EWOs (Education Welfare Officers) have the job of dealing with all the welfare problems of children which are related to their education. The most notorious task of the EWO is 'securing regular attendance of all children of school age'. By and large this means checking up on truancy. The most striking single fact about the Education Welfare Service is that it is grossly understaffed.

29 Although in many schools teachers take a register at each lesson, absentee figures from such schools *would* include post-registration truants.

30 GALLOWAY, 'Size of School', *British Journal of Educational Psychology*, Vol. 46. Social hardship was assessed by the numbers of children receiving free school dinners.

31 GALLOWAY, D. (1976) 'Persistent Unjustified Absence from School', *Trends in Education*, Vol. 4 (pp. 22–7).

32 Ibid., p. 27.

33 Department of Education and Science Press Notice, 25 July 1974.

34 RANKIN, LESLIE (1960–1) 'Irregular Attendance of Children at School', *Educational Review* (Birmingham), Vol. 13 (p. 124).

35 TYERMAN, MAURICE J. (1958) 'A Research into Truancy', *British Journal of Educational Psychology*, Vol. 28 (pp. 217 onwards); RANKIN, 'Irregular Attendance of Children at School'; SANDON, FRANK (1961) 'Attendance through the School Year', *Educational Research*, Vol. 3 (pp. 153 onwards); TYERMAN, M. J. (1968) *Truancy*. London: University of London Press Ltd; CLYNE, MAX B. (1966) *Absent*. London: Tavistock publications (chapter 2); DENNEY, A. H. (1973) *Truancy and School Phobias*. London: Priory Press.

36 COX, C. B. and BOYSON, RHODES (eds) (1975) *Black Paper 1975*. London: Dent (p. 3).

37 By a process of deduction I think the figure is based on a miscalculation of some figures mentioned in a speech which Rhodes Boyson read about in *The Times Educational Supplement* in 1973.

38 BOYSON, *The Crisis in Education* (p. 13). It is difficult to square this claim with the assertion six pages earlier that the National Survey of reading standards gave a deceptively high average score for fifteen-year-olds because many of the worst pupils were truanting.

39 TYERMAN, M. J. (1958) 'A Research into Truancy', *British Journal of Educational Psychology*, Vol. 28, p. 219.

40 Survey conducted in May 1976 and reported by the Research and Statistics Branch to the ILEA Schools Sub-Committee. It is true that in May secondary schools no longer have the fifth-year 'Easter leavers', amongst whom absenteeism is greatest. But the secondary school figure for May 1976 (87.4 per cent attendance at morning registration and 86.9 per cent at afternoon registration) was rather better than the figure of 85.2 per cent for ILEA secondary schools found in the January 1974 survey (conducted in the course of the nationwide DES enquiry). In that January 1974 survey, some 5.8 per cent of secondary pupils were found to have been absent with 'no adequate reason'.

2.4 School size: its influence on pupils

W. J. Campbell

The studies of school size undertaken by the Midwest Psychological Field Station at the University of Kansas indicated that while students in large schools were exposed to a larger number of school activities and the best of them achieved standards in many activities that were unequalled by students in the small schools, students in the small schools participated in more activities, their versatility and performance scores were consistently higher, they reported more and 'better' satisfactions, and displayed stronger motivation in all areas of school activity. Although there has long been evidence from industrial psychology that the larger and more bureaucratically efficient the organization the greater the degradation of the individual, this knowledge has had little influence upon schools, and the widespread concern for the organization man has not been accompanied by a similar concern for the organization child.

Introduction

The influence of school size upon pupils, like most educational issues, has given rise to considerable controversy. On the one hand, supporters of large schools claim that pupils benefit through better and more varied curriculums, better classifications, better facilities, especially in subjects like science and music, contact with better teachers, opportunities to participate in better and more varied extracurricular activities, wider social opportunities and experiences. On the other hand, the opponents claim that these 'advantages' are illusory, and, indeed, that large-school pupils lack intimate contact with teachers, especially principals, have fewer opportunities to participate in extracurricular activities, and lose the stimulation and challenge of small-school life. Barker, for example, writes:

To an outside observer, a school with many students is impressive: its imposing physical dimensions, its seemingly endless halls and numberless rooms, its hundreds of microscopes, its vast auditorium and great audiences, its sweeping tides of students, all carry the message of power, movement, vitality, purpose, achievement, certainty. In contrast, a small school with its commonplace building, its few microscopes, its dual-purpose gym-auditorium half-filled with students who assemble and depart, not in tides but in a tangle of separate channels, is not impressive. The members of the field-work team never ceased to marvel that the directly experienced differences between large and small schools were, in these respects, so compelling, like the differences between a towering mountain and an ordinary hill, between a mighty river and a meandering brook. But to an inside participant the view is different. When the field workers were able to participate in the functioning behaviour settings of schools, they saw the small schools as in some

Source: *Journal of Educational Administration*, Vol. III, No. 1, May 1965.

respects more coercive and dominating than the large schools ... There is, indeed, an inside-outside perceptual paradox, a school size illusion.[1]

On general theoretical grounds, members of small units (be they schools, tutorial groups, business organizations, or voluntary associations), in comparison with those of large units, are likely to encounter stronger and more varied pressures associated with their participation. There is nothing mysterious about this: it is simply a matter of arithmetic. Again, on general theoretical grounds, some of the behavioural consequences are likely to be:

1 *Greater effort:* in a small organization, failure to find a replacement for one of two office boys means that the other one must work either harder or longer.

2 *More difficult and more important tasks:* in the absence of a large and strong Senior class, some of the Sub-Seniors will be called into positions of responsibility.

3 *Wider variety of activities:* in the small Parents and Citizens Committee, the Secretary might also be Treasurer; in the small school the Principal might also be the 7th Grade class teacher.

4 *Less sensitivity to and less evaluation of differences between people:* when essential personnel are in short supply, one must be tolerant of those who are available.

5 *Lower level of maximal performance:* the University professor who is unable to specialize in research, teaching, or administration, is less able to excel in one of these; his work is affected, too, by the versatility demanded of his colleagues, subordinates, and superiors.

6 *Greater functional importance within the setting:* with increasing scarcity of population, those who remain become even more essential; in a three-man organization, each member could be a key person.

7 *Greater responsibility:* when the membership in a valued association is large, we can afford occasional absences, but when it is small, we must attend lest the association collapses.

8 *Lower standards and fewer tests for admission:* in an over-manned setting, like a present-day university, it is easy to be highly selective, but in the small family the five-year-old and even the parent are frequently welcomed into the soccer game.

9 *More frequent occurrences of success and failure:* the twelve-year-old 8th Grade pupil who, in the absence of more experienced players, captains the under-fourteen basketball team is placed in a situation where the opportunities for quick success and recognition, but also for failure and lowered esteem, are greater.

Again, these theoretical consequences are not mysterious; they are almost common-sense inevitabilities of small units. Research conducted in a variety of areas provides overwhelming support for their occurrence. Thus concerning:

1 *Frequency, depth and range of participation.* Persons in smaller groups:

   (a) are absent less often;

(b) resign positions less often;

(c) are more punctual;

(d) participate more frequently when participation is voluntary;

(e) function in positions of responsibility and importance more frequently and in a wider range of activities;

(f) are more productive;

(g) demonstrate more leadership behaviour;

(h) are more important to the groups and settings;

(i) have broader role conceptions;

(j) are more frequently involved in roles directly relevant to the group tasks

(k) are more interested in the affairs of the group or organization.

2 *Communication and social interaction.* Small groups give rise to:

(a) greater individual participation in communication and social interaction, and less centralization of the communication around one or few persons;

(b) more greetings and social transactions per person;

(c) facilitated communication, both through greater clarity and decreased difficulty;

(d) greater group cohesiveness and more frequent liking of all fellow group members.

3 *The reported experiences of persons.* Persons in smaller groups:

(a) receive more 'satisfaction';

(b) are more familiar with the settings;

(c) report being more satisfied with payment schemes and with the results of group discussions;

(d) find their work more meaningful.

Studies of school size support the general findings summarized above.

In 1949 Larson[2] related size of high school to students' activities and relations to peers. A higher percentage of students in small schools as compared with medium and large schools reported that it was easy to make friends and that they liked all their school acquaintances. Higher percentages of students in large schools than in medium and small schools reported that they engaged in no activities or only one, and that they experienced difficulty in getting into activities.

Isaacs[3] in 1953 reported that the per cent of retention (inverse of drop-outs) was negatively related to size of high schools in Kansas.

A questionnaire study by Anderson, Ladd, and Smith[4] in 1954, involving 2,500 high school graduates, found that the per cent of graduates who reported that their school experiences were 'very valuable and useful' was negatively correlated with school size. Coleman[5] in 1961 found the following to be negatively related to size of high school: *(a)* per cent of boys who participated in football; *(b)* ability to name an outstanding fellow student in certain areas; *(c)* consensus about persons in the student body who were outstanding in certain areas.

The Kansas Study

The most comprehensive and sophisticated studies of school size yet reported were undertaken at the Midwest Psychological Field Station at the University of Kansas, and published in 1964 under the editorship of Barker and Gump.[6] A total of 218 high schools with student populations ranging from 18 to 2,287 were involved in the cluster of studies. The research workers at Kansas were interested mainly in identifying the different experiences encountered by pupils who were similar in many respects but who were attending schools that differed in size, and, except on rare occasions, they do not go beyond their data to the effects that these different experiences are likely to have upon the growth and development of the pupils. However, in this paper, I shall follow a brief review of the Kansas findings with a few speculative comments concerned with: (*a*) likely effects upon pupils, and (*b*) implications for administrators.

1 *Judged in terms of existing behavioural units* (Barker calls these 'behaviour settings') the large school is likely to appear infinitely rich, and the small school impoverished. Thus, Capital City with 2,287 pupils had 499 distinct settings, and Otan with 35 pupils had only 60 settings. Nevertheless, even from these figures one can see that the setting density is much higher in Capital City (4.58 pupils per setting) than in Otan (0.58 pupils per setting). School settings do not increase at the same rate as pupils, and, moreover, setting varieties increase least of all. Thus Capital City, compared with Otan, had 65 times as many students, eight times as many settings, but only 1.5 times as many setting varieties (43.29). Finally, the evidence suggests that, as schools increase in size, it is the operational settings that increase most. This finding is in accord with other research which shows that as units increase, higher proportions of energy and facilities are devoted to unit maintenance.

2 *Judged in terms of the number of subjects taken* the small-school students appeared to be at an advantage, for they tended to take more courses each, and, in particular, a greater number of non-academic courses. Thus students in schools with a population of 300 were averaging 6 courses, while those in the 1,800 group were averaging 5. No data were gathered on the quality of the classes, or the depth of student participation in them. These are matters which, at least theoretically, can be separated from the issue of school size.

3 *Judged in terms of inter-school cultural participation* the small-school students appeared to be at an advantage, for participation percentages started at 28 in the smallest schools, rose to 45 in schools with enrolments between 76 and 115, and thereafter fell steadily to four. This trend emerged even though the large schools, as schools, were the strongest supporters of the inter-school activities, and, of course, the large school competitors secured most of the prizes. Their degree of specialization was greater.

Versatility scores, too, suggested that pupils from the small schools had the advantage in these inter-school activities. Thus when the maximum score was 8, seniors from the small schools were averaging 4.8, while those from the large schools were averaging 2.2. In the smallest school, 53 per cent of the seniors scored 5 or more, and in the largest school only 4 per cent scored similarly.

4 *Judged in terms of participation in extracurricular activities* the small-school pupils appeared to be at an advantage, for, although the large schools provided a somewhat larger number and wider variety of activities, actual participations were higher among small-school pupils. This was most apparent when participations were graded according to extent of penetration, thus level 1: 'watched', 'listened'; level 2: 'practised in the play'; level 3: 'ushered at the play'; level 4: 'acted a part in the play'. If levels 3 and 4 are classified as 'performances' and levels 1 and 2 as 'entries', performance ratings are found to be much higher among small-school students. Thus, in the largest school, 794 juniors were exposed to 189 extracurricular activities and, on the average, achieved a performance score in 3.5 of these; in the smaller schools, 23 juniors were exposed to 48 extracurricular activities, and, on the average, achieved a performance score in 8.6 of these. Almost one-half of the extracurricular participations of students in the very small schools were performances. This proportion fell to around the 40 per cent mark for the schools in the 83–221 range, to the 30 per cent mark for the schools in the 339–438 range, and to about 15 per cent in the very large school.

Finally, as far as extracurricular activities were concerned, small-school pupils were found to participate in a wider variety of activities.

5 *Judged in terms of 'satisfactions' associated with school* the small-school students appeared to be at an advantage. This is not surprising since numerous studies have suggested that levels of satisfaction in group activities are closely associated with levels of participation. The small-school students not only reported more activities from which they received satisfaction, and a larger number of satisfactions per activity mentioned, but their *kinds* of satisfactions differed from those of large-school students. While the latter mentioned mainly vicarious enjoyment and satisfactions arising from belonging to a large group, the former mentioned mainly satisfactions related to competence, challenge, and activity.

6 *Judged in terms of attractions and pressures to participate in school activities* the small-school students appeared to be at an advantage. They reported more attractions (e.g. 'I thought that I might learn something there', 'I thought that it would be lots of fun'), more internal forces or pressures (e.g. 'I had a responsibility with the activity', 'I knew this activity needed people'), and more external pressures (e.g. 'I was expected to go', 'Others wanted me to go'). They were more aware than pupils in large schools of claims associated with wishes, expectations, demands, and requirements of other persons and they also mentioned more frequently claims associated with personal responsibilities which they held or perceived themselves as holding. In other words, the small-school students were more

strongly motivated to participate. Many students in the large schools experienced few, if any, forces to participate.

In summary, students from the large schools *were exposed* to a larger number of school activities, and the best of them achieved standards in many activities that were unequalled by students in the small schools; on the other hand, students in the small schools *participated* in more activities – academic, inter-school, cultural, and extracurricular; their versatility and performance scores were consistently higher, they reported more and 'better' satisfactions, and displayed stronger motivation in all areas of school activity.

At several points in the statement of findings, it has been suggested that the small-school students were 'at an advantage', because of the difference in experiences which they encountered. To the extent that one man's meat may be another man's poison, it is difficult to argue the case on the basis of experience alone. Nevertheless, knowledge in child development is sufficiently advanced to enable one to infer some general effects.

Inferences from the Kansas Study

External pressures aimed at increasing participation

The finding that students in the small schools experience more external pressures would seem to have important implications for the development of a sense of confidence in oneself. In the early years of life, a sense of security, worth, and importance is gained largely through membership within the family, but sooner or later the child must cast aside this support and establish himself as a worthy, independent being. The school can make a useful contribution here by fostering feelings of success and mastery within the formal curriculum, but many students are likely to derive their patterns of security, adequacy, and other ego attributes in the more informal extracurricular activities. It is here that the small schools have an important advantage, for whether weak, strong, inept, skilful, young, or experienced, each pupil really is important; often the activities cannot continue without his participation. Thus one would speculate that the increased external pressures would enhance the development of what is currently called primary status among students in the small school. This enhancement, in its turn, could be expected to foster development in most other areas.

Sense of personal responsibility associated with school activities

Again we could speculate on the developmental implications of the heightened sense of personal responsibility that the small-school students appear to have in connection with school activities. Nevertheless, here we seem to be dealing with a different order of phenomenon, not an experience, in the sense that external pressures are experiences, but rather an index of development. In our society a child is expected to progress from a state of egocentrism towards one in which due attention is given to the welfare of an ever-widening circle of individuals and groups. Thus he learns, or is expected to learn, respect for the interests of family, peer group, school, church, community, nation, and human race in roughly that sequence, and he is expected, too, to contribute to these groups according to his abilities. To the extent that the small-school students were more conscious of responsibilities of this kind, we can hypothesize greater maturity on their part.

Penetration of school settings

If an entry penetration (for example, 'listening', 'watching', etc.) is rated equal with a performance one (for example, 'spoke to the class', 'acted in the play', etc.) students are likely to gain equally at small and large schools. However, without underestimating the value of watching or listening to high-quality performances (and performances at the larger school are likely to be of a higher quality), the research on child development overwhelmingly endorses the view that more active participation is more stimulating. In general, it is better to play than watch, to contribute actively rather than to sit passively, and it is surely no coincidence that the small-school students report greater satisfaction with school, and, in particular, mention more values associated with physical well-being, acquisition of knowledge, development of self-concept, and plain enjoyment. These are some of the characteristics that one would expect to be fostered by the increased performances, and the reporting of these by the students themselves increases the confidence which can be placed in the expectations.

Variety of settings, situations, and activities

An item somewhat similar to the one just discussed is that concerned with the variety of settings, situations, and activities. In general (although this generalization like the earlier one concerned with penetration could be pushed too far) students benefit in a large number of ways through active participation in a variety of activities. Thus, in most cases at the child and adolescent levels, one gets more enjoyment, develops a keener self-concept, and receives greater all-round stimulation if one participates in varied activities rather than concentrates upon one, or upon those that are alike. The small-school student is not allowed to be selective; versatility is prized more than specialization. The large-school student, on the other hand, spends most of his time on a few activities and participates less frequently in clubs, music, hobbies, excursions, and the like. These miscellaneous activities can be particularly beneficial since they frequently provide the few opportunities that students have for experimentation and the pursuit of their own interests.

Although there has long been evidence from industrial psychology that the larger and more bureaucratically efficient the organization the greater the degradation of the individual, this knowledge has had little influence upon schools, and the widespread concern for the organization man has not been accompanied by a similar concern for the organization child. On the contrary the enlargement of schools has often been accepted not as an unfortunate necessity but as a welcome educational improvement. This evaluation is usually based upon the assumption of a direct positive relationship between the properties of schools and the experiences and behaviours of their pupils, e.g. the assumption that a rich curriculum means rich experiences for students, or that a comprehensive programme of extracurricular activities means strong individual involvement. Obviously good facilities provide good experiences only if they are used. The educational process is a subtle and delicate one about which we know little: but it surely thrives upon participation, enthusiasm, and responsibility. Without participation, education cannot occur, however excellent the arrangements may be. All of the research findings reveal a negative relation between school size and individual student participation. To the degree that this is true it means that when better facilities are purchased at the expense of larger size they are discounted by lower participation on the part of the students.

From the child development viewpoint, how big should a school be? Even from this narrow viewpoint the question is difficult to answer because so much depends upon the facilities that can be provided. Nevertheless, one can answer with Professor Roger Barker: 'A school should be sufficiently small that all of its students are needed for its enterprises. A school should be small enough that students are not redundant.' Once enrolments pass the 400 mark it is probably difficult to ensure that students do not become redundant. A scientific answer to the question would probably be expressed in terms of the ratio of students to settings, and, although no conclusive data are available, this ratio probably should not exceed 2.5:1.

Implications for school administration

Assuming that increases in school size beyond a certain point almost inevitably result in a poorer set of experiences for the students, what are the implications for school administrators? Four that occur to me concern school consolidation, school developments in new and expanding areas, means by which the advantages of the large schools can be taken to the small ones, and means by which the advantages of the small schools can be taken to the large ones. My intention now is to discuss briefly each of the first three of these.

1 *Consolidation of schools.* Consolidation is variously defined, but the essential elements are: (*a*) commuting to a school outside the local community boundary, and (*b*) attendance at a larger school than the one that had previously existed, or could exist, in the local community. The advantages and disadvantages of consolidation then will, in many respects, be identical with those of increases in school size. To the best of my knowledge, only one study has examined the effects of consolidation upon pupil experiences, and this is to be found in the Midwest cluster of studies. Eastern Kansas in 1962 presented an excellent field laboratory for the study of these effects. In many districts consolidation at the high school level had already taken place, and schools that were formerly used for secondary students were being used for primary students or were standing idle. On the other hand, there was no dearth of small local high schools that were still functioning actively.

Three groups of pupils were carefully matched and then compared with respect to school experiences:

Group 1: small local – students in attendance at small rural high schools within the boundaries of their own communities. There were two schools involved here and each had a student population of 53. Each, too, was situated within a small town of about 200 persons.

Group 2: consolidated – students who came from communities that were similar in size to those in group 1, but who were transported daily by bus to a county high school with an enrolment of 370 students within a larger district.

Group 3: larger local – students in attendance at the larger county high school referred to above, but who came from the community (population 551) within which the school was situated.

This, I imagine, is a fairly typical consolidation picture [. . .] the investigator was able to show very conclusively that the other-community students who were transported to it suffered decreases in *pressures, claims, performance participations, variety of participations*, and *satisfactions*. These were all attributed to a size increase from 50 pupils to 370. In addition, as a result of commuting, these students suffered decreases in the range of non-school situations and activities, and in neighbourhood and community participations.

These findings suggest that the current assumption of consolidated school superiority is, in at least some aspects, like the first report of Mark Twain's death – exaggerated! Consolidation ought not to be embarked upon lightly and indiscriminately and, when it does occur, special efforts are demanded from both the school and the local community. Through its structural organization, its instructional procedures, and its extracurricular activities, the larger school needs to ensure that *all* its students participate actively and acquire a genuine sense of attachment and contribution to group goals. There is a temptation in a larger school to concentrate upon extracurricular goals and standards which can be achieved by only the most talented students at the expense of the rest. Similarly the local community from which the pupils are drawn must take special pains to so arrange its recreational programmes and community tasks that its young members are appropriately challenged and stimulated. Once consolidation has taken place, there is a temptation for the community to discard some of its obligations to its children and adolescents, whereas the data suggest the need for a still more determined effort to meet those obligations.

2 *School development in expanding areas.* During the last few years many new suburbs have sprung up within Australian cities, and small rural schools have been transformed into bulging city ones. To take only one example close to home, although Kenmore school was established about 1900, it remained until 1958 a one-teacher school serving a rural community. In the space of six short years, enrolments have risen to well over the 500 mark, and there is every indication of continuing increases. It is true that the building programme has kept pace with enrolments, so that now the school has thirteen permanent classrooms, an office, two staff rooms, library, four store rooms, a health room, and a permanent lunch room. Nevertheless, it is clear that the stage is past when school enrichments can keep pace with enrolments. Instead of maintaining a policy of adding to the present site, bringing pupils from wide distances to the present school, and transferring headmasters at regular intervals, the education authorities might well push ahead vigorously with the establishment of additional schools within the Kenmore area.

We have the research techniques to answer this important administrative problem of the number of schools needed for a given population, but no serious Australian attempt has been made to gather data scientifically. Too frequently, as Sir Fred Clarke has suggested,[7] we proceed by 'common sense' or 'blind', according to one's viewpoint.

If we conducted our medical and engineering services and our industrial production with the same slipshod carelessness, the same disregard for precision of thought and language, the same wild and reckless play of sentimentality or class prejudice or material interest masquerading as principle, with which we carry on our public discussion about education, most patients would die, most bridges would fall down, and most manufacturing concerns would go bankrupt.

Seldom if ever does a discussion about education proceed in a medium of clearly defined terms, used in an agreed sense by all participants; seldom if ever does it escape contamination and distortion by the intrusion of some sectional prejudice or vested interest which usually knows how to disguise itself in a speciously attractive colouring ... It is no more than a wild dream to imagine that the same kind of close precision can be imparted to thinking about education that belongs properly to physics or chemistry or even law and economics. But it is my central conviction that the educational thinking of all of us who attempt it is gravely in need of that kind of discipline ... Education has at least as much claim to systematic study as animal husbandry or rural economy or coal-mining ...

Systematic, courageous and uncontaminated thinking about national education touches our national salvation.

I am suggesting that we should take scientific steps to determine at what stage our schools here make their greatest contribution to the development of our children and then take what steps we can to ensure that the optimal size is reached and not exceeded.

3 *Taking the advantages of the large school to the small school.* If, as the research evidence suggests, the negative relationship between school size and individual participation is deeply based, and difficult, if not impossible, to avoid, it may be easier to bring specialized and varied behaviour settings to small schools than to raise the level of individual participation in large ones. [. . .] This is already done to some extent in such fields as guidance, music, physical education, etc., but I suspect that it could be extended very considerably. The use of more itinerant specialists, the appointment of bright, enthusiastic teachers to positions of area advisers, and the encouragement of greater inter-school cooperation, through the transporting of teachers and equipment, rather than students, are some suggestions aimed at ensuring that our pupils enjoy the best of both worlds. Certainly, many of our very small schools are dreary and impoverished educational centres as they now stand, but these characteristics are not inevitabilities of small size.

It may well be, also, that some of the innovations which are cautiously being introduced into the educational system will enrich the small schools. self-teaching machines, taped school courses, television classes, wired television linking separate schools, new conceptions of the contributions of the community to educational objectives [. . .], and new materials and standards for school construction could all mean that the specialization and variety which are available to, but seldom able to be capitalized upon by, the large-school pupil, would be within the grasp of the small-school pupil under conditions of maximum opportunity.

Schools are specialized environments, established and manipulated in order to produce certain educational opportunities and effects. We are in need of more investigations, employing new concepts and methods, in order to determine the nature and consequences of these environments.

References

1 BARKER, R. G. and GUMP, P. V. (eds) (1964) *Big School, Small School.* Stanford, Calif.: Standard University Press.
2 LARSON, CAROL M. (n.d.) *School Size as a Factor in the Adjustment of High School Seniors.* State College of Washington Bulletin No. 511, Youth Series No. 6.
3 ISAACS, D. A. (1953) 'A Study of Predicting Topeka High School Drop-Outs One Year in Advance by Means of Three Predictors'. Doctoral dissertation, University of Kansas.

4 ANDERSON, K. E., LADD, G. E. and SMITH, H. A. (1954) *A Study of 2,500 Kansas High School Graduates*. University of Kansas, Kansas Studies in Education No. 4.

5 COLEMAN, J. S. (1961) *The Adolescent Society*. Glencoe, Ill.: Free Press (later New York).

6 BARKER and GUMP, *Big School*.

7 CLARKE, F. (1943) *The Study of Education in England*. Oxford: Oxford University Press (pp. ii–iv).

2.5 Power and the paracurriculum[1]

D. Hargreaves

Introduction

From whom, one wonders, is the hidden curriculum now hidden? Like examination papers, what was once unseen is now revealed. Certainly it has proved to be a popular concept among social scientists working in the field of education, partly perhaps because in unmasking the hidden they felt able to bring 'news' both to their lay audience and to fellow social scientists. Once published, social scientific news soon loses its novelty, if less rapidly than journalistic news. The alternative names for the hidden curriculum – unwritten, unstudied, tacit, latent, unnoticed – have the same disadvantage, and if the phenomenon is to have more than a temporary place in our studies it seems right to give it a more appropriate name. I suggest the term 'paracurriculum' – that which is taught and learned alongside the formal or official curriculum.

The literature on the paracurriculum is now fairly extensive, though to my knowledge no one has attempted a systematic analysis of its various subjects and pedagogies to match our analysis of the formal curriculum. And hitherto most attention has been devoted to the paracurriculum that is learned by learners rather than to the paracurriculum that is learned by our teachers, even though it might be claimed that the latter is at least as important as the former.

'Internal' aspects of the paracurriculum

My initial purpose is to offer a brief analysis of the previous literature. The earliest writing on the paracurriculum focused on what I might call its 'internal' aspects, by which I mean its role within the school itself. Here the analysis is essentially social psychological and concentrates upon how members of an institution, particularly those in positions with little formal power, adapt to the relatively unnoticed constraints of the institution. The claim made is that the members must learn and conform to the paracurriculum if they are to succeed, and perhaps merely survive, in the institution. The most sophisticated exponent of this approach, who took little interest in schools and who did not use the concept of the hidden curriculum, is the symbolic interactionist Erving Goffman (1961) in his analysis of 'total institutions'. This work, rich with insightful observations and conceptual inventions, has proved to be a major source of ideas which

Source: RICHARDS, C. (ed.) (1977) *Power and the Curriculum: Issues in Curriculum Studies*. Driffield: Nafferton Books.

can usefully be applied to the paracurriculum in education right up to the present day (e.g. Woods, 1977). Becker (1961, 1968), also a symbolic interactionist, followed this tradition in his study of medical students and Snyder (1971) and Miller and Parlett (1976) offered further applications within higher education. At the school level, the most significant contributions were made by the anthropologist Henry (1955) and by Jackson (1968). For Henry, the paracurriculum teaches docility to pupils; for Jackson, it is patience. On this view, the paracurriculum is an inherent and inevitable feature of life in institutions; the analysis is, in a sense, conservative. It is most neatly characterized by Jackson:

Here then are four unpublicized features of school life: delay, denial, interruption and social distraction. Each is produced, in part, by the crowded conditions of the classroom. When twenty or thirty people must live together within a limited space for five or six hours a day most of the things that have been discussed are inevitable. Therefore, to decry the existence of these conditions is probably futile, yet their pervasiveness and frequency is too important to be ignored. One alternative is to study the ways in which teachers and pupils cope with these facts of life and to seek to discover how that coping might leave its mark on their reactions to the world in general (p. 17).

For Jackson, there is little point in trying to reform schools so that the 'facts of life' which lie behind his view of the hidden curriculum – namely, crowds, praise and power – are eliminated. In this, as in other respects, Jackson follows Goffman whose analysis (some would say indictment) of mental hospitals never led him to become a social reformer.

In the second strand of work on the 'internal' paracurriculum the emphasis is less on institutional demands and more on the dissonance or conflict that arises between the paracurriculum and the formal curriculum. Here the paracurriculum is held to undermine and even to achieve primacy over the formal curriculum. This theme runs through the work of Becker and Snyder but the most influential writer here is, perhaps, Carl Rogers (1969) who, believing that the paracurriculum is not inevitable, enthusiastically begins to explore personal and institutional reform. The title to one of his papers, 'Current assumptions in graduate education: a passionate statement', is a telling one and contrasts markedly with Jackson's dispassionate social scientific approach. At the school level, passion turns to anger, especially in the writing of Holt (1964) and other New Romantics such as Kohl, Herndon, etc. Holt, like Jackson, examines the strategies that pupils adopt to cope with the institution and the teacher's power, but interprets them as profoundly anti-educational; for him, the successful learning of the paracurriculum is achieved only at the cost of the destruction of love of learning, interest and curiosity, intelligence and creativity. The paracurriculum instils not patience, but fear. The difference is crucial. Patience is a socially approved virtue which is acquired when a person adapts to constraints which are inevitable or to powers which are legitimately exercised. To describe the same reaction as fear is to imply both that the reaction is undesirable and that it is a product of power that is exercised illegitimately, arbitrarily or unwisely. In his later writing (1966) Henry is closer to Holt than to Jackson. On reading Jackson's account we smile knowingly as he wittily draws our attention to the taken-for-granted; on reading Henry, whose writing is based on the same mundane and trivial classroom events, we recoil with horror and shock from the picture we see reflected in his mirror.

It is simply that the child must react in terms of the institutional definitions or he fails. The first two years of school are spent not so much in learning the rudiments of the three Rs, as in learning definitions (p. 240). . . . School is indeed a training for future life not because it teaches the three Rs (more or less), but because it instils the essential cultural nightmare fear of failure, envy of success and absurdity (p. 250).

From Jackson's patience, and Holt's fear, we have moved to hatred and absurdity as the consequences of the successful learning of the paracurriculum.

The analysis of the 'internal' or social psychological aspects of the paracurriculum, then, can be divided into two strands. In the first or conservative position, the adaptation of members, particularly those with little power, to the demands of the institution is described, but the analysis is not used as the basis for an attack upon the nature of institutions (schools) or those in positions of power (teachers). In the second or radical position, the conflict between the paracurriculum and the official ideology or goals of the institution is stressed. The values of the analyst become more explicit and the critical or condemnatory attitudes permeate both the characterization of the paracurriculum and the alternatives that are proposed.

'External' aspects

In contrast to this essentially social psychological approach, sociologists have taken greater interest in the 'external' aspects of the paracurriculum. On this view the learning of the paracurriculum is not merely a situation-specific adaptation to school but a fundamental, extensive and pervasive contribution to socialization which has profound effects both outside school and beyond the years spent in formal education. There are, of course, traces of such ideas in Henry and Holt, but a more systematic treatment is provided by sociologists who (significantly) tie their analysis much less closely to carefully observed mundane classroom events. At this level there are again two strands which parallel those at the social psychological level. The first is exemplified in the work of Dreeben (1967, 1968) who, in a functionalist account which closely follows the earlier work of Parsons, highlights the contribution that schooling makes to the acquisition of general social norms – independence, achievement, universalism and specificity. Here the school's paracurriculum acts as an important bridge between early socialization in the home and preparation for adult membership in Western society. Like all functionalist accounts, Dreeben's is open to the accusation that it is implicitly conservative; Dreeben anxiously warns that his analysis should not be taken as a defence of national values. The second strand can be illustrated through Illich's (1971) version of the paracurriculum. On this view the paracurriculum teaches, *inter alia*, that learning can occur only in schools and only as a consequence of teaching by professional, qualified teachers. This, it is claimed, makes a massive contribution to the creation of the passive consumers who populate modern society. There is no risk that this analysis might be read as conservative; Illich proceeds on the basis of his account to propose the complete abolition of schools.

In the present climate it is de-schooling, not schooling, which is dead; Illich's analysis was sociologically too naïve to last. Current sociological work, which nevertheless maintains some interesting continuities with the functionalist approach, stresses the contribution of the paracurriculum to the complex process of cultural and social reproduction. The writing of Bourdieu (e.g. 1973) is important here, and in its impact on Bernstein (1975). The Marxist analysis of Bowles and Gintis (1976) neatly exemplifies an important contemporary sociological analysis of the paracurriculum:

The educational system operates in this manner [i.e. in fostering types of personal development compatible with the relationships of dominance and subordination in the economic sphere] not so much through the conscious intentions of teachers and administrators in their day-to-day activities, but through a close correspondence between the social relationships which govern personal interaction in the work place and the social relationships of the educational system. Specifically, the relationships of authority and control between administrators and teachers, teachers and students, students and students, and students and their work replicate the hierarchical division of labour which dominates the work place... (pp. 11–12)

The correspondence between the social relation of schooling and work accounts for the ability of the educational system to produce an amenable and fragmented labour force. The experience of schooling, not merely the content of formal learning, is central to this process... (p. 125)

The educational system, through the pattern of status distinctions it fosters, reinforces the stratified consciousness on which the fragmentation of subordinate economic classes is based.... To reproduce the social relations of production, the educational system must try to teach people to be properly subordinate and render them sufficiently fragmented in consciousness to preclude their getting together to shape their own material existence... (p. 130)

The perpetuation of the class structure requires that the hierarchical division of labour be reproduced in the consciousness of its participants. The educational system is one of the several reproduction mechanisms through which dominant élites seek to achieve this objective... (p. 147)

Through the educational encounter, individuals are induced to accept the degree of powerlessness with which they will be faced as mature workers (p. 265).

The new Open University collection of essays (Dale *et al.* 1976) contains several similar contributions. For instance, Karier writes:

... the second-grade child learns that some people look different and speak differently from others, and that some know more, learn more, and have more wealth than others. Differences in wealth seem to be associated with both knowledge and ability, and they are treated as phenomena as natural as differences in speech or appearance. If the second grader learns this lesson well, he has taken an important step in his socialization – the acceptance and justification of an economically determined social system. The school in both the nineteenth and twentieth centuries not only taught those values that normally sustain a commercial culture, but it also effectively taught the social myths necessary to sustain the social-class system that was a product of the economic order (p. 24).

The analysis is more sophisticated than that of either Dreeben or Illich, and the analysts' values are quite overt. The impact of the paracurriculum cannot be subverted merely by reform of schools or teacher practices. Rather, a full-scale democratic socialist revolution is required. The paracurriculum is in part mediated through the teachers' power, but teachers are powerless to eliminate the paracurriculum's effects by changing what they do in school, unless it takes the form of self-conscious, collective, politicised action.

Power and the use of space

The theme of power and authority as a part of the paracurriculum permeates the literature from Jackson's social psychological analysis to the sociological/political economy account of Bowles and Gintis. My own interest in power and the paracurriculum stems from none of this literature but, as befits a social psychologist, from the literature on non-verbal communication. In particular, I have been concerned with the use of space (an important concept in the work of E. T. Hall's anthropological work as well as in ethnological studies) in schools as both a symbolic expression of, and as a mechanism for creating and maintaining, the power relation that exists between teachers and pupils. The significance of the physical layout of the classroom, the pupils clustered together in their desks facing the teacher at the front, did not escape comment from social psychologists interested in non-verbal communication. Thus Sommer (1969) notes:

The straight rows tell the student to look ahead and ignore everyone except the teacher; the students are jammed so tightly together that psychological escape, much less physical separation, is impossible. The teacher has fifty times more free space than the students, with the mobility to move about. He writes important messages on the board with his back to his students. The august figure can rise and walk about among the lowly who lack the authority even to stand without explicit permission (p. 99).

In similar vein Richardson (1967) writes:

The teacher figures as the person who should be the focus of all eyes, the central authority who tends either to be asking all the questions or supplying all the answers, the presiding adult through whom all communication must go (p. 85).

Power and authority are communicated in a congruent way in assembly, where the youngest ('junior') pupils are seated at the front and the oldest at the back. The headteacher, sometimes with a retinue of staff and prefects, frequently enters to a silent and standing audience and slowly mounts the platform from which he conducts proceedings. Evans (1971) provides an insightful commentary on assembly:

The arrangements for the staging of authority in the school hall seem to show where the school authorities are most inclined to position themselves in relation to the past, and in relation to the crises in authority through which the nation has battled since the sixteenth century. In some, but not all, Catholic schools the arrangements for assembly takes us back to before the Act of Supremacy. Here, power continues to inhere in the transcendental order. Assembly is conducted with curtains closed, acting like the rood screen to obscure the ultimate mysteries of the chancel. The headteacher stands not on the stage, but on the same level as the pupils and a large crucifix hangs above the heads of all. Next we come to the Divine Right of Kings, symbolized by the throne or great chair. Court etiquette long decreed that the sovereign alone should occupy a chair, other persons present being seated on stools. This usage was governed by rigorous court etiquette right down to the early Georgian period. It is this symbolism which seems to have ossified in many of the public schools, where the great chair is retained and the headmaster sits alone on the stage. It has diffused more widely. In the majority of the schools in this study, the head teacher continued to take assembly alone. Sometimes there are three chairs rather than one. This may be related to the arrangements in the House of Lords, where there are thrones for the King and Queen at the centre and for the heir apparent at the side. But besides being a symbol of regal authority, the chair has also, as the throne of God, been the symbol of divine authority, so there may be some trinitarian flavour about this triple arrangement.... Since 'chairs' are also offered to professors, the chair can also symbolize academic authority and it begins to emerge that the great chair, long used in schools, and retained in many, is a ritual symbol with a high degree of ambiguity which can supply rich associative links of a generalized character and permit a transition between levels of meaning. When the head of one public school was asked who sat in the three big leather chairs at the front of the stage, he looked the investigator straight in the eye and replied 'I do' in a tone which combined the authority of holy trinity, demonic trilogy, male triad and Goldilocks legend.

Space in schools is divided into distinct territories – hall, classrooms, corridors, playgrounds – but on the whole it is soon made clear that it is the staff who 'own' this territory. It is only they who are free to move where they want when they want, with the exception of the headteacher's room. They have free access to what is the closest to being pupil territory, their lavatories. Even territory which is officially shared between teachers and pupils, the classroom, is frequently termed 'My room' by the teacher, who has complete control over entry, exits and movement within the room. Teachers have a more private territory in the form of the staffroom, from which pupils are often carefully excluded.

In a very real sense, then, the pupils have no legitimate territory of their own, not even what Goffman calls a 'temporary tenancy'. Wherever they are, they are subject to surveillance and control. This is even true of the playground: its ambiguous status with regard to ownership is betrayed by the fact that many teachers on playground duty feel slightly uneasy at appearing to invade pupil territory. Wherever a pupil is in school, he must be ready to be called to account, to explain and justify his location. Thus pupils on corridors must always be 'going somewhere' lest they be accused of 'loitering' with or without intent. In the allocation, use and control of space in school, the teacher's power and authority are constantly represented and reinforced. He is observably a powerful person.

Power and time

The structuring, allocation and control of time in school by teachers can be subjected to a similar analysis. Of the various contributions to the literature on time none is more relevant or fecund in ideas than E. P. Thompson's paper on 'Time, work-discipline and industrial capitalism' (1968). His focus is the transformations in the understanding and effects of time in the light of the industrial revolution and the claim is that:

Puritanism, in its marriage of convenience with industrial capitalism, was the great agent which converted men to new valuations of time; which taught children even in their infancy to improve each shining hour; and which saturated men's minds with the equation, time is money (p. 95).

The Protestant ethic's message was to redeem the time; the factory owner's gospel was to come to work on time, on regular days, for regular periods, and to work hard for money under the master's discipline. Thompson draws some very telling parallels between the structures of factories and Sunday schools, a common feature of which is the emphasis on punctuality. Compare the duties of the warden of the mill as listed in the Law Book of the Crowley Iron Works:

Every morning at 5 a clock the Warden is to ring the bell for beginning to work, at eight a clock for breakfast, at half an hour after for work again, at twelve a clock for dinner, at one to work and at eight to ring for leaving work and all to be lock'd up (p. 82).

with this extract from the Rules for the Methodist School of Industry at Pocklington.

The Superintendant shall again ring – when, on a motion of his hand, the whole School rise at once from their seats; – on a second motion, the Scholars turn; – on a third, slowly and silently move to the place appointed to repeat their lessons, – he then pronounce the word 'Begin' ... (p. 85).

How heavily the past weighs upon the modern school, with its day divided into periods, signified by electronically controlled bells. Sandwiched between these work periods are the 'breaks', lunch-time and home-time, all carefully pre-programmed and punctuated by the bells. And through this we teach the pupils how to make sharp distinctions between work and play. For lessons are work-times taking place in work-places (classrooms), whereas play has its own appointed time (break or playtime) in its own appointed place (the playground). For the majority of the pupils this scheduling will soon be replaced by leisure-time in the evening and at the week-end and by work-time at the factory or office, punctuated by *clocking* on and off.

In school, as in the factory, time belongs to those who wield power and authority. Just as pupils own no territory, so they have little time they can call their own. It is school-time in several senses. Pupils must be ready to give an account of their use of that time, for of all pupil sins *wasting* time is one of the most common and the most serious, and the seriousness of the offence rises if the pupil wastes not only his own time but that of the teacher as well. Good children, like good Christians, *devote* their time to higher and important things. They have 'their own time' only when they are in the playground or not in school at all.

Space, time and the paracurriculum: claims and research

The interesting question to ask is how all this analysis relates to the social psychological and sociological literature, either conservative or radical. Into which of these sectors of the literature does the argument fit? The answer is into all four of them. The 'facts' with which I have been dealing do not speak for themselves; I must speak for them. Where I locate the 'facts' depends upon whether I (or you) wish to operate at the purely social psychological level or to ground a macro-sociological account in micro-data; and it depends upon whether my (or your) values are conservative or radical. It can be argued that my analysis simply amplifies the Bowles and Gintis thesis. But it is equally justifiable to interpret the ideas in a totally different way. Some teachers, I believe, would argue that it is right that schools should prepare pupils for relatively passive adult roles in industrial society and that obedience to authority is as vital as it is desirable. If the schools foster such attitudes through the non-verbal aspects of the paracurriculum, this merely shows that schools undertake their proper task more thoroughly and systematically than perhaps we had realized. Indeed, such teachers might argue that such attitudes are not being taught effectively enough; for them, the lesson to be drawn from the studies of the paracurriculum is that we must intentionally increase and improve the means by which we prepare the young for an acceptance of their roles in industrial society. Such a position accepts the 'facts' of writers on the paracurriculum, from Jackson to Bowles and Gintis, but it inverts the neo-Marxist evaluative interpretation of those 'facts'.

Not all classrooms are like those I have described above. Many primary schools (and a very few secondary schools) structure space and time in very different ways – they offer an alternative paracurriculum. Indeed among 'progressive' writers the impact of this paracurriculum of time and space in relation to the teacher's authority is no longer a hidden dimension but a conscious deliberation and intentional planning. Take these extracts from Kohl's *The Open Classroom* (1970):

The assignment of seats, perhaps the first act the teacher performs during the school year, can stand symbolically for many things that occur in authoritarian classrooms. It is the teacher who assigns the seats and the pupils who must obey . . . An open classroom is different. Pupils are free to choose and change their seats. So is the teacher (p. 22) . . . It is no accident that spatial memories are strong. The placement of objects in space is not arbitrary and rooms represent in physical form the spirit and souls of places and institutions. A teacher's room tells us something about who he is and a great deal about what he is doing. Often we are not aware of the degree to which the space we control gives us away . . . [In the open classroom] the teacher's desk might not even be the teacher's any more, the teacher settling for a desk like the pupil's and abandoning his privileged piece of furniture to some other use (p. 35).

One way to begin a change is to devote ten minutes a day to doing something different. There is never any problem in finding ten minutes to play with, since what the pupils 'must cover' is usually padded in order to fill up the time. During that ten minutes present the class with a number of things they can choose to do. Present them with options you feel may interest them. Allow them the option of sitting and doing nothing if they choose. Moreover, make it clear that nothing done during that period will be graded . . . That ten minutes is to be their time and is to be respected as such . . . It is not unlikely that those ten minutes may become the most important part of the day, and after a while may even become the school day (p. 71).

To what kind of paracurriculum – now far from hidden – are such conceptions of space and time contributing? How does this aspect relate to other features of the hidden curriculum? How does this paracurriculum, overt and hidden, relate to the formal curriculum? And how does it all relate to 'cultural and social reproduction' and life after school? Are Bowles and Gintis justified in claiming that such 'tinkering' is pointless because the effects are negligible?

The answer, of course, is that we do not know. Massive claims have been made and continue to be made for the paracurriculum. It is argued that it is learned more fully than the formal curriculum and that it has primacy over the formal curriculum in its short-term and long-term effects. At the present time the literature on the paracurriculum consti-tutes a set of claims. Different authors, with different perspectives, levels of analysis and values, have offered different, if overlapping, accounts of the paracurriculum and its effects. But should we believe these claims? Is there any good evidence for them? Or is the present literature on the paracurriculum, ironically, little more than the rhetoric which formerly surrounded claims for the formal curriculum? Most of the social scientific accounts are plausible and some of them are persuasive. But do they tell us anything more than the value position of the analyst?

If the concept of the paracurriculum (or whatever term is preferred) is not to do too much work or be the subject of too grandiose claims, future work must devote itself to two main tasks. First, we must clarify and elaborate the concept itself. What are the contents ('subjects') of the paracurriculum and how do they relate to one another? The first part of this paper showed some of the many subjects that are allegedly part of the paracurriculum and then devoted itself to just one of them, that of power and authority. In itself that is not enough. We need to know how the contents vary, whether (and when) some parts are hidden, and whether there is a crucial 'core paracurriculum' that is common to both progressive and traditional schools. Perhaps the nearest we have come to such a conceptual clarification is in Bernstein's (1975) paper on visible and invisible pedagogies, though it is obviously much stronger on the sociological than psychological aspects, and its probable brilliance is matched only by its impenetrability.

Second, we must root the claims much more firmly in empirical evidence. On the one hand we must descriptively document and detail the contents and pedagogy of the paracurriculum, and on the other we must systematically evaluate the effects of the paracurriculum. For some this will mean presenting the claims in some falsifiable form and then subjecting them to empirical test – though how one would handle Bernstein here I do not know. For others, scarred by their experiences of attempting to evaluate the official curriculum, this may mean opting for some kind of 'illuminative evaluation' of the paracurriculum. Many questions are there to be asked and answered. Does lack of congruence/conflict both within the paracurriculum and between the paracurriculum and the formal curriculum matter? If the teachers change some features of the paracurriculum (e.g. *à la* Kohl) will there be any notable effects? How is the curriculum taught and who are its most effective teachers? What variations are there in the paracurriculum with regard to pupils of different sex, age, ability, stream, etc.? What individual differences are there in pupils' ability/readiness to master the paracurriculum? What are the consequences of success/failure in the paracurriculum, both in general and in relation to the formal curriculum? How does the school's paracurriculum relate to the paracurriculum of other institutions (e.g. the home, the youth club, the church, etc.)? How does the school's paracurriculum relate to the pupils' transition from school into work and adult life? Some current research endeavours will relate to these questions to a degree – see for instance the work of Willis (1977), or consider the recent interest in the influence of the school on the moral and political socialization of adolescents, which will inevitably consider features of the paracurriculum – but that is not the same as posing the question directly.

Social scientists working in the field of education are powerful people, for some teachers and many students listen to what they say. The concept of the 'hidden curriculum' has, in my experience, proved to be as fascinating a topic to teachers as 'the self-fulfilling prophecy'. In those areas where their power to influence is great, social scientists must be especially cautious that their readers do not mistake a plausible sketch of some ideas for a carefully refined and evidenced theory. No doubt social scientists should investigate the paracurriculum on which their own power rests, but most of us would, I imagine, regard that as quite another story.

Note

1 The middle section of this paper is a shortened form of an unpublished paper entitled 'The hidden curriculum: time, space and the teacher's authority' first presented in a series of open lectures on the circumstances of learning by the School of Education, University of Manchester, in 1975.

References

BECKER, H. S. *et al.* (1961) *Boys in White: Students Culture in Medical School.* Chicago: University of Chicago Press.

BECKER, H. S. *et al.* (1968) *Making the Grade: The Academic Side of College Life.* New York: Wiley.

BERNSTEIN, B. (1975) *Class, Codes and Control,* Volume III. London: Routledge and Kegan Paul.

BOWLES, B. and GINTIS, H. (1976) *Schooling in Capitalist America.* London: Routledge and Kegan Paul.

BOURDIEU, P. (1973) 'Cultural Reproduction and Social Reproduction', in BROWN, R. (ed.) *Knowledge, Education and Cultural Change.* London: Tavistock.

DALE, R. *et al.* (eds.) (1976) *Schooling and Capitalism.* London: Routledge and Kegan Paul.

DREEBEN R. (1967) 'The Contribution of Schooling to the Learning of Norms'. *Harvard Educational Review,* 37.

DREEBEN, R. (1968) *On What is Learned in School.* Reading, Mass: Addison-Wesley.

EVANS, K. (1971) The Symbolic Culture of the School', unpublished M.A. (Econ.) thesis, University of Manchester.

GOFFMAN, E. (1961) *Asylums.* Harmondsworth: Penguin Books.

HENRY, J. (1955) 'Docility or Giving Teacher What She Wants'. *Journal of Social Issues,* 11:1.

HENRY, J. (1966) *Culture Against Man.* Harmondsworth: Penguin Books.

HOLT, J. (1964) *How Children Fail.* Harmondsworth: Penguin Books.

ILLICH, I. (1971) *Deschooling Society.* Harmondsworth: Penguin Books.

JACKSON, P. W. (1968) *Life in Classrooms.* New York: Holt Rinehart and Winston.

KARIER, C. J. (1976) 'Business Values and the Educational State' in DALE, R. *et al.* (eds) *Schooling and Capitalism.* London: Routledge and Kegan Paul.

KOHL, H. (1970) *The Open Classroom.* London: Methuen.

MILLER, C. M. L. and PARLETT, M. (1976) 'Cue-Consciousness' in HAMMERSLEY, M. and WOODS, P. (eds.) *The Process of Schooling.* London: Routledge and Kegan Paul.

RICHARDSON, E. (1967) *The Environment of Learning.* London: Nelson.

ROGERS, C. R. (1969) *Freedom to Learn.* Columbus: Merrill.

SOMMER, R. (1969) *Personal Space.* Englewood Cliffs, N.J.: Prentice-Hall.

SNYDER, B. R. (1971) *The Hidden Curriculum.* New York: Knopf.

THOMPSON, E. P. (1968) 'Time, Work-Discipline and Industrial Capitalism'. *Past and Present,* 38.

WILLIS, P. (1977) *Learning to Labour.* London: Saxon House.

WOODS, P. (1977) 'Teaching for Survival' in WOODS, P. and HAMMERSLEY, M. (eds.) *School Experience.* London: Croom Helm.

2.6   Learning to teach

D. H. Lawrence

The first week passed in a blind confusion. She did not know how to teach, and she felt she never would know. Mr Harby came down every now and then to her class, to see what she was doing. She felt so incompetent as he stood by, bullying and threatening, so unreal, that she wavered, became neutral and non-existent. But he stood there watching with that listening-genial smile of the eyes, that was really threatening; he said nothing, he made her go on teaching, she felt she had no soul in her body. Then he went away, and his going was like a derision. The class was his class. She was a wavering substitute. He thrashed and bullied, he was hated. But he was master. Though she was gentle and always considerate of her class, yet they belonged to Mr Harby, and they did not belong to her. Like some invincible source of the mechanism he kept all power to himself. And the class owned his power. And in school it was power, and power alone that mattered.

Soon Ursula came to dread him, and at the bottom of her dread was a seed of hate, for she despised him, yet he was master of her. Then she began to get on. All the other teachers hated him, and fanned their hatred among themselves. For he was master of them and the children, he stood like a wheel to make absolute his authority over the herd. That seemed to be his one reason in life, to hold blind authority over the school. His teachers were his subjects as much as the scholars. Only, because they had some authority, his instinct was to detest them.

Ursula could not make herself a favourite with him. From the first moment she set hard against him. She set against Violet Harby also. Mr Harby was, however, too much for her, he was something she could not come to grips with, something too strong for her. She tried to approach him as a young, bright girl usually approaches a man, expecting a little chivalrous courtesy. But the fact that she was a girl, a woman, was ignored or used as a matter for contempt against her. She did not know what she was, nor what she must be. She wanted to remain her own responsive, personal self.

So she taught on. She made friends with the Standard Three teacher, Maggie Schofield. Miss Schofield was about twenty years old, a subdued girl who held aloof from the other teachers. She was rather beautiful, meditative, and seemed to live in another, lovelier world.

Ursula took her dinner to school, and during the second week ate it in Miss Schofield's room. Standard Three classroom stood by itself and had windows on two sides, looking on to the playground. It was a passionate relief to find such a retreat in the jarring school. For there were pots of

Source: LAWRENCE, D. H. (1915) *The Rainbow*. London: Heinemann.

chrysanthemums and coloured leaves, and a big jar of berries: there were pretty little pictures on the wall, photogravure reproductions from Greuze, and Reynolds's *Age of Innocence,* giving an air of intimacy; so that the room, with its window space, its smaller, tidier desks, its touch of pictures and flowers, made Ursula at once glad. Here at last was a little personal touch, to which she could respond.

It was Monday. She had been at school a week and was getting used to the surroundings, though she was still an entire foreigner in herself. She looked forward to having dinner with Maggie. That was the bright spot in the day. Maggie was so strong and remote, walking with slow, sure steps down a hard road, carrying the dream within her. Ursula went through the class teaching as through a meaningless daze.

Her class tumbled out at mid-day in haphazard fashion. She did not yet realize what host she was gathering against herself by her superior tolerance, her kindness and her *laisser-aller*. They were gone, and she was rid of them, and that was all. She hurried away to the teachers' room.

Mr Brunt was crouching at the small stove, putting a little rice-pudding into the oven. He rose then, and attentively poked in a small saucepan on the hob with a fork. Then he replaced the saucepan lid.

'Aren't they done?' asked Ursula gaily, breaking in on his tense absorption.

She always kept a bright, blithe manner, and was pleasant to all the teachers. For she felt like the swan among the geese, of superior heritage and belonging. And her pride at being the swan in this ugly school was not yet abated.

'Not yet,' replied Mr Brunt, laconic.

'I wonder if my dish is hot,' she said, bending down at the oven. She half expected him to look for her, but he took no notice. She was hungry and she poked her finger eagerly in the pot to see if her brussels sprouts and potatoes and meat were ready. They were not.

'Don't you think it's rather jolly bringing dinner?' she said to Mr Brunt.

'I don't know as I do,' he said, spreading a serviette on a corner of the table, and not looking at her.

'I suppose it is too far for you to go home?'

'Yes,' he said. Then he rose and looked at her. He had the bluest, fiercest, most pointed eyes that she had ever met. He stared at her with growing fierceness.

'If I were you, Miss Brangwen,' he said, menacingly, 'I should get a bit tighter hand over my class.'

Ursula shrank.

'Would you?' she asked, sweetly, yet in terror. 'Aren't I strict enough?'

'Because,' he repeated, taking no notice of her, 'they'll get you down if you don't tackle 'em pretty quick. They'll pull you down, and worry you, till Harby gets you shifted – that's how it'll be. You won't be here another six weeks' – and he filled his mouth with food – 'if you don't tackle 'em and tackle 'em quick.'

'Oh, but –' Ursula said, resentfully, ruefully. The terror was deep in her.

'Harby'll not help you. This is what he'll do – he'll let you go on, getting worse and worse, till either you clear out or he clears you out. It doesn't matter to me, except that you'll leave a class behind you as I hope *I* shan't have to cope with.'

She heard the accusation in the man's voice, and felt condemned. But still, school had not yet become a definite reality to her. She was shirking it. It was reality, but it was all outside her. And she fought against Mr Brunt's representation. She did not want to realize.

'Will it be so terrible?' she said, quivering, rather beautiful, but with a slight touch of condescension, because she would not betray her own trepidation.

'Terrible?' said the man, turning to his potatoes again. 'I dunno about terrible.'

'I *do* feel frightened,' said Ursula. 'The children seem so—'

'What?' said Miss Harby, entering at that moment.

'Why,' said Ursula, 'Mr Brunt says I ought to tackle my class,' and she laughed uneasily.

'Oh, you have to keep order if you want to teach,' said Miss Harby, hard, superior, trite.

Ursula did not answer. She felt non-valid before them.

'If you want to be let to *live*, you have,' said Mr Brunt.

'Well, if you can't keep order, what good *are* you?' said Miss Harby.

'An' you've got to do it by yourself' – his voice rose like the bitter cry of the prophets. 'You'll get no *help* from anybody.'

'Oh indeed!' said Miss Harby. 'Some people can't be helped.' And she departed [...]

Ursula felt her heart faint inside her. Why must she grasp all this, why must she force learning on fifty-five reluctant children, having all the time an ugly, rude jealousy behind her, ready to throw her to the mercy of the herd of children, who would like to rend her as a weaker representative of authority. A great dread of her task possessed her. She saw Mr Brunt, Miss Harby, Miss Schofield, all the schoolteachers, drudging unwillingly at the graceless task of compelling many children into one disciplined, mechanical set, reducing the whole set to an automatic state of obedience and attention, and then of commanding their acceptance of various pieces of knowledge. The first great task was to reduce sixty children to one state of mind, or being. This state must be produced automatically, through the will of the teacher, and the will of the whole school authority, imposed upon the will of the children. The point was that the headmaster and the teachers should have one will in authority, which should bring the will of the children into accord. But the headmaster was narrow and exclusive. The will of the teachers could not agree with his, their separate wills refused to be so subordinated. So there was a state of anarchy, leaving the final judgment to the children themselves, which authority should exist.

So there existed a set of separate wills, each straining itself to the utmost to exert its own authority. Children will never naturally acquiesce to sitting in a class and submitting to knowledge. They must be compelled by a stronger, wiser will. Against which will they must always strive to revolt. So that the first great effort of every teacher of a large class must be to bring the will of the children into accordance with his own will. And this he can only do by an abnegation of his personal self, and an application of a system of laws, for the purpose of achieving a certain calculable result, the imparting of certain knowledge. Whereas Ursula thought she was going to become the first wise teacher by making the whole business personal, and using no compulsion. She believed entirely in her own personality.

So that she was in a very deep mess. In the first place she was offering to a class a relationship which only one or two of the children were sensitive enough to appreciate, so that the mass were left outsiders, therefore against her. Secondly, she was placing herself in passive antagonism to the one fixed authority of Mr Harby, so that the scholars could more safely harry her. She did not know, but her instinct gradually warned her. She was tortured by the voice of Mr Brunt. On it went, jarring, harsh, full of hate, but so monotonous, it nearly drove her mad: always the same set, harsh monotony. The man was become a mechanism working on and on and on. But the personal man was in subdued friction all the time. It was horrible – all hate! Must she be like this? She could feel the ghastly necessity. She must become the same – put away the personal self, become an instrument, an abstraction, working upon a certain material, the class, to achieve a set purpose of making them know so much each day. And she could not submit. Yet gradually she felt the invincible iron closing upon her. The sun was being blocked out. Often when she went out at playtime and saw a luminous blue sky with changing clouds, it seemed just a fantasy, like a piece of painted scenery. Her heart was so black and tangled in the teaching, her personal self was shut in prison, abolished, she was subjugate to a bad, destructive will. How then could the sky be shining? There was no sky, there was no luminous atmosphere of out-of-doors. Only the inside of the school was real – hard, concrete, real and vicious.

She would not yet, however, let school quite overcome her. She always said, 'It is not a permanency, it will come to an end.' She could always see herself beyond the place, see the time when she had left it. On Sundays and on holidays, when she was away at Cossethay or in the woods where the beech-leaves were fallen, she could think of St Philip's Church School, and by an effort of will put it in the picture as a dirty little low-squatting building that made a very tiny mound under the sky, while the great beech-woods spread immense about her, and the afternoon was spacious and wonderful. Moreover the children, the scholars, they were insignificant little objects far away, oh, far away. And what power had they over her free soul? A fleeting thought of them, as she kicked her way through the beech-leaves, and they were gone. But her will was tense against them all the time.

All the while, they pursued her. She had never had such a passionate love of the beautiful things about her. Sitting on top of the tram-car, at evening, sometimes school was swept away as she saw a magnificent sky settling down. And her breast, her very hands, clamoured for the lovely flare of sunset. It was poignant almost to agony, her reaching for it. She almost cried aloud seeing the sundown so lovely.

For she was held away. It was no matter how she said to herself that school existed no more once she had left it. It existed. It was within her like a dark weight, controlling her movement. It was in vain the high-spirited, proud young girl flung off the school and its association with her. She was Miss Brangwen, she was Standard Five teacher, she had her most important being in her work now.

Constantly haunting her, like a darkness hovering over her heart and threatening to swoop down over it at every moment, was the sense that somehow, somehow she was brought down. Bitterly she denied unto herself that she was really a schoolteacher. Leave that to the Violet Harbys. She herself would stand clear of the accusation. It was in vain she denied it.

Within herself some recording hand seemed to point mechanically to a negation. She was incapable of fulfilling her task. She could never for a moment escape from the fatal weight of the knowledge.

And so she felt inferior to Violet Harby. Miss Harby was a splendid teacher. She could keep order and inflict knowledge on a class with remarkable efficiency. It was no good Ursula's protesting to herself that she was infinitely, infinitely the superior of Violet Harby. She knew that Violet Harby succeeded where she failed, and this in a task which was almost a test of her. She felt something all the time wearing upon her, wearing her down. She went about in these first weeks trying to deny it, to say she was free as ever. She tried not to feel at a disadvantage before Miss Harby, tried to keep up the effect of her own superiority. But a great weight was on her, which Violet Harby could bear, and she herself could not.

Though she did not give in, she never succeeded. Her class was getting in worse condition, she knew herself less and less secure in teaching it. Ought she to withdraw and go home again? Ought she to say she had come to the wrong place, and so retire? Her very life was at test.

She went on doggedly, blindly, waiting for a crisis. Mr Harby had now begun to persecute her. Her dread and hatred of him grew and loomed larger and larger. She was afraid he was going to bully her and destroy her. He began to persecute her because she could not keep her class in proper condition, because her class was the weak link in the chain which made up the school.

One of the offences was that her class was noisy and disturbed Mr Harby, as he took Standard Seven at the other end of the room. She was taking composition on a certain morning, walking in among the scholars. Some of the boys had dirty ears and necks, their clothing smelled unpleasantly, but she could ignore it. She corrected the writing as she went.

'When you say "their fur is brown", how do you write "their"?' she asked.

There was a little pause; the boys were always jeeringly backward in answering. They had begun to jeer at her authority altogether.

'Please, Miss, t-h-e-i-r,' spelled a lad, loudly, with a note of mockery.

At that moment Mr Hardy was passing.

'Stand up, Hill!' he called, in a big voice.

Everybody started. Ursula watched the boy. He was evidently poor, and rather cunning. A stiff bit of hair stood straight off his forehead, the rest fitted close to his meagre head. He was pale and colourless.

'Who told you to call out?' thundered Mr Harby.

The boy looked up and down, with a guilty air, and a cunning, cynical reserve.

'Please, Sir, I was answering,' he replied, with the same humble insolence.

'Go to my desk.'

The boy set off down the room, the big black jacket hanging in dejected folds about him, his thin legs, rather knocked at the knees, going already with the pauper's crawl, his feet in their big boots scarcely lifted. Ursula watched him in his crawling slinking progress down the room. He was one of *her* boys! When he got to the desk, he looked round, half furtively, with a sort of cunning grin and a pathetic leer at the big boys of Standard VII. Then, pitiable, pale, in his dejected garments, he lounged under the menace of the headmaster's desk, with one thin leg crooked at the knee and the foot stuck out sideways, his hands in the low-hanging pockets of his man's jacket.

Ursula tried to get her attention back to the class. The boy gave her a little horror, and she was at the same time hot with pity for him. She felt she wanted to scream. She was responsible for the boy's punishment. Mr Harby was looking at her handwriting on the board. He turned to the class.

'Pens down.'

The children put down their pens and looked up.

'Fold arms.'

They pushed back their books and folded arms.

Ursula, stuck among the back forms, could not extricate herself.

'*What* is your composition about?' asked the headmaster. Every hand shot up. 'The –' stuttered some voice in its eagerness to answer.

'I wouldn't advise you to call out,' said Mr Harby. He would have a pleasant voice, full and musical, but for the detestable menace that always tailed in it. He stood unmoved, his eyes twinkling under his bushy black brows, watching the class. There was something fascinating in him, as he stood, and again she wanted to scream. She was all jarred, she did not know what she felt.

'Well, Alice?' he said.

'The rabbit,' piped a girl's voice.

'A very easy subject for Standard Five.'

Ursula felt a slight shame of incompetence. She was exposed before the class. And she was tormented by the contradictoriness of everything. Mr Harby stood so strong, and so male, with his black brows and clear forehead, the heavy jaw, the big, overhanging moustache: such a man, with strength and male power, and a certain blind, native beauty. She might have liked him as a man. And here he stood in some other capacity, bullying over such a trifle as a boy's speaking out without permission. Yet he was not a little, fussy man. He seemed to have some cruel, stubborn, evil spirit, he was imprisoned in a task too small and petty for him, which yet, in a servile acquiescence, he would fulfil, because he had to earn his living. He had no finer control over himself, only this blind, dogged, wholesale will. He would keep the job going, since he must. And his job was to make the children spell the word 'caution' correctly, and put a capital letter after a full-stop. So at this he hammered with his suppressed hatred, always suppressing himself, till he was beside himself. Ursula suffered bitterly as he stood, short and handsome and powerful, teaching her class. It seemed such a miserable thing for him to be doing. He had a decent, powerful, rude soul. What did he care about the composition on 'The Rabbit'? Yet his will kept him there before the class, threshing the trivial subject. It was habit with him now, to be so little and vulgar, out of place. She saw the shamefulness of his position, felt the fettered wickedness in him which would blaze out into evil rage in the long run, so that he was like a persistent, strong creature tethered. It was really intolerable. The jarring was torture to her. She looked over the silent, attentive class that seemed to have crystallized into order and rigid, neutral form. This he had it in his power to do, to crystallize the children into hard, mute fragments, fixed under his will: his brute will, which fixed them by sheer force. She too must learn to subdue them to her will: she must. For it was her duty, since the school was such. He had crystallized the class into order. But to see him, a strong, powerful man, using all his power for such a purpose, seemed almost horrible. There was something hideous about it. The strange, genial light in his eye was really vicious, and ugly, his smile was one of torture. He could not be impersonal. He could not have a clear, pure purpose, he could only exercise his own brute will. He did not believe in the least in the education he kept inflicting year after year upon the children. So he must bully, only bully, even while it tortured his strong, wholesome nature with shame like a spur always galling. He was so blind and ugly and out of place. Ursula could not bear it as he stood there. The whole situation was wrong and ugly.

The lesson was finished, Mr Harby went away. At the far end of the room she heard the whistle and the thud of the cane. Her heart stood still within her. She could not bear it, no, she could not bear it when the boy was beaten. It made her sick. She felt that she must go out of this school, this torture-place. And she hated the schoolmaster, thoroughly and finally. The brute, had he no shame? He should never be allowed to continue the atrocity of this bullying cruelty. Then Hill came crawling back, blubbering piteously. There was something desolate about his blubbering that nearly broke her heart. For after all, if she had kept her class in proper discipline, this would never have happened, Hill would never have called out and been caned.

She began the arithmetic lesson. But she was distracted. The boy Hill sat away on the back desk, huddled up, blubbering and sucking his hand. It was a long time. She dared not go near, nor speak to him. She felt ashamed before him. And she felt she could not forgive the boy for being the huddled, blubbering object, all wet and snivelled, which he was.

She went on correcting the sums. But there were too many children. She could not get round the class. And Hill was on her conscience. At last he had stopped crying, and sat bunched over his hands, playing quietly. Then he looked up at her. His face was dirty with tears, his eyes had a curious washed look, like the sky after rain, a sort of wanness. He bore no malice. He had already forgotten, and was waiting to be restored to the normal position.

'Go on with your work, Hill,' she said.

The children were playing over their arithmetic, and, she knew, cheating thoroughly. She wrote another sum on the blackboard. She could not get round the class. She went again to the front to watch. Some were ready. Some were not. What was she to do?

At last it was time for recreation. She gave the order to cease working, and in some way or other got her class out of the room. Then she faced the disorderly litter of blotted, uncorrected books, of broken rulers and chewed pens. And her heart sank in sickness. The misery was getting deeper.

The trouble went on and on, day after day. She had always piles of books to mark, myriads of errors to correct, a heartwearying task that she loathed. And the work got worse and worse. When she tried to flatter herself that the composition grew more alive, more interesting, she had to see that the handwriting grew more and more slovenly, the books were filthy and disgraceful. She tried what she could, but it was of no use. But she was not going to take it seriously. Why should she? Why should she say to herself, that it mattered, if she failed to teach a class to write perfectly neatly? Why should she take the blame unto herself?

Pay day came, and she received four pounds two shillings and one penny. She was very proud that day. She had never had so much money before. And she had earned it all herself. She sat on the top of the tram-car fingering the gold and fearing she might lose it. She felt so established and strong, because of it. And when she got home she said to her mother:

'It is pay day to-day, mother.'

'Ay,' said her mother coolly.

Then Ursula put down fifty shillings on the table.

'That is my board,' she said.

'Ay,' said her mother, letting it lie.

Ursula was hurt. Yet she had paid her scot. She was free. She paid for what she had. There remained moreover thirty-two shillings of her own. She would not spend any, she who was naturally a spendthrift, because she could not bear to damage her fine gold.

She had a standing ground now apart from her parents. She was something else besides the mere daughter of William and Anna Brangwen. She was independent. She earned her own living. She was an important member of the working community. She was sure that fifty shillings a month quite paid for her keep. If her mother received fifty shillings a month for each of the children, she would receive twenty pounds a month and no clothes to provide. Very well then.

Ursula was independent of her parents. She now adhered elsewhere. Now, the 'Board of Education' was a phrase that rang significant to her, and she felt Whitehall far beyond her as her ultimate home. In the government, she knew which minister had supreme control over Education, and it seemed to her that, in some way, he was connected with her, as her father was connected with her.

She had another self, another responsibility. She was no longer Ursula Brangwen, daughter of William Brangwen. She was also Standard Five teacher in St Philip's School. And it was a case now of being Standard Five teacher, and nothing else. For she could not escape.

Neither could she succeed. That was her horror. As the weeks passed on, there was no Ursula Brangwen, free and jolly. There was only a girl of that name obsessed by the fact that she could not manage her class of children. At week-ends there came days of passionate reaction, when she went mad with the taste of liberty, when merely to be free in the morning, to sit down at her embroidery and stitch the coloured silks with a passion of delight. For the prison house was always awaiting her! This was only a respite, as her chained heart knew well. So that she seized hold of the swift hours of the week-end, and wrung the last drop of sweetness out of them, in a little, cruel frenzy.

She did not tell anybody how this state was a torture to her. She did not confide, either to Gudrun or to her parents, how horrible she found it to be a school-teacher. But when Sunday night came, and she felt the Monday morning at hand, she was strung up tight with dreadful anticipation, because the strain and the torture was near again.

She did not believe that she could ever teach that great brutish class, in that brutal school; ever, ever. And yet, if she failed, she must in some way go under. She must admit that the man's world was too strong for her, she could not take her place in it; she must go down before Mr Harby. And all her life henceforth, she must go on, never having freed herself of the man's world, never having achieved the freedom of the great world of responsible work. Maggie had taken her place there, she had even stood level with Mr Harby and got free of him: and her soul was always wandering in far-off valleys and glades of poetry. Maggie was free. Yet there was something like subjection in Maggie's very freedom. Mr Harby, the man, disliked the reserved woman, Maggie. Mr Harby, the schoolmaster, respected his teacher, Miss Schofield.

For the present, however, Ursula only envied and admired Maggie. She herself had still to get where Maggie had got. She had still to make her footing. She had taken up a position on Mr Harby's ground, and she must keep it. For he was now beginning a regular attack on her, to drive her away out of his school. She could not keep order. Her class was a turbulent crowd, and the weak spot in the school's work. Therefore she must go, and someone more useful must come in her place, someone who could keep discipline.

The headmaster had worked himself into an obsession of fury against her. He only wanted her gone. She had come, she had got worse as the weeks went on, she was absolutely no good. His system, which was his very life in school, the outcome of his bodily movement, was attacked and threatened at the point where Ursula was included. She was the danger that threatened his body with a blow, a fall. And blindly, thoroughly, moving from strong instinct of opposition, he set to work to expel her.

When he punished one of her children as he had punished the boy Hill, for an offence against *himself*, he made the punishment extra heavy with the significance that the extra stroke came in because of the weak teacher who allowed all these things to be. When he punished for an offence against *her*, he punished lightly, as if offences against her were not significant. Which all the children knew, and they behaved accordingly.

Every now and again Mr Harby would swoop down to examine exercise books. For a whole hour, he would be going round the class, taking book after book, comparing page after page, whilst Ursula stood aside for all the remarks and fault-finding to be pointed at her through the scholars. It was true, since she had come, the composition books had grown more and more untidy, disorderly, filthy. Mr Harby pointed to the pages done before her régime, and to those done after, and fell into a passion of rage. Many children he sent out to the front with their books. And after he had thoroughly gone through the silent and quivering class he caned the worst offenders well, in front of the others, thundering a real passion of anger and chagrin.

'Such a condition in a class, I can't believe it! It is simply disgraceful! I can't think how you have been let to get like it! Every Monday morning I shall come down and examine these books. So don't think that because there is nobody paying any attention to you, that you are free to unlearn everything you ever learned, and go back till you are not fit for Standard Three. I shall examine all books every Monday—'

Then in a rage, he went away with his cane, leaving Ursula to confront a pale, quivering class, whose childish faces were shut in blank resentment, fear, and bitterness, whose souls were full of anger and contempt of *her* rather than of the master, whose eyes looked at her with the cold, inhuman accusation of children. And she could hardly make mechanical words to speak to them. When she gave an order they obeyed with an insolent off-handedness, as if to say: 'As for you, do you think we would obey *you*, but for the master?' She sent the blubbering, caned boys to their seats, knowing that they too jeered at her and her authority, holding her weakness responsible for what punishment had overtaken them. And she knew the whole position, so that even her horror of physical beating and suffering sank to a deeper pain, and became a moral judgment upon her, worse than any hurt.

She must, during the next week, watch over her books, and punish any fault. Her soul decided it coldly. Her personal desire was dead for that day at least. She must have nothing more of herself in school. She was to be Standard Five teacher only. That was her duty. In school, she was nothing but Standard Five teacher. Ursula Brangwen must be excluded.

So that, pale, shut, at last distant and impersonal, she saw no longer the child, how his eyes danced, or how he had a queer little soul that could not be bothered with shaping handwriting so long as he dashed down what he thought. She saw no children, only the task that was to be done. And keeping her eyes there, on the task, and not on the child, she was impersonal enough to punish where she could otherwise only have sympathized, understood, and condoned, to approve where she would have been merely uninterested before. But her interest had no place any more.

It was agony to the impulsive, bright girl of seventeen to become distant and official, having no personal relationship with the children. For a few days, after the agony of the Monday, she succeeded, and had some success with her class. But it was a state not natural to her, and she began to relax.

Then came another infliction. There were not enough pens to go round the class. She sent to Mr Harby for more. He came in person.

'Not enough pens, Miss Brangwen?' he said, with the smile and calm of exceeding rage against her.

'No, we are six short,' she said, quaking.

'Oh, how is that?' he said, menacingly. Then, looking over the class, he asked:

'How many are there here to-day?'

'Fifty-two,' said Ursula, but he did not take any notice, counting for himself.

'Fifty-two,' he said. 'And how many pens are there, Staples?'

Ursula was now silent. He would not heed her if she answered, since he had addressed the monitor.

'That's a very curious thing,' said Mr Harby, looking over the silent class with a slight grin of fury. All the childish faces looked up at him blank and exposed.

'A few days ago there were sixty pens for this class – now there are forty-eight. What is forty-eight from sixty, Williams?' There was a sinister suspense in the question. A thin, ferret-faced boy in a sailor suit started up exaggeratedly.

'Please, Sir!' he said. Then a slow, sly grin came over his face. He did not know. There was a tense silence. The boy dropped his head. Then he looked up again, a little cunning triumph in his eyes. 'Twelve,' he said.

'I would advise you to attend,' said the headmaster dangerously. The boy sat down.

'Forty-eight from sixty is twelve: so there are twelve pens to account for. Have you looked for them, Staples?'

'Yes, Sir.'

'Then look again.'

The scene dragged on. Two pens were found: ten were missing. Then the storm burst.

'Am I to have you thieving, besides your dirt and bad work and bad behaviour?' the headmaster began. 'Not content with being the worst-behaved and dirtiest class in the school, you are thieves into the bargain, are you? It is a very funny thing! Pens don't melt into the air: pens are not in the habit of mizzling away into nothing. What has become of them then? They must be somewhere. What has become of them? For they must be found, and found by Standard Five. They were lost by Standard Five, and they must be found.'

Ursula stood and listened, her heart hard and cold. She was so much upset, that she felt almost mad. Something in her tempted her to turn on the headmaster and tell him to stop, about the miserable pens. But she did not. She could not.

After every session, morning and evening, she had the pens counted. Still they were missing. And pencils and india-rubbers disappeared. She kept the class staying behind, till the things were found. But as soon as Mr Harby had gone out of the room, the boys began to jump about and shout, and at last they bolted in a body from the school.

This was drawing near a crisis. She could not tell Mr Harby because, while he would punish the class, he would make her the cause of the punishment, and her class would pay her back with disobedience and derision. Already there was a deadly hostility grown up between her and the children. After keeping in the class, at evening, to finish some work, she would find boys dodging behind her, calling after her: 'Brangwen, Brangwen – Proud-arce.'

When she went into Ilkeston of a Saturday morning with Gudrun, she heard again the voices yelling after her:

'Brangwen, Brangwen.'

She pretended to take no notice, but she coloured with shame at being held up to derision in the public street. She, Ursula Brangwen of Cossethay, could not escape from the Standard Five teacher which she was. In vain she went out to buy ribbon for her hat. They called after her, the boys she tried to teach.

And one evening, as she went from the edge of the town into the country, stones came flying at her. Then the passion of shame and anger surpassed her. She walked on unheeding, beside herself. Because of the darkness she could not see who were those that threw. But she did not want to know.

Only in her soul a change took place. Never more, and never more would she give herself as individual to her class. Never would she, Ursula Brangwen, the girl she was, the person she was, come into contact with those boys. She would be Standard Five teacher, as far away personally from her class as if she had never set foot in St Philip's school. She would just obliterate them all, and keep herself apart, take them as scholars only.

So her face grew more and more shut, and over her flayed, exposed soul of a young girl who had gone open and warm to give herself to the children, there set a hard, insentient thing, that worked mechanically according to a system imposed.

It seemed she scarcely saw her class the next day. She could only feel her will, and what she would have of this class which she must grasp into subjection. It was no good, any more, to appeal, to play upon the better feelings of the class. Her swiftworking soul realized this.

She, as teacher, must bring them all, as scholars, into subjection. And this she was going to do. All else she would forsake. She had become hard and impersonal, almost avengeful on herself as well as on them, since the stone throwing. She did not want to be a person, to be herself any more, after such humiliation. She would assert herself for mastery, be only teacher. She was set now. She was going to fight and subdue.

She knew by now her enemies in the class. The one she hated most was Williams. He was a sort of defective, not bad enough to be so classed. He could read with fluency, and had plenty of cunning intelligence. But he could not keep still. And he had a kind of sickness very repulsive to a sensitive girl, something cunning and etiolated and degenerate. Once he had thrown an ink-well at her, in one of his mad little rages. Twice he had run home out of class. He was a well-known character.

And he grinned up his sleeve at this girl-teacher, sometimes hanging round her to fawn on her. But this made her dislike him more. He had a kind of leech-like power.

From one of the children she took a supple cane, and this she determined to use when real occasion came. One morning, at composition, she said to the boy Williams:

'Why have you made this blot?'

'Please, Miss, it fell off my pen,' he whined out, in the mocking voice that he was so clever in using. The boys near snorted with laughter. For Williams was an actor, he could tickle the feelings of his hearers subtly. Particularly he could tickle the children with him into ridiculing his teacher, or indeed, any authority of which he was not afraid. He had that peculiar jail instinct.

'Then you must stay in and finish another page of composition,' said the teacher.

This was against her usual sense of justice, and the boy resented it derisively. At twelve o'clock she caught him slinking out.

'Williams, sit down,' she said.

And there she sat, and there he sat, alone, opposite to her, on the back desk, looking up at her with his furtive eyes every minute.

'Please, Miss, I've got to go an errand,' he called out insolently.

'Bring me your book,' said Ursula.

The boy came out, flapping his book along the desks. He had not written a line.

'Go back and do the writing you have to do,' said Ursula. And she sat at her desk, trying to correct books. She was trembling and upset. And for an hour the miserable boy writhed and grinned in his seat. At the end of that time he had done five lines.

'As it is so late now,' said Ursula, 'you will finish the rest this evening.'

The boy kicked his way insolently down the passage.

The afternoon came again. Williams was there, glancing at her, and her heart beat thick, for she knew it was a fight between them. She watched him.

During the geography lesson, as she was pointing to the map with her cane, the boy continually ducked his whitish head under the desk, and attracted the attention of other boys.

'Williams,' she said, gathering her courage, for it was critical now to speak to him, 'what are you doing?'

He lifted his face, the sore-rimmed eyes half smiling. There was something intrinsically indecent about him. Ursula shrank away.

'Nothing,' he replied, feeling a triumph.

'What are you doing?' she repeated, her heart-beat suffocating her.

'Nothing,' replied the boy, insolently, aggrieved, comic.

'If I speak to you again, you must go down to Mr Harby,' she said.

But this boy was a match even for Mr Harby. He was so persistent, so cringing, and flexible, he howled so when he was hurt, that the master hated more the teacher who sent him than he hated the boy himself. For of the boy he was sick of the sight. Which Williams knew. He grinned visibly.

Ursula turned to the map again, to go on with the geography lesson. But there was a little ferment in the class. Williams' spirit infected them all. She heard a scuffle, and then she trembled inwardly. If they all turned on her this time, she was beaten.

'Please Miss –' called a voice in distress.

She turned round. One of the boys she liked was ruefully holding out a torn celluloid collar. She heard the complaint, feeling futile.

'Go in front, Wright,' she said.

She was trembling in every fibre. A big, sullen boy, not bad but very difficult, slouched out to the front. She went on with the lesson, aware that Williams was making faces at Wright, and that Wright was grinning behind her. She was afraid. She turned to the map again. And she was afraid.

'Please Miss, Williams –' came a sharp cry, and a boy on the back row was standing up, with drawn, pained brows, half a mocking grin on his face, half real resentment against Williams – 'Please Miss, he's nipped me' – and he rubbed his leg ruefully.

'Come in front, Williams,' she said.

The rat-like boy sat with his pale smile and did not move.

'Come in front,' she repeated, definite now.

'I shan't,' he cried, snarling, rat-like, grinning. Something went click in Ursula's soul. Her face and eyes set, she went through the class straight. The boy cowered before her glowering, fixed eyes. But she advanced on him, seized him by the arm, and dragged him from his seat. He clung to the form. It was a battle between him and her. Her instinct had suddenly become calm and quick. She jerked him from his grip, and dragged him, struggling and kicking, to the front. He kicked her several times, and clung to the forms as he passed, but she went on. The class was on its feet in excitement. She saw it, but made no move.

She knew if she let go the boy he would dash to the door. Already he had run home once out of her class. So she snatched her cane from the desk, and brought it down on him. He was writhing and kicking. She saw his face beneath her, white, with eyes like the eyes of a fish, stony, yet full of hate and horrible fear. And she loathed him, the hideous writhing thing that was nearly too much for her. In horror lest he should overcome her, and yet at the heart quite calm, she brought down the cane again and again, whilst he struggled making inarticulate noises, and lunging vicious kicks at her. With one hand she managed to hold him, and now and then the cane came down on him. He writhed, like a mad thing. But the pain of the strokes cut through his writhing, vicious, coward's courage, bit deeper, till at last, with a long whimper that became a yell, he went limp. She let him go, and he rushed at her, his teeth and eyes glinting. There was a second of agonized terror in her heart: he was a beast thing. Then she caught him, and the cane came down on him. A few times, madly, in a frenzy, he lunged and writhed, to kick her. But again the cane broke him, he sank with a howling yell on the floor, and like a beaten beast lay there yelling.

Mr Harby had rushed up towards the end of this performance.

'What's the matter?' he roared.

Ursula felt as if something were going to break in her.

'I've thrashed him,' she said, her breast heaving, forcing out the words on the last breath. The headmaster stood choked with rage, helpless. She looked at the writhing, howling figure on the floor.

'Get up,' she said. The thing writhed away from her. She took a step forward. She had realized the presence of the headmaster for one second, and then she was oblivious of it again.

'Get up,' she said. And with a little dart the boy was on his feet. His yelling dropped to a mad blubber. He had been in a frenzy.

'Go and stand by the radiator,' she said.

As if mechanically, blubbering, he went.

The headmaster stood robbed of movement and speech. His face was yellow, his hands twitched convulsively. But Ursula stood stiff not far from him. Nothing could touch her now: she was beyond Mr Harby. She was as if violated to death.

The headmaster muttered something, turned, and went down the room, whence, from the far end, he was heard roaring in a mad rage at his own class.

The boy blubbered wildly by the radiator. Ursula looked at the class. There were fifty pale, still faces watching her, a hundred round eyes fixed on her in an attentive, expressionless stare.

'Give out the history readers,' she said to the monitors.

There was dead silence. As she stood there, she could hear again the ticking of the clock, and the chock of piles of books taken out of the low cupboard. Then came the faint flap of books on the desks. The children passed in silence, their hands working in unison. They were no longer a pack, but each one separated into a silent, closed thing.

'Take page 125, and read that chapter,' said Ursula.

There was a click of many books opened. The children found the page, and bent their heads obediently to read. And they read, mechanically.

Ursula, who was trembling violently, went and sat in her high chair. The blubbering of the boy continued. The strident voice of Mr Brunt, the roar of Mr Harby, came muffled through the glass partition. And now and then a pair of eyes rose from the reading-book, rested on her a moment, watchful, as if calculating impersonally, then sank again.

She sat still without moving, her eyes watching the class, unseeing. She was quite still, and weak. She felt that she could not raise her hand from the desk. If she sat there for ever, she felt she could not move again, nor utter a command. It was a quarter past four. She almost dreaded the closing of the school, when she would be alone.

The class began to recover its ease, the tension relaxed. Williams was still crying. Mr Brunt was giving orders for the closing of the lesson. Ursula got down.

'Take your place, Williams,' she said.

He dragged his feet across the room, wiping his face on his sleeve. As he sat down, he glanced at her furtively, his eyes still redder. Now he looked like some beaten rat.

At last the children were gone. Mr Harby trod by heavily, without looking her way, or speaking. Mr Brunt hesitated as she was locking her cupboard.

'If you settle Clarke and Letts in the same way, Miss Brangwen, you'll be all right,' he said, his blue eyes glancing down in a strange fellowship, his long nose pointing at her.

'Shall I?' she laughed nervously. She did not want anybody to talk to her.

As she went along the street, clattering on the granite pavement, she was aware of boys dodging behind her. Something struck her hand that was carrying her bag, bruising her. As it rolled away she saw that it was a potato. Her hand was hurt, but she gave no sign. Soon she would take the tram.

She was afraid, and strange. It was to her quite strange and ugly, like some dream where she was degraded. She would have died rather than admit it to anybody. She could not look at her swollen hand. Something had broken in her; she had passed a crisis. Williams was beaten, but at a cost.

Feeling too much upset to go home, she rode a little farther into the town, and got down from the tram at a small tea-shop. There, in the dark little place behind the shop, she drank her tea and ate bread-and-butter. She did not taste anything. The taking tea was just a mechanical action, to cover over her existence. There she sat in the dark, obscure little place, without knowing. Only unconsciously she nursed the back of her hand, which was bruised.

When finally she took her way home, it was sunset red across the west. She did not know why she was going home. There was nothing for her there. She had, true, only to pretend to be normal. There was nobody she could speak to, nowhere to go for escape. But she must keep on, under this red sunset, alone, knowing the horror in humanity, that would destroy her, and with which she was at war. Yet it had to be so.

In the morning again she must go to school. She got up and went without murmuring even to herself. She was in the hands of some bigger, stronger, coarser will.

School was fairly quiet. But she could feel the class watching her, ready to spring on her. Her instinct was aware of the class instinct to catch her if she were weak. But she kept cold and was guarded.

Williams was absent from school. In the middle of the morning there was a knock at the door: someone wanted the headmaster. Mr Harby went out, heavily, angrily, nervously. He was afraid of irate parents. After a moment in the passage, he came again into school.

'Sturgess,' he called to one of his larger boys. 'Stand in front of the class and write down the name of anyone who speaks. Will you come this way, Miss Brangwen.'

He seemed vindictively to seize upon her.

Ursula followed him, and found in the lobby a thin woman with a whitish skin, not ill-dressed in a grey costume and a purple hat.

'I called about Vernon,' said the woman, speaking in a refined accent. There was about the woman altogether an appearance of refinement and of cleanliness, curiously contradicted by her half-beggar's deportment, and a sense of her being unpleasant to touch, like something going bad inside. She was neither a lady nor an ordinary working man's wife, but a creature separate from society. By her dress she was not poor.

Ursula knew at once that she was Williams' mother, and that he was Vernon. She remembered that he was always clean, and well-dressed, in a sailor suit. And he had this same peculiar, half transparent unwholesomeness, rather like a corpse.

'I wasn't able to send him to school today,' continued the woman, with a false grace of manner. 'He came home last night *so* ill – he was violently sick – I thought I should have to send for the doctor. – You know he has a weak heart.'

The woman looked at Ursula with her pale, dead eyes.

She stood still with repulsion and uncertainty. Mr Harby, large and male, with his overhanging moustache, stood by with a slight, ugly smile at the corner of his eyes. The woman went on insidiously, not quite human:

'Oh yes, he has had heart disease ever since he was a child. That is why he isn't very regular at school. And it is very bad to beat him. He was awfully ill this morning – I shall call on the doctor as I go back.'

'Who is staying with him now, then?' put in the deep voice of the schoolmaster, cunningly.

'Oh, I left him with a woman who comes in to help me – and who understands him. But I shall call in the doctor on my way home.'

Ursula stood still. She felt vague threats in all this. But the woman was so utterly strange to her, that she did not understand.

'He told me he had been beaten,' continued the woman, 'and when I undressed him to put him to bed, his body was covered with marks – I could show them to any doctor.'

Mr Harby looked at Ursula to answer. She began to understand. The woman was threatening to take out a charge of assault on her son against her. Perhaps she wanted money.

'I caned him,' she said. 'He was so much trouble.'

'I'm sorry if he was troublesome,' said the woman, 'but he must have been shamefully beaten. I could show the marks to any doctor. I'm sure it isn't allowed, if it was known.'

'I caned him while he kept kicking me,' said Ursula, getting angry because she was half excusing herself, Mr Harby standing there with the twinkle at the side of his eyes, enjoying the dilemma of the two women.

'I'm sure I'm sorry if he behaved badly,' said the woman. 'But I can't think he deserved treating as he had been. I can't send him to school, and really can't afford to pay the doctor. – Is it allowed for the teacher to beat the children like that, Mr Harby?'

The headmaster refused to answer. Ursula loathed herself, and loathed Mr Harby with his twinkling cunning and malice on the occasion. The other miserable woman watched her chance.

'It is an expense to me, and I have a great struggle to keep my boy decent.'

Ursula still would not answer. She looked out at the asphalt yard, where a dirty rag of paper was blowing.

'And it isn't allowed to beat a child like that, I am sure, especially when he is delicate.'

Ursula stared with a set face on the yard, as if she did not hear. She loathed all this, and had ceased to feel or to exist.

'Though I know he is troublesome sometimes – but I think it was too much. His body is covered with marks.'

Mr Harby stood sturdy and unmoved, waiting now to have done, with the twinkling, tiny wrinkles of an ironical smile at the corners of his eyes. He felt himself master of the situation.

'And he was violently sick. I couldn't possibly send him to school today. He couldn't keep his head up.'

Yet she had no answer.

'You will understand, Sir, why he is absent,' she said, turning to Mr Harby.

'Oh, yes,' he said, rough and off-hand. Ursula detested him for his male triumph. And she loathed the woman. She loathed everything.

'You will try to have it remembered, Sir, that he has a weak heart. He *is* so sick after these things.'

'Yes,' said the headmaster, 'I'll see about it.'

'I know he is troublesome,' the woman only addressed herself to the male now – 'but if you could have him punished without beating – he is really delicate.'

Ursula was beginning to feel upset. Harby stood in rather superb mastery, the woman cringing to him to tickle him as one tickles trout.

'I had come to explain why he was away this morning, Sir. You will understand.'

She held out her hand. Harby took it and let it go, surprised and angry.

'Good morning,' she said, and she gave her gloved, seedy hand to Ursula. She was not ill-looking, and had a curious insinuating way, very distasteful yet effective.

'Good morning, Mr Harby, and thank you.'

The figure in the grey costume and the purple hat was going across the school yard with a curious lingering walk. Ursula felt a strange pity for her, and revulsion from her. She shuddered. She went into the school again.

The next morning Williams turned up, looking paler than ever, very neat and nicely dressed in his sailor blouse. He glanced at Ursula with a half-smile: cunning, subdued, ready to do as she told him. There was something about him that made her shiver. She loathed the idea of having laid hands on him. His elder brother was standing outside the gate at play-time, a youth of about fifteen, tall and thin and pale. He raised his hat, almost like a gentleman. But there was something subdued, insidious about him too.

'Who is it?' said Ursula.

'It's the big Williams,' said Violet Harby roughly. '*She* was here yesterday, wasn't she?'

'Yes.'

'It's no good her coming – her character's not good enough for her to make any trouble.'

Ursula shrank from the brutality and the scandal. But it had some vague, horrid fascination. How sordid everything seemed! She felt sorry for the queer woman with the lingering walk, and those queer, insidious boys. The Williams in her class was wrong somewhere. How nasty it was altogether.

So the battle went on till her heart was sick. She had several more boys to subjugate before she could establish herself. And Mr Harby hated her almost as if she were a man. She knew now that nothing but a thrashing would settle some of the big louts who wanted to play cat and mouse with her. Mr Harby would not give them the thrashing if he could help it. For he hated the teacher, the stuck-up, insolent high-school miss with her independence.

'Now, Wright, what have you done this time?' he would say genially to the boy who was sent to him from Standard Five for punishment. And he left the lad standing, lounging, wasting his time.

So that Ursula would appeal no more to the headmaster, but, when she was driven wild, she seized her cane, and slashed the boy who was insolent to her, over head and ears and hands. And at length they were afraid of her, she had them in order.

But she had paid a great price out of her own soul, to do this. It seemed as if a great flame had gone through her and burnt her sensitive tissue. She who shrank from the thought of physical suffering in any form, had been forced to fight and beat with a cane and rouse all her instincts to hurt. And afterwards she had been forced to endure the sound of their blubbering and desolation, when she had broken them to order.

Oh, and sometimes she felt as if she would go mad. What did it matter, what did it matter if their books were dirty and they did not obey? She would rather, in reality, that they disobeyed the whole rules of the school, than that they should be beaten, broken, reduced to this crying, hopeless state. She would rather bear all their insults and insolences a thousand times than reduce herself and them to this. Bitterly she repented having got beside herself, and having tackled the boy she had beaten.

Yet it had to be so. She did not want to do it. Yet she had to. Oh why, why had she leagued herself to this evil system where she must brutalize herself to live? Why had she become a school teacher, why, why?

The children had forced her to the beatings. No, she did not pity them. She had come to them full of kindness and love, and they would have torn her to pieces. They chose Mr Harby. Well then, they must know her as well as Mr Harby, they must first be subjugate to her. For she was not going to be made nought, no, neither by them, nor by Mr Harby, nor by all the system around her. She was not going to be put down, prevented from standing free. It was not to be said of her, she could not take her place and carry out her task. She would fight and hold her place in this state also, in the world of work and man's convention.

2.7 Strategies, decisions and control: interaction in a middle school classroom

Andy Hargreaves

[...] Although some primary and middle school classrooms may be organized almost entirely on 'traditional' lines, there will be occasions in most such schools when the teacher addresses, organizes and disciplines the class as a whole. This would appear to be the case in even the most progressively organized institutions.

The substantive focus of this paper is on one such occasion in an inner-city middle school. I shall argue that the specific techniques used by the teacher to organize the school class in instances of this type can be embraced within a more widely defined coping strategy where the teacher is engaged in actions which can be described as policing. In contrast to the general features of the management of pupil behaviour within such a coping strategy, I shall also document the ways in which teachers handle one particular deviant pupil, Charlie, in an attempt to avoid direct confrontation with him in the classroom. The two coping strategies of *policing* and *confrontation-avoidance* will be analysed in terms of the degree of their mutual compatibility. I shall argue, in fact, that basic incongruity between these two coping strategies results in unintended consequences which affect both the 'efficient' management of classroom life by teachers, and the process of identity-formation on the part of the deviant (Charlie).

More generally, such a substantive analysis, I suggest, provides a focal point for considering the relationship between power and decision-making in the educational process. Here, situationally specific decisions will be viewed as *negotiative strategies*. These are considered qualitatively different from the more generalized definitions of teaching behaviour embraced by the concept *coping strategy*.[1] [...]

Organizing the school class: the role of policing

[...]

Second-level decisions

My concern here is with one particular way in which the school class can be and often is organized. [...] The specific type of occasion I explore is

Source: EGGLESTON, J. (ed.) (1979) *Teacher Decision-Making in the Classroom.* London; Routledge and Kegan Paul, pp. 135–168.

one where the teacher employs a coping strategy which I shall call Policing. This entails the management in bodily terms of a large crowd of pupils by a single teacher or, in this instance, two teachers. The management of pupil control over their own bodies is, in this coping strategy, also accompanied by the close monitoring of pupil talk.

The data analysed here were collected as part of a small project carried out in an inner-city middle school in a social priority area.[2] The group of children concerned are thirty nine- to ten-year-olds in the first year of that school. Their open-plan classroom is situated in a wooden terrapin building adjacent to the main lower school block. For much of the day, the children work within an integrated-day system which was initially imposed by the headmaster against many of the staff's wishes. After stimulus periods, pupils work on one of three alternative areas of the curriculum. The work is often heavily programmed in the form of work cards (especially in the 'linear' subjects) and checks are systematic and rigorous. These occur through step-by-step evaluation of pupil work, where the teacher ticks off individual work cards when assignments have been satisfactorily completed. This is a necessary condition that must be fulfilled before the pupil is allowed to move on to work in any other area of the curriculum. Spot checks are also carried out daily to ensure that pupils are seated in the right place for the task on which they are engaged. This checking involves the momentary (and momentous) suspension of classroom activity so that checks can be conducted in a formal, public manner.

The general pattern of classroom life is therefore one of individually based learning where strong control is nevertheless exerted through the heavily programmed character of pupil learning and through a rigorous, systematic procedure of evaluation. This general pattern is complemented by a set of occasions when the class is addressed as a whole. These include 'stimulus' periods, story time and, as in the example offered here, drama lessons. The public, repeatable and testable character of teacher-pupil interaction and the rules it embodies in such situations contrast sharply with the more private individuated forms of interaction which constitute the general pattern of classroom life.

The particular lesson under scrutiny is a drama lesson, predominantly taught by one member of staff, though assisted by another. Under normal circumstances, drama is held in the school hall (which is allocated to classes at specific times for this purpose), but on this particular day, the hall is being used for a concert rehearsal by another year group. As a result, if drama is to be held at all, then it must take place within the classroom area and the architectural restrictions [. . .], which that imposes upon the possibilities for drama activity.

In the circumstances, the teachers are initially presented with two second-level decisions that need to be made. By second-level decisions, I mean those decisions which are made and resolved before a lesson actually begins. These decisions possess defining features and frame the para-

meters within which classroom activity is to take place.[3] Given the very
real constraints which a terrapin building and the clutter of classroom
furniture place upon the teaching of drama, it would be quite justifiable to
substitute another learning activity more suited to the surroundings. Such
flexibility in arrangements would not be inconsistent with the general
philosophy of integrated teaching. Yet, in opting to continue with drama
despite the difficult circumstances, the teachers seem hardly to have made
a conscious decision at all. Discussion between them centred around what
kind of drama should take place rather than whether indeed it should
occur. When I asked if they had considered alternative activities, one
teacher stated that 'the pupils expect it [drama] at this time' and asserted
also that 'they like to know where they are'. These remarks are quite
probably empirical statements of fact. It is a mundane point that if events
have occurred routinely at the same time on the same day, then it is
reasonable to expect affairs to continue in this way. But expectation might
additionally mean desire. In this sense, to expect drama to be the next
lesson is to look forward to it. Where, from the pupils' point of view,
subjects are hierarchically organized in terms of their desirability, i.e.
their approximation to play rather than 'real work', then to remove a
'desirable' subject not only violates a pupil's sense of order but also
amounts to the imposition of a sanction. The maintenance of such 'soft
options' even in conditions of adversity is therefore reasonable from the
teacher's point of view not only on 'humanitarian' grounds but also in
terms of the maintenance of social order, for 'truce' situations between
teacher and pupil are partly predicated on the assumption that desirable
and undesirable subjects are traded off against one another in the preservation of a precarious equilibrium (Woods, 1977).[4]

The third assumption contained within the teachers' justifications is
that not only do pupils actually *have* an appreciation of orderly relations,
but that they also *need* a sense of social order. The ambiguity of the
statement 'They like to know where they are' captures and intertwines
both these possibilities. The justifications, as they are offered, break down
the demarcation line between structurally produced expectations and an
imputed set of moral imperatives couched in terms of pupils' needs. The
view that the pupil *should* know where he is can here be equated with the
injunction of Plowden that the deprived *need* 'affection, stability and
order'.[5]

The other second-level decision involves the choice of a *particular* drama
activity. After brief discussion the teachers opted to do mime 'because it's
less chaotic than anything else'. Despite all the cognitive benefits which
might accrue to pupils from their participation in mime, the teachers'
decision here is clearly related to its potential for social control. For this
very reason, mime is something of an 'old chestnut' for teachers and is
employed in many classrooms where drama activity cannot take place in a
spacious hall or studio. This is by no means universally the case, however,
for I have occasionally witnessed exciting incidents of spoken drama in the

tricted space of school classrooms which were, unlike the lesson under
view, also near other classes.

The choice of mime as the most suitable drama activity cannot, there-
e, be related solely to the constraints imposed by the physical confines
the classroom, although these matters are not insignificant. Mime also
ers greater potential for the surveillance of pupil behaviour than other
rms of drama. By the suppression of legitimate talk (that which is seen as
cessarily related to cognitive learning), illegitimate talk (perceived as
related to learning) is identified more easily. So deviant activity can be
ashed at its inception. Even if legitimate talk is integral to lesson
tivity (e.g. planning a group mime), conditions can be invoked (e.g.
hispering) which allow surveillance.[6]

Consequently, mime is selected not only because of a set of physical
nstraints but also because of its surveillance potential under the felt
reat of impending anomie. As Becker (1952)[7] has pointed out, the
perience of such a threat and the problems of teaching and behavioural
ntrol intensify when the clientele predominantly comprises children
hose parents are lower class. For this reason, I suggest that in social
riority area schools, the primary orientation of classroom teaching will
e towards the moral dimensions of school life rather than towards the
gnitive ones, though legitimation may derive from the latter. [...]

This is not to say that the cognitive dimension is irrelevant in the
aching of lower working class pupils, only that the moral aspect takes
rimacy. In this sense, social control becomes inseparable from cur-
culum planning, preferred styles of teaching and classroom organiza-
on. It can often come to constitute the definition of teaching.[8] For this
eason, I wish to regard the use of 'mime' as a means of social control. Its
election by teachers provides the grounds upon which specific decisions
vithin the lesson can be made and negotiated. [...]

Coping strategies have a predefinitional quality about them. In so far as
hey involve second-level decisions and assumptions about the selection of
appropriate' curricular items (e.g. mime as a means of social control) and
bout pedagogical styles (e.g. policing), all subsequent action is framed
vithin these predefined parameters. Nevertheless, the second-level
ecisions and assumptions which make up coping strategies must still be
accomplished through the practice of teacher-pupil interaction. The prac-
ical techniques of control and instruction employed by teachers and the
egotiations which arise between teachers and pupils are the necessary
neans by which coping strategies are affirmed or modified. Each coping
strategy implies its own degree of latitude in first-level decision-making.
Policing, I suggest, implies a narrow range of possible negotiation in
classroom practice. The boundaries of power, autonomy and decision-
naking are explicitly demarcated through the utilization of techniques
which make up this pedagogical style. It is to a detailing of such techniques that I now turn.

First-level decisions

Philip Jackson (1968)[9] has emphasized that 'crowds' are one of the m[]
pervasive features of classroom life. Although his concern was with t[]
effect this had on the decoding of the hidden curriculum by pupils, t[]
phenomenon is also crucially relevant to the techniques of classroo[]
management which teachers employ. In this sense the teacher acts []
policewoman in so far as she engages in 'crowd control'. Crowd cont[]
entails first-level decisions about exclusion (who is allowed to be part []
the crowd), the movement of the crowd as a whole, and the movement []
individuals within the crowd. The orderly organization and spatial di[]
tribution of pupils is the essence of good policing.

The first specific decision concerns who is to be included in the crow[]

T2   Donald, are you in this?
D   No, Miss.
T2   Will you move towards the wall, then. (lines 173–8)

Pupils may be excluded purely for the preservation of classroom harmon[]
This kind of decision has its parallels in the placing of disruptive childre[]
outside the classroom, in the setting up of special isolation units and in th[]
practices of suspension and expulsion. But the practice takes on anothe[]
dimension when desirable activities are involved. Any crowd may in to[]
be denied access to the desirable activity. An analogous situation here i[]
the disciplinary stipulation that soccer clubs play several crucial game[]
away from their home supporters when the latter have been held account[]
able for disruptive behaviour. The threat of action involving the im[]
position of unpleasant alternatives may be used in classrooms as a mean[]
of establishing pupil conformity:

T1   You do it without making a lot of noise (raised voice), otherwis[]
      we won't bother. We'll just come and sit down here and you'll ge[]
      your reading books. (57–60)

The threat of expulsion is linked in this pedagogical style to the statemen[]
of a rule, e.g. 'making a lot of noise'. The combination of the threat o[]
exclusion and the articulation of a rule may also be applied to individua[]
pupils. The first example here refers to the rule of 'being sensible'.

T1   Right now, you've got to be really sensible because if Mrs H see[]
      anybody being silly or I see anybody you will come and you will sit
      down. You won't take part in it again this afternoon. (71–4)

The link between the threatened sanction, the rule, and behaviour which
violates that rule may require more inference on the part of the pupil,
though in the public situation characteristic of this coping strategy the
data from which inferences can be drawn are readily available. For
example,

T1   What we're going to do this afternoon is something that only very, very sensible people can do. You'd better put your foot down, Terry Carter. People who behave like Terry Carter can't do it. (6–10)

Inappropriate positioning of the body can here be linked to a breaking of the rule, 'being sensible'.

In acting as policewoman, apart from decisions regarding exclusion and expulsion, the teacher also makes decisions regarding the movement and positioning of the crowd *en masse*. As a consequence of the successful enactment of these decisions, pupils, through their occupation of a particular position within the classroom and through their common adoption of a certain position (e.g. sitting), are more open to surveillance. Such crowd control techniques may be articulated prescriptively or proscriptively, and may refer either to the occupation of a particular space or to the way in which that space is occupied. For example, all children may be required to occupy a particular part of the classroom:

T1   The people over there; can you move over here so that whoever's doing it can (Pause) be in front of you. (95–7)

The need to maintain easy surveillance also necessitates the proscription of certain areas which become 'out of bounds':

T1   You can go anywhere in my area, in the little corner or anywhere in Mrs H's area where we can see you. (30–2)

Pupils are more easily surveyed and controlled when they adopt certain bodily positions rather than others. That pupils are seated, for example, while the teacher stands, places the latter in a 'superior' position both physically and symbolically. Sitting may be prescribed,

T1   Right, sit down on your bottoms, all of you. (101)

or movement may be proscribed:

T1   Don't you dare move. You're liable to get your heads chopped off. (106–7)

The occupation of space and its manner of occupation may be combined. The last example illustrates this in the form of a proscription. An alternative one shows how such an injunction may be expressed in the form of a prescription,

T1   Right, all of you, sit on the carpet. C'mon (Pause) Go sit on the carpet. (1–2)

Policing may also involve the separation into and the handling of subgroups. Although such decisions *may* take the form of *segregation* for social control purposes, in this extract the formation of groups would seem to be integral to the teaching of mime.

> T1   I want you to get into little groups of four. (11–12)

Such movement within the mass increases the possibility of disorder and is therefore accompanied by the explicit statement of rules according to which this separation into groups is to be accomplished, i.e.

> T1   ... without fussing (Pause) without talking and shouting or whatever.... (10–11)

Even such stringent safeguards do not ensure that the teacher's requirements will be fulfilled automatically. Simple mathematical difficulties may entail some negotiation about the formation of the groups.

> P   There's only two of us – me and Colin ⎤
> T1   Well you can still do.... ⎬ complex interchange
> P   We've got two ⎦
> T1   There's two of you. Right, well you four join together then.
> P   Miss, there's only three of us.
> T1   Well go (inaudible) then. It doesn't matter. (75–81)

Apart from the interestingly exceptional case of Charlie, who will be discussed later, the latitude allowed for negotiation here is extremely restricted. Consequently, the negotiative decisions tend to rotate around minor points of classroom order and procedure.

The third major form of crowd control involves the close monitoring of individual pupils with respect to their position within the crowd and to their gestures and general demeanour. Pupils may be ordered to change positions in the classroom:

> T1   Right Pam, c'mon over here. (23)

More typically, strict control is exercised over posture:

> T1   You'd better put your foot down, Terry Carter. (8)

The teacher here acts less like a policewoman and more like a puppeteer in the extent to which she governs the most detailed movements of pupils in her charge. Otherwise idle hands are, through such techniques of puppeteering, allotted a specific function and their mischievous potential is thereby removed. The success of such techniques is marked by the degree to which they become employed routinely and ritualistically. The placing of hands upon heads as a means of preventing or suspending all deviant activity is one such commonly used device (lines 18–27).

Policing implies most of the above techniques, though for others, the metaphor of puppeteering would seem more appropriate. The utility of policing as an adequate metaphor is lost, however, when consideration is given to the particular techniques which the teacher employs in the control of pupil talk. In the extent to which she facilitates, delimits, terminates or reformulates such talk, the teacher, in fact, is more akin to a barrister.

References to pupil talk are almost always proscriptive in form. The major exception is when the pupil is invited to make contributions through the system of participation which the teacher organizes. Invocation of the 'no talking' rule can vary from explicit statement to para-linguistic indication.[10] The following are explicit statements,

T1 Now then, without fussing (Pause), without talking and shouting or whatever, I want you to get into little groups of four. I said without talking, so sit down again. (10–13)

or:

T1 Your group. C'mon in this space. Now then, you will have to be *really* quiet. (112–13)

Rather than a statement of the rule which is being broken, a noise like 'Sssshhh!' which is conventionally associated with the suppression of noisy rule-breaking behaviour, might be uttered instead (e.g. lines 52 and 115).

As another alternative, the teacher may merely state the behaviour in which the pupil is indulging, leaving the latter to infer that, by its very remarkability, such behaviour constitutes the infraction of a rule. For example,

T2 You are talking. (124)

The teacher may also criticize pupil behaviour in a more diffuse manner, where the pupil must infer that 'talking' is the specific behaviour that has to end.

T1 Are you listening? You're being very bad mannered, Barry. (60–1)

The grounds for such inference would still appear to be explicitly available in the teacher's speech, however. Given the fact that within the coping strategy of policing those grounds comprise strict rules about talking and the use of the body, the fixed attention of the teacher through the use of 'the look' (55–6, 62) on any particular pupil will be sufficient to indicate to him both his characterization as deviant and also the grounds of his deviance.

Under the experienced conditions of impending anomie, stringent control over pupil talk and bodily movement becomes a central feature of teacher behaviour. It is not surprising, therefore, that infractions often involve a combination of talk *and* bodily movement (e.g. lines 56–9, 81–2).

Possibly the most interesting and disturbing feature of the coping strategy of policing is the extent to which the moral features of classroom life take priority over the cognitive. In this sense, forms of teaching (at the second level of decision-making) and particular negotiative strategies[11] (at the first level) which are organized primarily around principles of social control come to be, at the very least, indistinguishable from forms of teaching which are cognitively based. The strong element of this thesis

would state that in schools comprising mainly lower working class pupil
teaching decisions at both levels are taken on largely moral grounds an
the cognitive dimension becomes merely a weak legitimation of th
former. Under these circumstances, social control passes for teaching.

I have already pointed out how the choice of mime (at the second leve
as a curricular item contains marked advantages for social control in so fa
as it enables an efficient separation of legitimate from illegitimate talk. T
some extent, the principles lying behind the choice of a curricular iter
re-emerge at the first level of decision-making in the classroom.

(1)   T1   Now then, we'll give you about five minutes in which to get ..
           your mime ready. You do it without making a lot of nois
           (raised voice), otherwise we won't bother. We'll just come an
           sit down here and you'll get your reading books.... And the
           when you've done it ... you're all going to show us in you
           groups in turns and we're going to see if we can guess wha
           you've been doing. So you've got to be very quiet because if yo
           stand over there and shout 'Oh, let's do this, let's all be milk
           men' – everybody'll know before you even start. So you ge
           together and you whisper very quietly and then ... you work i
           out and you go practise it – very quietly. (55–69)
(2)   T1   Right, very quietly, in your groups. (81–2)
(3)   T2   Stop! Everybody stop! What's a mime? Nora?
      N   It's when you don't speak.
      T2   There is no speaking *at all*. So it's no good saying 'Well, I'
           come and so and so to you and you do such and such to me'
           There's got to be no talking at all. So really we shouldn't hea
           any sound from you at all. (86–93)

Within these extracts, the teachers, through their employment of strategi
decisions, specify more closely the meaning and definition of 'mime' fo
their pupils. In the first extract, the cognitive and the moral reasons fo
maintaining quietness in producing a mime are closely bound together
When this close specification of the curricular item, mime, fails to restric
pupil speech to 'acceptable' noise levels, then a further, rather specious se
of conditions is involved. In the third extract the teacher draws a tenuou
connection between the silence required in order to perform a mime and
the required behaviour in planning such a mime. It is difficult to see how
effective planning within a group could in fact be achieved without the use
of pupil talk to elaborate meanings and intentions.

The reasons both for choosing mime and for the particular way in whicl
this curricular item is transformed into a pedagogical strategy are, I
should argue, primarily moral in character. There is, of course, an
interpretive problem in assessing the status of cognitive factors as either
implementing reasons or legitimating justifications. My reason for opting
for the latter alternative is the way in which the teachers, in an ad hoc
manner, *extend* the relevance of the 'no talking' rule to all behaviour

beyond the mime itself. Through this procedure the cognitive justification becomes extremely attenuated. Yet, it is the very binding together of (albeit attenuated) cognitive justifications and moral reasons within the teachers' talk which not only presents the observer with interpretive difficulties but also marks the process by which social control passes for valid teaching.

To expose the moral basis of policing is not to make an indictment of teachers' attitudes and behaviour. It should not be thought that teachers are unenlightened repressors of pupil spontaneity. [. . .] Teachers themselves, it must be remembered, work in an environment of abundant social constraints. These constraints may be so severe in a school of social priority area status that teaching necessarily becomes organized around survival (Woods, 1977). The coping strategy of policing is under these circumstances a reasonable, constructively articulated adaptation to the demands imposed by a school which caters predominantly for lower working class pupils. [. . .]

To sum up, the coping strategy of policing comprises three elements: The first is rigorous and systematic control over pupil talk and bodily movement. The second is an explicit articulation of the rule system and a public display of the hierarchical relationship which obtains between teacher and pupil. This is manifested in the detailed first-level negotiative strategies included under the first-element but is also exemplified by other features of classroom life. These include the frequent use of imperatives; the repeated use of attention maintaining devices and signals which indicate a switch in the phase of the lesson and hence the rules which are appropriate to that phase (D. Hargreaves *et al.*, 1975),[12] e.g. 'Right'; and finally the use of non-voluntarist modes of speech, e.g.,

T1   *You're going to* get together and *you're going to* think of something to mime. (32–3; see also lines 61–9)

The third element arises because of the problems presented by lower working class children in a school environment. Coping strategies of policing and second-level decisions about the curriculum, in addition to specific negotiative strategies at the first-level of decision-making, are all based primarily on the necessity to maintain social control. Where cognitive justifications are invoked in order to legitimate such strategic decisions, control may well pass for teaching.[13] Survival strategies can, according to Woods (1977), 'appear as teaching, their survival value having a higher premium than their educational value'.[14]

Confrontation avoidance: an alternative coping strategy

[. . .]

My second concern is with a coping strategy which I term 'confrontation avoidance',[15] and the consequences which this has for the identity and self of the pupil. Particular strategies of confrontation avoidance can be found in earlier work on the sociology of the classroom. Werthman (1971)[16] describes how some teachers attempted to 'bribe' gang member of whom they were afraid with high grades. Wegmann (1976)[17] has illustrated how pupil challenges to teacher authority may be redefined by the teacher as literal contributions to democratic rational discourse, so that some semblance of order can be sustained within the classroom. In the classroom with which I am concerned here, the salient feature of confrontation avoidance is either a refusal to act upon pupil challenges or a minimization of response to such challenges. In the maintenance of this low profile orientation, it should be remembered that any refusal to act does not constitute the absence of action because

> no action at all ... can have fully serious clear-cut consequences and hence constitute a move 'in effect'.[18]

Second-level decisions

The child who is the object of such (in)attention is Charlie, a ten-year-old West Indian boy. Charlie carries a nefarious past in tow because he was expelled from his previous school after committing acts of violence (throwing furniture) against the headmistress.[19] The possibility that such action might recur is an understandably frightening prospect for teachers and presents them with the acute problem of how this potentially explosive and volatile individual is to be handled. The chosen coping strategy is the avoidance of confrontation with Charlie wherever possible. Within the individualized learning process of the integrated day system, this seems to reap *some* rewards from the teachers' point of view. The general policy is summed up by the head of the year group:

> We're not too bothered if Charlie doesn't do much work providing he's reasonably quiet.

To the amusement of the teachers, Charlie could often be seen wandering about the classroom looking out of the window, drawing, singing to himself or talking to other children. Through broadening the latitude of acceptable behaviour beyond conventional bounds little of Charlie's behaviour became sanctionable and peace often prevailed.

The second-level coping strategy of confrontation-avoidance was sometimes realized in more subtle ways:

> If we want Charlie to do something, we don't tell him. We don't say, 'Charlie, get in the queue.' We say, 'C'mon Charlie, which end of the queue do you want to go to, front or back?' He thinks he's got a choice.

The essence of the strategy here is the close specification of the framework within which Charlie is to make decisions. That framework comprises a *finite* set of alternative possible decisions from which Charlie is able to choose rather than a set of conformist or *oppositional* decisions involving compliance or non-compliance which would be opened up by the use of direct commands and orders.

The intention contained within these second-level decisions which make up the coping strategy of confrontation avoidance is to frame the parameters of interaction such that Charlie will be made organizationally proper. The teachers here can be seen to be 'making a proper Charlie' of him. This is a deliberate use of irony on my part, for the implementation of such a coping strategy may have fatal consequences for Charlie's self and identity, even though it may defuse his explosive potential.

There are strong connections between involvement in social interaction, the presentation, implementation and mutual recognition of identities and the development or sustenance of the self. Now, although the coping strategy of policing and other explicit, formal, public modes of classroom interaction involve a depersonalization of the pupil (i.e. he is manifestly treated as one of a type rather than as a unique individual), nevertheless the explicit, public character of such forms of interaction makes available the hierarchical nature of the relationship which obtains between teacher and pupil and hence establishes the communication and imposition of an identity upon the pupil by the teacher. Such identities are not necessarily accepted by the pupil. They need not be incorporated into the definition of his self. Indeed, Goffman has pointed out that through the employment of secondary adjustments 'the individual stands apart from the role and the self that were taken for granted for him by the institution'.[20]

The totalitarian quality of classroom life characteristic of policing entails the exertion of teacher control over the most detailed of pupil actions and it closely circumscribes the latter's autonomy. Yet it also facilitates the recognition of *an* identity, and the preservation of the self through a distancing off from such institutionally imposed identities. In individualized patterns of classroom interaction, these possibilities are reduced. The avoidance of confrontation, where it comes to constitute the avoidance of interaction, can lead to the removal of communicable identities and hence can invite dissolution of the self. Such is the case with Charlie. Since the self is constituted reflexively through interaction with others, where such interaction is seriously diminished, then the absence of communicated identities might well lead to the self perceiving itself as a non-entity. Had individualized interaction been the only form of classroom discourse, then it would have been reasonable to have hypothesized the dissolution of the self in Charlie's case.

There are two factors which obviate such a process, however. First, Charlie, like other actors, is more than merely a passive recipient of an imposed social order and possesses the ability to respond constructively to pressures which he experiences. Secondly, the presence of some formal, explicit, public classroom contexts (e.g. policing) provides a platform upon which Charlie can present and assert witnessable definitions of his own existence and worth.

First-level decisions

Charlie, then, has an interest in presenting a definition of his self – in asserting an identity, possibly *any* identity. [...] Charlie's need to establish an identity coupled with the teachers' wish to avoid confrontation result in 'interesting' negotiative processes at the first level of decision-making.

Early in the lesson one of the teachers sets about organizing the class into groups of four to construct and perform their mimes. The teacher counts slowly up to five to allow time for this to be completed.

T	Four (class is now quiet – three-second pause) Five.
Ch	We haven't got four.
T1	Right. Everybody's ready. Now then, what you're going to do with your group.... (26–30)

A true, 'legitimate' statement uttered by Charlie (there were only three in his group) is here ignored by the teacher. Charlie seeks attention by stating that his group does not come up to organizational requirements. The teacher responds by not responding, i.e. she does not engage in any (spoken) interaction with Charlie. That this would seem to be a reaction to Charlie-making-the-statement, rather than to the statement itself, is confirmed when another pupil in Charlie's threesome reiterates the problem.

P	Miss, there's only three of us.
T1	Well go (inaudible) then. It doesn't matter.... (80–1)

Because the transcription is inaudible at one point, it is not perfectly clear whether or not the teacher's response constitutes a rejection of the legitimacy of the pupil's observation. The important point, however, is that this pupil receives recognition whereas Charlie did not.

Charlie's second contribution to the proceedings constitutes the first instance of rule transgression on his part. Martyn Hammersley (1974)[21] has noted how, in formally organized classrooms, pupils are often invited and required to participate in lessons when the teacher signals that this is appropriate. The complex procedure of participation is rule governed partly for the maintenance of orderly social relations within the class. Charlie succeeds skilfully in breaking one important and fundamental rule of participation – not speaking out of turn. In this instance, the teacher is inviting suggestions for a mime:

P	Tidying up
T1	Tidying up ∧
P	Clearing up
T1	Clearing up ∧
P	Being the milkman
T1	Yes ∧
P	Going to school

T1	Going to school. ∨ It can be anything you can think of.
Ch	Swimming.
T1	Sssshhhh-er-If we see anybody being silly, you'll come and sit down here and you won't take part in the lesson. . . . (43–53)

The requirement for continued participation is here indicated by upward intonation in the teacher's voice.[22] The downward intonation in line 50 signals the termination of legitimate suggestions. This signal is reinforced by the closing statement, 'It can be anything you can think of.' It is at this point that Charlie again asserts his existence by inserting a suggestion at an inappropriate point, one reserved for teacher talk. In effect, Charlie temporarily takes the teacher's talk away from her. Although the teacher's next utterance 'Sssshhhh' appears to be a response to Charlie, in fact it was directed more to the class as a whole, many of whom were now shuffling and muttering considerably. Again, therefore, Charlie's 'contribution' is ostensibly ignored through another non-response on the teacher's part. To reiterate an earlier point, this non-response is not inconsequential, for it constitutes an action of *intended* avoidance. The likelihood follows that Charlie will make additional moves in order to have an identity recognized and witnessed. Yet the teacher too is intent on avoiding overt conflict with Charlie. The negotiative strategies hence proceed and escalate. Consider the next extract, where the pupils are attempting to guess what has just been mimed. Several suggestions have already been offered:

T	Charlie?
Ch	Eating sweets and taking 'em off 'em. . . . putting 'em up at wall.
M	We're not eating sweets.
P	Eating bubbly gum.
M	(Shakes head)
Ch	Eatin' sausage roll.
P's	(Slight giggles)
T2	We've already said they're eating sweets. (141–9)

Charlie first offers what would appear to be an authentic suggestion of what is being mimed. This guess is incorrect. After another incorrect pupil attempt to guess the mime, Charlie puts forward a more comic suggestion. It is somewhat equivocal whether or not this suggestion constitutes an intentionally deviant act. Though our own common sense would tell us that a guess is incorrect because it wrongly identifies the action (eating) rather than the object (sweets), such a distinction is not drawn within the mimic's reply, 'We're not eating sweets', nor anywhere else in the transcript so far. It is therefore *possible* that Charlie's second guess ('Eatin' sausage roll') is an honest contribution, although the smile which accompanied his remark might indicate the opposite. If there is any initial doubt, however, the pupils' giggles in response to his suggestion retrospectively confer upon it a deviant status. This is the first time that Charlie's remarks produce an effect (giggling) upon the rest of the class. Interestingly, it is also the first time that his remarks merit a spoken response on the part of the teacher.[23] It is therefore at least plausible that the intervention of the teacher is connected to the potential threat of the wider breakdown of classroom order which Charlie's remark creates.

In view of the teacher's intention to avoid confrontation, the substance of her response is especially interesting. It is, in fact, a lie. The teacher's non-controversial response imputes an alternative intention to Charlie's utterance. In re-defining the remark as a reasonable contribution rather than an intended challenge, direct confrontation is avoided (Wegmann, 1976).[17] Charlie's contribution is treated as incorrect rather than inappropriate. As a result, Charlie's intentions are not besmirched by the teacher. However, I am not suggesting that the felt necessity to avoid direct confrontation has led the teacher to construct a calculated lie. Rather, the urgency of strategically avoiding confrontation would seem to engender a particular structuring of perceptions which might then lead to the inadvertent statement of 'false' reasons on the part of the teacher.

In producing a response from the teacher and hence a witnessable recognition of his existence, Charlie has had an initial glimpse of 'success'. The 'silly foods' theme, from Charlie's point of view, is worth developing.

P   Being naughty.
M   No.
T2   You'll never guess.
Ch   Got fish and chips.
T1   Charlie! (150–4)

Charlie's contributions are amusing in so far as they constitute a re-definition of the game (What's my mime?) as one of guessing increasingly absurd objects as opposed to actions. In so doing he undermines the teachers' conventional definition of mime and thereby constitutes a threat to classroom order. The teachers are confronted with an escalating series of challenges from Charlie which present them with increasingly difficult decisions whereby the necessity to maintain classroom order must be traded off against a wish to avoid direct confrontation when dealing with Charlie. This dilemma is exploited with great skill and success by Charlie in his development of the 'silly foods' theme. At this point the trade-off results in the teacher paying attention to Charlie and, through her tone, indicating to him that he is being deviant. By 'naming' Charlie, his deviance is pointed out but the exact nature of Charlie's deviant act is not explicitly stated. When a teacher only *names* the miscreant, then the nature of his deviance must be *inferred* by all who hear this naming (D. Hargreaves *et al.*, 1975).[12] The act, and the identity that attaches to the act, are not in this instance spelt out.

Charlie has thus far transformed the response of the teacher to him from one where she avoids interaction altogether to one where, by being named, Charlie's deviant behaviour and deviant character are implied. Charlie takes the process one step further and achieves startling results after the next mime (delivering milk) has been performed.

T1 Right, well don't look at me, ask them.
M Charlie?
Ch You're having a bag of chips.
M No.
T1 Right, we're not going to ask Charlie in future 'cos he's being silly.
(197–202)

The highly lucrative 'silly foods' theme is here extended to its ultimate conclusion – its insertion into a situation where the actions involved in the mime could not, even by the most imaginative speculation, be regarded as embodying any kind of eating. The absurdity of Charlie's contribution and the alternative definition of classroom events which he thereby puts forward pose a more serious threat to orderly classroom relations. The teacher abandons the delicate process of trading off alternatives and opts instead for more direct confrontation. Charlie is named as a deviant, his deviant acts are explicitly stated and notice is given of his future exclusion and the grounds for this exclusion.

Charlie, it could be argued, has proved victorious. Using an ingenious set of negotiative strategies, he has succeeded in having an identity recognized and publicly proclaimed. For a brief moment, through having to make a first-level decision which resulted in a confrontation with Charlie, the teacher has been momentarily prised out of the framework circumscribed by the coping strategy of confrontation avoidance. Yet any success on Charlie's part is a Pyrrhic victory. It is true that the negotiative strategies he employed and the counter-strategies which these induced may well have averted the wreckage and loss of the self, but fatal consequences have followed in the hardening of a deviant career.[24]

The classroom negotiations in which Charlie has been involved can be seen as one small phase in the much broader process of deviancy amplification. Such a process involves a hardening of the deviant's identity[25] and the committing of further deviant acts largely as a result of the way in which social control agencies define and treat him. In this process of secondary deviation (Lemert, 1951),[26] the deviant (Charlie) develops defence mechanisms in order to cope with the problems created by the reaction of the control agents to him as a deviant.

To sum up, through his expulsion from a previous school and through the reports accompanying that expulsion, Charlie is defined as a deviant. On the basis of this definition, teachers adopt a coping strategy of confrontation avoidance in an attempt to frame the parameters within which subsequent interaction can occur. As these second-level decisions are translated into first-level decisions which initially involve the general evasion of interaction with Charlie, problems are created for him. These problems concern the threats posed to the maintenance of the self through the difficulty of having an identity recognized and witnessed by others.

Charlie, therefore, at the second level of decision-making adopts th
coping strategy of identity recognition. This coping strategy is translate
into first-level decisions which are enacted as negotiative strategies. Thes
involve the presentation of alternative definitions of classroom events an
the breaking of organizational (interactional) rules. As these strategie
escalate in severity, the teachers are increasingly constrained into recog
nizing Charlie's new deviance and into explicitly stating the precis
nature of his deviance. Through this process, Charlie's deviant identity i
confirmed, hardened and perpetuated. In the establishment of ominou
future careers, strategic interaction and the decisions which it incorpo
rates can indeed have both fateful and fatal consequences.

From the above evidence, two specific conclusions can be drawr
although these clearly require substantiation in further research. First, th
coping strategies of policing and of confrontation-avoidance are mutuall
incompatible. The former, indeed, provides the grounds for the negatio
of the latter. Charlie would have found much greater difficulty in assertin
his identity and provoking confrontation in a less explicit and less publi
interactional context. Second, the unintended consequence of th
employment of these strategies in combination is that the very devianc
which teachers are seeking to eliminate or control is exacerbated. Th
management of classroom life no longer remains efficient and where thi
situation continues, the strategy of expulsion will be turned to as the las
resort. This ultimately happened in Charlie's case and marked anothe
definitive stage in the development of his deviant career. [. . .]

Transcript of a drama lesson

Key

T1	1st teacher
T2	2nd teacher
P	Pupil
M	Mimic
Ch	Charlie
∧	Upward intonation
∨	Downward intonation

1	T1	Right, all of you, sit on the carpet. C'mon.
2		(Pause)

3		Go sit on the carpet.
4		(Pause – children settle down on the carpet while
5		teacher & researcher talk)
6		Right. (Pause) What we're going to do this afternoon
7		is something that only very, very sensible people can
8		do. You'd better put your foot down, Terry Carter.
9		People who behave like Terry Carter
10		can't do it. Now then, without fussing (Pause)
11		without talking and shouting or whatever, I want you to
12		get into little groups of four. I said without talking,
13		so sit down again. Penny Dawson, sit down. When you're
14		in your groups, put your hands on your head so we can
15		see you're ready.
16		(Long pause – some noise as children organize into
17		groups)
18		Right, by the time I count five, I want you all sitting
19		with your hands on your heads without talking.
20		One (three-second pause)
21		Two (four-second pause)
22		Three – Who's got four? Which group has got four?
23		Right Pam, c'mon over here.
24		(Eight seconds pass after the word 'three' is uttered
25		and before the utterance below)
26		Four (class is now quiet – three-second pause)
27		Five.
28	Ch	We haven't got four.
29	T1	Right. Everybody's ready. Now then, what you're going
30		to do with your group. You can go anywhere in my area,
31		in the little corner or anywhere in Mrs H's area where
32		we can see you. You're going to get together and you're
33		going to think of something to mime. Now then, what
34		sort of things can it be?
35	P	Doing baking.
36	T1	Doing baking. ∧
37	P	At the shop.
38	T1	At the shop. ∧
39	P	Playing.
40	T1	Playing. ∧
41	P	Sewing.
42	T1	Sewing. ∧
43	P	Tidying up.
44	T1	Tidying up. ∧
45	P	Clearing up.
46	T1	Clearing up. ∧
47	P	Being the milkman.
48	T1	Yes. ∧

49	P	Going to school.
50	T1	Going to school. ∨ It can be anything you can think of.
51	Ch	Swimming!
52	T1	Sssshhhh. -er- If we see anybody being silly, you'll come
53		and sit down here and you won't take part in the lesson.
54		Are you listening, John Clarkson?
55		Now then, we'll give you about five minutes in which
56		to get (pause – looks at child talking to another child)
57		your mime ready. You do it without making a lot of
58		noise (raised voice), otherwise we won't bother. We'll
59		just come and sit down here and you'll get your reading
60		books. Are you listening? You're being very bad
61		mannered, Barry. And then when you've done it (pause –
62		look) you're all going to show us in your groups in
63		turns and we're going to see if we can guess what you've
64		been doing. So you've got to be very quiet because if
65		you stand over there and shout 'Oh, let's do this, let's
66		all be milkmen' – everybody'll know before you even
67		start. So you get together and you whisper very quietly
68		and then (pause – look) you work it out and you go
69		practise it – very quietly. When you're ready and when
70		I tell you, come and sit down and then we'll let you do
71		it in your groups. Right now, you've got to be really
72		sensible because if Mrs H sees anybody being silly or I
73		see anybody you will sit down. You won't take part in
74		it again this afternoon.
75	P	There's only two of us – me and Colin⎤
76	T1	Well you can still do. . . . ⎬Complex interchange!
77	P	We've got two ⎦
78	T1	There's two of you. Right, well you four join together
79		then.
80	P	Miss, there's only three of us.
81	T1	Well go (inaudible) then. It doesn't matter. Right,
82		very quietly, in your groups.
83		(Pupils now prepare their mimes. They are talking in
84		order to organize their mimes, but some are also
85		incorporating talk into their 'mime'.)
86	T2	Stop! Everybody stop! What's a mime? Nora? (pupil's
87		name)
88	N	It's when you don't speak.
89	T2	There is no speaking *at all* (raised voice). So it's no
90		good saying 'Well, I'll come and so and so to you and
91		you say such and such to me'. There's got to be no
92		talking at all. So really we shouldn't hear any sound
93		at all from you at all.
94		(Preparation continues)

95	T1	Right, now. (Pause) Now. Right. The people over there,
96		can you move over here so that whoever's doing it can
97		(Pause) be in front of you.
98		(Children move around)
99	T1	Don't be stupid.
100		(Long pause)
101	T1	Right, sit down on your bottoms, all of you.
102	P	(inaudible)
103	T1	On your bottoms, every single one of you. Now, people
104		round there can't see.
105	T2	There's plenty of space over here.
106	T1	Don't you dare move. You're liable to get your heads
107		chopped off.
108	T2	Look at that space there.
109	T1	Right. Now then. Which group would like to volunteer
110		to go first?
111		(Hands are raised)
112	T1	Ivy had her hand up first. Your group, c'mon, in this
113		space. Now then, you will have to be *really* quiet.
114		(Group moves towards front of audience)
115	T1	Sssshhhh! Sit *down*. Colin! David! Sandra! On your
116		bottom! They can't see for you. *You*, on your bottom
117		like everybody else. You can see through that gap as
118		well as anybody else. Right. You ready?
119		(Mime is now in progress. The particular mime is of
120		a situation involving poor table manners and the
121		offenders being placed up against a wall as
122		'punishment by their teacher'. The following
123		utterances occur whilst the mime is in progress.)
124	T2	You are talking.
125	P's	(Inaudible)
126	T2	Now watch her. (Referring to the mime.)
127	T1	Remember, you've to guess what they're doing.
128	D	You've not to eat in school.
129	T2	Don't be silly about it, John.
130	T1	Have you finished? Right.
131		Well don't look at me. It's them you're asking.
132		(Addressed to the audience.)
133	P	Eating sweets in school and getting into trouble.
134	M	No.
135	T1	Does anyone know?
136	P.	(Inaudible suggestion)
137	M	No.
138	P	Eating....
139	T.	Charlie?
140	P.	... food (continuation of line 138)

141 T   Charlie?
142 Ch   Eating sweets and taking 'em off 'em ... putting 'em
143   up at wall.
144 M   We're not eating sweets.
145 P   Eating bubbly gum.
146 M   (Shakes head)
147 Ch   Eatin' sausage roll.
148 P's (Slight giggles)
149 T2   We've already said they're eating sweets.
150 P   Being naughty.
151 M   No.
152 T2   You'll never guess.
153 Ch   Got fish and chips.
154 T1   Charlie!
155 P   They've both been bad mannered at table and been put in
156   t'corner.
157 M   Yes.
158 T1   That's right.
159 T2   Very good.
160 T1   That's fifteen team points for you, Matthew. You guessed.
161   right. Now which group would like to go next?
162 T2   Sssshhhh.
163   (Hands are used to indicate who would like to go next.)
164 T1   (Selects a person) Is that the group who guessed it?
165 P   Yes.
166 T1   The group who guessed it. Right, Matthew, you, your group.
167   (Mime takes place. The subject this time is delivering.
168   milk. Talk again takes place during the performance.)
169 T1   (Inaudible)
170 T2   Right, any silliness and you'll sit back down. (Addressed
171   to the mimics)
172 D   Yeah!
173 T2   Donald, are you in this? (Donald opted initially to be
174   excluded from the proceedings and has been drawing at
175   the side of the mimed performance but periodically moves
176   forward to observe the proceedings or to pass comment.)
177 D   No, Miss.
178 T2   Will you move towards the wall, then.
179   (Players are still on stage but have not yet started
180   the performance.)
181 M   Miss, Gary isn't here.
182 T1   C'mon, Gary. C'mon. Take your jumper off or is that
183   necessary. (Gary has a jumper tied round his neck.)
184   Right. Have you started (addressed to mimics)? Have
185   you started, Trevor?
186 M   Yeah.

187   (Performance now definitely under way.)

188 T1 I can't see what you're doing for Paul.

189 M's (Much quiet giggling.)

190 T1 I think you're being a bit silly. Can you do it without
191   giggling, Terry?

192 M Yeah.

193 T1 Donald, I suggest you go and sit down (Donald has moved
194   across to view proceedings again.) Right, have you
195   finished?

196 M Yes, Miss.

197 T1 Right, well don't look at me, ask them.

198 M Charlie?

199 Ch You're having a bag of chips.

200 M No.

201 T1 Right, we're not going to ask Charlie in future 'cos he's
202   being silly.

203 P Playing marbles.

204 M's No.

205 P (Inaudible)

206 M What?

207 P Meals on wheels?

208 M No.

209 P Playing about.

210 M No.

211 P Getting a drink o' water.

212 M No.

213 P Goin' to t'shop?

214 M No.

215 P Delivering milk?

216 M Yeah.

217 T1 Well done. That's fifteen team points for you, Terry, and
218   your group.

    (And so on after the tape has run out, with three
    more mimes.)

Notes

1 For a more detailed outline of the concept *coping strategy* in the context of progressive education see HARGREAVES, A. (1977) 'Progressivism and Pupil Autonomy', *Sociological Review*, Vol. 23, No. 3, pp. 585–621.

2 The choice of evidence from the small project rather than the major case study in two suburban middle-class schools is an act of deliberate selection on my part. The reason for my choice is that the salient features of policing and confrontation-avoidance are, I wish to argue, more clearly displayed in a school where the majority of the pupils are lower working class in origin.

3 See the final section for a more precise explication of this point.

4   WOODS, P. (1977) 'Teaching for Survival', in WOODS, P. and HAMMERS-
    LEY, M. (eds) *School Experience*. London: Croom Helm.
5   Plowden Report (1967), p. 195.
6   This point is developed in the analysis of the transcript.
7   BECKER, H. S. (1952) 'Social Class Variations in the Teacher-Pupil Relation-
    ship', *Journal of Educational Sociology*, Vol. 25, pp. 451–65
8   The question of the relationship between 'teaching' and social control is an
    urgent one and is of central importance to the sociology of education. In this
    paper, I can offer only some brief comments which might aid clarification. One
    point I particularly wish to stress is that it should not be thought that it is
    somehow possible to devise a method whereby the polluting force of social
    control could be filtered out of the schooling process, and that the task of social
    science is to discover an efficient technique of filtration which would leave
    behind pure 'teaching'. [. . .]
        There is a sense in which, in capitalist societies, education *is* social control in
    that it plays a preparatory and supportive role in reproducing the social
    relations of production, i.e. in perpetuating the structured relations of domi-
    nance and subordinacy in the society. My reference to social control in this
    paper is thus a narrower one and concerns its more explicit manifestation as a
    'gentling of the masses'. This definition is probably closest to teachers' and
    educators' phenomenal awareness of social control as discipline and placation
    in circumstances where they are faced with such pressing matters as RoSLA or
    of the 'problems' presented by children in deprived areas, for example. Using
    social control in this sense, I would therefore argue that it is possible to
    distinguish it from something else which we might call teaching where the
    imparting and creation of school-relevant knowledge is considered the primary
    concern. Likewise, it is therefore legitimate, at this level, to distinguish
    between the cognitive and the moral components of schooling.
9   JACKSON, P. W. (1968) *Life in Classrooms*. New York: Holt, Rinehart and
    Winston.
10 Explicit statements are those where the meaning is expressed literally. By
    literal meanings I refer to those which are least dependent on the social context
    for their sense.
11 By negotiative strategies, I mean those which must be implemented through
    and witnessed in on-going interaction. Negotiation here should not be taken to
    mean a process of reaching common agreement. Where interactional rights
    and power resources are distributed so unevenly, negotiative strategies could
    clearly not be part of a free bargaining procedure.
12 HARGREAVES, D. H., HESTER, S. K. and MELLOR, F. J. (1975) *Deviances in
    Classrooms*. London: Routledge and Kegan Paul.
13 See n. 8.
14 P. 274.
15 The term 'avoidance of confrontation' is used in Hammersley's (1976) study of
    interaction in a secondary modern school: HAMMERSLEY, M. 'The Mobiliza-
    tion of Pupil Attention', in HAMMERSLEY, M. and WOODS, P. (eds) *Process of
    Schooling: A sociological reader*. London: Routledge and Kegan Paul (p. 109).
16 WERTHMAN, C. (1971) 'Delinquents in Schools: A test for the legitimacy of
    authority', in COSIN, B. *et al.* (eds) *School and Society*. 2nd edn 1977. London:
    Routledge and Kegan Paul.
17 WEGMANN, R. (1976) 'Classroom Disciplines: An exercise in the maintenance
    of Social Reality', *Sociology of Education*, Vol. 49, pp. 71–9.

18 GOFFMAN, E. (1970) *Strategic Interaction*. Oxford: Blackwell (p. 91).

19 This information was given to me by the teachers.

20 For an account of the process of secondary adjustment, see GOFFMAN, E. (1961) *Asylums*. Harmondsworth: Penguin Books (p. 172).

21 HAMMERSLEY, M. (1974) 'The Organization of Pupil Participation', *Sociological Review*, Vol. 22, No. 3, August 1974, pp. 355–68.

22 The indication through upward intonation that more participation is required does not always mean that pupil responses have been *accepted*. This is the case only where the teacher is eliciting alternative suggestions. Where she is after a 'right answer', then the signal for continued participation implies a *rejection* of previous contributions.

23 Indeed, the teacher's reply, 'We've already said they're eating sweets', could have been intended not only for Charlie's ears but for those of the whole class. (There are no grounds either in the transcript or in the original recording to assess how far this was true, however.)

24 Charlie now attends a residential school for the maladjusted.

25 This is despite the fact that ostensibly the teachers seek to *avoid* communicating this identity to the pupil.

26 LEMERT, E. (1951) *Social Pathology*. New York and London: McGraw-Hill.

2.8 Teaching styles and pupil progress

Neville Bennett

This investigation set out to answer two basic questions which lie at the heart of pedagogic practice: 'Do differing teaching styles result in disparate pupil progress?' and 'Do different types of pupil perform better under certain styles of teaching?' Although no research study is perfect, a number of improvements were incorporated in design, methodology and measurement in order to overcome the perceived inadequacies of previous investigations. These improvements resulted in a clear definition of terms, a more valid typology of teaching styles, a randomly selected sample of teachers, but not of pupils, a wide ranging set of measures for which there is evidence of reasonably high reliability and validity, and a design which allowed the study of possible effects over a reasonable time scale, i.e. one school year.

The creation of the teaching typology required a large scale survey of schools from which it was possible to assess the common belief that informal teaching is relatively widespread, or, as the Plowden Report put it, 'represents a general and quickening trend'. This was not found to be the case in the upper primary school in the geographical area covered by the survey. From the responses of 88 per cent of the 871 schools sampled, a fairly generous estimate is that some 17 per cent of teachers teach in the manner prescribed by Plowden, while at the other end of the teaching continuum approximately one in four teaches formally. The majority of teachers use what have been termed mixed styles, incorporating elements of both formal and informal practice.

It could of course be argued that the schools in the region covered by the survey are not typical of schools in Britain as a whole. There could be some justification in this argument since there are, for example, more church schools in the north-west than elsewhere. But typicality is difficult to define in this context. Teaching methods in Church of England schools, for example, were found to be similar to those in state schools, although those in Roman Catholic schools did tend to be more formal. Similarly there are certain counties in England and Wales whose schools are renowned for their informal ideology, but these too are unlikely to be typical of schools in general.

It is therefore worth noting that other surveys of this kind tend to support the pattern apparent in the north-west. Studies in the west and east Midlands and in Northern Ireland have been carried out, and in the latter it was found that in a 10 per cent sample of the primary schools 'ratings of teaching methods used for mathematics and reading in the

Source: BENNETT, N. (1976) *Teaching Styles and Pupil Progress*. London: Open Books, pp. 149–163.

upper and lower primary school revealed the majority of teachers as neither formal nor radical in approach but as favouring a mixture of formal practice and practical activities ... The pupils of all but a few schools were allocated to classes by age and were in ability groups within the class' (Trew 1974). Although not concerned with detailing classroom practice the study lent support to the suggestion of the Northern Ireland Advisory Council for Education that the vast majority of pupils were still being taught by traditional methods.

These findings taken together provide little evidence for a wholesale movement towards informality. But neither do they support the assertion that teachers are moving back towards more formal approaches. The Plowden statement was a subjective, and perhaps hopeful, assessment rather than one based on a comprehensive survey. There are no comparable data on which to base statements about trends. All the data do suggest is that the estimates of writers such as Blackie and Silberman, who assert that some 30 per cent of teachers are following informal approaches, are likely to be optimistic.

In discussing trends in teaching it is obviously important to ascertain what factors influence teachers in their decision to adopt a particular style or approach. This was not investigated in any systematic way but some of the evidence gathered does throw light on this area, particularly the data relating to teaching aims and teacher opinions, and that on the external constraints impinging on the classroom process.

A strong relationship was found between teacher aims and opinions and the way teachers actually teach. This link between aims and methods probably comes as no surprise since it supports other studies, noticeably that by Ashton and others (1975). Teachers aim to engender different outcomes in their pupils. The biggest disagreements about aims occur between formal and informal teachers, with mixed teachers adopting a more middle of the road approach. Formal teachers lay much greater stress on the promotion of a high level of academic attainment, preparation for academic work in the secondary school, and the acquisition of basic skills in reading and number work. Informal teachers on the other hand value social and emotional aims, preferring to stress the importance of self-expression, enjoyment of school and the development of creativity.

These differences in emphasis were again demonstrated in the marked disagreements in opinions about teaching methods. The results illustrate how wide the opinion gap is. Formal teachers defend their methods in entirety and disagree with all the arguments made against them by informal teachers. This is also true of informal teachers, who defend the efficacy of their methods except on the question of discipline, where two-thirds agree that their methods could create discipline problems. On the other hand informal teachers are prepared to concede certain points to formal methods, e.g. that they teach basic skills and concepts effectively, and provide an environment in which pupils are aware of what to do, and minimize time wasting and daydreaming. Formal teachers for their part

concede that informal methods are likely to encourage responsibility an
self-discipline, and to teach pupils to think for themselves. Mixe
teachers, although generally aligning themselves more with form;
teachers, agree and disagree with a number of opinions expressed by both

These results would seem to indicate that aims and opinions ar
strongly held and that they relate closely to actual classroom practice
They do, however, seem to be mediated to some extent by external factor
such as the characteristics of the children taught, the church affiliation c
the school, and more powerfully, the presence of the eleven-plus selectiv
examination. The individual effects of these factors are difficult to disen
tangle since many operate simultaneously, but the eleven-plus was clearl
related to a more formal approach. Similarly rural schools tended to b
more informal, and Roman Catholic schools more formal.

Teaching styles and pupil progress

The review of related research had indicated that little difference i
progress might be expected under different teaching methods, althoug
there was a suggestion that creativity might be enhanced in informa
schools and that reading might be fostered in a more formal environment
These findings are somewhat confounded by poor sampling and th
insistence that all teachers can be adequately described by the use of tw
categories such as progressive and traditional. The Richards and Bolto
study on performance in mathematics did seem to indicate that perhap
the middle way was the best way – moderation in all things!

To assess the impact of differing teaching styles on pupil progress
thirty-seven teachers were chosen to represent seven of the twelve teach
ing styles isolated in the typology. Because of the twin constraints o
finance and staffing it was not possible to sample all twelve styles, but th
seven chosen adequately represented the full range. The pupils wh
entered the classroom of these teachers in September 1973 were tested on ;
wide range of attainment and personality tests on entry, and again th
following June. From these data, analyses were computed to ascertain th
effect of teaching style across the group of pupils as a whole, on pupils o
different sex, on pupils of differing achievement level and on pupils o
differing personality type.

The results form a coherent pattern. The effect of teaching style i
statistically and educationally significant in all attainment areas tested. In
reading, pupils of formal and mixed teachers progress more than those o
informal teachers, the difference being equivalent to some three to five
months' difference in performance. In mathematics formal pupils are
superior to both mixed and informal pupils, the difference in progress
being some four to five months. In English formal pupils again out-
perform both mixed and informal pupils, the discrepancy in progress
between formal and informal being approximately three to five months. It

is interesting to note that these differences are very similar to those which have been found in the most recent American research (cf. Solomon and Kendall 1975; Ward and Barcher 1975).

Marked sex differences rarely appear, but differences among pupils of similar initial achievement, but taught by different methods, are often quite marked. In all three attainment areas boys with low achievement on entry to formal classrooms underachieved, i.e. did not progress at the rate expected. This was not true of girls of a similar achievement level, who often over-achieved. At the other end of the scale pupils who had entered formal classrooms with a high level of achievement showed much greater progress than pupils of a similar achievement level in informal classrooms. Formal pupils were also superior to their counterparts in mixed classes in mathematics.

These findings will be disturbing to many teachers and parents since they indicate that the teaching approaches advocated by the Plowden Report, and many of the educational advisory staff and college lecturers, often result in poorer academic progress, particularly among high performance of low ability boys under formal teaching. It has been noted in other research that formal teaching can result in a widening of the achievement gap between the bright and not so bright pupils. Why this underachievement only occurs in boys is not clear.

The realism of these findings rests heavily on the validity of the measures used. As far as possible the measures chosen were specifically developed to take into account differences in teaching approach. As an added check one third of the teachers taking part in the study were interviewed after the data collection stage to acquire feedback on their perceptions of the conduct of the study. Two questions in the interview schedule are of relevance in this context. The teachers were asked 'Do you think that the attainment tests used were adequate measures of achievement? If not, why?' In reply every teacher thought that they were adequate although one or two felt that the reading test was fairly difficult for low ability pupils. Two teachers remarked that the mathematics test was particularly good in that it really did assess mathematical concepts – 'The children had to think and apply knowledge.'

Also gratifying was the finding that all the teachers said that the results on these tests were in line with what they had expected and tallied well with those from internal tests administered. There was only one exception to this where the scores from the reading test did not match too well those of an internal test in one class.

A common criticism of standardized tests is that they are, in some way, biased against informal teaching. The teachers were therefore asked the question 'Did you feel that the tests showed bias towards either formal or informal types of teaching?' One third felt that there was no bias, one sixth said they were biased towards informal teaching, and the rest that there was some degree of bias towards formal teaching. Some informal teachers felt that the bias was only apparent in the administrative procedures while others felt the bias to be 'very slight', or that it was only apparent in the English test.

The allegation of bias did not all come from informal teachers complaining that the tests favoured formal teaching. The opposite effect was also noted, i.e. formal teachers feeling that the tests might be biased towards informal methods.

In general this feedback would indicate that the teachers were happy with the choice of attainment tests, feeling that they accurately reflected the achievements of their children.

In order to encompass a wider range of pupil attainment, samples of imaginative and descriptive stories were also analysed. These analyses allowed an assessment of the equivocal link between creative writing and informal teaching, and also of the frequently heard criticism that informal teaching tends to depress skills in grammar, punctuation and spelling.

Each script was impression-marked by three teachers, one formal, one mixed and one informal, in order to achieve high reliability in the marking and also to partial out any systematic bias in marking which could be attributed to teaching style.

The findings were not altogether as expected. Girls produced better quality work than boys, a fairly common result among pupils of this age, but no difference was found in either story that could be attributed to a teaching style effect. The pupils in all types of classroom gained very similar marks.

A detailed category schedule was developed to investigate punctuation and spelling errors, and was used to mark the scripts of a matched sample of pupils from the three types of classroom. The results indicated that the frequency of punctuation errors was much smaller in the written work of formal and mixed pupils than in that of informal pupils. Spelling errors were divided into three categories and here the findings showed sex rather than teaching style disparities. Overall the frequency of spelling errors was slightly higher in the scripts of informal pupils but the differences were marginal.

The evidence suggests that formal and mixed pupils are better at punctuation, and no worse at creative or imaginative writing, than pupils in informal classes. The link between the quality of creative output and informality is not supported whereas that between formality and punctuation skills is. Creativity and formal grammar often seem to be incompatible objectives in the minds of many educationists, but from this evidence formal and mixed teachers appear to be achieving both.

As an aside it is worth noting how valuable the teachers found marking these scripts. This was spontaneously mentioned by two-thirds of the teachers in the interview. They found it particularly interesting to compare and contrast the work of their own pupils with work from similar classes elsewhere. It made one teacher reappraise her own approach, feeling that she had been 'stressing the creative use of language at the expense of use of imagination'. Primary school teachers rarely gain the opportunity to examine the work of pupils other than those in their own school. This approach might therefore be a useful one for in-service courses. Finally, on the debit side, one teacher criticized the stimulus for the imaginative story which she thought was not exciting enough.

Personality and progress

There is current concern about the effect of open plan schools on certain types of pupil and this concern is echoed in relation to informal teaching. The review of evidence pertaining to this problem clearly pointed to the fact that anxious, insecure children prefer, and perform better in, more structured environments. There was also some evidence that extroverted children cope more easily with less structured situations, and that motivation improves.

The findings on anxiety and motivation were supported in this study, and both showed a similar pattern. Degree of change was as expected in formal classrooms, less than expected in mixed and more than expected in informal classes. Motivation, in the form of attitudes to school and school work, does seem to improve under informal teaching, but at the expense of anxiety which also increases. This increase in anxiety can be interpreted in a number of ways, but perhaps the explanation of greatest theoretical validity is that a more nebulous structure, more often found in informal settings, is not conducive to the needs of many children. Indeed many adults react anxiously when placed in ambiguous situations.

However, the major purpose of the analyses was not to establish links between personality *traits* and academic progress, but to explain the relationships between *types* of pupils and their progress. Pupils who had a similar personality profile were therefore grouped together, producing eight personality types. It was then possible to answer the question 'Do pupils of the same personality type progress at similar rates under differing teaching styles?' The answer is unequivocally 'No.' Differences were noted among all types of pupil but particularly among those groups containing a larger proportion of high achievers, i.e. the motivated stable extroverts (type 1) and the 'saints' (type 8). But similar differences were also evident for the unmotivated stable extroverts (type 3) and motivated neurotics (type 4).

Teaching style clearly has a more powerful effect on progress than pupil personality does, since most pupil types show better progress under formal teaching. This is particularly noticeable among those pupils whose attributes include a high level of anxiety and neuroticism, who work harder and are more attentive under formal teaching. These findings suggest that formal teaching contains or controls the overt behavioural manifestations of personality whereas informal teaching allows or encourages them. This is no doubt because informal teachers wish to foster self-expression in their pupils, but it should be recognized that this seems to lead to more behaviour which tends to work against effective learning such as general social gossip, gazing into space or out of the window and various negative behaviours.

It would appear that a number of pupils cannot cope effectively in a less controlled setting, and are unable to accept the responsibility of self directed activity, if indeed they recognize or are told what this responsibility implies. For these pupils a decrease in teacher control often seems to lead to an increase in time wasting.

These results fit neatly into the underlying theoretical model adopted in this study. This model is expounded succinctly by Sells (1973), who argues that the utility of a personality model must be judged on the basis of its capacities to predict and explain behaviour. To do this effectively both the person and the setting in which the person is located must be specified. In Sell's scheme personality represents a unique set of behavioural repertoires consisting of patterns of traits and behaviour in settings, the latter being actual behaviours in the settings in which the person is functioning. He claims that settings limit the behaviours that can occur, and influence their occurrence. It is therefore useless to ascertain personality alone without any details of the setting. This model gains support from the findings presented here since the settings, i.e. formal or informal classrooms, have different influences upon the overt behaviour of pupils with similar personalities. This has obvious connotations for future research on the relationships between personality and school attainment.

Mechanisms of progress

The analyses of the different progress of pupils in the three general teaching styles show clearly the general efficacy of formal methods in the basic subjects. It was felt that these analyses may have been unfair to mixed teaching since this includes a more heterogeneous set of teaching approaches. Analyses were therefore computed for all seven teaching styles sampled, the results of which are less reliable because of smaller sample size. Nevertheless, they indicate that only three of the seven styles were associated with progress above that expected from initial achievement. These were the two formal styles and the mixed style which conjoined a form of integrated day with strict teacher control of content and pupils. Some mixed styles thus appear to be more effective than others.

It is therefore important to attempt to identify those factors within the classroom context which seem to be instrumental in creating these discrepancies in pupil progress. The observation of pupils' behaviour, which unfortunately had to be limited to formal and informal classrooms, provides some evidence on these factors. Pupils in formal classrooms engaged in work related activity much more frequently, the differences being most marked among pupils whose initial achievement level was high. Such children in informal classes engaged in the lowest amount of work related activity, preferring to talk about their work or indulging in purely social interaction. The same general pattern was also true of low achievers in informal classrooms, who engaged in significantly less work than pupils of a similar level in formal situations.

The same pattern also applies when differences in pupil personality are taken into account. All types of pupils engaged in more work activity in formal classrooms. Anxious pupils tended to work less than others but among these large discrepancies were noted in the two types of classroom. The motivated neurotic (type 4) pupils for example were observed to be working four times more often in the formal situation. On the other hand informal pupils interact more both in relation to their work and in general social gossip.

This suggests the juxtaposition low work-low performance in informal classrooms and high work-high performance in formal. Adams (1970a) has argued that 'education is empirically and theoretically bereft', but there is an emerging body of theory relating work activity and attention to academic performance which provides pointers to the likely mechanisms underlying differential pupil progress.

The basic propositions of this theory can be seen in the writings of Rothkopf and Anderson. Rothkopf (1970) contends that 'in most instructional situations what is learned depends largely on the activities of the student'. In other words it depends on the use made by students of the materials and learning experiences provided by the teacher. This accords with Anderson's (1970) general thesis that 'the activities the student engages in when confronted with instructional tasks are of crucial importance in determining what he will learn'. The propositions conform to an earlier model of school learning put forward by Carroll (1963), who contended that, everything else being equal, attainment mastery is determined by the opportunities provided by the teacher for a pupil to study a given content, and the use made of that opportunity by the pupil. This relationship has been investigated by Samuels and Turnure (1974) among six-year-olds, by McKinney and others (1975) among eight-year-olds, by Cobb (1972) among eleven-year-olds and by Lahaderne (1968) among twelve-year-olds. In each study a high correlation was found between work related activity and achievement. McKinney synthesized the findings of these studies and presented a picture of what he called the 'competent child', who is attentive, intelligent and task orientated.

Competence, defined in these terms, is likely to depend on the quality of the teacher-pupil interface since it is much easier for a child to be attentive and task orientated in a classroom in which the teacher imposes an unambiguous structure, as is often the case in formal approaches. In settings where the structure is more inchoate the pupil has the added burden of providing his own structure. Wiley and Harnishfeger (1975) recognize the duality of this effect in a recent paper.

As we conceive it the realities of teaching and learning and the ways in which we structure and understand them are the ways to fundamental policy issues in education. We strongly emphasize the focal role of the pupil and his pursuits as the commonly missing link in a chain mediating all influences on pupil acquisitions. We also stress the teacher as the second vital link. She is the major instrumentalit for curriculum implementation.

They, like Carroll, regard time on task as the crucial factor in attain ment, their approach deriving from two strong convictions. The first i: that 'the total amount of active learning time on a particular instructiona topic is *the* most important determinant of pupil achievement on tha topic', and the second that 'there is enormous variation in time fo learning for different pupils, their time devoted to specific learning topics. and their total amount of active learning time'. They further argue tha the investigation of learning time has been neglected – 'the usual fate of the obvious'.

Although this study did not set out to investigate the relationship between work activity and progress the results do, *ex post facto*, fit into this conceptual framework. They suggest that careful and clear structuring of activities together with a curriculum which emphasizes cognitive content are the keys to enhanced academic progress. These in fact are the two elements which differentiated the high gain informal classroom from the rest. The teacher was informal in attitude and behaviour, reflecting her type 2 classification (i.e. not the most informal group). But almost half of the classroom activities were on some aspect of English and mathematics, the structuring of which was clear and sequenced. It therefore seems to be curriculum emphasis and organization rather than classroom organiza tion factors such as seating, grouping, and degree of movement and talk, which are crucial to pupil performance. This is not to deny that the quality of the environment in which children work is important, merely to suggest that its effect may be relatively marginal in fostering learning. And learning, as Pluckrose (1975), a teacher dedicated to informal teaching, recently pointed out, is still 'the teacher's prime function'.

The relationships found would seem to require a restatement of the obvious – that it is important how pupils spend their time and on what, and what content and learning experiences the teacher provides. The impression gained is that many teachers base their practice on the line of the old song which runs 'It ain't what you do but the way that you do it', but for teaching and learning 'It is what you do, not the way that you do it' would seem more appropriate in the light of this evidence.

The consideration of the mechanisms underlying the superiority of pupil performance in formal classrooms has so far been limited to the behaviour patterns of pupils. These obviously interact with the actions of the teacher and in this context two other explanations are worth consider ing: firstly the possibility that the results may not reflect badly on informal methods themselves, but on the way these methods are put into practice; secondly – a different possibility – that the results accurately reflect the aims of informal teachers.

It seems generally accepted that to teach well informally is more difficult than to teach well formally. It requires a special sort of teacher to use informal methods effectively – one who is dedicated, highly organized, able to work flexibly, able to plan ahead and willing to spend a great deal of extra time in preparatory work. How many teachers do we have who could meet these specifications? Bantock was quoted in chapter 1 [not reprinted here] as being concerned about this problem, and Burt (1969) also alluded to it in his critique of informal methods:

With younger children, particularly those drawn from overcrowded homes in drab surroundings, they [informal methods] have at times undoubtedly achieved a conspicuous success: the duller pupils are surprisingly happy, and the brighter make remarkable progress. But these results are exceptional: they are the work of exceptional teachers provided with an exceptional amount of space and equipment – usually able and ingenious enthusiasts who have themselves devised the techniques they practise. But when copied by the young teacher fresh from college, the outcome, more often than not, is utter failure.

A supporter of the integrated day sounds the same warning:

The integrated day can be outstandingly successful; and it can be dismally bad. It is unfortunately a fact that when it does not work the results can be almost totally unprofitable for the children, and demoralizing and exhausting for the teacher. It is probably no exaggeration to say that with a more formal structure somebody is almost certain to learn something on the way, whereas with a disorganized Integrated Day it is perfectly possible for no child to make any real progress at all except that which comes about more or less by accident. (Taylor 1971)

Burt laid some of the blame on teacher training courses for substituting for work on teaching methods lectures on the principles of education, 'hammered home by a stock set of clichés and catchwords'. The education of teachers, like the education of children, would seem to need much closer examination. One is all too aware of the fate of the American progressive education movement when informal methods spread from the hands of the exceptional teacher in the university laboratory schools to the average teacher in the state system. It would be a pity if this extreme reaction were to happen in Britain.

The second explanation is that the poorer academic progress of informal pupils is an accurate reflection of the aims of informal teachers. It will be recalled that formal teachers stress academic aims while informal teachers prefer to stress the importance of self expression, enjoyment of school and the development of creativity. These aims are less easy to evaluate both for the teacher and the researcher, but the evidence that can be brought to bear on them would seem to argue that the aims are only partially achieved.

Creative arts were not investigated, but creative or imaginative writing proved to be no better in informal than formal classrooms, although it should be remembered that these data are weaker inferentially than those on academic progress. The aim for greater enjoyment of school does seem to have been fulfilled since attitudes to school and school work did show an improvement over the school year, but this was at the expense of an increase in anxiety.

It is difficult to know what specific outcomes informal teachers intend in developing self-expression. Informal pupils certainly interact more, but the benefits derived from this are not clear from the evidence gathered. Improvements in sociability and self-esteem are no different from those in formal schools, time wasting tends to be manifested more often and there is no academic pay-off, providing some support for the doubtful efficacy of 'learning by talking' commented upon by Froome (1975).

In summary, formal teaching fulfils its aim in the academic area without detriment to the social and emotional development of pupils, whereas informal teaching only partially fulfils its aims in the latter area as well as engendering comparatively poorer outcomes in academic development.

The central factor emerging from this study is that a degree of teacher direction is necessary, and that this direction needs to be carefully planned, and the learning experiences provided need to be clearly sequenced and structured. Experts in the fields of reading and mathematics have recently echoed this same view (Southgate 1973; Biggs 1973). It would seem less than useful for a teacher to stand by and leave a child alone in his enquiries hoping that something will happen. As Bruner (1961) pointed out, 'discovery, like surprise, favours a well prepared mind'.

This study has concentrated on what is rather than what ought to be. The latter is a much more difficult question since there is not, nor is there likely to be, consensus on what should constitute a primary education. Nevertheless it is hoped that the evidence presented will enable a more informed debate on primary school methods to be conducted. It is surely time to ignore the rhetoric which would have us believe that informal methods are pernicious and permissive, and that the most accurate description of formal methods is that found in Dickens's *Hard Times*.

If the key to effective progress lies in the direction and planning provided by teachers, then perhaps another 'ought' is for teachers, and the teachers of teachers, to submit their practices to critical scrutiny. To question critically the bases of one's accepted values and practices can be a disturbing process, but it is an essential one, not only for teachers, but also for the children whose education is the teacher's prime responsibility. In the words of Lady Plowden (1973), 'it is not sufficient to say "this is *what* we do", it is also necessary to know, and to be able to say "this is *why* we do it". It is this deeper understanding which needs to underlie what all teachers do.'

References

ADAMS, R. S. (1970) 'Perceived Teaching Styles', *Comparative Education Review*, 50–9, February 1970, pp. 39–40.

ANDERSON, R. C. (1970) 'Control of Student Mediating Process during Verbal Learning and Instruction', *Review of Educational Research*, Vol. 40.

ASHTON, P., KNEEN, P., DAVIES, F. and HOLLEY, B. J. (1975) *The Aims of Primary Education: A study of teachers' opinions*. London: Macmillan.

BIGGS, E. E. (1973) 'Forward and Back', *Education Three to Thirteen*, Vol. 1, October 1973, pp. 83–7.

BRUNER, J. S. (1961) 'The Act of Discovery', *Harvard Educational Review*.

BURT. C. (1969) 'The Mental Differences between Children', in COX, C. B. and DYSON, A. E. (eds) *Fight for Education: A Black Paper*. Critical Quarterly Society.

CARROLL, J. B. (1963) 'A Model of School Learning', *Teachers' College Record*, Vol. 64, pp. 723–33,

COBB, J. A. (1972) 'Relationship of Discrete Classroom Behaviours to Fourth Grade Academic Achievement', *Journal of Educational Psychology*, Vol. 63, pp. 74–80.

FROOME, S. (1975) 'Note of Dissent' in *A Language for Life* (the Bullock Report). London: HMSO.

LAHADERNE, H. M. (1968) 'Attitudinal and Intellectual Correlates of Attention: A study of four sixth grade classrooms', *Journal of Educational Psychology*, Vol. 59, pp. 320–4.

MCKINNEY, J. D., MASON, J., PERKERSON, K. and CLIFFORD, M. (1975) 'Relationship between behaviour and academic achievement', *Journal of Educational Psychology*, Vol. 67. pp. 198–203.

PLOWDEN REPORT (1967) *Children and their Primary Schools*. Report of the Central Advisory Council for Education (England). London: HMSO.

PLOWDEN, Lady (1973) 'Aims in Primary Education', *Education*.

PLUCKROSE, H. (1975) 'Openness is All', *Times Educational Supplement*, 10 October 1975.

ROTHKOPF, E. Z. (1970) 'The Concept of Mathematical Activities', *Review of Educational Research*, Vol. 40.

SAMUELS, S. J. and TURNURE, J. E. (1974) 'Attention and Reading Achievement in First Grade Boys and Girls', *Journal of Educational Psychology*, Vol. 66, pp. 29–32.

SELLS, S. B. (1973) 'Prescriptions for a Multivariate Model in Personality and Psychological Theory', in ROYCE, J. R. (ed.) *Multivariate Analysis and Psychological Theory*. New York: Academic Press.

SOLOMON, D. and KENDALL, A. J. (1975) 'Individual Characteristics and Children's Performance in Open and Traditional Classes'. Paper read at AERA annual conference, Washington.

SOUTHGATE, V. (1973) 'Reading: three to thirteen', *Education Three to Thirteen*, Vol. 1, April 1973, pp. 47–52.

TAYLOR, J. (1971) *Organizing and Integrating the Infant Day*. London: Allen and Unwin.

TREW, K. (1974) 'Classroom Practices in the Upper Primary School'. Internal report. Belfast: Northern Ireland Council for Educational Research.

WARD, W. D. and BARCHER, P. R. (1975) 'Reading Achievement and Creativity as related to Open Classroom Experience', *Journal of Educational Psychology*, Vol. 67.

WILEY, D. E. and HARNISHFEGER, A. (1975) 'Distinct Pupils, Distinctive Schooling: Individual differences in exposure to instructional activities'. Paper read at AERA annual conference, Washington.

2.9   A little learning is a dangerous thing: true or false?

Banesh Hoffmann

On the otherwise unmemorable day, Wednesday 18 March 1959, *The Times* of London printed the following letter to the editor:

Sir,—Among the 'odd one out' type of questions which my son had to answer for a school entrance examination was: 'Which is the odd one out among cricket, football, billiards, and hockey?'

I said billiards because it is the only one played indoors. A colleague says football because it is the only one in which the ball is not struck by an implement. A neighbour says cricket because in all the other games the object is to put the ball into a net; and my son, with the confidence of nine summers, plumps for hockey 'because it is the only one that is a girl's game'. Could any of your readers put me out of my misery by stating what is the correct answer, and further enlighten me by explaining how questions of this sort prove anything, especially when the scholar has merely to underline the odd one out without giving any reason?

Perhaps there is a remarkable subtlety behind it all. Is the question designed to test what a child of nine may or may not know about billiards – proficiency at which may still be regarded as the sign of a misspent youth?

Yours faithfully,

T. C. BATTY

This question of the four sports makes a fascinating party game. There are many reasons for picking the various answers, and one had only to read the question aloud to start a party off in high gear, with everyone joining in the fun. Any number can play. There is only one drawback: after a while the fun suddenly stops and the party becomes indignantly serious. This happens as soon as someone asks what sense there is in giving children such questions on tests; for then, right away, the fat is in the fire. Parents begin recalling similar questions that their own children had on tests. College students complain that such questions are by no means confined to children. Graduate students and older people push the age limit higher as they recount their own experiences. And soon there is an awed realization that there may, in fact, be no age limit at all.

But before the party reaches this solemn stage – and before this book does – there is fun to be had. Even the staid London *Times* could not resist enjoying it. On 19 March, the day after the appearance of Mr Batty's letter, it printed the following two letters, in this order, without comment:

Sir,—'Billiards' is the obvious answer . . . because it is the only one of the games listed which is not a team game.

Source: HOFFMANN, B. (1962) *The Tyranny of Testing*. New York: Crowell-Collier reissued 1978 by Greenwood Press, Westport, Conn., pp. 17–20 and 67–73.

Because the answer is so simple and does not require the child answering it to have a detailed knowledge of the games referred to, I should have thought it a very suitable question for an intelligence test.

Sir,— . . . football is the odd one out because . . . it is played with an inflated ball as compared with the solid ball used in each of the other three [games].

At this stage I managed to tie myself into an intellectual knot that still has me slightly bewildered. When I had read these letters it seemed to me that good cases had been made for football and billiards, and that the case for cricket was particularly clever, but that the case for hockey was dubious at best. At first I thought this made hockey easily the worst of the four choices and, in effect, ruled it out. But then I realized that the very fact that hockey was the only one that could be thus ruled out gave it so striking a quality of separateness as to make it an excellent answer after all – perhaps the best.

Fortunately for my peace of mind, it soon occurred to me that hockey is the only one of the four games that is played with a curved implement. But what if I had not thought of that? The problem haunts me still.

In the meantime, *The Times* had not been idle. On 20 March it published the following letter from an eminent philosopher:

Sir,—Mr T. C. Batty . . . has put his finger on what has long been a matter of great amusement to me. Of the four – cricket, football, billiards, hockey – each is unique in a multitude of respects. For example, billiards is the only one in which the colour of the balls matters, the only one played with more than one ball at once, the only one played on a green cloth and not on a field, the only one whose name has more than eight letters in it. Hockey is the only one ending in a vowel. And so with each of the others.

It seems to me that those who have been responsible for inventing this kind of brain teaser have been ignorant of the elementary philosophical fact that every thing is at once unique and a member of a wider class. Mr Batty's son, in his school class, could be underlined as the only member who was Mr Batty's son. Similarly with every member of his class.

The next day *The Times* printed a tongue-in-cheek letter of typically British insularity, based as it was on the purely amateur status of hockey in the British Isles:

Quite clearly 'hockey' is the correct answer. . . . Every child should know that of the four games quoted hockey is the only example of one which, at present, no player is ever paid to play. The examiners are plainly anxious to discover how aware the child is of the problems of choosing a career.

Finally, after a day of meditative silence, *The Times* grew more serious and printed this letter:

Sir,—In reply to Mr Batty's letter . . . I wonder if he would be interested in the results I obtained from a class of eleven-year-old children of more than average intelligence and who recently sat for the common entrance examination for secondary education?

I asked them to choose the 'odd one out' and then to give their reasons for doing so. The results were as follows:—Football 18, Billiards 17, Hockey 3, Cricket 1.

The reasons they gave were mainly those already submitted by Mr Batty.

I agree with your correspondent and wonder how far this question and questions of a similar nature are a true and reliable guide in the testing of intelligence.

Having enjoyed its romp and returned full circle to the crucial, fun-dampening question, *The Times* dropped the whole topic from its letter columns. The incident was over, and an opportunity for action had been lost. [. . .]

[This raises the problem of how, if at all, ambiguity in test questions of this kind can be avoided.] [. . .]

The quickest way to understand the virtual inevitability of ambiguity in multiple-choice tests is to try making up a multiple-choice question.

Suppose we try it here. We can even use the above sentence. It is not a very good one, and I am not suggesting that reputable test-makers would be likely to use it. But it is well suited to our present purpose, which is to show how the multiple-choice format exerts its influence on the test-maker. Let us convert the sentence into a multiple-choice question of the sentence-completion type. We merely leave out a word and offer five choices for filling the gap, like this:

The quickest way to understand the .... inevitability of ambiguity in multiple-choice tests is to try making up a multiple-choice question.

        (A) ....
        (B) virtual
        (C) ....
        (D) ....
        (E) ....

That seems simple enough. All we have to do is to think of four words for the wrong choices, A, C, D, and E.

We might try (A) rainy, (C) loving, (D) blonde, (E) cosy. But these words obviously do not fit the sentence at all. They make the question too easy. Besides, as any competent psychologist would quickly realize, they betray that our mind was not on our work: we have been unconsciously making free associations, stimulated by the word *virtual*.

So, back to work. We do not want to make the question trivially obvious. How can we make it difficult? One way is to use relatively obscure words , for example: (A) anti-phonal, (C) unifoliate, (D) succinic, (E) refrangible. Now we have a harder question – quite a difficult one, it would seem. Yet a person who knows what these four words mean will find it as simple as before. None of them is in the least relevant. Indeed, even a person who does not know the meanings of these four words may well recognize the word *virtual*, see that it obviously fits, and so take a guess that the others do not.

We had better try again. What we want are relatively well known words that will entice the weaker students away from the wanted answer, *virtual*, by the very plausibility with which they seem to fit into the gap in the sentence. Finding them takes some thought. After a while we may come up with the following: (A) equal, (C) simple, (D) sinister, (E) emotional. Each of these words yields a quite plausible sentence. But none makes as good a sentence as *virtual* does. None is the 'best' answer. So at last we have a good multiple-choice question that will discriminate between the good and the bad students.

But have we? What makes us so sure that *virtual* makes the 'best' sentence? Could it not be the fact that we have known all along what the sentence actually was? If we look at the sentence less subjectively, with less pride of authorship, trying to forget that the word we deleted was *virtual*, we begin to wonder whether *virtual* really does make the 'best' sentence. *Sinister* would change the meaning of the sentence *as we had conceived it*, but it would nevertheless make an excellent sentence (certainly a more powerful one – 'the sinister inevitability' is strong stuff), and if a sense of the sinister is what the sentence was meant to convey, a much better one.

The candidate does not know that we had *virtual* in mind. He comes to the questions with no preconceptions as to the intended meaning of the sentence. To him *sinister* may seem particularly apt.

He may also regard *emotional* as a strong candidate. And he may approve the quiet power of the sentence that results from using the word *simple*. As for *equal*, it gives the sentence yet another nuance of meaning, and he must make up his mind whether the fact that the sentence then requires a preceding sentence for its meaning to be complete is a valid reason for rejecting *equal* or not.

In trying to make our question difficult, we have made it ambiguous. Of course, we are just amateurs. But the professionals face the same problem we did. And their solution is too often the same as ours: to create a spurious difficulty by introducing ambiguity. They have an advantage over us. They can try their questions out and look for statistical indications of ambiguity. But these indications are of limited value.

It is not without significance that the professional testers refer to the 'wrong' answers as 'distractors', 'misleads', and 'decoys'. The decoys are deliberately designed to seem plausible. They are, in fact, deliberate traps. Were they always traps baited with definitely spurious bait one might tolerate them, even though their presence gives the test an air of trickery and deception that is not altogether becoming. But too often the traps are baited unfairly. For it is difficult to draw a sharp line between legitimate wile and illegitimate deceit, and the temptation to trespass on the shadowy no-man's-land between the two is hard to resist. (Harder, even, than the temptation to change metaphors in mid-argument.)

Purely factual questions can be made difficult by merely using obscure, unimportant facts. Making genuinely difficult multiple-choice questions by other means is far from easy, and, under pressure to produce many hard questions, the test-makers tend to succumb to the lure of ambiguity.

How difficult it is to produce a hard multiple-choice question that has precisely one good answer and is free from ambiguity, can be seen from the following question, which was made up by a psychologist as part of a test in a college course in psychology:

A scientific hypothesis must be

    A. true
    B. capable of being proven true
    C. capable of being proven false
    D. none of these

While a psychologist is not necessarily an expert in the art of making up multiple-choice tests, he must be classified as somewhat more than a rank amateur. The above question was designed to test whether the student understood the nature of scientific 'proof', the idea being that while experimental verifications of a hypothesis serve to bolster faith in the truth of the hypothesis they can not *prove* the hypothesis true, whereas a single experiment can suffice to prove a hypothesis false. Thus the wanted answer was C. And when we know what is in the tester's mind the question, at first sight, seems quite a good one. Certainly, in this case there was no deliberate attempt to be ambiguous.

When we do not know what the tester had in mind, though, the question can be puzzling. And if we examine it carefully we find in it all sorts of unsuspected defects.

For example, *mathematical* hypotheses are neither true nor false. They are just hypotheses – axioms on which to build a mathematical structure. Thus neither the wanted answer, C, nor answer A, nor answer B would be valid here, and the best answer would seem to be D. However, one can argue in rebuttal that the phrase 'a scientific hypothesis' was not meant to include mathematical ones, any more than it was meant to include purely logical ones. Let us proceed, then, to other difficulties.

We can imagine a scientist accidentally hitting on a true scientific hypothesis. He may not be able to prove it true, but it could be true none the less. Such a scientific hypothesis could not be proved false. Thus in this particular case answer C would be incorrect; and the word *must* in the question therefore makes answer C in principle incorrect. Once more we seem to be led to answer D.

Again, we can make hypotheses using perhapsy, telltale words; for example, that *some* objects fall towards the earth. Such a scientific hypothesis can certainly be proved true, and can certainly not be proved false.

Even worse, if we prove a scientific hypothesis false, we automatically prove the negative of the hypothesis true, and the negative is itself a scientific hypothesis. So, because of the word *must*, answer C can not be valid – or so it would seem. Yet 'a scientific hypothesis' is ambiguous. Does it mean every scientific hypothesis or just some particular scientific hypothesis? We have automatically been assuming the former. But if we assume the latter, then both answer B and answer C can be justified.

The safest course – though it would actually have led to a zero score on the question – would seem to be to pick answer D. We can, moreover, justify answer D on verbalistic grounds. For no one would deny that a scientific hypothesis *must* be 'a scientific hypothesis' and this is neither answer A, nor B, nor C. Therefore it is 'none of these'.

And yet there is even difficulty with answer D, because of its poor wording. The usual phrasing of such answers is something like 'none of the above' or 'none of the others'. If answer D means this, it is the best answer, though it is not the wanted answer. Even so it is a poor answer, since we have no idea what a scientific hypothesis *must* be – beyond being a scientific hypothesis, this being in fact the deepest justification for answer D that we have given. But what if the phrase 'none of these' includes answer D itself, as well it might? Then we have a pretty puzzle. For we can argue that a scientific hypothesis *must* be 'none of these' if only because it *must* be a scientific hypothesis, but it can not be D because D is *one* of these. The logic here is not impeccable, but let us leave that to the professional logicians. We have seen, at least, that there can be more to a multiple-choice question than the test-maker imagines, and we can draw two morals, one for the test-maker, whether amateur or professional, and the other for the test-taker. For the former: you can not be too careful about wording – or about choice of answer. And, for the latter, the sort of advice that teachers find themselves having to give to students before they take multiple-choice tests: when in doubt, don't think – just pick.

In discussing the above question we have pushed the argument rather far, for there is no clear line of demarcation between what is cogent and what is not. Here this fact is of small moment. But on a multiple-choice test the decision as to what to regard as cogent can be crucial, making the difference between choosing a wanted answer and choosing an unwanted one. And because test-makers use different standards of cogency, relevance, subtlety, depth, and intellectual rigor in different questions on a multiple-choice test, the candidate can have no reasonable assurance that he is accurately gauging the tester's standard on any particular question.

When told that a particular multiple-choice question is vague or ambiguous, testers sometimes argue that the candidate is expected to recognize the context of the question. In so doing they seem not to realize that they are confirming that the candidate is expected to fathom what is in the tester's mind. Students are well aware that they are expected somehow to do this, though: among themselves they call these tests not 'multiple-choice' but 'multiple-guess'.

2.10   The side-effects of assessment

Derek Rowntree

The Competitive Aspects of Assessment

The side-effects of learning for the sake of extrinsic rewards are bad enough. But what when these extrinsic rewards are in short supply? When there are not enough to go round? The side-effects are then worsened by competition. In one sense, of course, there is more than enough knowledge available for everyone to have a sufficiency. As Robert Paul Wolff (1969, p. 66) points out: 'The Pythagorean theorem does not flicker and grow dim as more and more minds embrace it.' Learning is a 'free commodity'. But only so long as we are thinking of knowledge as a source of intrinsic, expressive rewards. Think instead of 'approved' knowledge, legitimated and reified as GCE 'passes', admissions to college, university degrees, and the like. No longer is the supply unlimited. For one person to get more, another must make do with less. A great many assessment systems are competitive in that the extrinsic rewards they offer are in short supply and each student who wants them is asked to demonstrate that he is more deserving than others, or others less deserving than he is.

Contesting with others over the extrinsic spoils of learning is one aspect of competitive assessment. Another, upon which it depends and which usually arises early in a child's educational career, before the extrinsic rewards have become so tangible and external, is his teacher's public comparison of one student with another. A child will not have been in school many days before he is made aware of individual differences among his classmates. Roy Nash (1973, p. 17) discovered that pupils as young as eight years were able to say which children in the class were better than them at reading, writing and number; and their self-perceived class rank correlated highly with the rankings made by the teacher at the researcher's request (and therefore not explicitly available hitherto for communication to the children).

Such awareness can encourage learning that is motivated (extrinsically) by what John Holt called 'the ignoble satisfaction of feeling that one is better than someone else'. Jules Henry (1969) describes how a classroom atmosphere of competitive assessment fosters such a tendency. Eleven-year-old Boris is out at the blackboard publicly trying to simplify a fraction while his teacher is being excruciatingly patient and restraining the rest of the class who are bursting to put Boris right. Boris is mentally paralysed by the situation, however. So teacher finally asks Peggy, who can be relied on to know the correct answer.

Source: ROWNTREE, D. (1977) *Assessing Students: How Shall we Know Them?* London, Harper and Row, pp. 51–61, 64 and 68–71.

Thus Boris' failure has made it possible for Peggy to succeed: his depression is the price of her exhilaration, his misery is the occasion of her rejoicing. This is the standard condition of the American elementary school.... To a Zuni, Hopi, or Dakota Indian, Peggy's performance would seem cruel beyond belief, for competition, the wringing of success from somebody's failure, is a form of torture foreign to those noncompetitive Indians.... (p. 83)

But why should it be that Peggy gets a lift from knowing that she has 'beaten' Boris? To say that she has been publicly compared with him and proved superior in fraction-simplification is insufficiently explanatory. No doubt the teacher too is superior but she would hardly be expected to feel joyful on that account. Why, for instance, does Peggy not get satisfaction instead from trying to eradicate the difference between herself and Boris, e.g. by helping him reach the answer himself rather than telling him? And if she has already enjoyed the satisfaction of having climbed a new standard of proficiency, higher than she has been before, why should she care one way or another to know that others have not yet reached this standard? Perhaps the reason is that she has been persuaded that teacher-approval, and whatever other more tangible extrinsic rewards may follow, are in short supply and to gain what she needs she must not simply (or even necessarily) improve but also get (or merely stay) ahead of others.

Students generally have been led to believe that they cannot all achieve a worthwhile level of learning. They, and for the most part their teachers, often assume that only a few can do very well, the majority doing moderately only, and a few doing poorly or even failing. This expectation is seen institutionalized among teachers who 'grade on the curve'. (The practice is to be found in education everywhere, although the terminology is American – see Terwilliger 1971, pp. 74–100 for a discussion of this and related techniques.) Such teachers, marking students' work with, say, the grades 'A', 'B', 'C', 'D', 'F', will set out with a predetermined grade-distribution in mind. ('E' is often skipped over because by 'happy' coincidence, the next letter is the initial letter of failure!) Among 100 students, for example, they may expect to award about 10 A's, 20 'B's, 40 'C's, 20 'D's and 10 'F's. (Figure 1 shows this expected distribution graphically – and also the underlying 'normal distribution curve' from which the method gets its name.) The teacher who is 'grading on the curve' may, on marking a given set of students, allow himself to vary the proportions slightly. But he would likely feel uneasy if, say, twice as many students as expected appeared to deserve an 'A' or a 'B'. He might also fear being reproached by colleagues for lowering standards. Some teachers guard against this by making it a principle *never* to award an 'A'. According to a French adage quoted by Remi Clignet (1974, p. 349), the maximum '20 is given only to God, 19 to his saints, 18 to the professor's professor, 17 to the professor himself' – so the student of French composition can't be expected to score more than 16!'

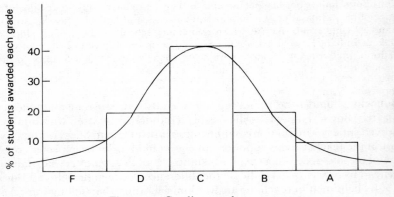

Figure 1   Grading on the curve

The expectation that students with 'A' or 'B' (or their equivalents in other systems for dispensing approval) will be in the minority has a strong hold in classrooms. Too easily it becomes a self-fulfilling prophecy: 'We can't expect the majority of students to do very well – so don't blame us for the failures.' When year after year the General Nursing Council failed one-third of candidates taking SRN examinations after three years of preparation, few questioned the proportion (*Nursing Times* 1972). Fear of passing too many students is still preventing the Esperanto Teachers' Association from getting Esperanto examined as a GCE O level subject. They are told the language is 'too easy'. Too many students would get top grades.

The competitive nature of public examinations was brutally brought home to me a few years ago when I was first impressed by the instructional potential of programmed learning. In an excess of enthusiasm I suggested to a GCE examiner that with the help of well-written programmes, we'd soon enable nearly all students to pass O-level mathematics. 'Oh no you won't,' he said, 'we'll just raise the standard.' Conversely, the Black Paper pessimist (see Pollard 1971) can accuse this same self-fulfilling mechanism of disguising the fact that standards are falling as the quality of candidates declines!

Such viewpoints I have since found elaborated in Brereton (1944) who records, almost as an educational 'law', that: 'the standard of an examination adjusts itself to the standard of those taking it' (p. 43). While suggesting the possibility that, as a result of the war, children may become more aware of and more knowledgeable about geography, he considers it obvious that School Certificate examinations should continue to give credit only to about half the candidates. He justifies this implicit raising of the required standard partly in order to encourage pupils to continue caring about geography lessons (as opposed to reading the newspapers) and partly because it would be unfair to give pupils taking geography a better chance of reaching university than pupils taking, say, physics under the war-time difficulties caused by shortage of laboratories and physics teachers.

In such situations – where the best X% of students are to get the 'A's, the next best nX% the 'B's, and so on – the grade awarded to a student depends not on the absolute level of performance he attains but on how he performs *relative to* other students. That is, he may improve his performance by 100 per cent, but if everyone else improves similarly his grade will be no higher than before. To get a better grade he must take it from one of the students above him by out-performing him.

What are the side-effects of an assessment system believed by students (whether rightly or wrongly) to be competitive? For most students they are centred in the need to come to terms with failure. The psychiatrist Ronald Laing suggested once that 'to be a success in our society one has to learn to dream of failure'. And Bergman's film *Wild Strawberries* shows us an elderly professor at the peak of his career, about to receive the highest academic honour in the land, who dreams the night before of failing an examination.

For a few to emerge as outstandingly successful the majority must fail – to varying degrees. The failure may be only partial. Indeed, had the student been in a different (e.g. less selective) school or college, his performance might well have made him a success. But, by comparison with those he has been led to emulate, he has fallen short. Of course, it should be possible for a student who has 'failed' at one learning task to compensate by his success on another task. Unfortunately, the ethos of competitive assessment often leads the student who has failed on a few tasks (e.g. learned more slowly than other people) to feel that he has failed *as a person*. As a 'failure' himself he may then become less capable of succeeding in subsequent tasks. His only consolation may be that most of his friends will soon be those who are failing at about the same level as he is. Between them they may be able to construct mutually defensive attitudes to those above them and those (if any) below them in the hierarchy.

These defensive attitudes, based on fear, envy, resentment and self-hatred, may be of various kinds. The least active response is what Philip Jackson (1968, p. 27) describes as 'devaluing the evaluations to the point where they no longer matter very much'. Perhaps this attitude of 'cooling it', 'turning off', 'keeping his head down', 'disengaging' on the part of the failing student is a special case of what Roy Cox (1967) had in mind when he said: 'It is clear that where students are assessed in a way which is not seen to be relevant to what they are aiming at they will tend to distort and degrade the assessment so that it does not become a source of esteem.'

More actively, students who cannot 'adjust' equably to being labelled 'failures' may seek alternative sources of esteem. Perhaps through their attempts to pull school (or society) apart out of hours. As Dr Samuel

Johnson pointed out: 'By exciting emulation and comparisons of superiority, you lay the foundation of lasting mischief; you make brothers and sisters hate each other.' A US Senate subcommittee survey of 1975 reports the case of a seventeen-year-old Detroit schoolgirl who was awarded massive damages after being beaten up and stabbed with pencils by thirty girl classmates who apparently resented that she was more attractive than they and received better grades. This case may be an example, more physical than usual, of what Arnold Wesker calls 'Lilliputianism – the poisonous need to cut other people down to size'. Who knows how much of the physical damage done to property and people arises out of the resentment and frustration smouldering on from school-days? (See Hargreaves 1967, and Lacey 1970, for accounts of the 'D'-stream sub-culture in secondary schools.)

Peter Vandome and his colleagues (1972) neatly sum up some of the pernicious side-effects of competitive assessment at college level:

Students feel they will gain through the poor performance of others and suffer by imparting their own knowledge to fellow students. In this way, a potentially rich source of knowledge – communication of ideas among students – tends to be stifled. To the extent that it does take place, any exchange is biased by the way in which a student's 'self-image' and his image of his fellows is affected by their grades. A 50 per cent student for instance will think twice before putting forward one of his ideas for discussion with a group of 60 per cent students. This is relevant not only to informal interchange between students but also to tutorial discussion. Competitive rather than cooperative behaviour may be manifested in other ways such as the 'illegal borrowing' of library books.

Sadly, teachers too are sometimes caught up in a competitive assessment system – perhaps even as beneficiaries. While the students compete for honours within their class, the teacher may be looking to the class as a whole, competing with other teachers' classes, to bring *him* esteem and promotion. The following quotation from Norman Conway, a grammar school chemistry teacher interviewed by Brian Jackson and Dennis Marsden (1962), shows how the competition for scarce university places (and ultimately for a better job for teacher), especially in the context of bureaucratic mass-assessment which is what we are going on to look at in the next section, can allow the instrumental pursuit of extrinsic rewards to drive out the expressive 'educational side':

I reckon I can do A level chem. in four terms. Four terms flat out mind. We have to go really fast. We have tests twice a week, but we get the results. For instance, last year I got an open at Pembroke, Cambridge, and an exhibition at Trinity Hall Cambridge, and then I got half-a-dozen places. I've got fourteen places in the last two years and then these opens. I do pretty well; my results are all right. The way we teach, we teach for results. I want the passes, the schols and all those things. Tests all the time, and scrub the teaching methods, forget about the educational side .... What I want now is a head of department in a really good school, and then I'd do what our head of department has done. I'd put on the pressure, really hard. Really work those children, tests, tests, tests, and get the results. Get them the results they should have, and that would establish me, wouldn't it? It would give me a reputation. People would know that I could do the job. I might slacken off when I got established – perhaps after ten years or so. I might start looking round and thinking more about the educational side. But you've got to establish yourself first, haven't you? (pp. 36–7)

The bureaucratic aspects of assessment

When is assessment bureaucratic? Consider an extreme scenario: You have been summonsed to appear in court, some months in the future, to be tried on a number of offences which you may or may not have committed prior to your trial. In due course, you arrive in court only to find it empty of judge, jury and counsel. Nothing but a tape-recorder and a set of instructions await you. You are instructed to defend yourself as best you can on a number of standard charges within a strictly limited time-period. You are not told the precise nature of the evidence against you. Nor do you know sufficient about the alleged nature of the offences to be quite sure what evidence would count best in your defence. Judgment is to be made on the basis of the tape-recorded defences you leave behind. You have no idea who laid the charges against you in the first place; nor, when the verdict of the court is mailed to you some weeks later, do you know who made the judgment and decided the various restrictions that are to be imposed on your future movements. There is no means of appeal. Your only consolation is that thousands of others are being judged by identical process.

I do not need to point out all the parallels between this Kafkaesque experience and that of the candidate in a public examination. The feature I am interested in at present is its *impersonality*. It is impersonal in two senses. Firstly, in that you cannot identify the persons who are assessing you. Secondly, in that they, whoever they are, choose not to regard you as an individual or meet you personally to hear your case.

Norman Morris (1969) neatly exposes the bureaucratic approach: '. . . as likely as not the examiner has no interest in us as individuals. He is merely assessing us in order to maintain the efficiency of something else. In this sense the examination is an instrument of policy, designed to preserve a preconceived standard elsewhere.' Bureaucracies deal in huge numbers, following laws, formulating policies, seeking objectivity, preferring standardized routines, disliking exceptions and special cases, venerating, above all, administrative convenience. They are not normally staffed – whether in government, the health service, big business, the armed services, the trade union movement, education, or whatever – by people who take pleasure in celebrating the quirky individualities of other persons.

In their study of assessment in a university, Carolyn Miller and Malcolm Parlett (1973) explicitly distinguish between the 'bureaucratic' and

the 'personalized' style. They see the predominant style as reflecting th
extent to which the teaching-learning setting is impersonal or personal:

In the first setting, for instance, the tutor (who was the only individual to know
student's work in any detail) neither set nor marked the exam papers of h
students. The student did not know who his examiner was. And the tutors, thoug
they got to know their students 'quite well' were still often surprised by results tha
struck them as 'odd'. In the constrasting setting . . . , the lecturer was also interna
examiner, setting and marking student's papers while having a clear idea of th
abilities, interests and previous performances of the students. Moreover, th
student knew who the examiner was, (and in some cases also the name of th
external examiner). (p. 15)

The Open University operates a highly bureaucratic assessmer
system, combining both continuous assessment and examinations. A
intervals during his course, the student sends in his assignments to th
University's headquarters. These assignments may be objective tests fc
marking by the computer, or they may be essays for marking by a huma
tutor. The student may or may not be in occasional face-to-face, c
telephonic, contact with the tutor who marks his assignments. Thousand
of students, up and down the nation, may all have been faced by the sam
assignment questions at the same time, though they may have bee
offered some limited choice. Examinations are compulsory even for
course that is the equivalent of less than a term in a 'conventiona
university. Students produce answer-papers under normal test condition
and their papers are sent off to a set of markers who do not know th
student's previous work and who give him no feedback at all, though it i
usually possible for him to work out his overall grade on the exam. Th
bureaucracy generated by the need to cope centrally with tens c
thousands of 'remote' students is tempered with considerable humanit
by the tutorial and counselling staff spread around the Open University'
thirteen regions. As one senior counsellor, David Kennedy (1973), cau
tions: 'this University, with its complex academic and administrativ
processes, will grow in moral stature only to the degree it indulges i
self-questioning and heart-searching over the fall of even one sparrow
(p. 1).

But, by and large, bureaucratic assessment is less the rule in a student
university years than in those examination-dominated years immediatel
preceding them. (See Montgomery 1965, for a history of English examir
ations as 'administrative devices'.) In Britain nowadays, the student i
first likely to become aware of bureaucratic assessment as he approache
the age of 'sixteen-plus'. Here, if he is considered a likely candidate, he wi
prepare for the examinations leading to a Certificate of Secondary Educa
tion or General Certificate of Education (ordinary level) – one 'certificate
for each subject he 'passes'. This sixteen-plus assessment is big busines:
In the summer of 1974 more than 800,000 GCE candidates were takin
more than 2¼ million subject papers between them. (In the same yea
rather fewer CSE candidates generated almost as many subject entries.

All the GCE students' scripts (and most of the CSE scripts) have, of course, to be routed around Britain to the 'out-workers' who do the marking, and eventually results have to be returned to the students. The postal bill must be enormous for the annually growing traffic of items, and it is scarcely surprising that one GCE examining board alone (and there are eight) has an annual expenditure well over £2¼ million. Naturally figures like this would pale into insignificance beside those current in the United States where mass testing supports a multi-million dollar test-publishing industry. One non-profit organization alone – Educational Testing Service, whose battery of tests and examinations helps control entry to the US meritocracy – has an annual income of $50 million (see Rein 1974). Yet size in itself is not a feature that damns the system. Giants can be benign. And large numbers of sixteen-year-olds could be satisfactorily assessed, for all reasonable purposes, without suffering the baleful effects of this particular giant system. No, these side-effects spring not so much from size as from *standardization*. In its zeal to claim comparability between large numbers of candidates (though the need would still arise, if less painfully, were there only two candidates), the examining authority imposes uniform conditions on candidates. (We won't examine you in Esperanto because it doesn't reach the same standard of difficulty as other languages. We won't examine you in anything except on our standard syllabus. We won't examine you at all if you have left school and are studying the syllabus under non-standard conditions.) The underlying assumptions are laid bare by Oppenheim *et al* (1967) who, although explicitly referring to university examinations, might well be analysing the sixteen-plus:

Behind this lies the ideology of 'equality of opportunity', so that all students have an equal chance to fail, to pass or to distinguish between themselves. This uniformity is somewhat mitigated by allowing students a *choice* of questions. This practice makes very little allowance for the individual patterns of growth and interests of candidates. (In some cases we *do* set individual examinations for *higher* degrees.)

The ideology of 'equality of opportunity' is itself part of broader ideas about fair play – all students must receive equal tuition, and sit for the same examinations, with no favours. This attitude is reinforced by the power of universities to bestow social mobility. The question is always: is this examination practice fair to other students? and not: is this practice fair to this particular student?

The reality of this last dilemma is well-caught in the example posed by Brereton (p. 54) who seems to settle for unfairly devaluing the knowledge of geography students in order not to be unfair to physics students. The 'fairness to whom' criterion is an important one when we consider the main bastion of standardized, bureaucratic assessment – the uniform syllabus.

To treat people equally is not necessarily to treat them fairly. Indeed, people being so different, equal treatment probably means injustice for most. If I wish to offer myself as a candidate for an O-level GCE in law, I

must demonstrate my ability on the same set of syllabus topics as everyon
else. Are these the only topics that could be considered to constitute 'law'
No, there are many viable ways of construing the subject. Then why can't I (and al
others who care to) choose a set of viable topics to suit my own interests
Because this might give you an advantage over others who tackle the set syllabus an
would anyway make you difficult to compare with others, especially if everyone did it
So we must all forgo the chance of being assessed on what most interests u
and what we are most likely to be best at? *Yes, but it's the same for everybody.* I
doesn't seem fair. *Perhaps it's not fair to individuals, but it's fair to students as*
whole.

Of course, the standard examination syllabus has long been accused c
providing a mechanism whereby the ruling interests in society can defin
what is to count as knowledge – and determine what is learned. Thorstei
Veblen (1918) cannot have been the first to identify industrial leaders a
the real clients of the university and claim that the pressure for examin
ations and grading arises out of their need for a bureaucratically efficien
estimate of graduates' usability. Similarly, the universities, who contro
most of the GCE exam boards, have traditionally been chided fo
imposing criteria appropriate to university selection not only on likel
applicants, but also, through syllabus uniformity, on students who hav
no intention of ever going near a university. 'Why should the curriculur
of the rest be determined so largely by that required for the universit
students?' asked C. W. Valentine (1938) at a time when only about 5 pe
cent of secondary school pupils went on to university. (Even withi
universities it is sometimes claimed that a syllabus is geared not to th
needs of the majority of students but to those of the precious few who wi
go on to become researchers.)

Nowadays the same examinations are used, as Harry Judge (1974
points out: 'to assist everybody to select everybody else for everything' (
47). The lure of a prestigious standard examination syllabus is strong
William Taylor (1963) shows how it helped subvert the new ideas for
'secondary modern' curriculum as, in all fairness, schools began enterin
their pupils, who had failed the eleven-plus, for GCE. The need fo
external recognition fed upon itself, more and more examination wor
was demanded, traditional subjects and teaching methods regaine
dominance, streaming and segregation fostered success-rates, an
thus secondary modern schools largely failed to develop an identit
separate from the grammar schools whose assessment procedures the
were aping. [...]

We have scarcely yet begun to search for ways of coming to know wha
the student can do (let alone what he is) rather than whether he can d
certain standardized tasks. Elliott Eisner (1972, p. 211) reminds us tha
'It's one thing to ask, "Did the student learn what (he or I) intended?" It i
another to ask, "What did the student learn?"' One thing we can be sur
of is that such enlightened assessing is likely to cost a great deal more tha
the current methods. It may well not even be possible on principle, if th

bureaucratic ideals of uniform procedures and impersonal 'objective' standards are to be adhered to. [...]

The giving of grades

Much of the criticism of assessment is aimed at 'the grading system'. Thus we might expect to find that the giving of grades has a crop of side-effects peculiarly its own. This, however, is not the case. The side-effects usually blamed on grades are, in fact, those we have already seen associated with other aspects of assessment systems – emphasis on the easily-measured, unfairness, standardization, competition, extrinsic rewards. The giving of grades no doubt aggravates and facilitates such effects but mostly they could survive in its absence. So are grades an empty symbol, guilty by association but harmless in themselves? Not quite. Their special 'sin' is simply less obvious, being one of omission. (Remember Sherlock Holmes's clue of the dog that *didn't* bark in the night?) Grades are more to be blamed for what they don't do than for what they do do.

And what grades don't do is tell all that is known about the student's performance or abilities. Information is lost. Consider the assessment process. Someone – teacher, examiner, 'assessor' – observes the student at work, or perhaps interacts with him in some way, or more commonly analyses products of the student's work. The assessor forms impressions of the qualities and attainments discernible in the student's work – his interests and aversions, hang-ups and hobby-horses, strengths and weaknesses. These impressions he could perhaps spell out, verbalizing them for the benefit of the student and anyone else who has a legitimate interest in knowing how the student is seen by people close to him. Sometimes he will do this for an individual assessment event (e.g. in commenting on an essay):

You have shown a general understanding of the assignment, but could have improved your answers by closer attention to detail. In the first section (music) you failed to answer the part of the question that asked why the particular form used was appropriate, rather than the other forms available. In the second section, although you noted some of the imagery and discussed it intelligently, you often moved too far away from the imagery itself and relied on an 'outside' view of the poem (what you thought it must be about) to interpret it. In the final section you did pay close attention to detail, but it remained only observation of detail. You failed to connect the various elements together or to move *through* the detail to the larger issues of the painting. See the introductory section in the Unit and its explanation of the movement from meaning to form. It is a matter of working-at, responding to the detail, exploring the 'resonances' of the detail and moving from this to a full appreciation of the total effect. (Tutor's comments on an Open University student's assignment, quoted in Kennedy 1974)

Such comments are more illuminating, particularly for the student, but also for anyone else concerned, than is a mark or grade or percentage label. (That student's essay, by the way, was graded 'C'.) But when the assessor is expected merely to grade the product he will keep such insight to himself. Worse still, he perhaps never articulates them at all unless he expects to have to spell them out. And the tutor's impressions of one student are unlikely to remain vivid after he has looked at the work of a few more students. Thus his students will probably receive from him no feedback of a kind that might help them learn from his response to their work. Donald McIntyre (1970) illustrates what is missing when he suggests that the 'result' of a pupil's mathematics exam, *instead of* 40 per cent might be recorded as a 'diagnostic profile' thus:

Has mastered ideas of variable and one-to-one correspondence; not yet clear about functions; gets confused with problems of proportions; still has difficulty in structuring verbal problems (lack of grammatical understanding?); geometry generally competent, but has not learned terminology adequately; considerable skill in analysing visual problems.

Important qualities and features differentiating one student from another are obliterated by the baldness of grades. Thus several students who've got the same grade may have tackled quite different problems and in quite different ways. As a trivial example, one student may have scored five out of ten on his arithmetic test by answering the five additions correctly and the five subtractions incorrectly while his friend is given the same score for precisely the converse performance! Frances Stevens (1970) in reviewing the marking of examiners in A-level English literature, compares the gradings given to two particular scripts and reveals how much information has been lost in labelling the girl 'C' and the boy 'D':

Is the more optimistic forecast to be made of the dutiful immature girl who has some mildly appreciative responses, knows her books and has paid careful attention to what she has been told to think, but who has few independent ideas and writes with neither firmness nor joy; or of the mature and independent boy, who may not have studied his notes or perhaps his texts so thoroughly, but who has a sense of relevance, whose judgments are valid, who writes with assurance and betrays in his style . . . that he has made a genuine engagement with the literature he has encountered? (p. 130)

Whether or not the assessor's criteria were exactly the same as Frances Stevens's is neither here nor there. They are unlikely to have been less subjective – or contestable. Translating them into a grade is an act of reification, erecting a pseudo-objective façade on what is a very delicate personal judgment. One effect of this façade is to repel debate. The grade seems god-given and immutable whereas the grounds on which it was decided might seem only too human and open to dispute. If an assessor were to respond to the girl mentioned above in the terms of Frances Stevens's assessment, he might well find her anxious to draw his attention to other qualities of her work which had been overlooked and which might revise his overall assessment. Certainly it could lead to a valuable teacher-learner dialogue. In the context of bureaucratic assessment, however, it could only be regarded as 'noise in the system'.

Whether or not we're always aware of the fact, grades act like *averages*. They smooth out and conceal irregularities and variability. One essay may have both first-class and abysmal features and yet be graded neither 'A' nor 'F'; instead it may get a 'C' which fails altogether in letting us know that it differs from another essay graded 'C' which is consistently of that quality in all its parts. Similarly, of two 60 per cent examination scripts, one may contain answers both of failure quality and distinction quality while the other is 60 per cent-ish throughout. And of course, the same variability may lie behind the all-concealing degree class of 'lower second' or a diploma class of 'satisfactory' – for all we know. In short, numbers and labels do not allow us to discriminate even between stable performers and those not infrequently found (see Stevens 1970, p. 125) 'in whose papers near-brilliance alternates with near-nonsense'.

Grades, percentages and category labels are hopelessly inadequate to convey the load of meaning that we sometimes believe we are putting into them and which other people desperately try to get out from them again. How could a single letter or number possibly tell as much, for example, as is contained in descriptive reports or profiles? [. . .] There is a well-known Peanuts cartoon by Charles Schulz in which a girl is sitting at her school desk querying the 'C'-grade she's been given for her 'sculpture' made from a coat-hanger. She wants to know whether she was judged on the piece of sculpture itself; and if so is it not true that time alone can judge a work of art? Or was she judged on her talent; if so, is it right that she should be judged on a part of life over which she has no control? If she was judged on her effort, then she regards the judgment as unfair since she tried as hard as she could. Was she being judged on what she had learned about the project and if so, wasn't the teacher being judged on how well he had transmitted knowledge and therefore should he not share the 'C'-grade? And finally, was she perhaps being judged by the inherent quality of the coat-hanger itself out of which her creation was made; and if so why should she be judged by the quality of the coat-hangers on which garments are returned by the laundry her parents patronize – since that's their responsibility shouldn't they share her grade? Her teacher's reply is not recorded.

I cannot applaud the rosy vision of a senior colleague whose spirited defence of grading (and rejection of profiles) climaxed as follows:

Grading is a method of achieving a shorthand synthesis of every possible quality that one might wish to be included in a profile, consolidated into a symbol which examiners understand pragmatically with reference to a platonic point of reference existing in the minds of a group of examiners who have worked together, while a profile, however detailed, can never be more than an attempt to put down all those qualities.

To which perhaps the only reply is St Augustine's lament:

> For so it is, O Lord my God, I measure it;
> But what it is that I measure I do not know.

References

BRERETON, J. L. (1944) *The Case for Examinations*. Cambridge: Cambridge University Press.

CLIGNET, R. (1974) 'Grades, examinations, and other check-points as mechanisms of social control', Chap 10 in *Liberty and Equality in the Educational Process*. New York: Wiley (pp. 327–58).

COX, R. (1967) 'Examinations, Identity and Diversity'. Talk given at the symposium on Recent Results of Research in Higher Education, organized jointly by South Birmingham Technical College and the Society for Research into Higher Education, Midlands Branch.

EISNER, E. W. (1972) *Educating Artistic Vision*. New York: Macmillan.

HARGREAVES, D. H. (1967) *Social Relations in a Secondary School*. London: Routledge and Kegan Paul.

HENRY, J. (1969) 'In suburban classrooms' in GROSS, R. and B. (eds.) *Radical School Reform*. New York: Simon and Schuster.

JACKSON, B. and MARSDEN, D. (1962) *Education and the Working Class*. London: Routledge and Kegan Paul.

JACKSON, P. W. (1968) *Life in Classrooms*. New York: Holt, Rinehart and Winston.

JUDGE, H. (1974) *School is not Yet Dead*. London: Longman.

KENNEDY, D. (1974) 'Preliminary Report on case study project in the Yorkshire Region'. Leeds: Open University (limited internal circulation).

LACEY, C. (1970) *Hightown Grammar: The School as a Social System*. Manchester: Manchester University Press.

MCINTYRE, D. (1970) 'Assessment and teaching' in RUBENSTEIN, D. and STONEMAN, C. (eds) *Education for Democracy* (2nd edn). Harmondsworth: Penguin Books.

MILLER, C. and PARLETT, M. (1973) 'Up to the Mark: a Research Report on Assessment'. Occasional Paper 13: University of Edinburgh Centre for Research in the Educational Sciences.

MONTGOMERY, R. J. (1965) *School Examinations: An Account of their Evolution as Administrative Devices in England*. London; Longman.

MORRIS, N. (1969) 'An Historian's view of examinations' in WISEMAN, S. (ed.) *Examinations and English Education*. Manchester: Manchester University Press (first published 1961).

NASH, R. (1973) *Classrooms Observed: the teacher's perception and the pupil's performance*. London: Routledge and Kegan Paul.

NURSING TIMES (1972) 'And still they failed', editorial in *Nursing Times*, 27 July 1972.

OPPENHEIM, A. N., JAHODA, M. and JAMES, R. L. (1967) 'Assumptions underlying the use of university examinations'. *Universities Quarterly*, June 1967, pp. 341–5.

POLLARD, A. (1970) 'O and A level: Keeping up the standards'. pp. 72–9 in COX, C. B. and DYSON, A. E., (eds) (1970) *Black Paper Two*. Critical Quarterly Society.

REIN, R. K. (1974) 'Educational Testing Service: the examiner examined'. *Change*, Vol 6, No. 3 (pp. 40–6).

STEVENS, F. (1970) *English and Examinations*. London: Hutchinson.

TAYLOR, W. (1963) *The Secondary Modern School*. London: Faber and Faber.

TERWILLIGER, J. S. (1971) *Assigning Grades to Students*. Glenview, Ill. Scott, Foresman.

VALENTINE, C. W. (1938) *Examinations and the Examinee*. Birmingham: The Birmingham Printers.

VANDOME, P. *et al.* (1973) 'Why Assessment?' Paper given limited circulation in the University of Edinburgh.

VEBLEN, T. (1918) *The Higher Learning in America*. New York: B. W. Heubsh.

WOLFF, R. P. (1969) *The Ideal of the University*. Boston: Beacon.

2.11   The myth of subject choice

Peter Woods

I Introduction

The study of subject choice urgently needs the attention of sociologists who will not only illuminate the interactional processes that bear on subject choice, thus complementing the several personality studies that have been made, but will also, at the systems level, ask questions about the functions of the process within the general policy of the school and society at large.[1]

It was with this in view that, while engaged in a long-term observation project in a Secondary Modern School,* I undertook a study of the subject choice process. My engagement at the school enabled me to monitor the process through the summer term, and to follow it up the next year. I talked to all the pupils in the third year, at least once, in interviews ranging from ½ to 2 hours, and discussed freely with teachers from day to day. I sent a questionnaire to all parents of 3rd year pupils, and visited as many as I could before the end of term (25 per cent). This involvement over a long period enabled me to cross-check results, follow up promising leads, and to explore in some depth the reactions of those concerned.

II A sociological model of subject choice

In making sense of the data, I employed certain concepts. I was then able to link these in a general model which seeks to put the process into some sociological perspective.[2] For convenience and intelligibility I will give this theoretical framework here.

The first important concept arising from my discussions with pupils, was that of *group perspectives*. As used by Becker,[3] these refer to 'modes of thought and action developed by a group which faces the same problematic situation. They are the customary ways members of the group think about such situations and act in them ... which appear to group members as the natural and legitimate ones to use in such situations.' They arise when people face 'choice points', where previous thought and experience does not guide their actions, though if a particular kind of situation recurs frequently, the perspective will probably become an established part of a person's way of dealing with the world. They develop and gain strength as a result of group interaction and they are situationally specific. I shall show in section IV how, among the pupils, two broad 'group perspectives' developed.

Source: *British Journal of Sociology*, Vol. 27, No. 2, June 1976, pp. 130–149.

The second key concept, focusing more on pupils' parents, discussed in section v, is *social class*. The relationship between social class and educational experience is well known, as is the culture clash between working class children and teachers.[4] My materials show that parental definitions of the situation differ along class lines, and thus the parental influences brought to bear on children in making their choices are both quantitatively and qualitatively different in accordance with these broad groupings. There is a strong connection between social class and the development of group perspectives. Underpinning these are different frames of reference and self-conceptions,[5] which are products of the position a family occupies within the overall class structure.[6] How these frames of reference are stabilized and reinforced by the child's experience of others within the school (thus facilitating the development of group perspectives) has been discussed by others.[7]

However, school decisions such as subject choice are triangular affairs, involving children, parents and teachers. I found the latter important as *choice mediators* operating within a framework of *institutional channelling*. These concepts owe a great deal to the work of Cicourel and Kitsuse.[8] As against explanations of academic attitudes and achievements mainly or directly in terms of class-related differentials and peer group culture,[9] Cicourel and Kitsuse in their study of the American 'Lakeshore High School' presented an alternative view which saw the differentiation of students as a consequence of the administrative organization and decisions of personnel in the school. The counsellor's role in students' ultimate admission to college was shown to be crucial. Assignment to college and non-college courses was dependent upon the interpretations of a student's ability and aptitude by admissions personnel; since parents knew little about college entrance requirements, his opportunities were to a great extent decided by counsellor's perceptions of him.

Cicourel and Kitsuse explain their counsellor's actions in terms of motivation in celebration of the self within the framework of professionalization, and in the self-fulfilling outcomes of bureaucratic structures. There were other factors bearing on teachers in my account, which I term *critical area influences*. To a great extent they direct and constrain teacher actions and thus serve to modify the Cicourel and Kitsuse conclusions above, at least in relation to this particular school. I shall expand on this in section vi.

How I relate these concepts together in a general model is illustrated in Diagram 1. Differences in social class origins produce different educational experiences. These are reflected in school structure, which is serving societal rather than individual aims, and hence feeds back into social structure. From all of these, singly and collectively, values, attitudes and actions form. Group perspectives develop in reaction to 'pedagogical orientation', which includes aims, methods and organization of teaching, themselves determined by teacher philosophies and ideologies and sustained or intensified by critical area influences (these are frequently

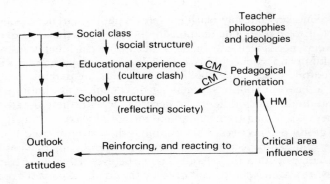

CM = Choice Mediation   HM = Headmaster Mediation

Diagram 1   A social structural model of subject choice

mediated by the headmaster). The particular pedagogical orientation dominant in a school then bears on life in the school (culture) and the school's organization (structure). Most educational decisions in school including subject choice, are made within this framework.

III The school's system of subject choice

All pupils are required to complete a form expressing their choice of subjects. The rhetoric behind the scheme is governed by four crucial criteria: (1) Prevailing custom, which allows choice. (2) Prevailing state of knowledge and current patterns of educational career, largely dictated by the extended examination system, the requirements of further education and employers and the disposition of pupils. Thus there are the traditional subjects, and traditional groupings available (e.g., Sciences, Arts, Commerce, Non-examination subjects); English, Maths and Games are considered so important as to be compulsory. (3) Type of child. All the pupils had been unsuccessful at the eleven-plus examination and it was considered that six examination subjects were the optimum number for them. (4) Resources (size of school, number of teachers, space and equipment).

IV The pupils: the development of group perspectives

I asked each pupil his or her reasons for each of the original choices.[1] Table I summarizes the results. There appear to be two main factors, an affective one (liking or disliking) and a utilitarian one (career and ability) and they seem to hold in roughly equal proportions overall. However there are some interesting differences within, illustrative of two basic group perspectives. The positive reasons (liking, good ability) are much stronger in 3a and 3b than in 3c, where good ability is hardly a factor at all. 'Liking for subject' includes of course a strong teacher element. The like/dislike teacher categories are for responses indicating direct personal reasons. This was a factor in only 7 per cent of cases, with nearly three times as many girls being involved as boys. The like/dislike of subject response focuses on the subject as mediated by the teacher. But this response begs a further question – why do they 'like' certain subjects? The interviews showed these reasons to fall into two types which point up the contrast between 3a and 3c more vividly. Thus the former tended to like subjects for official, counter-cultural, social reasons. Thus the first type might like a subject because the teacher makes it interesting, is well-organized, can keep order, and gives them to feel that they are learning something; the second type for almost directly opposite reasons, such as having few demands made on them, having great freedom and even 'having a muck-about'.

Table 1   Pupils' reasons for choices

Forms	Nos	Liking for subject	Dislike of others	Job	Good ability	Poor ability at others	Liking for teachers	Dislike of teachers	Others
3a Boys	15	29	5	15	19	1	1	2	8
Girls	21	29	26	44	12	5	5	11	2
Total	36	58	31	59	31	6	6	13	10
3b Boys	14	18	9	12	23	6	1	3	10
Girls	20	31	17	13	8	5	3	1	5
Total	34	49	26	25	31	11	4	4	15
3c Boys	15	13	6	10	3	13	0	1	2
Girls	15	9	22	8	0	3	0	1	2
Total	30	22	28	18	3	16	0	2	4
All Boys	44	60	20	37	45	20	2	6	20
All Girls	56	69	65	65	20	13	8	13	9
Total	100	129	85	102	65	33	10	19	29

Another striking result, again indicative of group perspectives, was the difference in number of responses among forms. The average number of responses per pupil decreases with stream, with a big drop in 3c. I take this, as with their reasons for likes and dislikes, to be a reflection of their basic attitudes to school. For 3c, it is largely characterized by estrangement from its main objectives. As one of the teachers said to me, 'You won't find many of their parents [i.e. of 3c pupils – P.W.] here tonight [at the headmaster's talk – P.W.], they know it's not for them.' Such pupils, alienated from the school's processes, go through the organizational motions that are required of them, inventing their own rationale for existence. It is hardly surprising then that when faced with making a decision of their own relating to the school's processes, many were lost. It was an unreal situation for them.

EXAMPLE 1

Dave: I filled that form in in about 20 seconds. (*laughs*)
P.W.:   Did you ask anybody's advice about what to do?
Dave: I didn't 'ave time. See, I filled my paper in, I took it 'ome, see what me dad think, an' I forgot all about it, an' then, oh, (deputy head) came in and gi' me another form an' I filled it in quick so I wouldn't lose it, because I've got a bad memory, I always forget things an' I just filled it in quick.
P.W.:   Did you talk about it amongst yourselves?
Dave and *Philip:* No.
Kevin: We just said what we were doing.

EXAMPLE 2

P.W.:   What subjects did you choose?
Paul: The non-exam ones.
P.W.:   Why did you choose those?
Paul: Because I ain't no good at anything so I chose those.

EXAMPLES 3 and 4

Malcolm, though with three of his friends, seemed to know very little about the process, what was required of him, as well as how he met it. Though he had chosen four subjects, he was unable to say why he had chosen them. Sheila did the same as her sister because 'She was no good at anything'; in fact her sister filled in the form for her, and she was unable to remember the subjects she had chosen, even when shown the list.

EXAMPLE 5

Gary: I only done two out of these, I didn't fill the other two places in.
P.W.:   Why is that?
Gary: All the others I'm not any good at.

EXAMPLE 6

P.W.:   What subjects have you chosen, Susan?
Susan: I dunno. I forget. (*I show her the form.*) I think it was (4 subjects).
P.W.:   Why did you choose those?
Susan: I dunno.
P.W.:   Did you ask anybody's advice?
Susan: Yeah, I asked Mr Lewis's. First of all, I put all sciences down because I want to be a nurse . . . and he said they're no good . . .

P.W.: Why did he say that?
Susan: I dunno.

EXAMPLE 7
Claire: I'm doing the non-exam course.
P.W.: Why?
Claire: Because I don't like any of the other courses.
P.W.: Why do General Science non-exam rather than General Science exam?
Claire: Because that's an exam course in't it?
P.W.: How do you know you won't like it?
Claire: I don't like Science anyway.
P.W.: Why put down for it then?
Claire: Well I 'ad to pick something, din't I?

These suggest the nature of the non-event it was for many pupils. In example 1, Dave turns the procedure into material for his own use, as he does for many other events relating to school. He makes a laugh of it. Examples 2, 3 and 4 illustrate the problems set up by pupils' lack of success by the school's single criterion of ability. Examples 3, 4 and 6 perhaps give some idea of the massive vagueness or unawareness that some of these pupils displayed. Example 7 shows the unerring logic of a pupil with a sound grasp of the situation.

For these pupils then, there is no much 'choice'. Inasmuch as they 'choose' at all, it is a diffident, social, counter-cultural choice. They employ the following kind of dichotomous model:

Kinds of subjects

1. Hard work	Easy
2. Examination	Non-examination
3. Nasty, horrible	Fun
4. Boring	Interesting
5. Without friends	With friends
6. Control	Freedom

There is a sense of immediate gratification, and jocular acceptance of ultimate destiny. Years of interactions, tests and examinations have taught them their place. By the time of the 3rd year, these processes have completed the sifting, and groups have worked out their *modi vivendi*. They may choose only within their pre-ordained route, and for some in 3c, as we have seen, that means no choice at all.

For another group of pupils, mostly found in 3a, subject choice, like all other school decisions, is a real and positive affair, and is defined in school terms. For them, society is a contest system and they are in the contest with a chance. Comparative success in assessment and selection mechanisms reinforced by social factors (like within-group pressure and parental encouragement), will have cued them in to this. This means they do see the future in progressively structured terms, and they do believe their choices have relevance to their future careers. Thus they are much more likely to think in terms of career, ability, examination success, and other factors that promote it. Here is an example of the sort of reasoning involved:

Stephen: I chose Chemistry instead of Geography because someone advised me it would be better for the RAF than Geography. I thought Geography would be better, but the bloke next door thought Chemistry. He knows a bloke in the Air Force, pretty important, and he was talking to Mum and Dad one night and he said Chemistry was more important. I would much rather do Chemistry myself than Geography because you can't do Geography 'O' level, but you can Chemistry.

p.w.: Why Physics?

Stephen: Well, the only other one I thought of was English Literature and I'm not really interested in that, so I chose Physics.

p.w.: The others are out are they?

Stephen: Yeah – General Science – I'm already doing Chemistry. I'm not interested in Biology, so I might as well do Physics and specialize in something else rather than do General Science.

p.w.: Tell me about Technical Drawing.

Stephen: Well, I wanted to do both that and History, I just couldn't make my mind up.

p.w.: What was hard about it?

Stephen: Well if I join the RAF, I want to be a draughtsman, so Tech. Drawing is obviously the one to do. But I'm interested in History and I enjoy it. I put History down first then thought again and changed it later.

p.w.: Did you talk to anybody about it?

Stephen: No. I told Mum and Dad I was thinking of changing it, and they said we won't say yes or no either way.

p.w.: And why Woodwork in group 6?

Stephen: Well I'm not good at Metalwork, I don't do Needlework or Housecraft, I'm no good at Music, shan't mention French. I quite enjoy Woodwork, but I'm not much good at it.

Contrast this with the replies given on pp. 218–19. The close commitment to school values, the logical and ebullient application to the task in hand, the instrumental reasoning tinctured with the educational reciprocation all point to this pupil's close approximation to the 'ideal', and emphasizes the distance the others are away from it. His major criteria in choosing are:

Job-related	Non-related
Good ability	Poor ability
Good learning situation	Poor learning situation
Interest	No interest

The existence of two polar sub-cultures in the school and their connection with school organization is well documented.[11] My study again illustrates the connection with school structure, but further shows the existence and illustrates the different perspectives of these two broad groups of pupils confronted with the specific problem of subject choice. They employ different interpretative models, distinguished by instrumentalism on the one hand, and social and counter-institutional factors on the other. These underwrite the more general and potentially misleading affective factor of 'liking' or 'disliking', which applies to some degree to both groups. The values and attitudes which provide the bases of these group perspectives derive in large part, I suggest, from position in the social class structure.[12]

V Parents: some differences emerging from social class

Conversations were held with six pairs of parents on subject choice, and on the basis of these a questionnaire was devised and sent to all parents of all 3rd year children in the middle of the summer term when pupils were resolving their choices. Replies were received from 73 per cent of homes. Also I visited 25 per cent of homes of all 3rd year children before the end of the summer term.

Parental advice

The responses were analysed by form. Unfortunately, insufficient precise detail of father's occupation was available for it to be of use. However, the connection between social class and stream is so well known for us to assume reasonably that it holds in this case, an assumption well supported by the interviews.

The questionnaire replies supported the social structure model in some respects, in that 3c parents in making certain different responses from 3a showed that they do hold different, less supportive attitudes towards school. Their replies on how they would advise their children, and on what influenced them as parents were particularly revealing in this respect. Table IIa summarizes the replies on projected 'advice to children'.

Fewer thought 'teacher advice' as important as some of the others, but 3c parents thought it even less so than others. 3c parents would be more inclined than others to say 'do those subjects you want to', and they also put more emphasis on doing subjects with the best teachers, and

Table IIa   Parents' projected advice to children

	Very important			Quite important			Of some importance			Not very important			Not at all important		
	3a	3b	3c	3a	3b	3c	3a	3b	3c	3a	3b	3c	3a	3b	3c
Ability	23	21	22	8	24	8	2	3	0	0	0	1	0	0	0
Interest	19	28	27	12	16	7	2	1	0	0	0	0	0	0	0
Best teachers	8	9	15	8	7	8	12	20	8	3	9	0	2	1	1
Own choice	15	19	27	11	20	3	7	5	3	0	1	0	0	0	0
Good job	20	25	26	7	13	4	6	7	3	0	1	0	0	0	0
Teacher advice	12	13	9	18	17	10	2	13	8	1	1	2	0	0	3

(compared with 3a) 'interest'. These results are consistent with a model implying a differential fit between outlook of parents of different class, and aims and ethos of school. The 'own choice' and 'teacher advice' differences in particular suggest less involvement and perhaps suspicion of teachers among 3c parents. More of these proportionately also put more emphasis on 'interest'. Interviews showed that 3a parents were inclined to be more involved, and to use more complex reasoning. Thus they would be less likely to settle first for interest, best teachers, or own choice and would more closely accord with the school's policy of 'guided choice', reasoning their way through a complex set of factors; while the replies of parents in the lower form accord with the 'drop-out' syndrome shown by many of their children. This squares with replies to question 1 which asked if their children consulted them about what subjects to choose. Table IIb shows there are signs of less consultation in 3c than in 3a.

Table IIb   Parental consultation: parents' views

	3a	3b	3c	*Totals*
Yes	26	33	21	80
No	7	13	15	35
Totals	33	46	36	115

This was supported by pupils' own responses, and reflected in attendance rates at the parents' meetings convened at the school to discuss the matter. Stronger attachment to unofficial functions of the school by 3c parents is also suggested by the replies on school aims. A much larger proportion of 3c parents attached great importance to 'keeping children occupied till they go out to work', than did other parents.

On influences bearing on their views of the child's suitability for certain groups of subjects (see Table IIc) fewer 3c parents reckon they are influenced by school reports, examination results or teachers' recommendations (i.e. a 'school' factor). With others, most of them claim to b

Table IIc   Perceived influences on parents

	Very influential			Quite influential			A little			Not very influential		
	3a	3b	3c	3a	3b	3c	3a	3b	3c	3a	3b	3c
Reports	10	12	3	17	22	19	4	8	9	2	0	5
Examinations	11	12	2	15	22	15	4	6	13	3	0	2
Own knowledge	25	23	23	7	14	11	0	3	1	1	1	0
Family knowledge	10	9	18	8	11	9	3	7	3	9	13	5
Teachers	11	13	5	19	22	13	2	5	7	1	1	8
Child's view	12	17	7	16	20	23	4	4	2	1	2	3
Other children	0	2	4	2	12	9	6	10	10	17	17	10

strongly influenced by a 'personal' factor (own knowledge of the child, knowledge of the rest of the family). This again squares with the social, uncommitted outlook of their children and a distancing from official policy and processes.

Table III   Distribution of types of parental influence

Type of influence	Middle class			Total	Working class			Total
	3a	3b	3c		3a	3b	3c	
Compulsion	0	2	0	2	0	0	0	0
Strong guidance	1	3	0	4	1	0	1	2
Mutual resolution	2	1	0	3	1	4	1	6
Reassurance	3	0	0	3	0	1	2	3
Little/Nil	0	0	0	0	0	1	2	3
Total	6	6	0	12	2	6	6	14

From my interviews with pupils and parents, I identified five types of parental influence: 1. Compulsion. 2. Strong guidance. 3. Mutual resolution. 4. Reassurance. 5. Little or nil. Table III shows how these were spread among the 27 homes that I visited. Though numbers are small, the trend towards stronger counselling for the middle-class child is clearly visible.

Compulsion. This seems to have been used in cases where parents greatly feared their child was in danger of selecting the 'wrong' route with all its disadvantageous consequences. I only found middle-class parents using it, and it is another instance of how the middle-class child who, for whatever reason might have adopted the social, counter-cultural model, can be cushioned against a possible fall into the drop-out zone. (If this cushion is lacking, teachers might provide an alternative one.)

Linda, for example, who wanted to be a hairdresser, and had wanted the non-examination course, was coerced into opting for Commerce by her mother, because she 'wanted her to work in an office'. Many such parents showed a high degree of status consciousness, being very sensitive to the difference between the two main routes. Jane, daughter of a managing director, told me she would have preferred to carry on in the same way rather than be forced to choose. Her father explained to me at length the reasoning behind *his* selection on her behalf.

Strong guidance contains an element of persuasion, often subtly concealed in the continual involvement typical of the middle-class parent

It goes back over a period of time. There's been a careful channelling of opportunities as they've presented themselves. From experience of life, I'm biassed towards a child going into secretarial work, because if you're not academic, the only alternative is factory work. It goes back two or three years really. I would say if you don't get good results you'll land up in a factory on the line, and you've seen them factory girls in their hair nets. Sara actually made her own choice – I think I influenced her unknowingly. She told me she wanted to be a secretary, and that's what I've wanted her to do! None of the subjects on the bottom line would be helpful to her in the sort of occupation I wanted her, so I chose housecraft for her, for general use, later. (*Factory manager*.)

Having steered the child on the right courses, middle-class parents can then provide resources to see that he or she gets accepted, as when the estate agent's wife advised her son, who had done such a poor examination that he should by that teacher's stated rule have been automatically excluded, to apologize to the teacher and promise to try hard in the future. This he did, and was accepted to the annoyance of some who had scored higher. 'Why didn't you do what he did?' I asked one of these. 'I'm unlucky in things like that,' he said.

Mutual resolution, with reassurance, was the most common form among those I interviewed. Working-class families were well represented here. However, though they might show as much concern as middle-class families, their guidance tended to be less well informed. Middle-class parents told me in detail how they monitored their children's thinking on the matter, making sure that they themselves were well informed, by, for example, frequent consultations with teachers; then employing this knowledge, and that of the child, and of the world in general to feed gently into the decision-making process when requested. By contrast, working-class parents seemed as puzzled as their children. To many of these, school is an alien though desirable agency, where professionals practise their considerable expertise behind well-defined boundaries. They have little idea either of their own child's achievements and capabilities or of the career prospects and how they are associated with educational routes. Another 'disadvantage' for working-class parents was that they tended to be less instrumentally oriented than middle-class, though every parent I met thought primarily of the child's future career. *Reassurance* also differed along class lines, middle-class parents supporting their children through confidence in them to make the best choices, working-class parents supporting their children as they would in any enterprise as part of the socio-emotional bond between them. As the table shows, I only found working-class parents giving *very little* or *no* advice.

In this section I have shown that there are different kinds and amounts of parental advice and influence operating on the different groups of pupils identified previously. These show a connection with social class.[13] Middle-class parents are likely to be more involved with school processes, show more complex reasoning in accordance with school criteria in advising their children, be more persuaded by 'school' factors. Working-class parents display less 'involvement', are less instrumentally oriented, possibly entertain suspicions of school and teachers, have less consultation with teachers and their own children, are more likely to be persuaded by 'personal' factors. Middle-class parents tend to give strong guidance, be well informed, critical and coercive, instrumentally oriented and status conscious. Working-class parents tend to give less guidance, and to be uninformed. Indications have been given of the subtle ways in which class can work towards differential opportunity, for example, though 'knowledge of the world' and 'how to handle men'. It also operates of course through the teachers.

VI The teachers: choice mediators

Teachers of course acknowledge that there is not a completely free choice, but there is a belief that the advice and guidance offered is given in the best interests of the pupil. This is a view I wish to contest in this section. As with Cicourel and Kitsuse's Lakeshore High School, this school's structure is determined by what happens at the end of the pupil's career, in this case the taking (or not) of examinations. Pupils are streamed and/or put in sets in the early years to facilitate optimum overall academic performance as defined by skills and knowledge deemed useful in the 5th year examinations. As at Lakeshore, early decisions can be crucial. Of one 5L group I was able to trace back, 27 out of 31 had come through the school in the bottom stream. This institutional channelling creates its own effects,[14] and in association with the group perspectives that form within the channels and the development of teachers' typifications,[15] brings about a crystallization of opportunities at a very early stage.

This is vividly illustrated by one aspect of the subject choice process, the rechannelling of misdirected choices. Teachers view pupils' subject choice in a way akin to Diagram 2.

This shows four basic types of choice from the teachers' point of view. The 'system acceptive' type pupil is one who interprets correctly the school and its processes and his relationship to it, and hence the implications of the subject choice, be it for examination or non-examination subjects. The 'system disruptive' pupils however have misinterpreted the cues, and made unrealistic choices, selecting examination subjects when they should have chosen non-examination (by ability), or vice-versa. The

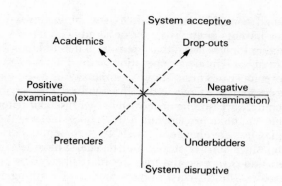

Diagram 2

problem for teachers then becomes one of moving pupils along the lines indicated.

But who are these 'pretenders' and 'underbidders'? Table IV shows the changes that were made from pupils' first choices to final allocation. 'Positive' changes are those from non-examination to examination subjects; 'negative' vice-versa; and 'neutral' are changes within the same standard. 44 per cent of the whole, and proportionately twice as many boys as girls had at least one subject changed from his or her original

Table IV   Choices changes

Form	Nos	No in form	Changes	Positive	Negative	Neutral
3a Boys	5	15	10	2	5	3
Girls	3	21	3	1	0	2
Total	8	36	13	3	5	5
3b Boys	15	17	24	2	12	10
Girls	10	20	16	2	7	7
Total	25	37	40	4	19	17
3c Boys	9	15	15	0	13	2
Girls	4	15	10	0	9	1
Total	13	30	25	0	22	3
All Boys	29	47	49	4	30	15
All Girls	17	56	29	3	16	10
Total	46	103	78	7	46	25

choice, and 60 per cent of these changes were 'negative' ones. Nearly half of these came from 3c, even though many in that form had already made negative choices and therefore did not come into the reckoning. Most of the rest came from 3b, which is here showing its 'in-between' status, having some 'good' pupils, some 'bad'. 3a had two or three 'bad' boys who blotted 3a's copybook. 62 per cent of the boys were involved in changes, compared with 30 per cent of the girls. Clearly the vast majority of those requiring rechannelling came from the lower part of the streaming structure.

There is another problem, again shown by Diagram 2, namely the line between academics and non-academics. There can be no appeal to an absolute standard in drawing this line just as with the line separating success and failure in the eleven-plus. It is determined by the teachers, each for his own subject, and as with the eleven-plus, it might fall at different points, for much the same reason – resources. If more pupils choose one subject than another, more have to be excluded from that subject.

This points up the uneven nature of the redistribution problem. But teachers will already have exerted influence to try to achieve these results less brutally beforehand. Their teaching and assessment, culminating in the all-important examinations at the end of the 3rd year, gives most pupils a sound idea of their 'ability' at school subjects.

This is the most powerful factor underlying all others in the acceptance of pupils to subjects – i.e., teachers' definitions of success and failure.[16] We have already seen in the section on the pupils how many of them (and their parents) had internalized these definitions, accepted the consequences and chosen 'realistically'.

To guard against 'unrealistic' choices, a teacher might use special pre-option techniques. The teacher of one popular subject, for example, possibly anticipating a big redistribution problem, gave a talk which had the effect of cooling out several 'pretenders'.

P.W.:   Why didn't you choose subject 4 in that group?
June: We'd get too much homework.
Mavis: Yeah! She don't 'alf put it on . . . 'you'll 'ave to work all the time' – an' homework! You think 'oh I can't do that – oh!' Talking about it made me feel ill.

As with Cicourel and Kitsuse's counsellors, teachers' judgments are not based simply on past achievement.

I asked the teacher of one 'popular' subject what were her principles of exclusion. In making up the optimum number she employed three – (1) the 'best ones'; (2) those who seemed to have the 'right' attitude; and (3) from 3c, the three who seemed a 'cut above the rest'. It was no good having problem people like John Church. 'He's too lazy, he lays around, and if he gets his pen out, he lolls around saying "Oh Miss!" I can't

take the risk, it spreads like a cancer. Who starts it, initiates it, I don'
know.

'It's cruel I know, but what else can I do? I haven't time to motivate
inspire, correct for behaviour and so on, so you must cut out all the
miscreants and thickies. You just haven't got time. They do drag you
down. Now Sharon Brown, nice girl, parents didn't want her in that form,
I think once she gets out and in with this other lot, they'll pull these three
(from 3c) up.'

This teacher is articulating the system's rules, and by tidying up the
'misplacements' illustrates how the wedge is even more firmly driven
between two types of pupil. These two types, and who falls into them, are
clearly identified, as is their within-group influences. So also are the
criteria for success, which include apart from past performance, 'attitude'
and a 'cut above the rest'. The social undertones and divisiveness become
explicit towards the end. Family background can be decisive. It can rescue
or condemn at the eleventh hour.

Apparent also is the classic dilemma of the upper secondary school
teacher – concern for the individual while operating within the constraints
of a structure which allows very little room for manoeuvre. There is an
overlap among O level, CSE, and non-examination routes. For teachers,
these overlap areas can be high tension generators, for there is pressure on
the teacher to achieve a high proportion of examination passes. Usually
this might be interpreted, as Cicourel and Kitsuse did with their counsellors, purely through the concept of professionalization. Here, however, a
critical external influence increases the pressure; indeed, for some
teachers, could be held responsible for it. In the ordinary course of events,
a teacher might gain relief by ensuring that the overlap is as small as
possible, ideally non-existent, which would mean 100 per cent examination passes; or, of course, he might not feel under any pressure, especially
if his results are deemed reasonable. But at this particular point in the
school's history, numbers are seen to be very important. For the school is
about to become a Comprehensive, and to receive pupils formerly admitted to the high status town grammar and high schools. The strain towards
better and better examination results is seen by the teachers[17] as a public
relations exercise in honour of the parents of such children to convince
them of the school's credibility as a respectable academic institution. One
of the effects on teachers is to cause them to monitor the selecting of
subjects with great care. It is unavoidable, even in traditionally less
constrained subjects like creative design.

'A lot choose Art, yes, and you know why don't you? I'm not fooled. I
say to them, "Why do you want to do Art?" I say, "*I* know, but come on,
you tell me," and they say, "Huh, I don't want to do old Biology or
whatever, all that homework and so on." It's an easy option, and they go
for it on both lines. My results this year were pretty poor which rather
proves my point. But what I do is this. I pick those with most artistic
ability and I like it to be seen to be fair. I don't spring this on them either. I

tell them all this at the beginning of the third year. I tell them they'll be judged on the quality of work that goes into their folders, and then towards the end of the year, I get them to lay it all out, so they can all see, and of course some are very good and some are pathetic. There's no other way, not if they want to take the exam. If they just want to skive they can do it somewhere else.'

Here is 'justice' being seen to be done, and opportunity given for pupils to make their cases. With its free and informal atmosphere, and its different, non-exacting work-task, the 'Art' options are a natural attraction for the diffident counter-cultural chooser. But the Art teacher is subject to the same forces as his colleagues, and the same criteria must apply.

What direct counselling of children by teachers came to my attention also seemed directed towards the preservation of institutional channels, while expounding the rhetoric which legitimated it. In his address to the 3rd year pupils, for example, the headmaster showed a conservative selection-oriented, instrumental and élitist approach, emphasizing the virtues of 'ability' and 'usage' as against 'interest', the essential link with the occupational structure, the functionalist need for 'all sorts', and the predicating of all considerations on the system as it stood. As might be anticipated, the diffident, counter-cultural choosers at least took in little, if any, of this advice. The same applies to the senior master's 'counselling'. Empowered with responsibility for running the scheme, he had more involvement in it overall than any other teacher. But his individual 'counselling' came at the end of the chain, and, as we have seen, was channel-restorative. It appears therefore that teacher mediation does not operate in the interests of the individual pupil, but is predicated rather on considerations of status, career and professionalization, rendered particularly acute by the critical external influence of parental pressure. Mediation then takes the form basically of alerting pupils to the ideal-types (and their own approximations to them) which serve the purpose of those ends through the agency of 'good examination results'.

Why then have a system of subject choice at all? I would suggest that, within the system, schemes like this have four main functions: (1) There is some option within groups of subjects, if not of routes. However, we have seen that some groups of pupils have more option than others. (2) It does give some pupils and parents an opportunity to relate, to some extent, their school careers with prospective occupations. For those on the 'deviant' route, for whom school has a different meaning, it is an opportunity to select those subjects which best support that meaning, though there will be problems if a subject is also an examination one, as with Art, above. (3) It helps to consolidate the image of the school as a meritocratic and democratic institution. (4) It serves as a kind of hiatus in the school programme which can be used as yet another motivating device.

However, in a wider sense, the subject choice scheme is serving the implicit school policy of selection in as much as (1) subjects are grouped in accordance with recognized patterns associated with occupation career; (2) two broad channels allow for those who 'opt in' and those who 'opt' or are ruled 'out'. The non-examination provision can be viewed therefore as a form of social control;[18] (3) pupils are encouraged to choose those subjects in which they have most ability and which are most related to their likely future occupational careers; (4) in rationalizing the picture that emerges from the last point, teachers apply those criteria which promise to lead to the best overall examination results; priority is given to the élite; (5) 'interest' and 'liking' are played down.

VII Conclusion

The four within-system functions therefore are serving a system of sponsorship mobility behind a 'contest' mask.[19] There is an illusion of a range of choice, of selection of personnel delayed to the last moment (immediately prior to the commencement of examination courses), of a common starting line (everybody in with a chance), and of common fare (roughly the same subjects up to the end of the 3rd year). In fact, the range of choice is variable among the pupils, non-existent for some; the pupils have been 'channelled', that is to say selected (at eleven-plus, and no doubt earlier), and selected again (in the school's streaming arrangements, and possibly 'hidden' streaming before) long before they come to the 3rd year; different social origins lead to different educational experiences, the difference being reinforced by the prevailing pedagogical paradigm; and these differences have repercussions for what is taught to different groups. Despite meritocratic overtones, by the third year most pupils have developed group perspectives; they know their places, having internalized teacher definitions of success and failure and their application to themselves with the usual labels ('thick', 'dibby', 'lazy', 'pest').

For them, subject choice has different meanings. Generally speaking to the initiated, generally middle-class pupil it is his choice, and he makes it carefully with a view to job, ability and prospects. To the estranged, generally working-class pupil it is a line of least resistance, and even that at times presents problems. This scenario is complicated, but sharpened still further, by the changing status of the school wherein the unseen and unspoken influence of potential 'sponsoring' parents is felt by teachers to exert great pressure on them, through the mediation of the headmaster, to produce better and better examination results. While this ultimately might mean more joining the élite ranks of the examination pupils, it does not of course alter the basic division and the principles on which it rests; in fact it increases it, since teachers will feel compelled to sharpen their selective and pedagogic techniques to guard against the increased risk of 'contamination'.

With these powerful forces structuring their policies and activities, teachers 'mediate', choosing the arena, making the rules and providing most of the equipment (including the pupil's own view of himself) for the game of subject choice. For them, the game is to guide pupils into the right channels to get the bell of examination results to ring. The criteria they use are past achievement and future potential. For all of these factors, we know that there is a strong connection with social class, though it is not a simple one. The middle-classes are at home in this arena, the working-classes strangers. It is in this sense, most powerfully, that pupils' subject choice is socially structured. But we have seen also how, even within these severe limitations, social factors such as degree and type of parental advice, within-group influences, cultural impressions on teachers (a 'cut above the rest') or simply parents' *savoir-faire* of the middle-class milieu, can exert an influence and indeed at times retrieve apparently lost situations.

'Progressive' measures in schools, such as team teaching and mixed ability classes, have come under fire from both right and left lately. To the former they are fomenting disorder and decay, to the latter they are merely scratching at the edges of an outmoded but curiously resilient system. Pupils' subject choice might be regarded as one of these so-called 'progressive' measures owing something to fashionable child-centred philosophies, and how one regards it might depend ultimately on one's political position. However one thing is clear. Changes in the subject choice system alone will not make a fundamental difference. Extending the range of choice can only be of benefit, but while the social structure of its intake and the school's general aims remain the same, changes in constraint will be of degree rather than of kind.

Notes

* My greatest debt is to the pupils and teachers of the school, who gave so generously of their time. I am particularly grateful to those teachers at the school who read and made comments on an earlier draft of this paper. Their reactions cannot be included here, but will be incorporated in the larger study of which this paper is a part. My thanks are due too, to my colleagues D. F. Swift and I. R. Dale for their comments on the first draft. I am solely responsible of course for the views expressed and the faults that remain.

1 To date, the field has been the preserve mainly of psychologists interested in correlations between personality factors and subject choice. The most well-known one perhaps is Liam Hudson's famous distinction between divergent and convergent thinkers, and their predisposition for Arts and Science subjects respectively. See HUDSON, L. (1966) *Contrary Imaginations*. London: Methuen; in a recent review of the literature, five times as much space is taken up with personality factors as 'other possible causes'. See PITT, A. W. H. (1973) 'A review of the Reasons for Making a Choice of Subjects at the Secondary School Level', *Educational Review*, Vol. 26, No. 1, November 1973; the most recent work

on subject choice is policy research, taking for granted the general context of both school and society. See REID, M. I., BARNETT, B. R., ROSENBERG, H. A. (1974) *A Matter of Choice*. Slough: NFER.

2 This follows the methodology recommended by GLASER, B. G. and STRAUSS, A. L. (1968) *The Discovery of Grounded Theory*. London: Weidenfeld and Nicolson.

3 BECKER, H. S. *et al.* (1961) *Boys in White*. Chicago: University of Chicago Press.

4 For useful summaries and recent reflections on this position, see Section V of EGGLESTON, J. (ed.) (1974) *Contemporary Research in the Sociology of Education*. London: Methuen.

5 These terms are used by D. N. Ashton in 'Careers and Commitment: The movement from school to work', in FIELD, D. (ed.) (1974) *Social Psychology for Sociologists*. London: Nelson.

6 BERNSTEIN, B. (1972) 'A Socio-Linguistic Approach to Socialization: with some reference to educability', in BERNSTEIN, B., *Class Codes and Control*, Volume 1. London: Routledge and Kegan Paul.

7 E.g. D. N. Ashton, op. cit.

8 CICOUREL, A. V. and KITSUSE, H. I. (1963) *The Educational Decision-Makers*. New York: Bobbs-Merrill.

9 As, for example, in PARSONS, T. (1958) 'General Theory in Sociology', in MERTON, R. K. et al., *Sociology Today*. New York: Basic Books; HOLLINGHEAD, A. B. (1949) *Elmtown's Youth*. New York: Wiley; COLEMAN, J. S. (1961) *The Adolescent Society*. Glencoe, Ill.: Free Press.

10 Pupils were interviewed in friendship groups of 2 or 4 pupils previously ascertained by sociometry and observation. I have no doubt that this aided free and frank discussion. It might be argued that they would influence each others' responses. But I believe this to have been a beneficial influence, in that our discussions frequently drew upon discussion they had had amongst themselves on the subject, and they assisted each other's recall.

11 HARGREAVES, D. H. (1967) *Social Relations in a Secondary School*. London: Routledge and Kegan Paul; LACEY, C. (1970) *Hightown Grammar*. Manchester: Manchester University Press; KING, R. A. (1969) *Values and Involvement in a Grammar School*. London: Routledge and Kegan Paul.

12 See Bernstein, op. cit.

13 It might equally be said that they show a connexion with academic achievement, but of course I am assuming also a connexion between *that* and social class. Also, as pointed out previously, I was able to establish from the interviews that the connexion with social class predominated over connection with academic stream.

14 For the effects of streaming see JACKSON, B. (1964) *Streaming: An educational system in miniature*. London: Routledge and Kegan Paul; CENTRAL ADVISORY COUNCIL FOR EDUCATION (England) (1967) *Children and their Primary Schools* (Plowden Report). London: HMSO; LUNN, J. B. (1970) *Streaming in the Primary School*. Slough: NFER.

15 For teachers' knowledge of pupils based on institutional channelling, see KEDDIE, N. (1971) 'Classroom Knowledge', in YOUNG, M. F. D. (ed.), *Knowledge and Control*. London: Collier-Macmillan.

16 For a discussion along these lines, related to subject choice in a girls' secondary school, see BEECHAM, Y. (1972) 'The Making of Educational Failures', *Hard Cheese Two*, May 1973.

17 It is important to note that the teachers did not feel this directly. Pressure was put on them by the headmaster, and from his words and actions they thought this the most likely, indeed the sole, explanation.

18 BERNSTEIN, B. (1971) 'On the Classification and Framing of Educational Knowledge', in HOPPER, E. (ed.), *Readings in the Theory of Educational Systems*. London: Hutchinson.

19 TURNER, R. H. (1971) 'Sponsored and Contest Mobility and the School System', in E. Hopper (ed.), op. cit.

Part Three

Schooling and social change

The controversy over whether educational standards are falling is, as we have argued in our introductory paper, a complex one. So is the debate about which standards matter, and why. As the contributions in Part One illustrate, there are many different views on what schooling should be for, and thus on why improving the standards reached in different kinds of learning is important. In this part of the collection we shall be looking largely at some aspects of the relationships between schooling and social change. As Crosland's contribution to Part One illustrates, a central issue in educational controversy since the Second World War has been how, if at all, schooling can be used to promote greater social mobility and to decrease class differences within our society.

One major obstacle to achieving these aims has been thought to be the existence of unequal access to educational provision for different social groups. If, as was assumed, the key to greater social equality lay in the socially integrating and compensatory effects of education, it would be obvious that greater equality of access to education was of the first importance. This belief led on the one hand to the progressive raising of the school leaving age, and on the other to attempts to increase the total amount of post-compulsory education available.

Cantor and Roberts discuss some aspects of this latter development, charting the growth and development of the further education sector in the 1970s. The paper by McIntosh which follows notes that the same phenomenon of overall growth has also occurred in higher education. However, she goes on to identify a range of factors which separately constitute partial barriers to access to higher education. These factors include social class, previous qualifications, school background, choice of subject area, financial resources, sex and age. The cumulative effect of the existence of these hindrances is to create a complex differentiation of access to higher education for various groups in society. She concludes with an analysis of the extent to which one new institution, the Open University, has succeeded in at least partially reducing the effects of some of these barriers.

Heath's paper takes up the theme of social class as a barrier to access at the secondary school level. He describes the main findings of a study of the social backgrounds and educational careers of several thousand men aged between twenty and sixty at the time of the survey. In the paper he concentrates upon the relationships between class background and an individual's chances of gaining access to various categories of secondary schools, ranging from fee-paying independent to the secondary modern. He argues that social class membership has had a significant effect upon an individual's chances of gaining entry to the more selective categories of school, independently of the IQ of the individual, an effect diminished somewhat but not eliminated by expansion of educational provision. One response (and indeed it is Heath's own) to this finding is to suggest that the advent of the comprehensive schools might well modify this picture.

The paper by Ford suggests that comprehensivization in itself, may not alter the situation to any significant degree. In a comparative study (carried out in the 'sixties) of a streamed comprehensive, a grammar school and a secondary modern, Ford concluded that, with IQ differences allowed for, there was little evidence that 'comprehensive education as it is practised at present will modify the characteristic association between social class and educational attainment'.

With this reference to educational attainment we may usefully move from the topic of what affects access to schooling to the question of the effects that that schooling subsequently has, upon individuals and society in general.

The papers in this collection reveal a number of assumptions about why schooling might be valued. Individuals may look, more or less consciously, to their schooling to assist them in moving into a different social class or preferred occupation. They may view it as a way of gaining useful skills or knowledge which, although of no particular economic or career value, they see as intrinsically interesting or significant. On the other hand they may be concerned only to gain the paper qualifications that success in schooling can provide, as a means to later benefits that have no conceivable intrinsic relationship to what they have been obliged to study.

Needless to say, these different reasons for valuing schooling are ones that we seldom separate out so neatly from one another in real life. But for purposes of political polemic, educational research, or policy discussion (or any combination of these activities), such distinctions are often drawn, as this collection itself illustrates.

In the same way, the question of the overall effects upon society of schooling is one which in reality ideally requires very subtle and complex study of a kind and scale beyond the scope of this collection (or indeed of the course with which it is associated). Instead we must be content to pick out only certain aspects of the question for further discussion, leaving others largely out of consideration. The papers in Part Three which we have not yet mentioned are largely concerned with the effects upon social class structure and national economic performance of schooling in its various forms. They do not look at the careers of particular individuals, but at the overall effects on society as a whole, or on large groups within it, of the multiplicity of detailed educational and social activities in which we as individuals engage.

The paper by Bowles and Gintis questions the belief that in modern technological societies it is a person's IQ which, by and large, determines their economic success in life. Similarly they argue that there is no statistical basis for the beliefs that genetic factors or the level of schooling are major determinants of economic success, although IQ, family memership and level of schooling are all correlated with such success. They suggest that these correlations are not signs of any direct causal relationships, but are created by the fact that all three of the assumed causal factors are actually themselves correlated with a fourth, namely social class. It is this last element, they argue, which is the main influence upon the level of economic success achieved. They then suggest that the belief amongst many liberals that IQ and schooling are crucial factors illustrates the way in which the basic structure of a late capitalist society distorts the perceptions of its supporters so as to provide apparently plausible but actually misleading accounts of the social processes at work.

The connection between schooling and economic development is the central topic in the paper by Ginzberg which follows. In a favourable review of the research carried out by Berg, he suggests that this research indicates that, beyond a certain basic level, the education people receive is largely irrelevant to their subsequent success. (Whether it is of any relevance to the quality of their life or the level of culture that their society can sustain are two of the topics with which this collection does not deal.) If, however, the contribution of schooling to the creation of remunerative skills is minimal, then why do people wish continually to increase the amount of schooling they receive, especially if, as Ginzberg claims, the effect of such overeducation is to make people dissatisfied with their work?

One answer to this is offered in Thurow's paper. He suggests that in the competition for more desirable jobs employers often cannot distinguish between applicants on the basis of differences in relevant skills, either because the employers have no way of judging such differences accurately, or because they are also looking for certain general capacities and attitudes (such as discipline and good work habits) which are neither job specific nor easily checked in a short interview. So instead they use educational attainment, as indicated by paper qualifications, as an important indirect indication of the candidate's possession of desired attitudes and general capacities. If Thurow is correct, it is here that we must look for one motivating force pressing people towards ever rising levels of certified success in schooling.

Support for Thurow's view here is provided in Dore's paper. He makes an international comparative study of the relationships between social mobility and 'credentialism' (i.e. the drive towards possession of certificates of schooling success) in a number of developed and developing countries. He suggests that such a study shows that credentialism is increasing, and increasing fastest in those countries most recently beginning the move towards industrial and technical development. In this process the schools become of ever greater importance, not because of the learning they provide, but because of the certificates that they issue. Yet this increased importance itself creates pressures feeding back into the schools, to adjust their purposes ever more firmly towards credentialism rather than education. Quite how far the process has gone is unwittingly revealed in Dore's own assertion that the view of education as being about

moral and intellectual uplift and enlightenment is a fiction, albeit
important one. If by this he means that much schooling fails to live u
(or even aspire to) such a conception of education, he may well be rig
But if he means that, as an ideal, it is a conception that is somehow
defensible than conceptions of education that achieve greater succ
simply by aspiring to very little, then that takes us again into issues w
which this collection does not attempt to deal, although in their v
different ways Freire, Lawrence and Peters all begin to direct our att
tion towards them.

.1 Further education in the 1970s

Leonard M. Cantor and I. F. Roberts

In the second edition of our book, *Further Education in England and Wales*, we began by describing the phenomenal post-war growth in further education by which the number of students doubled from 1,595,000 in 1946 to 3,174,000 in 1970 and the number of teaching staff increased even more dramatically during that period from under 5,000 to 50,000. In the 1970s, the figures reveal a continuing growth so that by 1976, for example, further education establishments contained almost 4,000,000 students taught by over 76,000 teachers. However, as we shall see, this growth is partly due to the movement of the former colleges of education into the further education sector. The optimism and expectancy of continued expansion, particularly in regard to higher education, which infused education as recently as 1972 has, at the time of writing, been replaced by a more realistic appreciation of the situation. Two main factors are responsible for this radically changed position: the economic recession resulting in large part from the oil crisis following the 1973 Middle East war and the sharply declining birth rate of the late 1960s and early 1970s.

The first years of the 1970s were marked by a public debate on the nature and content of teacher education and training, a debate which had rumbled on for many years but which came to a head at this time. Public concern led to the setting up of the James Committee, which issued its report, 'Teacher Education and Training', in January 1972. Although the report proposed no major institutional changes in the colleges of education sector, it did recommend that the colleges themselves should cease to be monotechnics providing only courses in teacher-training and should diversify their provision in the form of a two-year course of general education to be known as the Diploma of Higher Education (Dip.HE).

In December of the same year, the Conservative Government of the day issued its White Paper, 'Education: A Framework for Expansion', which, as its title indicates, still envisaged a period of continued growth, especially in higher education. Accordingly, it recommended that student places in higher education should be increased from under 500,000 in 1972 to 750,000 in 1981, the places to be shared equally between the universities and the further education sector. In other words, the public sector colleges should accommodate 375,000 students by 1981. This was to be accomplished partly by merging the great majority of the colleges of education, hitherto a separate sector of higher education, with polytechnics and other further education colleges. The White Paper, recognizing that there was some decline in the birth rate and that this would require a cut-back in the

Source: CANTOR, L. M. and ROBERTS, I. F. (1979) *Further Education Today.* London: Routledge and Kegan Paul, pp. 1–7.

output of trained teachers, announced that the number of teacher-traini places in the public sector colleges would be reduced from a maximum 114,000 in 1972 to between 75,000 and 85,000 initial and in-service plac by 1981. Finally, it strongly advocated the introduction of the Dip.HE recommended by the James Report.

In the following March, the DES issued Circular 7/73, 'The Develo ment of Higher Education in the Non-University Sector', asking loc authorities and voluntary bodies to put forward detailed plans for t re-organization of the colleges of education which for the most part wou be expected to move into the public sector. Clearly, at that time it was n envisaged that very drastic surgery would be required as the planne increase in student numbers would more than compensate for the redu tion in teacher-training places. However, as the full impact of the stee decline in the birth rate, 832,000 live births in 1967 to just over 600,000 1975, began belatedly to be recognized by the DES, so it felt it necessar successively to reduce the number of teacher-training places in the co leges. The final target figures, announced at the end of 1977, are 45,00 places by 1981, including some 9,000 for in-service courses for practisir teachers. The fall-out from these decisions has had far-reaching effect the college of education sector has virtually disappeared; a number colleges of education have closed altogether; the merger of the remainin colleges with further education colleges has created a new group of instit tions known generally as Colleges or Institutes of Higher Education; an the further education sector has now acquired a substantial stake teacher training, albeit considerably smaller than that envisaged in th 1972 White Paper. As a result, the institutional structure of furthe education has changed substantially in recent years (Figure 1).

Closely linked with these developments has been the growth of th Diploma of Higher Education. From the introduction of the first tw courses in September 1974, student numbers have gradually increased t about 5,000 in 1977 on some 50 courses. However, these numbers are ver tiny when compared to those of students on degree courses in furthe education who number more than 100,000 and, in any case, many of th Dip.HE programmes are, in effect, the first two years of an integrate degree course. It is therefore still too early to tell whether the Dip.HE ha firmly taken root.

The growth of higher education in the further education sector ha inevitably focused attention on the management of those institutions notably the polytechnics, which are very largely concerned with th provision of advanced courses. Not surprisingly, they measure themselve against the universities and envy them their powers of self-validation o courses and, more especially, their relative freedom of financial manage ment within agreed budgetary limits. By contrast, the polytechnics ar constrained by the necessity of advanced course approval through th Regional Advisory Councils and by complex financial procedures exer cised by the parent local education authorities and through the 'pool'

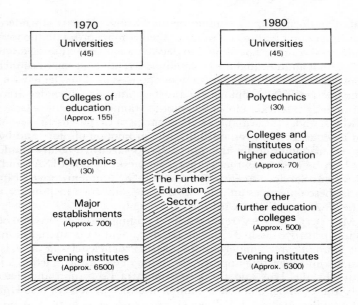

Figure 1 The pattern of further and higher education in the 1970s

These problems have been further complicated by the arrival on the scene of the Colleges and Institutes of Higher Education and their public airing has culminated in the 1978 Oakes Report, 'The Management of Higher Education in the Maintained Sector'. The Oakes Report recommended the establishment of a national body for England to oversee the development of maintained higher education, a recommendation that was taken up by the Labour Government which decided to press for the establishment of two national bodies, to be known as Advanced Further Education Councils (AFECs), one for England and one for Wales. This proposition was incorporated in an Education Bill which, by Spring 1979, had reached the Committee stage of the House of Commons when the general election intervened. At the time of writing (April 1979), it is uncertain whether the recommendations of the Oakes Report will be given legislative effect; should this occur, it will remain to be seen how far they succeed in resolving the management problems of the polytechnics and colleges of higher education.

The 1970s have also witnessed far-reaching changes in the field of industrial training. The structure created by the Industrial Training Act of 1964, based upon the creation of industrial training boards, was coming under increasing criticism by the beginning of the decade on the grounds that the boards had had only limited success in increasing the quantity and improving the quality of training. Consequently, the Government conducted a review of their work resulting in the publication in 1972 of a consultative document, 'Training for the Future'. It recommended th establishment of a National Training Agency to co-ordinate the work the industrial training boards and to develop a national training advisor service, and it adumbrated the possibility of creating a general council o manpower services. These recommendations soon bore fruit with th passing in 1973 of the Employment and Training Act which declared th Government's intention of establishing a Manpower Services Commis sion (MSC) under the aegis of the Department of Employment. The MS(would have as its main responsibility the promotion of more and bette industrial training and for this purpose two executive bodies would b created, to be known as the Training Services Agency (TSA) and th Employment Services Agency (ESA). The Government moved rapidl towards these objectives and the MSC was established in January 197 and the TSA and the ESA in April 1974.

In May 1975, the TSA (renamed the Training Services Division of th MSC in April 1978) issued a discussion document, 'Vocational Prepara tion of Young People', underlining the serious deficiencies in the existing provision and suggesting appropriate action. This, in turn, led to a join initiative by the TSA and the Department of Education and Science namely the establishment of a limited number of schemes of Unified Vocational Preparation (UVP) which came into being in 1977. Althoug they cater for relatively small numbers of young people, these schemes are of considerable significance in that they represent a joint venture by the majority forces in industrial training and education respectively.

Of considerably greater scope and significance in this respect is th Youth Opportunities Programme (YOP), operated by the Special Pro grammes Division (SPD) of the MSC. Set up in April 1978 to provide a comprehensive national scheme for over 200,000 unemployed school-leavers and stemming from the Holland Report, 'Young People and Work', published in May 1977, YOP is essentially an endeavour to prepare young people for work by means of Job Creation projects, work experience schemes and specially prepared programmes of further educa-tion. It is of great significance for the colleges in that it is introducing to further education a group of young people for whom they have scarcely catered before. This thrusts upon teachers in the colleges a considerable challenge, namely that of working out the most suitable provision for a group of youngsters many of whom have few or no qualifications and who in the course of their schooling were apathetic or even hostile towards education.

Another group of school-leavers who have been entering further educa-tion in increasing numbers in recent years are those between the age of sixteen and nineteen enrolled on full-time courses in the colleges. Rela-tively highly motivated, they are mainly undertaking courses leading to GCE awards, both at O and A levels, Ordinary National Diplomas, and CGLI [City and Guilds of London Institute] awards. Many could have remained at school to continue their GCE studies; instead, for a variety of reasons, they have opted for the further education college. In some areas of the country, however, all provision for the sixteen to nineteen age group is made in one institution, known as the Tertiary or Junior College. As the effects of the sharp decline in the birth rate in the late 1960s and the first half of the 1970s begin to work their way through the education system, so it will become increasingly necessary to coordinate post-sixteen provision, presently made in school and further education colleges. In such circumstances, some local education authorities may well turn to the tertiary college as an attractive solution to their problem.

Another major area of further education which came under the microscope of public opinion in the late 1960s was technician education. The Haslegrave Committee issued its Report on Technician Courses and Examinations in 1969, advocating the introduction of a unified pattern of courses of technical education for technicians in industry and in the field of business and office studies. The Report recommended the establishment of two new councils, the Technician Education Council (TEC) and the Business Education Council (BEC), to devise and approve an entirely new pattern of courses spanning both advanced and non-advanced further education. Although these recommendations were accepted by the Government, there was a long delay before the new councils were created, so that it was not until March 1973 that TEC came into existence and May 1974 before BEC appeared upon the scene. Since then, however, as a result of the activities of the two councils, a completely new pattern of technician training is emerging, embracing not only education for technicians in industry and business but also some aspects of art and design education. In addition, it seems likely that the lower-level courses in agriculture will shortly be brought within the remit of TEC.

A belated and encouraging development in recent years has been the increase in teacher-training and staff development for further education, partly stimulated by curriculum changes wrought by bodies such as TEC and BEC and the CNAA [Council for National Academic Awards]. With the recommendations of the 1975 Haycocks Report on the training of full-time teachers of further education having been accepted by the Government, we may well be on the eve of a very considerable expansion of provision.

Wales, like England, has been subject to all these changes but events there have been given an added dimension both by the transfer to the Welsh Office of responsibility for all post-school education other than the university and also by the debate which preceded the referendum on devolution. Had the people of Wales voted in favour of devolution, it would have resulted in the creation of a Welsh Assembly with ultimate responsibility for all further education provision in Wales.

Finally, the present decade has witnessed an encouraging growth in research and curriculum development in further education. The number of research projects currently in operation is considerably larger than it was at the beginning of the 1970s. However, in terms of volume, it still lags far behind the amount of educational research sponsored by the universit and school sectors. Curriculum development has been given a fillip by th work of TEC and BEC and by the need to cater for youngsters under taking YOP and unified vocational preparation courses. The setting up, i January 1977, of the Further Education Curriculum Review and Development Unit (FEU) is a most welcome development and, if firs indications are anything to go by, it should contribute greatly to much needed curriculum development in the further education colleges.

Thus, during the 1970s, the further education sector has been, and indeed still is, undergoing a major transformation whose full effects have yet to be felt. The past decade has witnessed substantial changes in highe education within further education, like the creation of the new Colleges and Institutes of Higher Education and the introduction of the Diploma o Higher Education; major curricular developments are taking place in technician education as a result of the work of TEC and BEC; teaching training and staff development in further education are increasing; and the growing problem of unemployment has stimulated the provision by the MSC of industrial training and associated further education and highlighted the need properly to integrate education and training. Above all, perhaps, increasing public concern over these issues has been the stimulus which has led government, industry and the education service to take remedial and long-overdue action. How effective this will turn out to be only time will tell.

3.2 Access for whom?

Naomi E. S. McIntosh

The notion of equality of opportunity

The increase in absolute numbers entering higher education has been great over the past ten years. The questions we now want to ask are concerned with quality rather than quantity. Has access been increased for all? Does 'more' mean 'different' or are we, in fact, simply talking about 'more of the same'?[1] A recent report published by the Organization for Economic Cooperation and Development concluded that 'Big increases in education in the 1950s and 1960s ... brought about only marginal advances in equality of opportunity.'[2] We wish to examine whether the same types of people as before are simply benefiting proportionately more from the increase in available places or whether there has been any real change in the nature of those receiving higher education.

The notion of 'equality of educational opportunity' is a slippery one. As Neave points out, the concept is essentially relativistic, being dependent on ideologies and beliefs concerning the educability of individuals and the nature of the type of society one should be aiming for.[3] The various interpretations are based on different axioms related to intelligence; they result in different educational structures and they require different variables for their evaluation. Neave goes on to delineate three ideal-type interpretations which are briefly summarized as follows:

a) The élitist interpretation

Intelligence is innate and can be measured by psychometric tests taken in early puberty or slightly before.

*Editors' Note: The figure given in this article for the projected level of fees for students on first degree courses in 1977 were accurate at the time it was written. In fact, some differential between the fees charged to home and overseas students was maintained, and this has widened sharply since, to the disadvantage of the latter group.

Source: MCINTOSH, NAOMI E.S., WOODLEY, A and GRIFFITHS, M. (1978) *Access to Higher Education in England and Wales*. The Open University. Printed in (1978) *Innovation in Access to Higher Education*. New York: International Council for Educational Development, pp. 179–217.

Secondary education acts as a screening device to distinguish between the 'able' and the 'less able'.

Equality consists in the right of all children judged 'able', regardless of their social origin, to pursue studies to the highest level without financial hindrance. The success of an education system is judged by the quality and attainment of those students entering university.

(b) The socially oriented interpretation

Intelligence is influenced by 'private environment'. It can be measured but is subject to change and therefore can be determined only over a long period.

Secondary education is still a screening device but the period during which a pupil can gain qualification is prolonged.

Equality consists in educating all children through similar programmes, with a certain degree of compensatory education for the environmentally disadvantaged at the secondary level. The success of an education system is judged by the proportion of students remaining in school after the statutory leaving age.

(c) The individual-centred interpretation

Intelligence is influenced by both private and public environment and is a cultural phenomenon which cannot be meaningfully measured.

As far as possible the secondary school is free from filtering mechanisms.

Equality is measured in terms of the possibility of the individual to make use of and have access to the means of knowledge. The success of the system is judged by the degree to which it can provide for the diverse needs of all classes and individuals.

Although these three categories tend to overlap, the postwar developments in education systems, both at the secondary and postsecondary level, show a transition from the élite interpretation to the socially oriented or the individual-centred interpretation.

The extent to which this transition has been made varies greatly from country to country. Table 1, for instance, shows that little filtering out occurs at the secondary level in the US, with three quarters of the eighteen-year-olds still at school. The traditionally selective nature of the British school system, only recently starting to change, has effectively meant that large numbers of children have been screened out well before they could even have been expected to have aspirations to higher education. The rigorous admissions procedures employed by conventional universities have built on this selective basis, and in effect screened in only those likely to succeed.

Table 1   The percentage of 18 year olds still at school

	%		%
United States	75	Hungary	28
Belgium (Flemish-speaking)	47	Finland	21
		England	20
Belgium (French-speaking)	47	Italy	16
		Netherlands	13
Sweden	45	New Zealand	13
Australia	29	West Germany	9

Source: International Association for the Evaluation of Educational Achievement: Stockholm 1973.

To some egalitarians, to deny access to college is to deny equal opportunity. In the US this principle requires that all who want to try should have *access* to some form of postschool education. However, the extension of access almost invariably leads to an increase in dropout. Some advocates of egalitarianism, Burn[4] notes, confuse equality of opportunity with equality of outcome. But higher education is essentially meritocratic in nature: it seeks out and selects talent, differentiates between it, in the process widens disparities between people rather than levelling them and finally certifies those differences. A university cannot grant equal certification for unequal talents. Clark commented:

The conflict between open door admission and performance of high quality often means a wide discrepancy between the hopes of entering students and their means of realization.[5]

But it is vital both to the academic faculty and to external educationists and laymen that standards of performance and graduation are equivalent to other comparable institutions. It is even more vital to the students. Frank Newman commented on this dilemma in the following words:

In interpreting these findings, we *can* assume that society fulfills its obligations simply by providing the opportunity for as many people as possible to enter college. Success cannot and should not be guaranteed. High dropout rates are not inconsistent with our commitment to broad access, but rather reflect the maintenance of rigorous academic standards and our insistence that a college degree represents real achievement. *Or* we can assume that society's obligation (and its own self-interest as well) is to provide more than just the chance to walk through the college gate. There must also be access to a useful and personally significant education experience.[6]

It is no use extending access and giving to more people the right to enter, if that right simply becomes a right to fail.

England and Wales are still far from the provision of mass higher education, nor by any means does everybody agree upon it as a goal. Entry continues to depend upon the attainment of more or less rigorous entrance requirements. In what follows we take a wide-ranging look at the 'barriers' to access to higher education to see whether this basically élitist system is successfully drawing more 'able' students from traditionally underrepresented groups such as the working class and women. We also look at the development of more 'socially oriented' institutions such as comprehensive schools and polytechnics and evaluate their impact on access. Finally we consider The Open University which, with its absence of entry qualifications represents Britain's largest, if not only 'individually-centred' institution of higher education.

Barriers to access

There are several well-documented discussions of the problems involved in extending opportunity for higher education to minority groups. Crossland[7] provided a cogent summary of the barriers to access to higher education in the United States. He discussed the testing barrier, the barrier of poor preparation, the money barrier, the distance barrier, the motivation barrier, and the racial barrier. It is interesting that he omitted sex. The majority of Crossland's barriers also apply to working-class students in England and Wales. Even the racial barrier may well become significant over the next decade, as more second generation immigrants become qualified for, and expect access to, higher education as of right. These problems are common to many countries as the OECD report *Group Disparities in Educational Participation and Achievement*[8] shows. Much selection, in terms of background, has already taken place before the decisive *school* exams take place, and it is these exams which determine eligibility for selection for higher education.

Social class and universities

It is worth looking at some of these 'barriers' in more detail. To do this in our context is to realize that many of Crossland's barriers are subsumed under one heading, that of social class. Social class is more of a European than a North American phenomenon. It is still in England and Wales a powerful though difficult concept to define. This is not the place in which to embark upon a discussion of its complexities. Much as the concept is attacked, it continues to be the main discriminator used in much social and educational analysis.

The Robbins Committee[9] was well aware of the 'class problem' in higher education and discussed it in great detail. The report noted that there is a 'vast mass whose performance, both at entry to higher education and beyond, depends greatly on how they have lived and been taught beforehand'. This was quite clearly shown by the Robbins Committee when they looked at the progress of children in their sample who had the

Table 2   Progress of children born in 1940–41 with an I.Q. between 115 and 129

Level achieved:	Middle class %	Working class %
'O' levels	56	45
+ 'A' levels	23	14
Entry to full-time higher education	34	15
Entry to degree courses	17	8

Source: *Robbins Report*, 1963.

same I Q ratings but belonged in different social class backgrounds. Table 2 shows how the middle-class children had a far greater chance of entering into higher education and degree courses than their working class contemporaries. In terms of entrance to universities this trend has not changed much, if at all, over the past 20 years. Although greater numbers have been entering universities, in terms of their background they are still entering in the same proportions. Although both the 1966 census and the 1971 census which effectively cover this period showed just under two thirds of economically active males were employed in manual work, their offspring have consistently represented less than a third of accepted UCCA [Universities Central Council on Admissions] candidates (see Table 3). In contrast to this the children of professional staff/skilled technicians accounted for just over a third of UCCA accepted candidates in 1973 while their parents represented only 8 per cent and 9 per cent respectively of the working population in the 1966 and 1971 censuses. Indeed, the middle classes have actually gained ground over the last few years, a sorry state of affairs, 20 years after Robbins.

Table 3   The percentage of accepted UCCA home candidates by father's occupation

	Manual Worker %	Routine Non-manual %	Administrators and Managers %	Professional/ Technical etc. %
1968	28	28	14	30
1969	29	27	15	29
1970	29	17	15	29
1971	29	28	14	29
1972	27	27	14	32
1973	26	25	15	34
1974	26	25	15	34

Source: *UCCA Statistical Supplements*.

Social class and polytechnics

The situation according to this criterion does not seem any better in the polytechnics. The polytechnics did not, of course, leap into being over night. They are very much still a function of their past, many of them being formed as a result of the merging of two or more disparate institutions. Any analysis of their current structure has to bear in mind their origins. Some had strong technological traditions while others already had a major commitment to teaching London external degrees. Others were to incorporate art colleges with separate and distinct traditions.

The main thrust of the development of the binary policy was that these new institutions would be able to provide a comprehensive array of opportunities so that students could move up or down or sideways within them and so that courses at similar levels could be studied full- or part-time. Crosland made this clear in his Woolwich speech.[10]

There is an ever-increasing need and demand for vocational, professional and industrially based courses in higher education – at full-time degree level, at full-time just below degree level, at part-time advanced level and so on . . . . In our view it requires a separate sector with a separate tradition and outlook within the higher education system.

Table 4 shows, since the inception of the polytechnic policy, the range of 'advanced' provision within those institutions which were to be so designated. The early years show significant proportions of university degree work, mainly representing the external degree of London University, and of work in the area of professional studies. As the opportunity to move away from the straitjacket of the London external degree was increasingly taken, so the proportion of the CNAA degree students increases. The other main trend to emerge is, qualitatively, a more significant one. The numbers taking Higher National Certificates, a part-time qualification, have decreased dramatically. For some this is likely to have meant a real loss in opportunity since these courses have not just been transferred to other institutions, but have often been phased out. This interpretation is supported by Pratt and Burgess[11] who state:

A quite clear trend of the polytechnics had been to become less comprehensive in the most important ways. The substantial growth of full-time and sandwich advanced students has been at the expense of not only non-advanced students, as the (DES) policy implied, but of groups not implied in the policy. Part-time students are struggling to retain their position in the colleges, and those on HNC courses are steadily being shed.

An alternative and more sanguine view argued in government is that many who were previously forced to take part-time courses are now able to study full-time – a much more constructive situation. It is difficult to tell from available statistics which of these propositions is correct. It is certainly the case that such courses continue to be provided in Colleges of Further Education.

Table 4 Percentage distribution of advanced students in various courses in polytechnics 1965–1974

Year	First degree		Higher degree		Post- graduate+re- search	HND	HNC	Art	Profes- sional studies	Other	Total students
	Univ	CNAA	Univ	CNAA							
1966	14.0	4.9	0.7	–	2.6	6.0	29.1	4.4	30.5	6.5	77,920
1967	13.0	6.9	0.4	0.04	3.4	6.9	23.5	5.3	34.0	8.3	95,066
1968	12.6	9.4	0.6	0.07	3.5	7.6	21.2	5.0	32.7	7.4	100,813
1969	11.2	13.0	0.6	0.13	4.2	8.6	14.8	3.6	31.2	12.6	101,994
1970	9.7	20.0	0.3	0.32	4.8	10.6	12.4	3.8	28.7	9.4	91,080
1971	9.6	22.1	0.5	0.42	4.4	10.1	11.7	3.8	27.5	9.9	111,283
1972	7.9	26.0	0.4	0.65	4.6	9.4	10.9	4.0	26.3	9.8	114,147
1973	5.1	30.3*	0.3	0.75	4.7	8.8	10.1	4.3	25.6	10.0	116,496
1974	3.0	37.3*	0.2	0.96	4.3	8.0	9.4	0.3*	25.9	10.5	126,106

Sources: Neave, G. and DES, *Statistics of Education*, Vol. 3, Further Education, HMSO, by year.
*The changes in 1974 relate to amalgamation of the National Council for Diplomas in Art and Design with the CNAA.

Both the stated objectives of polytechnics, and the quantitative increase in numbers to be achieved through their establishment, might have been expected to lead to a qualitative change in the nature of their student population. There is little evidence of this. Donaldson[12] was already concerned that 'there is no institutionalized policy of making the polytechnics more accessible to the working class and the current evidence suggests that they are assimilating to the university pattern of social class composition.' Pratt and Burgess[13] commented on the 'social academic drift that appeared increasingly to be taking place in polytechnics. 'As part-timers are shed, the proportion of advanced full-time working-class students declines.' Both of these comments are supported by the findings of the first national survey of staff and students in polytechnics carried out in 1972-73. Whitburn, Mealing, and Cox[14] found that although there were differences between regions and between subject areas, 60 per cent of all students had fathers who were working in nonmanual occupations. The figure for students on degree courses was 64 per cent, and only among part-time students did it drop to nearly one half (51 per cent). The tendency for polytechnics to discontinue lower level and part-time courses is likely to have implications for this aspect of 'success'.

It has been argued that the higher status an institution has, the more remote and inaccessible its range of offerings will appear to potential students. Couper and Harris[15] studied the transition of Bath from a technical college to a College of Advanced Technology to a technological university, and found that the proportion of working-class students declined as the institution became a CAT and fell even further when university status was conferred. They suggested that one reason for this could be that the working class might perceive a university ethos and degree type work as unattractive or irrelevant for them. Whitburn *et al* were also concerned about this, noting 'it is possible that the composition of the student body in polytechnics partially determines and reflects their image or the perceptions which potential students have formed of what polytechnics have to offer.'[16] Of course this hypothesis is relevant only for that proportion of the population which remains interested in education. The majority of the working class are not in the business of discriminating between what two basically similar institutions of higher or further education are providing, since they are not in the market for that product anyway.

It is possible, with the increase of comprehensive schooling (76 per cent of school leavers in 1976 were from comprehensives), that this situation might now start to change, although the tracking that has traditionally taken place within the British educational system is unlikely to cease overnight. The past dominance of the private, direct grant and grammar schools as feeders for the older universities is well documented. There has always been a clearer route from the secondary modern or technical school to the local further education or technical college than to the university. And working-class people are more likely to be more reliant on and

fluenced by the in-school network for advice and their image of 'college'
the absence of knowledgeable parental support. There is also a much
·eater awareness of polytechnic opportunities in further education col-
ges than there is in grammar schools or even in the sixth forms of
omprehensives. In theory, provided polytechnics do not select out poten-
al applicants by reducing the range of provision available too drastically,
ιey should be able to continue to attract more working-class students. If,
ι the other hand, they continue their current emphasis on the develop-
ιent of CNAA degrees, often incorporating in them studies that would
reviously have been at diploma level, and at the same time reduce the
umber of part-time courses, then this is likely to result in a smaller
umber of working-class students. Looking at such a scenario it is not
ifficult to imagine polytechnics quite soon wishing to follow the route
ιken by the Colleges of Advanced Technology and becoming effectively
ιll-fledged universities. It is possible to suggest, if this were to happen
ιat the result of the polytechnic policy would be to have locked Britain
ιto maintaining an élite system of higher education, rather than to have
rovided an impetus to the development of a mass system.

There has never, of course, been a clear commitment in Britain to the
rovision of mass higher education. One might have expected to find it
lanned for as a natural concomitant of the move towards comprehensive
ducation. It may be that it is still too early for this to have started to
appen. It is ironic that the same Labour government which engaged in
ιe abolition of selection at eleven in order to introduce comprehensive
chools was at the same time effectively introducing more division at
ighteen.

If the early ideal outlined in Crosland's speech at Woolwich[17] had been
chieved, then the polytechnics would have been the best placed of all
·ritish institutions to provide opportunities for mass higher education.
Vith their tradition of being more accessible and receptive to the needs of
ιe local community, with less rigorous admissions criteria than univer-
ιties, and with a range of opportunities available at a variety of levels
ιithin and between institutions, more students could have been offered a
eal and continuing opportunity at one or other levels of higher education.

·he qualification barrier

Ίuch prior selection for higher education is, as we have noted, carried out
ιithin the schools. Until the raising of the school leaving age to 16 in 1972,
. substantial proportion of children left with no qualification at all. A
urther group took only O levels or CSE exams at around sixteen.
Although these proportions have increased substantially over the last
ιecade (see Table 5), the proportion of each cohort continuing on
ιntil A levels and thus in a position to take the key examinations is still
mall.

Table 5   Output from schools

The percentage of age-group leaving with	*1961–62*	*1966–67*	*1971–72*
5 or more O levels	15.4	18.7	22.7
1 or more A levels	8.9	12.4	15.6
2 or more A levels	7.1	9.9	12.2
3 or more A levels	4.7	6.4	7.9

Source: DES, *Statistics of Education*, Vol. 2.

There are also signs that further education is becoming an increasingly important additional path to A levels. The number of other children who got one A level in further education rose over the decade from 7,000 to 24,000 and the number who got two A levels from 3,000 to 11,000. Despite these advances, the use of A levels as a criterion for entry to higher level courses continues to act as an effective filter to remove many potential students, particularly those from working-class backgrounds.

Polytechnic admissions policies have to operate within the framework set nationally by the CNAA. This is roughly parallel to that operated by universities. But many polytechnics, particularly on some of their more innovatory programmes, interpret this liberally and demand only the minimum formal requirement.

It could be argued that this formal requirement, stipulating as it does only two subjects at Advanced level, and making no condition about level of grades, creates the lowest possible qualification barrier. However, a two A level requirement is in itself a formidable selection device. The new Diploma of Higher Education, now being offered or planned in nearly 40 colleges or polytechnics, also has a minimum entry requirement of two A levels. In this respect it is unlike the Higher National Diploma which has the less rigorous entry requirement of one A level or more. This is a curious difference in policy and one that is even more curious since the change in grant regulations that made grants for Higher National Diploma courses mandatory was a recent one (1975). Whether or not such an anomalous situation can or should be allowed to continue is a matter for discussion. Why should one set of students have mandatory grants on the basis of one A level and not others? From the point of view of educational accessibility one could argue that it is the Dip.HE that should be downgraded in terms of its entrance requirements, not the other way around.

Another problem arises with the reduction of places available for teacher education and their replacement by places on Dip.HE courses. Until the 1975 entry it was possible for students entering colleges of education to proceed to the degree of Bachelor of Education without first having to matriculate with two A levels at the beginning of the course. The regulations for the new degrees mean that this facility is now not available except for a small minority, e.g. mature students. Some colleges, it is true, are prepared to make retrospective matriculation arrangements allowing

tudents to switch to a degree course on the successful completion of a first
ear on another course. But the snag is that the other available course, the
Certificate of Teacher Education, is itself the subject of swingeing cuts.
Thus opportunities for those with less than two A levels are currently
eing substantially reduced. It could be argued that this will lead to a
welcome raising of standards. It has on the other hand been argued
ogently by Evans[18] that it will have a particularly damaging effect on
pportunities for girls who have hitherto provided the bulk of the students
1 teacher education courses. In 1974 Colleges of Education admitted
2,000 students of whom 24,300 were women. In 1975 again the women
umbered 22,300 of the 30,000 entries. Of these a sizeable proportion will
ot have had two A levels and on current form would be extremely lucky to
ain one of the few surviving teacher education places.

The question of sex as a barrier is one to which we shall return, but it is
vorth noting here that the introduction of the Diploma of Higher Educa-
ion with its traditional qualification barrier is likely to diminish rather
han increase opportunities for girls unless some new formula for pro-
visional matriculation is used on a large scale.

School background

Although many more places are now available in the various sectors of
higher education, there can be no doubt that different types of schooling
till play a dominant role in the selection system. This becomes most
apparent when we compare the destinations of school leavers from state
schools with those of leavers from the independent sector (Table 6). Pupils
rom independent schools are much more likely to enter higher education
n general, and universities in particular. Furthermore, their dominance is
most marked in those institutions generally accepted to be the 'ultimate'
n higher education, namely Oxford and Cambridge. In 1976, 55 per cent
of the male entrants and 44 per cent of the female entrants to Oxford were
educated in direct grant or independent schools. The state sector, while
catering to more than 90 per cent of the school population, provided only
45 per cent of Oxford entrants. This proportion has remained constant
over the last decade.

Direct grant grammar schools occupy an anomalous position, being
neither completely financially 'independent' nor 'state maintained'. The
majority of pupils pay fees but a certain number of free places are provided
on a competitive basis for local children. In recognition of this service past
governments have supported these schools with 'direct grants'. Their
achievements, when compared with those of state grammar schools, are
obviously great (Table 6). However, the present Labour government is at
the moment phasing out direct grant grammar schools. As their grants are
removed, such schools are forced to decide between becoming completely
independent or being absorbed into the state system. Supporters of the
direct grant system argue that such a move will not lead to equality of

Table 6 The Destination of School Leavers in 1974 (by type of school attended)

| | Type of School | | | |
Destination:	All state maintained n = 638,510 %	All independent n = 26,900 %	State grammar n = 70,520 %	Direct grant grammar n = 16,040 %
Oxford or Cambridge	0.3	6.7	1.5	5.4
Other universities	3.9	17.4	16.1	26.9
Degree courses in polytechnics and elsewhere	0.8	1.7	3.0	4.1
Teacher training	2.2	2.9	7.2	7.4
Higher National Certificate/ Diploma	0.3	1.0	1.0	1.0
Total entering full-time higher education	7.5	29.7	28.8	44.5

opportunity but will merely deny the opportunity of higher education to those bright working-class children who benefited under the old system. Whether this is a correct view or not will depend upon the performance of Britain's comprehensive schools.

There has been a large-scale move towards comprehensive secondary schooling in Britain over the last ten years. Comprehensive school pupils formed 76 per cent of school leavers in 1976 as opposed to 10 per cent in 1966. There has been much concern, especially in educational 'Black Papers', that this has produced a decline in standards. Evidence has been cited which purports to show the relatively small percentages of comprehensive school pupils entering higher education. However, as was pointed out earlier, other studies have shown that when one controls for the 'creaming off' of bright pupils by coexisting grammar schools, comprehensives appear to offer equal access to higher education. It is the hope of many supporters of comprehensive schooling that more and more pupils will be encouraged to stay on at school and hence overcome the qualification barrier to higher education. However, the recent raising of the school leaving age, coupled with the widespread reorganization of secondary education, means that it is still too early to see if their hopes will be realized. The fact that students entering university from state schools have formed a constant proportion of the total university intake during the period of massive reorganization in secondary education provides further evidence that comprehensive schools do not disadvantage aspiring pupils.

Subject areas

Although for some courses the simple possession of two A levels is sufficient academic qualification for entry, in some subject areas the excess of demand over places has meant that some institutions have been able to ask for and obtain much higher standards than the minimum formal requirements. In the university sector there have always been certain subjects that are considered to offer easy access and others which are oversubscribed by suitably qualified applicants. In recent years in the case of Arts subjects it has been possible for universities to ask for and obtain entrants with very high A level grades indeed. In engineering subjects, however, many students have obtained university places with the minimum entrance requirement of two grade 'E's.

Access in terms of subject area, then, will vary according to both the number of places which educational planners considered in the past to be appropriate for national needs, and also the popularity of a given subject among people currently applying for places. Taking the last point, there appears to be a trend towards vocational subjects (Table 7). Given the present economic climate and the fact that some 8 or 9 per cent of new graduates are still unemployed at least six months after graduating, it is perhaps not surprising that applicants are favouring courses which lead to specific jobs.

Table 7   Changes in the Preferred Subjects of Study of Applicants for University Admission

	Number of Applicants		
Subject	1971	1975	1975 as % of 1971
Dentistry	1,442	2,969	206
Pharmacy	1,471	2,679	182
Business management studies	1,805	2,675	148
Law	6,205	8,351	135
Medicine	8,971	12,046	134
Civil engineering	3,625	4,818	133
Combinations of languages and other arts	3,412	3,774	111
Electrical engineering	4,123	4,392	107
History	3,809	3,905	103
English	5,897	5,666	96
Mechanical engineering	3,540	3,350	95
Geography	4,432	4,128	93
Combinations of social administrative and business studies	7,622	7,078	93
Economics	3,417	3,107	91
Sociology	3,166	2,820	89
Physics	3,017	2,295	76
Mathematics	6,041	4,595	76
General Arts	2,978	2,210	74
Chemistry	3,405	2,292	67

Source: *UCCA Statistical Supplement to the 13th Report, 1974–75.*

The increased demand for vocational subjects has meant that applicants have faced stiffer competition for entry. In 1967, 13.2 per cent of the students accepted for courses in medicine had three A levels with Grade 'B' or higher whereas the corresponding proportion in 1975 had risen to 38.1 per cent. The proportions of highly qualified students accepted for engineering courses also rose slightly between 1967 (15.3 per cent) and 1975 (19.3 per cent). However, for both science and social subjects there was a drop in highly qualified students.

The financial barrier

Alexander Astin[19] in a discussion of equal access in the US looks at finance not as a barrier to access, but as a measure of equality of opportunity. Who pays what part of the costs? He found substantial differences in institutional expenditures both for tuition fees and for financial aid. He calculated a figure to indicate the extent to which student costs at public sector institutions are subsidized, and found that the smallest subsidy was in two-year colleges and the largest in the most selective universities. And, of course, the poorest students were found in the two-year colleges which were then the least subsidized.

This sort of effect is not likely to be so marked in Britain, since the possession of the offer of a place, together with the minimum entrance requirements, brings with it for full-time students the guarantee of a mandatory grant covering both tuition and maintenance. The maintenance element is, however, assessed on parental means, and neither the income scales employed nor the level of grant itself have kept up with inflation. Many students eligible for a partial grant have found their parents unable or unwilling to make up the difference. Students are likely to be better off coming from either rich or poor parents rather than in the middle of the income scale. There are also anomalies with respect to women who marry while studying, and problems about when students are judged to be independent of their parents.

In principle, however, the level of state support for full-time degree level study ensures that finance is not such a barrier as it is in the US [...] Approximately 90 per cent of all full-time students get a full or partial grant.

There are signs, however, that students are finding it increasingly hard to manage, and Gareth Williams[20] has argued that this is one of the factors involved in the declining level of demand. At the same time the government is consulting with universities about the possibility of cutting hidden subsidies in the form of residence and catering services, and charging a more economic price for such services. Unlike the US, there has been no tradition in Britain of paying economic fees for educational tuition at degree level. Even the élite universities are in that sense free. Again, unlike the US, the nature of the traditional British three-year tightly integrated degree programme is that it really has to be studied full-time. It is not possible to hold down a job and study at the same time in the way that many US students, for example, expect to be able to do.

Given this background, the financial barriers to access are more indirect. The basic decision rests with the government to expand the absolute number of places since it knows it will effectively have to find, at minimum 90 per cent of the total cost. The individual's commitment at this stage is a lesser one.

For the individual the critical decision is likely to have been taken earlier. For many children, particularly those from working-class homes, the real selection takes place at sixteen-plus, rather than eighteen-plus, when there is little or no financial incentive for them to stay on in full-time education. The level of maintenance grants for children who stay on at school after the compulsory school leaving age is very low and for many parents and children the need to earn is overwhelming.

The lack of financial support for those two critical years is one outstanding anomaly in the range of educational support in England and Wales. Awareness of it has been heightened by recent government policy in respect of the young unemployed who at the same age may now be given grants for pursuing training courses in colleges of further education. This early financial barrier is difficult to quantify, but is likely to continue as a significant one unless there is a change in government policy. Provided young people can survive those two years they are reasonably well provided for from then on through the mandatory grants system.

Support is not necessarily uniform as Wagner and Watts[21] argued in a recent study on the costs of being a student. They showed that generally speaking it was less costly to pursue full-time education at eighteen than to wait till later on in life. They also showed that part-time higher education was cheaper than the full-time alternative but that the gap was not large enough to make it an attractive option for eighteen-year-olds. A more unexpected finding was that students living away from home are financially better off than students living at home since the extra grant more than compensates for the extra cost. Not surprisingly, perhaps, in the light of this, the Public Accounts Committee is asking the DES to examine the case for increasing the number of home-based students 'as a matter of urgency'.[22]

The policy concerning mandatory grants is set nationally and is reasonably equitable, although there are some categories of students excluded from benefit as an act of policy while small numbers of others are debarred for more accidental reasons.

Prior to 1977, when tuition fees were set low for all but overseas students, these exceptions did not cause great hardship. With the rise in tuition fees to £650 for undergraduate students from both home and overseas in 1977, although the vast majority receiving mandatory grants will be no worse off, and those previously on minimum grant will be better off, those few with no grant are likely to be very hard hit. Indeed, initial estimates made by DES officials indicated that the swingeing increase in fees was expected to result in 7,000 fewer students in higher education in 1977–78, a drop of 2.5 per cent. Many of these it was anticipated, however, would be postgraduate and many would be from overseas.

We do not propose to discuss the difficult question of overseas students here, but there are other categories of debarred students which are of concern to us. Little is known about students who are not eligible for grants and how they have managed or will manage in the future. In an effort to find out about them Ernest Rudd studied all such students at Essex University.[23] One major group he found was those who already hold a qualification for which grants can be given. Note that they may not actually have received a grant for their studies. The previous qualification is frequently at subdegree level, e.g. a teaching certificate. People in this category may be married women returners, people who did badly in their first qualification and wish to return, or people who need further qualifications for promotion. Another group consisted of people who seemed to be eligible but who had been put off by the complexity of the form, by other people telling them they were not eligible, or by other misunderstandings. Other regulations concerning time of application and residence qualifications also hit some home students, often unfairly. He found that one in 15 of all undergraduate students at Essex had not got the minimum grant. Of these he estimated that one quarter already held a qualification which precluded them from a new grant. One third had fallen foul of the regulations in some way. A very small number had chosen not to apply. The balance are part of the more difficult overseas case. They are effectively overseas students who have acquired eligibility for the home tuition fee by dint of being resident here for over three years but have in some way become ineligible for maintenance, e.g. by not being in the country in September.

This last category is of less concern in this analysis but the other home students are likely to find the increased fees a major barrier to continued study and they are the types of groups which may occur more frequently among mature students, particularly as more transferability between institutions develops and there is any substantial move to continuing education.

There is much greater inequity in the area of grants for part-time study. Such grants come under the category of 'discretionary' awards and local education authorities make their own decisions about what are or are not deserving categories of students or types of courses. There are wide descrepancies in policy, even between adjacent areas. The assumption is that part-time students are usually adults who are working and can afford to pay. Many can, it is true, but many cannot, and the burden on younger low-paid workers, or housewives with no accessible income may be very great. The Equal Opportunities Commission has argued in evidence to the DES that the area of discretionary grants is particularly discriminatory against women who frequently cannot study full-time or wish to study on lower-level courses.[24]

The sex barrier

In Great Britain, women in higher education are quite clearly a minority group. The tradition, prevalent for so long, that the education of girls was less important than that of boys, and the cultural and social imperatives that have underlaid this, cannot be changed overnight. The Sexual Discrimination Act of 1975, together with the setting up of the Equal Opportunities Commission will, it is hoped, start to have some impact on existing practices, but old attitudes die hard, and the structure of existing institutions still continues to militate against women.

It is true that there are now signs of change. More girls are staying on longer at school, and more are applying to and being accepted by universities and polytechnics. Fifteen years ago Robbins had noted a cumulative negative effect: fewer girls were staying on at school, therefore, obtaining fewer A levels, and of those who were staying on fewer were attempting to take two or three A levels, as Table 8 shows.

Table 8   Percentage of School Leavers with 5 or More O Levels Obtaining Passes at A Level (by age of leaving) 1961

| Age of Leaving | A Level Passes | | | Numbers (= 100%) |
	3 or More %	2 or More %	1 or More %	
18 and over:				
Boys	51	73	85	26,940
Girls	34	58	78	19,450
Boys and girls	44	66	82	46,390
17:				
Boys	23	34	41	11,430
Girls	12	21	30	12,480
Boys and girls	18	28	35	23,910

Source: *Robbins Report*, Appendix One, Part 1, Table 5, p. 9.

By 1974, the situation had improved appreciably. The proportions of the sexes staying on at school (Figure 1) shows that the gap between girls and boys staying on had narrowed.

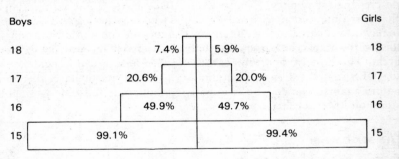

Figure 1   Proportion of boys and girls at school at given ages, 1974

To have stayed on at school and gained qualifications is only the beginning of the story. As Eileen Byrne[25] made clear, it is important to discover where school leavers go, and it is here that the differences emerge more strongly. While more girls overall go on to some form of further or higher education than boys, they go on to a lower level study. More go to colleges of education and colleges of further education, while fewer go to universities (Table 9). This is not in itself a serious difference, provided the lower level courses lead on adequately to desired occupations. However, the cuts in teacher training places will certainly diminish opportunities for girls. More significantly, while degree courses provide the main source of recruitment for many higher level jobs, the smaller number of girls getting A levels and even smaller numbers entering on degree courses, provides a serious limiting factor to the pool of women available for recruitment to top jobs.

Table 9   Destination of School Leavers 1973–1974

Destination:	Boys n = 349,650 %	Girls n = 331,810 %
Universities	6.9	4.2
Colleges of Education	0.9	3.9
Polytechnics	2.3	1.4
Other further education	6.8	13.5
All full-time further education	16.9	23.0

Source: DES, *Statistics of Education*, 1974, Vol. 2.

For the remainder, the number who do not go on to any full-time education, there is a more serious difference. The opportunities for girls to continue their education part time through day release are far less than for boys. Fewer than 10 per cent of girls in the relevant age groups get day-release education as compared with 40 per cent of boys.

The number of women applying to and being accepted by universities has increased steadily but slowly over the last few years, as Table 10 shows.

Table 10   Applications and Acceptances for Universities, Analysed by Sex (excluding overseas candidates)

	All Applicants		Accepted Applicants	
	Men %	Women %	Men %	Women %
1969	67.7	32.3	69.0	31.0
1970	68.7	31.3	67.2	32.8
1971	67.7	32.3	66.6	33.4
1972	66.9	33.1	65.5	34.5
1973	65.8	34.2	64.1	35.9
1974	64.8	35.2	63.6	36.4
1975	64.4	35.6	63.6	36.4

Source: *UCCA Statistical Supplements*.

However, the figures in the table also reveal that women are not favoured by the admissions process. Female applicants are slightly less likely to be accepted than male applicants.

Similar figures for polytechnics are hard to obtain, since as we have noted there is no central clearing house for polytechnic admission. For comparative information between sectors of higher education, then, we are confined to enrolment figures. These show the proportions of women steadily increasing over the decade both in universities and in polytechnics, although the figure for polytechnics is consistently lower than that for universities. Women continue to dominate in colleges of education but the figures do not show any clear trend (Table 11).

Subject differences have an important effect on opportunities open to girls and are likely to become more, not less, significant, at least in the short term. Many of the new colleges of higher education are developing CNAA degrees and diplomas in Arts, Social Sciences and Liberal Studies, capitalizing on their existing staff and experience, and these will provide some opportunities for girls provided they have two A levels. However, the national pressure for expansion of science and technology will certainly benefit men rather than women as the Secretary of State for Education, Shirley Williams, pointed out somewhat ruefully in a speech (*Guardian*, 10 February 1977).

It is ironic and potentially very serious that the growing interest and concern in the education of women comes at a time when economic and demographic factors are liable not just to militate against its expansion, but potentially to cut back on what is being currently achieved. The cutback in teacher training, the emphasis on science and technology, the arrival of the Dip.HE with its two A level entry, are all developments which are more likely to disadvantage than to advantage women.

If the country were to rethink its education of girls and if the social and psychological climate were to change sufficiently so that a similar proportion of girls as of boys gained A levels and went on to take a degree, then maybe we would discover that the forecasts of demand in the eighties would be too low. On current form this seems an unlikely prospect and a much greater urgency both within schools and in the country will be needed if women are not to continue as a minority group on degree courses for at least the next decade.

The age barrier

Mature students have become, both in the US and in Great Britain, a group of much interest to administrators and educationists, and now increasingly to politicians. They are seen, in particular, as a possible answer to those unfilled places in certain subject areas and in the future as a possible source of supply of students to fill the places which will become available in the mid-eighties as the demographic trends work their remorseless way through the education system. Some workers in adult education could be forgiven for looking at this newly awakened interest on the part of conventional universities with a somewhat jaundiced eye.

There is little agreement on what constitutes 'maturity'. Some institu-

Table 11 Location of Full-Time Students by Sex

	Universities		Further Education (advanced courses)		Colleges of Education	
	Male	Female	Male	Female	Male	Female
1965/66	73.5	26.5	76.8	23.2	28.4	71.6
1971/72	70.2	29.8	73.9	26.1	28.4	71.6
1972/73	69.1	30.9	72.3	27.7	29.5	70.5
1973/74	68.0	32.0	70.7	29.3	29.8	70.2
1974/75	66.9	33.1	69.2	30.8	27.7	72.3

Source: Central Statistical Office, *Social Trends*, London: HMSO, 1976.

tions class students as mature at over 23, some at over 35. Institutions vary in their entrance requirements for mature students; some demand standard qualifications; some set 'special' entrance tests and some accept essays. Mature students are not the homogenous body that the widespread use of the term implies.

A recent aspiring applicant to a Research Council for a grant to study mature students in the UK wished to study them as people 'marginal' to an institution. Ironically, only 25 years ago they would not have been a marginal case, but rather a very common occurrence in British universities. The Forces Education Training scheme ensured that large numbers of mature students from a wide variety of backgrounds entered and succeeded in higher education. It was the younger students who were often then more unusual. Now the situation is reversed. It seems unlikely that it was either the curriculum or the structure of higher education that was changed postwar. It is much more likely that it was the more practical questions, such as the provision of adequate financial support, that were the key to successful study then. These, allied with their motivation, enabled many adults to catch up on past missed opportunities.

The important distinction is not the question of what constitutes maturity, but the distinction between full- and part-time study. On the basis of the Open University experience we would propose that it may often be nonacademic factors which determine whether or not mature students study successfully. Many of them will already be married with children and often holding responsible and demanding jobs. It requires *adequate* funding to ensure that they *can* study without undue stress to their spouse and families. Rarely is this now available. It also requires some relaxation of the sets of bureaucratic and academic requirements which have been developed, maybe quite appropriately, for under 21s, but totally inappropriately for mature students. Some educationists argue the case for a different and 'relevant' curriculum for adult students. We are not convinced by this argument. On the other hand, the case for different structures, regulations, and finance is overwhelming.

The normal definition of 'mature' is over 25. Over the last decade the proportion of mature students in universities has crept up from 4.6 per cent in 1967 to 6.1 per cent in 1973. In polytechnics the percentages have been rather higher, culminating in 12.0 per cent on CNAA courses in 1973. In the university sector, each institution determines its own policy towards the admission of mature students and the chances of being accepted therefore vary widely. For example in 1975 mature students formed 20.0 per cent of the student population at Essex compared with only 3.0 per cent at Leicester. As a generalization, it seems to be the most popular universities that often take the smaller number of mature students. Several universities have shown interest in developing agreements between themselves and the Open University to enable mature students to transfer between them. It is clear that some of the initial interest in these arrangements was motivated by the desire of those univer-

Table 12   Age of Full-Time Students in Higher Education in the United Kingdom

	Men				Women			
	1971	1972	1973	1974	1971	1972	1973	1974
Base – all full-time students (1000's)	283.5	286.1	290.2	289.0	189.9	195.9	205.3	207.7
	%	%	%	%	%	%	%	%
Age 18 and less	10.7	10.6	10.3	10.4	17.0	16.6	15.6	15.5
19–20	35.8	35.6	35.4	35.2	45.0	44.8	43.5	43.2
21–24	37.7	36.7	36.8	36.2	24.5	24.9	26.7	26.7
25 and over	15.8	17.2	17.6	18.2	13.6	13.7	14.1	14.6

Note: Higher education includes universities, teacher training, and advanced further education.
Source: Central Statistical Office, *Social Trends*, 1976.

sities to find a new source of recruits for some of their empty places, particularly in science and technology.

The CNAA sets the overall policy for admission of mature students to polytechnics and is currently engaging in a major review of this policy which may well lead to a change in their entry requirements. While the number of full-time mature students in the country is increasing (see Table 12) the number of part-time students has, with the exception of the Open University, barely increased. Existing universities have not been successful in developing part-time courses which have proved attractive to significant numbers of students. They appear to have been more concerned to bend mature students to their existing structure and courses than to change the form of the courses to meet the needs of the students. And, surprisingly, it is only relatively recently that the polytechnic sector has started to increase its number of part-time degree courses significantly.

Academic inertia is hard to overcome. It is difficult to understand otherwise why conventional institutions are so reluctant to change their habits. It is obviously far cheaper for adults to study part-time, although it is not necessarily easier in terms of their personal life. The more people who can be encouraged and enabled to study part-time, the better it is likely to be for the country. If, on the other hand, all that existing institutions are prepared to do is to admit adult students on the institution's own 'irrelevant' terms, then it will not be surprising if many potentially very valuable students decide not to apply [...]

By admitting students of all ages and, perhaps more importantly, by demanding no entry qualifications, the Open University represents an attempt to create an establishment based on Neave's 'individual-centred interpretation' of educational opportunity within a system which, in varying degrees, contains the two other ideologies as well. In this model, education is no longer seen as a sequential process with pupils feeding directly into higher education having followed specific school 'tracking' systems, but rather may be taken up whenever the individual perceives the need....

References

1 ASHBY, ERIC (1973) The Structure of Higher Education – A World View, *Higher Education*, Vol 2, No. 2, May 1973, p. 143.

2 OECD (1970) *Group Disparities in Educational Participation and Achievement*, Paris: Organization for Economic Cooperation and Development.

3 NEAVE, GUY (1976) *Patterns of Equality*. Windsor: NFER.

4 BURN, BARBARA B. (1976) *Higher Education in a Changing World. Reflections on an International Seminar*. New York: International Council for Educational Development, Conference Report Number Three.

5 CLARK, BURTON (1960) 'The "Cooling Out" Function in Higher Education', *American Journal of Sociology*, Vol. LVX, No. 6, (p. 571). Chicago: University of Chicago Press, May 1960.

NEWMAN, FRANK. (1971) *Report on Higher Education*. Washington, D.C.: U.S. Government Printing Office (p. 3).

CROSSLAND, FRED E. (1971) *Minority Access to College. A Ford Foundation Report*. New York: Shocken Books.

OECD (1971) *Group Disparities in Educational Participation and Achievement*, Vol. IV. Paris: Organization for Economic Cooperation and Development.

Higher Education (1963) Report of the Committee Appointed by the Prime Minister under the Chairmanship of Lord Robbins 1961–63 (*The Robbins Report*), Cmnd. 2154. London: HMSO.

Speech by Anthony Crosland, Secretary of State for Education and Science, at Woolwich Polytechnic, 27 April 1965, printed in PRATT, J. and BURGESS, T. (1974) *Polytechnics: A Report*. London: Pitman Publishing (p. 204).

Op. cit., PRATT and BURGESS, p. 82.

DONALDSON, LEX (1971) *Social Class and the Polytechnics, Higher Education Review*. Autumn 1971 (pp. 44–68).

Op. cit. PRATT and BURGESS, p. 86.

WHITBURN, JULIA, MEALING, MAURICE and COX, CAROLINE (1976) *People in Polytechnics*. Guildford: Society for Research into Higher Education.

COUPER, M. and HARRIS, C. (1970) 'C.A.T. to University – The Changing Student Intake', *Educational Research*, Vol. 12, No. 2. (pp. 113–20).

Op. cit. Whitburn *et. al.*

Op. cit. Anthony Crosland.

EVANS, NORMAN (1976) 'Level Pegging', *Education Guardian*, 27 January 1976.

ASTIN, ALEXANDER W. (1975) *The Myth of Equal Access to Higher Education*. Los Angeles (mimeograph).

WILLIAMS, GARETH (1974) 'The Events of 1973–4 in a Long-Term Planning Perspective', *Higher Education Bulletin*, No. 3. Centre for Educational Research and Development, Lancaster University.

WAGNER, LESLIE and WATTS, ANNE (1976) *The Cost of Being a Student*. Polytechnic of Central London (mimeograph).

THES Report (30 September, 1977) on the Committee of Public Accounts Ninth Report, London: HMSO.

RUDD, ERNEST (1976) 'Tuition Fees: Those in greatest need will suffer most', *Times Higher Education Supplement*, 26 November, 1976.

'Award System Discriminates Against Women', *Times Higher Education Supplement*, 26 November, 1976.

BYRNE, EILEEN (1975) 'The Place of Women in the Changing Pattern of Further Education', *Women in Higher Education*, London: Institute of Education.

3.3 Class and meritocracy in British education

Anthony Heath

'The hereditary curse upon English education is its organization upo
lines of social class' (Tawney 1931, p. 142). These words are possibly th
most famous and the most quoted in the sociology of education in Britai
and they express succinctly the spirit of the 'political arithmetic' traditio
of British sociology – a tradition which has been the most important of th
indigenous schools of sociology and which has made some of the mo
influential contributions to educational reform.

The tradition has been a 'political' one insofar as it has always had
close association with social policy and the political reform of British (o
rather, more strictly, English and Welsh) education. Tawney's métier wa
impassioned rhetoric inveighing against the injustices within our educa
tional system. He was not the detached, impartial observer but th
convinced polemicist. Similarly, his successors have been concerned t
expose the defects of British education and thus to influence the politica
process. Like Tawney they have been on the political Left rather than th
Right – although they have usually had their Right-wing adversaries suc
as, in recent times, the contributors to the Black Papers.

Broadly subsumed under the heading of 'the class character of Britis
education' the questions which the political arithmeticians tackled hav
been ones of injustice and social waste – the social waste of able childre
who were denied effective access to secondary and higher education, an
the unjust distribution of opportunities for educational advancemer
granted to the children from different social classes. The goal to be aime
at, said Tawney, was simplicity itself. 'The idea that differences of educa
tional opportunity should depend upon differences of wealth amon
parents is a barbarity' (Tawney 1931; p. 145).

However, while writers in the political arithmetic tradition have unde
niably been 'politically motivated' in their aims and their choice of issue
to study, they have also (unlike the Black Paper writers) carried ou
rigorous empirical investigations of their own. These have provided muc
of the factual basis for our understanding of British education today. Som
of the major contributions of this kind have been Lindsay's *Social Progres
and Educational Waste* (1926), Gray and Moshinsky's paper on 'Ability an
Opportunity in English Education' (1938), Floud, Halsey and Martin'
Social Class and Educational Opportunity (1956) and Douglas' *The Home and th
School* (1964).

Halsey, Heath and Ridge's *Origins and Destinations* (1980) is the latest i
this line of research, and my intention is to describe some of its mai
findings on the class character of British education. I shall by no mean

Source: Commissioned by The Open University, January 1980.

tempt to summarize *all* the main findings of *Origins and Destinations*. I
all have nothing to say in this paper, for example, about the findings on
e 'reproduction of cultural capital' (Bourdieu's phrase), on the educa-
onal consequences of attending Independent, Grammar, Technical and
:condary Modern schools, or on the extent to which Part-time Further
lucation provides an effective 'alternative route' to educational success.
istead, I shall concentrate on class differences in access to different forms
id levels of education and the way in which these differentials have
langed over time. I shall tackle the questions, 'How did the class chances
` access to the Independent schools compare with those to the Grammar,
echnical and Secondary Modern schools?' 'Were these differences in
ass chances ones that could be justified by the distribution of talent in
ich class, or was there a wastage of working-class talent with working-
ass boys failing to win the places at Grammar and Technical school that
ley were entitiled to?' 'Did the 1944 Education Act reduce the class bias
. access to secondary education or did the "hereditary curse" remain as
otent after the ostensibly meritocratic reforms of the Act as it had before?'
nd finally, 'What are the current prospects for achieving the goals of
quality of opportunity of outcome?'

The data on which *Origins and Destinations* is based comes from a
ational sample survey of ten thousand adult men carried out in 1972.
·ur main interest lies in the eight thousand or so men who received their
lucation in England and Wales and who reported details which enabled
s to construct a measure of their social class origins. At the time of the
iterviews in 1972 these men were aged between twenty and fifty-nine
ears and they gave us detailed accounts of their own educational experi-
ice and qualifications. The youngest of them were thus reporting on an
lucation received in the 1960s while the oldest were reporting on an
lucation received almost forty years earlier. Accordingly, one of the main
ssets of *Origins and Destinations* is its ability to compare the educational
xperience of the different age-groups and thus to give an account of
le history of British education from the 1920s to the beginning of the
970s.

To obtain this historical account I and my co-authors divided the
ample into four birth cohorts consisting of men born from 1913 to 1922,
923 to 1932, 1933 to 1942, and 1942 to 1953 respectively. The members of
le first birth cohort were thus entering the primary schools in the 1920s
/hile some members of the last birth cohort were still receiving higher
lucation in 1972. Broadly speaking we can also say that the members of
le first two cohorts were educated before the 1944 Education Act came
ito effect after the Second World War while the members of the two
ounger cohorts went through the tripartite system of education (the
rammar, Technical and Secondary Modern schools) that was estab-
ished in the post-war period. By the 1960s, of course, the tripartite system
/as beginning to give way to comprehensive reorganization, but only a
iny proportion of our respondents were actually educated in Comprehen-

sive schools. In 1965, for example, 92 per cent of the children receivi
state secondary education were in schools organized along tripartite lin
and our data reflect this distribution. What the survey enables us to d
therefore, is to give an assessment of the tripartite system and to compa
it with the pre-war structure. As I shall try to argue, the lessons to
learned from such a historical study are not without their relevance
contemporary issues in state education, but we must remember that it is
the nature of such a survey that it gives us a look backwards and a way
monitoring past attempts at social reform rather than a preview of t
future.

However, before we can have our look backwards, we must first co
struct a measure of social class. The measurement of social class is one
the most contentious issues among professional sociologists and one that
responsible for considerable confusion among their readers. The layma
when pressed, will usually be willing to draw a distinction between t
middle and the working class, and when pressed further he may be willi
to make additional subdivisions into upper middle, lower middle a
perhaps even middle middle classes. When he does so he may well have
mind (among other things) differences in accent, style of life, consumptio
patterns or the use of 'U' and non-'U' English. These, however, a
criteria which the professional sociologist would associate more with *soci
status* than with *social class*. At any rate, they are *not* the criteria use
in the present paper.

Social status is now usually taken (following Max Weber) to be a matt
of social honour and respect accorded different social groups. Its presen
could be revealed, for example, by marks of respect such as addressing
person as 'Sir' or by according him precedence – allowing him to spea
first at a meeting or to enter the room first. Social class on the other hand
usually taken to be a matter of a group's economic and material interest
power and advantage, and in modern British society these will in tur
largely depend on that social class's position within the occupation
division of labour. For example, manual workers share common econom
interests in that their livelihood depends on their ability to sell the
labour-power in the economic market, in that they have little securit
of tenure in their jobs or promotion prospects, and in that they hav
relatively few 'fringe benefits' such as pension rights and sick pa
schemes.

However, while manual workers differ on average in these respects fron
non-manual workers, it would be quite wrong to treat non-manua
workers as a homogeneous group united by shared economic interests
While economic interests are by no means to be regarded as identical wit
income, it is still worth remembering that the routine clerical worke
actually earns less than many skilled manual workers while the profes
sional, manager, or senior administrator may earn three or four times a
much. Professionals and administrators also tend to have much greate
security of tenure than other groups, and once they have attained one o

these positions they are highly unlikely to move downwards to a subordinate one (see Goldthorpe 1980). They are also typically in positions of power and authority over others, unlike those at the lower levels of white-collar work.

The basic classification of social classes uses in *Origins and Destinations* is a threefold one and it is based on position within the occupational division of labour. It distinguishes between a 'service' class, an 'intermediate' class, and a 'working' class. The terms 'service' and 'intermediate' are used deliberately to indicate that we are *not* dealing with the old middle class of lay terminology, or with some subdivision of it into an upper and lower middle class. The service class, says John Goldthorpe who constructed the scheme, consists of those 'exercising power and expertise on behalf of corporate "authorities", plus such elements of the classic bourgeoisie, independent businessmen, and "free" professionals, as are not yet assimilated into this new formation' (Goldthorpe and Llewellyn 1977, p. 259). It contains professionals, administrators, officials in central and local government, managers in industrial establishments and 'large' proprietors (who run and own establishments of more than 25 employees). This includes both higher-level professionals such as doctors and lawyers as well as lower-level professionals like primary-school teachers and social workers. The latter Goldthorpe regards as a subaltern or cadet position of the service class, but all are in some sense exercising power and authority on behalf of the corporate authorities in contemporary society and to that extent share common interests.

Next comes the intermediate class. It consists of three rather disparate groups – routine white-collar workers such as clerical employees and sales personnel, 'small' proprietors and other self-employed workers, and lastly the classical marginal men of industry, the foremen, who are neither unambiguously part of the working class nor properly part of management. This is a rather heterogeneous collection of occupations, and we could not claim that they are united by common economic interest. Strictly speaking we should keep them separate in their three constituent groups, but it will keep the tables and the exposition simpler if we treat the intermediate classes as a single category. (For the more detailed breakdowns, see *Origins and Destinations*.)

In comparison the working class is a much more satisfactory category. It consists of manual workers in industry together with agricultural workers and smallholders. It is the most familiar of our three classes in its composition and hence we have felt able to use the familiar term 'working class'. We should perhaps note, however, that in many countries where agricultural workers form a much larger part of the labour force than they do in Britain, it would be necessary to draw a distinction between the industrial labourers and the farm population. In countries such as France or America we could well argue that their economic interests are radically different, but since British agriculture is relatively mechanized and since agricultural workers come to only 5 per cent of the labour force, we shall be doing no great violence to the class structure if we combine them into a single category.

So much for the preamble. Let us now turn to the evidence. We shall begin with a table showing the class differentials in access to secondary schools for our example as a whole before dividing them into the four birth cohorts. Table 1 gives this overview of class differentials and it brings out a number of indisputable if unsurprising features of the class character of British secondary education in the mid-twentieth century. First, we see gross inequalities in access to the Independent and Direct Grant schools. 11.8 per cent of service-class boys attended the élite Independent schools which belonged to the Headmasters' Conference whereas only a negligible proportion of working-class children, 0.3 per cent did so. This·means that a service-class boy was nearly *forty* times as likely as his working-class contemporary to get to one of these élite schools. In the case of the minor Independent schools which did not belong to the Headmasters' Conference (HMC), he was *eighteen* times as likely to gain a place, and with the Direct Grant schools he was *twelve* times as likely. These, relatively extreme, class differentials contrast with the much more egalitarian access to the state sector. The service-class boy was only *three* times as likely as the working-class to get to a Grammar school, and access to the Technical school was apparently the most egalitarian of all. Similar proportions from all three social classes attended these schools, and of all the types of school which we have seen in Britain this century (apart from the comprehensives), they are the only ones which contained anything like a representative cross-section of the population.

The same pattern of differentials emerges if we take the intermediate classes into account as well. They fall neatly in between the other two. For example, they had nearly twice the likelihood of working-class boys of getting to Grammar school but only about half the likelihood of service-class boys. Thus they may seem privileged if we compare them with the working-class, but if we compare them instead with the distribution of the school population as a whole they do not appear to have an 'unfair' share of places at the élite schools. Indeed, the intermediate class as a whole would be no worse off in a system which allocated places on the basis of chance alone. It is almost as though their sons had been shuffled randomly across the educational spectrum.

While the intermediate-class boys were the ones who came closest to receiving the 'chance' distribution of places, we should also note that there was considerable dispersion in the educational destinations of the other two classes as well. In looking at Table 1 we can either concentrate on the *columns* – comparing the class chances of access to given types of secondary schooling – or we can concentrate on the *rows* – comparing the educational destinations of children from the same class origins. If we do the latter, we observe very considerable homogeneity in the schooling of working-class boys: three-quarters of them attended Secondary Modern schools or their

Table 1 Attendance at Secondary Schools

(percentages)

Father's Class	Secondary Modern	Comprehensive	Technical	Independent (non-HMC)	Grammar	Direct Grant	Independent (HMC)
Service (N = 1072)	26.6	1.5	10.2	8.8	35.1	6.2	11.8
Intermediate (N = 2469)	59.1	1.3	12.9	3.3	19.6	1.8	2.1
Working (N = 4470)	74.7	1.6	11.4	0.5	11.1	0.5	0.3
All (N = 8011)	63.5	1.5	11.7	2.5	16.9	1.6	2.4

Source: *Origins and Destinations*, Table 4.4

pre-war equivalents the Elementary schools, and the great majority of the remainder attended Technical or Grammar Schools. Turning to the service-class boys, we see that the proportions are almost exactly reversed. Three-quarters of them attended some kind of selective school[1] and only one-quarter attended Secondary Modern schools.

It is easy enough to say 'only' one quarter, but it is a salutary point that one-in-four of the children from the most privileged class attended the least privileged educational institution. Indeed, we can speculate that the large number of service-class boys in the Secondary Modern schools may have formed the basis for public disquiet about the eleven plus. The service class undoubtedly had *in general* a substantial advantage over its intermediate or working-class competitors, but these advantages were not shared equally by all service-class boys. Moreover, if we focus on the service-class boys at selective schools, we are struck by the diversity in their educational destinations. It is only a minority who attended the élite Independent schools and even the private sector as a whole (defining the private sector to include HMC, non-HMC, Independent, and Direct Grant schools) took little more than a quarter of service-class boys. Whether through choice or necessity the great majority of the service class remained within the state sector.

There are, however, differences within the service class which are quite revealing. While the majority of the service class remained loyal to the state sector, the self-employed professionals – doctors, lawyers and the like – sent 65 per cent of their sons to the private sector while the 'large' proprietors – men who ran businesses of their own with more than twenty-five employees – sent 47 per cent of their sons to private schools. In other words, those whose work involved them most directly in market or capitalist relationships were the most likely to choose private education for their children. The same holds true of the intermediate class. The heaviest users there of the private sector of education were again those whose work involved them most directly in capitalism and the free market – the farmers and the 'small' proprietors. The salaried employees of state or commercial bureaucracies on the other hand were much more likely to choose state education or the Direct Grant schools – the latter being perhaps the more natural focus for their educational ambitions than the élite Independent schools.

Despite these complexities at the apex of the class structure, the overall pattern is clear enough. Class differentials were greatest in access to the most prestigious forms of secondary education; they narrow as we move down the academic hierarchy, effectively disappearing when we reach the Technical schools; and they then finally reverse when we move further down to the non-selective schools. However, *we cannot infer from this that the selection procedures of the more prestigious types of school were necessarily more biased than those lower down the academic hierarchy.* Simply because the Technical schools took equal proportions from all three social classes, it does not follow that they were unbiased in their selection procedures. After all, it could be that they took relatively few children from the service class simply because so many of them had already secured places at higher prestige institutions. Of those who were left in the competition a disproportionate number might still have been winning places at Technical schools.

What do we mean when we talk of 'bias'? Do we have to see *equal* proportions from each class attending the élite Independent or Direct Grant schools before we are willing to say that they have eliminated class bias, or is there some other yardstick which we can use? To say that a selection procedure is biased is to imply that certain children are unfairly treated, but the moment we raise the issue of fairness we are involved in the problem of social justice. There is no neutral *sociological* yardstick for deciding what is a fair or just allocation of educational resources. Whether we like it or not we are involved in *moral* and ethical arguments.

Throughout most of this century the dominant principle of social justice used in education has been that of equal opportunity for those with equal ability irrespective of their social origins – in other words, the principle of meritocracy. Thus the White Paper which preceded the 1944 Education Act established the canon that 'the nature of a child's education should be determined by his capacity and promise and not by the financial circumstances of his parents'. In effect, the official ideology of British education has been that there should be equal proportions of able children from each social class attending selective schools, and since the official measure of ability, the IQ test, showed class differences in average levels of ability this meant that there should be class differences in the proportions attending selective schools.

But while this may have been the dominant ideology, let us be quite clear that there have been other competing principles of social justice that can, and have been, advocated equally cogently. Thus the 1943 White Paper itself also pronounced that 'due regard should also be paid to the parents' wishes and the careers the children had in mind'. Here we have the germs of a different ideology – that of individual freedom. Parents and children should have the right to choose the kind of education that they want, and if some parents choose to spend their incomes on providing a superior education for their children while others prefer to spend their income on holidays abroad, then they should be free to do so. This is self-evidently the ideology that justifies the continued existence of the private sector and it could justify class differences too insofar as these were the result of differing parental preferences. Class differences in attendance at selective schools would thus be 'fair' if they reflected the differing extents to which the three social classes valued education. The logical extension of this principle would of course be a voucher system which allowed parents and children to choose where and when to have their education.

The principles of equality of opportunity and freedom of choice, ethical principles though they are, can none the less be attacked by the sociologists on empirical grounds. The class distribution of measured intelligence cannot be regarded as some neutral, factual datum which can provide an objective basis for evaluating the fairness of British education. Measured intelligence (particularly verbal ability) we now know to be affected by environmental factors, and so there is in this sense a prior 'class bias' in the measurement of intelligence. Equally, preferences are not autonomous, 'free' starting points for ethical argument. Everything that we know about socialization tells us that preferences for education are themselves the product of social experiences and upbringing. Marx's dictum that 'It is not the consciousness of men that determines their being, but, on the contrary, their social being that determines their consciousness' contains more than a grain of truth.

Many, sociologically informed, thinkers have therefore shifted from the principle of equality of opportunity to that of equality *per se*. This can take on a number of guises. At its simplest it says that equal proportions of children from all classes should secure superior education since neither meritocracy nor freedom of choice have provided satisfactory grounds for giving unequal treatment to different social classes. A stronger version holds that it is not the distribution of educational *inputs* – the proportion of places at selective school for example – which should be made equal but rather educational *outcomes* – the standards of achievement which children reach at the end of their schooling. This is a principle which justifies unequal treatment, only this time it is the social disadvantage groups which are to receive extra schooling. 'Compensatory education' or 'positive discrimination' become the key expressions. Children should receive the education they need in order to enable them to fulfil their roles as adult citizens of the society. Educational outcomes must be equalized since unequal education gives people unequal ability to exercise their civil and political rights and duties in modern democratic society.

I do not pretend that this is more than a sketch of the main principles of social justice that are employed in contemporary educational arguments. That the British educational system has fallen far short of justice according to the principles both of equality and of freedom of choice, cannot, however, be seriously in doubt whatever our ethical stance. On the other hand, the question whether British education has achieved its own professed goal of 'equality of opportunity for those of equal ability' in the post-war period, or at the least has contrived to come near it, is open to more argument. This, therefore, is the issue on which we shall concentrate.

It is one of the more astonishing facts about British education in the late twentieth century that there has been no official monitoring of the extent to which the educational system has achieved its own professed goals, leave alone the goals that other moral perspectives might advocate. The methods of HM Inspectorate of Schools are still those of the nineteenth century and the gentleman amateur. In the days of sample surveys and computerized data analysis we still do not have regular statistical surveys of the school population relating educational achievements to measured intelligence and social class. We comb the pages of *Statistics of Education* in vain for this. We are left to the sporadic efforts of sociologists to fill the gaps. Floud, Halsey and Martin in 1956 and J. W. B. Douglas in 1964 have shown clearly enough that among children of 'borderline ability' the middle classes had better chances of getting to Grammar school than the working class, but we have no serious study, official or unofficial, investigating whether British education has been getting closer to meritocracy over time. *Origins and Destinations* makes such an investigation, and while the answer it gives is not unchallengeable, I make no apology for that. It is simply the best effort we could make given the huge lacunae in the official records, and I shall spell the argument out in some detail so that the reader can check all its stages.

Let us begin with a highly simplified model of educational selection on meritocratic principles as a baseline against which to judge the actual workings of British education and the changes over time. Now we know that measured intelligence (whatever our reservations about it as a valid measure of children's native ability) is not distributed randomly. Children from the service class will have, *on average*, a higher measured IQ than their intermediate and working-class peers, although there will also be a great variation around the average within each social class; the differences *within* each class will be much greater than the difference *between* classes.[2] We must also remember that the three social classes differ in their size, and so although the service-class children may have on average a higher measured IQ, there could actually be a larger number of 'high IQ' children in the working class than in the service class.

We can represent this general picture of the distribution of IQ by Diagram 1. The area under each curve represents the number of boys in

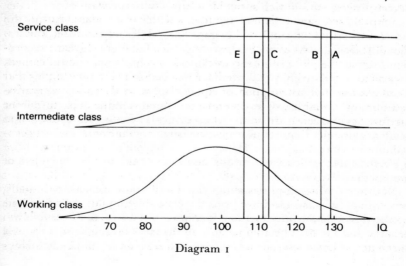

Diagram 1

our sample from that social class, the working class being by far the largest. The service-class curve is displaced to the right and the working-class curve to the left representing the class differences in average IQ. And the bell shape of each curve indicates the distribution of measured intelligence within each class, boys being concentrated towards the centre and the numbers falling off as we move towards the extremes of the IQ scale.

There can be little argument that this is in broad outline an accurate representation of the class distribution of measured IQ. The details, however, allow of more dissension. First, take the average intelligence of each class. From a number of sociological sources we have calculated that the average IQ of our service-class boys was probably of the order of 109, that of the intermediate class 102, and that of the working class 98. These figures are not based directly on IQ tests administered to our own sample. After all, we needed to know what our subjects' measured IQ was at the age of eleven not at the age they had reached when they were interviewed (which as we have said ranged from 20 to 59). So even if we could have persuaded our sample to submit to IQ testing, the resulting measurements would hardly have been helpful for the present task. What we had to do, therefore, was take the results of existing studies (such as Floud, Halsey and Martin's) and recalculate their estimates in order to compensate for the differences between their definitions of social class and our own. They provide as good an estimate as we can manage and we doubt if they are very far from the truth.

The next problem is the distribution of IQ within each class. We have drawn symmetrically bell-shaped curves, although in practice we know that within the population as a whole IQ has a slightly skewed distribution with the tail of very clever children being longer than the tail at the other end of the scale. Unfortunately, we do not know anything about the degree of skew within each social class, and so for the want of any better assumption we have assumed symmetry within each class. Again, the amount of scatter around the average may differ in the three classes; Floud, Halsey and Martin's evidence suggests that there is greater dispersion around the average in the working class, but since the differences appear to be relatively small, we have decided to make the simpler and more conservative assumption of equal dispersion. It is a conservative assumption in that it will lead to *reduced* estimates of the departure from meritocracy. Since we are on the whole critical of British education, good academic practice requires us to give the benefit of the doubt – where there is doubt – to its protagonists. Hence in choosing our assumptions we have preferred those which yield results more favourable to the defenders of meritocracy than to our own case.

Granting our assumptions about the distribution of measured intelligence, then, what would have been the class differentials if Britain had operated as a perfect meritocracy? One way to estimate this is as follows. Assume that the most prestigious schools take first pick, choosing enough of the ablest boys, irrespective of their social class, to fill all the places available. The next schools in the pecking order then cream off the ablest boys that are left, and so on down the queue. This can be represented on the diagram by a series of vertical lines. For the sake of argument let us place the élite Independent schools at the head of the line. They had 189 places available for members of our sample, and so if they were to take the 189 clevererst boys they would have taken all those with measured IQ above 129 – that is, all those to the right of line A. The fact that the line is vertical derives from our assumption that these élite schools were equally as happy to have a working-class boy with an IQ of 129 as a service-class boy of the same IQ – in other words that they were following meritocratic principles of selection.

Next in the pecking order let us place the Direct Grant schools. They had 131 places available and so would have needed to take boys with IQs of 126 to 128 to fill their places. They thus take all those between lines A and B. Next let us put the Grammar schools, and since they have a much larger number of places to fill, they have to drop their minimum IQ requirement a lot further – down to 112 according to the assumptions of our model.

The creaming process which this model postulates is by no means an unrealistic picture of the workings of selection within the state sector of education in England and Wales during the post-war period. Peaker's study of Manchester children, for example, showed that the average IQ of children at Direct Grant and Independent schools was higher than that of the Grammar-school children, which in turn was substantially higher than that of the Technical-school children (Peaker 1971). No one, however, could realistically claim that the Independent schools have been creaming off the cleverest boys in the way that the model assumes. Kalton's work on the Headmasters' Conference schools shows that they contained appreciable numbers of boys who had failed the eleven plus and thus, presumably, had relatively low IQs (many of them, it may be added, going on to get good results at O and A level: Kalton 1966). There are undoubtedly some very clever boys at the HMC schools (witness their record of winning scholarships to Oxford and Cambridge), but undoubtedly they also set out to provide education for less able children of wealthy or well connected parents. Meritocracy has not been their aim, and it is perhaps unfair to judge them by that yardstick.

There are, I think, two options for us here. One is to leave the Independent schools out of the analysis altogether. This is easy enough to do, and would leave us with a pecking order headed by the Direct Grant schools, which did indeed cream off able boys from the state schools in substantial numbers. The alternative is to include them while reorganizing their somewhat arbitrary placement in the pecking order. We have chosen the latter, since it is not without interest to estimate the relative extent of meritocracy within the independent and state sectors of education, but we have checked our results by carrying out the former analysis as well. As far as we can detect, the story we tell is substantially the same in both cases.

What we have done is to place the élite Independent Headmasters' Conference schools at the head of the pecking order, and by so doing we are presenting them in the most favourable light (if we are judging them according to the standards of meritocracy). Moving them down the order would have the effect of increasing the number of working-class recruits which meritocracy would have demanded, and hence of demonstrating that their actual, negligible proportion of working-class entrants was an even greater departure from meritocracy. We are in this sense bending over backwards to be fair to the Independent schools. The lesser, non-Headmasters' Conference schools on the other hand we have placed below the Grammar schools. There is considerable circumstantial evidence that these schools were a refuge for affluent parents whose children could not gain access to Grammar schools but who wished to provide an equivalent education for them, and it is certainly not an unreasonable place to put them if we judge them by their records at O and A level. (But we should note that if we move them up the academic hierarchy we increase the ostensible fairness of their selection processes.)

Let us now look at the pattern of class differentials that would have occurred if the assumptions of our meritocratic model had held strictly true. Table 2 gives the results. To recapitulate, it shows what would have happened if each type of school had selected its pupils solely on the basis of their measured intelligence, paying no attention whatsoever to their social class origins (and assuming always that each type of school took the cleverest pupils available once the schools higher up the pecking order had had their pick).

The first point to observe in Table 2 is that a perfectly meritocratic procedure, as we have defined it, would have led to a pattern of class differentials closely akin to that observed in the real world (shown in Table 1). The schools at the head of the academic hierarchy would have had the most extreme differentials; the Grammar schools would have been much more equal; the Technical schools would have had almost equal proportions from all three social classes; and the Secondary Modern schools at the end of the queue would still have had a predominance of working-class children. If the assumptions of our model are reasonably accurate, however, it is plain that the real world none the less deviated from the principle of equal opportunity for those of equal ability. In the real world the service-class boy was forty times as likely as his working-class peer to attend an élite Independent school, but in our meritocratic model, even when we put these schools at the head of the queue, the ratio is still only 7:1 not 40:1. There is thus sizeable deviation from meritocracy.

One way of measuring the magnitude of these deviations from meritocracy is to see how much the vertical lines in Diagram 1 need to be tilted in order to bring the class differentials of the model and the real world into alignment. For example, in the real world the élite Independent schools took 11.8 per cent of service-class children whereas the meritocratic model allowed them only 7.1 per cent. Now, even if these schools took only the

Table 2 Predictions of the Meritocratic Model
(percentages)

Father's Class	Non-selective	Technical	Independent (NON/HMC)	Grammar	Direct Grant	Independent (HMC)
Service	42.1	14.1	3.4	29.4	3.9	7.1
Intermediate	61.8	12.5	2.8	18.7	1.7	2.5
Working	72.1	10.6	2.1	13.0	1.0	1.2

Source: *Origins and Destinations*, Table 4.7

cleverest 11.8 per cent of the service class they would, on our assumptions about IQ, have had to lower their entry requirements for the service class from 129 to 126 IQ points. Equally, if they had been restricting themselves to the cleverest 0.3 per cent of the working class, that would have meant raising their standards for these boys to a minimum of 137 IQ points, giving a service-class/working-class disparity of 11 points. We can make the same calculations for the other schools, and we find that the disparity was 10 points for the Direct Grant schools, 7 for the Grammar schools, 9 for the minor Independent schools and 7 for the Technical schools.

It is not surprising that the Independent schools show the largest disparities and thus deviate the most from meritocracy. It is more interesting that the Technical schools and the Grammar schools now exhibit exactly the *same* degree of class bias (as we have redefined that concept): the apparent absence of class bias in the Technical schools which we observed in Table 1 proves not to withstand sustained examination. Rather, class bias extends throughout the secondary system. Outward appearances, as so often, are deceptive. *The marked tendency in Table 1 for class differentials to decline as we moved down the academic hierarchy is after all compatible with remarkably equal amounts of class bias at each stage in the pecking order.*

The major question to be tackled next is whether these class differences and deviations from meritocracy have changed over time. To do this we begin by dividing our sample into the four birth cohorts described earlier. First, we shall look at the changing class differences in access to selective schools (which we have defined as major and minor Independent, Direct Grant, Grammar and Technical schools). Then we shall go on to compare the observed trends with those that would have been predicted by our meritocratic model, and we shall test whether the two have come into closer alignment. One simple way to do this is to see if the service-class/working-class IQ disparities have become smaller. In other words, we will investigate whether the vertical lines of Diagram 1 need to be tilted *less* in the post-war period than they did before in order to bring the predictions of model and reality into alignment. But first, what has been the actual history of class differentials?

Table 3   Attendance at Selective Schools over Time
(percentages)

Father's class	Birth Cohort			
	1913–22	1923–32	1933–42	1943–52
Service	69.7	76.7	79.3	66.4
Intermediate	34.9	44.0	43.3	37.1
Working	20.2	26.1	27.1	21.6
All	29.6	37.0	38.8	34.8

Source: *Origins and Destinations*, Table 4.9.

Table 3 gives the story and it is perhaps a surprising one. Chances of getting to a selective school generally improved for the middle two birth cohorts who went through the secondary schools on either side of the war, but they then fell back again in the 1960s to levels not so very different from those of a generation earlier.[3] The pattern is repeated in all three social classes. For the service-class boy born in the late 1940s indeed the chance of getting to a selective school seems actually to have been worse than it was among his parents' generation thirty years earlier; 66 per cent of those born in 1943–52 won places at selective schools compared with 70 per cent of those born 1913–22. Class differentials followed a related pattern. Service-class boys from the oldest cohort were 3.5 times as likely as their working-class contemporaries to get to a selective school; in the next cohort the figure fell to 2.9, where it stayed for the third cohort; but for the youngest cohort it increased again to 3.1 True, this is rather better than the 3.5 of the oldest cohort but it is hardly startling evidence of social progress. The changes in class differentials all seem fairly minor, and the sceptic could be forgiven for denying that there had been any real changes at all.

What are we to make of this? Despite thirty years of political argument and social reform, little seems to have changed. Is social reform an idle venture after all? To answer this, let us try to account for the observed changes in class chances, such as they are. As well as the changes in governmental legislation over our period various other important changes were taking place in British social and educational structure. There was a gradual decline in the proportion of the male labour force engaged in industrial and agricultural manual occupations; the intermediate class remained more or less constant in size – although its composition changed somewhat, the petty bourgeoisie declining while the number of routine white collar workers increased; and above all the service class expanded, particularly in the case of the parents of our youngest cohort – of our respondents in the 1913–22 birth cohort only 9.9 per cent had service-class origins whereas in the 1943–52 birth cohort the proportion had almost doubled to 18.5. At the same time the number of selective schools had been increasing, with a particularly large expansion in the number of places at Grammar school. And perhaps most important of all the birth rate had been changing. There had been a baby boom in the years immediately after the First World War, but fertility then fell dramatically and remained low throughout the 1930s only to soar again in the post-war baby boom of 1946–7. This meant that there were simply far more children aiming for places at selective schools in the late 1950s than there had ever been before and pressure on the schools inevitably intensified.

We can look at the operation of these three 'demographic forces' with the aid of our meritocratic model of the educational system. We can calculate what would have happened if the number of places at selective schools, the size of the age-groups, and the relative sizes of the three classes changed in the way they actually did but the selection procedure remained perfectly meritocratic throughout. (For details of the calculations see *Origins and Destinations*.) The results are given in Table 4.

Table 4   Predictions of the Meritocratic Model over Time
(percentages)

Father's class	Birth Cohort			
	1913–22	*1923–32*	*1933–42*	*1943–52*
Service	52.8	60.4	62.0	55.3
Intermediate	33.5	40.7	42.3	35.8
Working	23.8	30.1	31.6	25.8

Source: *Origins and Destinations*, Table 4.10

The pattern of class differentials in Table 4 is remarkably similar to that of the real world given in Table 3. According to the model, expected chances of getting to selective school would have been better for all three classes in the two middle cohorts and then would have fallen back almost to those of a generation earlier in the final cohort. Again, in a perfectly meritocratic world service-class boys from the oldest cohort would have been expected to have had 2.2 times the chances of a working-class contemporary of getting to a selective school; this would have fallen to 2.0 in the two middle cohorts and widened again to 2.1 in the youngest cohort. As before, these are barely detectable changes, but such as they are they reveal the same overall pattern as the real world did. Demographic forces on their own, then, would have produced the same pattern as occurred in the real world.

True, the predictions of the meritocratic model do not tally with the real world in all respects. Hardly surprisingly, the class differentials of the real world were greater than those predicted by the model, but there is another more interesting discrepancy; the model predicts that the service-class boy in the youngest cohort would have had slightly *better* chances of getting to a selective school than his parents' generations from the oldest cohort, whereas in the real world the reverse was the case – his chances were actually slightly *worse*. If we compute the service-class/working-class IQ disparity as we did before we get the same story: the disparity narrowed slightly from 7 IQ points in the oldest cohort to 6 in the youngest. Was there, after all, a move towards greater meritocracy in the post-war period?

Unfortunately, the answer is almost certainly 'No'. In making our calculations for the meritocratic model we have assumed that the average measured intelligence of each social class remained constant over time. But this is not really a very good assumption. It is quite probable that when the service-class contained only 9.9 per cent of the school population (as it did in the oldest cohort) the average intelligence of its members would have been significantly higher than it was when the service class contained 18.5 per cent of the population, as it did in the youngest cohort. This is not at all the same as saying that the average intelligence of the population was falling – a fear that was often expressed in mid-century. Rather, it is a statement of the kind, 'The average IQ of the cleverest 10 per cent of the population is higher than that of the cleverest 20 per cent.' I do not want to imply for one moment that the service class contains all the cleverest members of the population. Indeed, our model has explicitly assumed otherwise. But as we have said, measured IQ is correlated with class, and to the extent that the correlation has remained constant over time, the point we made about the falling average IQ of an expanding service class will hold true. This will almost certainly wipe out the apparent move towards meritocracy which we noticed.

There seem, then, to be no good grounds for believing that British education became more meritocratic over the post-war years or that the 1944 Education Act brought us any nearer the goal of equality of opportunity. What the Act may actually have done by making Grammar school education free was to make it more attractive to parents who would otherwise have chosen the Independent schools. As we said in *Origins and Destinations*, 'Before the war a proportion of parents must have believed the educational (and social) advantages of the most prestigious private schools to outweigh the financial advantages of a subsidized place at a grammar school. But since the post-war reforms increased the financial advantages by making grammar-school education completely free, and probably did so without affecting their educational standing, this would alter the cost and benefits facing the minority of parents in a position to make a choice (namely the affluent parents of able children) and some of them might thus choose differently. By increasing the subsidy, therefore, the state may have tempted some parents of able children to forsake the private sector of education for the state one, and the extra competition from these children may thus have nullified any gains which the working-class would otherwise have obtained from the reforms. The point is an important and paradoxical one for social policy. A service is made free to enable the poor to take advantage of it, but this also makes the service more attractive to the rich' (pp. 69–70).

This may seem a depressing story that we have told so far. The changes that have occurred have been small, and even they can comfortably be explained by the demographic changes that have taken place over the thirty and more years covered by the study. But the story has a more cheerful chapter too. The discovery that demographic forces can account for changes in class differentials is in itself a theory of educational change that may give us some leverage on inequalities in the real world. In essence, it is a theory of supply and demand – the supply of places in selective schools and the demand for them from able children. If we expand the supply of places (that is, if we move the lines in Diagram 1 across to the left), then class differentials become smaller. And if we expand the demand for places (as the baby boom of the post-war period did), then class differentials become greater. In a nutshell, *our analysis means that expansion leads to greater equality between the classes while contraction leads to greater inequality*. Indeed, I would go so far as to posit this as one of the fundamental laws of educational policy.

The operation of this law can be seen clearly if we shift our attention from the selective schools as a whole to the Grammar schools in particular. The supply of Grammar school places increased steadily over our period and even in the post-war years managed to keep slightly ahead of the growth in the school population. In accordance with our law there was a corresponding equalization in the class chances of access to the Grammar schools: the service-class boy in the 1913–22 birth cohort was four-and-a-half times as likely as the working-class boy to attend Grammar school, but by the time of the 1943–52 birth cohort this figure had fallen to two-and-a-half.

But if we turn now to the Technical schools, we hear a very different story. Instead of expansion we find contraction, the proportion of the school population attending some kind of Technical school actually halving. As a result, what the working class had gained through the expansion of the Grammar schools they lost through the decline of the Technical schools. At the end of our period 100 working-class families sent an extra eight boys to Grammar school, but they sent eight fewer to Technical school. Putting the two together, of course, we get the 'no change' result that we have already described.

The decline of the Technical schools is one of the unsung tragedies of British education. True, the pre-war Technical schools were a motley collection of Central, Technical, and Senior schools, and they were really very different from the homogenous Grammar schools with their well-defined curriculum preparing children for the School Certificate and thence for University and administrative and professional occupation. But even in 1943, before the great expansion of the Grammar schools, the White Paper *Educational Reconstruction* had said that too many of the nation's abler children were being attracted into these schools whereas 'too few find their way into schools from which the design and craftsmanship sides of the industry are recruited. If education is to serve the interests both of the child and of the nation, some means must be found of correcting this bias and of directing ability into the field where it will find its best realization' (Para. 28).

Many of the assumptions of the White Paper may be objectionable, but the interests both of child and nation might well have been better met by an expansion of Technical rather than Grammar schools. Indeed, it is possible that one of the great ills of post-war British education has been its subjection to the ideals of the Grammar school and University rather than those of the Technical school. This is not merely because we train too few engineers and craftsmen – although this may well be true – but because the academic culture of the Technical school would probably have provided a much better basis for comprehensive reorganization than that of the grammar school. The academic culture of the Grammar school is one modelled on the non-vocational ideals of the university with its emphasis on learning for its own sake, on pure science and the liberal arts. This is a culture which flourishes in service-class homes but it is one that may well be alien to many in the intermediate and working-classes. Today, one of the great problems facing the Comprehensive schools is that of providing a common curriculum and common culture that will make sense to the whole range of their pupils, and it is one which the Technical schools might have helped solve. While the ex-Grammar-school Comprehensives may appear to be the most successful, if judged by success rates at O and A level, the size of their sixth forms, their entries to University and their popularity among service-class parents, they may none the less be failing the majority of their pupils, albeit the ones with less articulate or politically influential parents.

But bygones are bygones. The Technical school has withered and gone, and with it the tripartite system, even if many of its ideals live on in the minds of teachers and parents. But at least the issues of selection for secondary schooling have now largely disappeared into history. This does not mean, however, that the lessons we have learned about class differentials, meritocracy, and the forces of supply and demand have no relevance for the future of British education. Instead the focus will shift from the *beginning* to the *end* of compulsory secondary schooling. Access to the sixth form and class differentials in length of schooling will become the most visible targets for the sociologists' investigations (although this is not to deny the importance of prior but more covert 'class biased' processes such as residential segregation between comprehensive schools and streaming within them). The 'wastage of talent' of able boys from the Grammar schools through early leaving has long been an important issue in educational sociology, and in the Comprehensive era early leaving may become an even more prominent issue.

Table 5   Percentage Attending School at Different Ages

Father's class	*Age*			
	15	*16*	*17*	*18*
Service	88.2	70.0	48.1	28.8
Intermediate	67.3	32.6	15.1	7.7
Working	55.9	16.8	5.9	3.0
All	63.7	28.8	14.4	7.9

Source: *Origins and Destinations*, Table 8.2.

Table 5 gives the overall picture of school-leaving for the sample as a whole. The first point to notice is that class differentials become wider the higher up the educational ladder we go. Thus the service-class boys were *three* times as likely as the working class to attend selective schools of some kind; they were over *four* times as likely to be in school at seventeen; nearly *ten* times as likely to be in school at eighteen; and over *eleven* times as likely to attend University. These growing differentials illustrate another version of the fundamental law which we have already postulated: *the smaller the group that is being selected, the greater the class differentials.*

As before, this does not necessarily mean that selection becomes less meritocratic as we move up the educational ladder. The fundamental law would hold even if selection were perfectly meritocratic according to the criteria which we have used. What we actually find, using the same kind of calculations as those we used earlier in this paper to estimate the IQ disparities, is a more complex story. It will be remembered that there was a seven-point handicap for the working class in access to the Grammar and Technical school; that gap now widens to ten points at entry to the sixth form (which we take to be at the age of sixteen) but closes to slightly less than seven points at entry to University. The universities thus have the largest class differentials and accordingly have a population that is drawn predominantly from the service and intermediate classes – indeed, their social composition is not so very different from that of the élite Independent schools – yet they are at least as meritocratic in their selection as the Technical schools which contained a representative cross-section of the population.

Entry to the sixth form, then, is the least meritocratic stage of the educational ladder. The eleven plus and university entrance were distinctly more meritocratic. This pattern should not, however, surprise us much. After all, at eleven plus and again at university entrance ostensibly meritocratic selection procedures really were used, but at sixteen plus it was much more a matter of parents' (and children's) choice. Parents were influenced doubtless by the pressure and persuasion of schoolteachers, but the educational authorities did not exert quite the same decisive influence which they did both earlier and later in the child's school career. And of course the sixth form is also precisely the point where financial considerations will weigh most heavily. At eleven the families had no choice; even although pre-war there might have been fees to pay the Grammar schools, parents were still legally obliged to maintain their children at school somehow or other. But at sixteen the option of work is available, and even if there are no fees to pay, the maintenance costs of an adolescent will not be an insignificant burden to a working or intermediate-class parent. In the language of economists, the 'opportunity costs' of staying on at school are high – hence the working-class drop-out.

The boys who do decide to stay on at school will not, therefore, be a representative selection of working-class youngsters. They will tend to be those from homes which are more affluent or which place a higher priority on education, in short those who are closer to the service class in their circumstances and aspirations. Add to this the social and educational experience of schooling within a more and more service-class dominated sixth form, and we can see that the working-class and intermediate-class survivors will be progressively assimilated into the culture of the dominant class. If the universities show little class bias, therefore, this may reflect no particular virtue on their part. The relative meritocracy of their selection may simply reflect the fact that they are dealing with a culturally more homogeneous group of candidates. To have completed successfully a sixth-form career says a considerable amount about a child's educational aspirations and those of his parents, and to find that the universities are more meritocratic than the sixth forms is not therefore a matter for great congratulation; rather it is a matter for dismay that their selection is scarcely less biased than that of the eleven plus.

Table 6   Trends in School Attendance
Percentage staying on until 16 or later

Father's class	Birth Cohort			
	1913–22	*1923–32*	*1933–42*	*1943–52*
Service	52.4	61.0	77.3	78.6
Intermediate	16.1	23.9	34.6	48.5
Working	9.2	9.6	19.8	31.6
All	15.6	18.1	31.0	44.4

Source: *Origins and Destinations*, Tables 7.3 and 8.10.

None the less, early leaving would seem to be the more important problem, affecting as it does a larger number of pupils. What then has been its history, and what is the future likely to hold in store? Table 6 gives an overview of the history, but as so often, first appearances are deceptive. The first impression is that class differentials have narrowed considerably: in the oldest cohort the service-class children were nearly six times as likely as the working-class ones to stay on until sixteen whereas by the time of our youngest cohort they were less than three times as likely to do so. Here at last we seem to have found evidence of a move towards greater equality between the classes.

But this appearance is deceptive because, although *relative* class chances became more equal, the *absolute* gains were larger for the service class. Thus, comparing the oldest and youngest cohorts, we see that the percentage of service-class boys staying on until sixteen increased from 52 to 79. That is, for every hundred service-class boys, an extra 27 were staying on by the time of our youngest cohort. Compare this with the working-class history. Here the absolute gain is smaller, although the rate of increase is much greater: the proportion staying on more than trebled, but the absolute gain was only an extra 23 places for every hundred boys.

This distinction between absolute and relative increases is another one of fundamental importance in educational sociology. Indeed, we might be tempted (wrongly as it will transpire) to believe that we have here a second fundamental law, namely that in periods of expansion the larger absolute gains go to the privileged class while the larger relative gains go to the under-privileged. However, if we look at Table 6 more closely we see that the story is not quite so straightforward. The trends are not smooth, linear ones. In the pre-war period the service class showed both larger absolute gains and a higher rate of increase than the working class, and if we only had the pre-war data to go on, we would have reached a very pessimistic conclusion about the prospects for class differentials. But if we look only at the post-war period, we see exactly the opposite story; both relative and absolute gains were much bigger for the working-class, and optimism can replace pessimism.

One sensible moral to draw from this story is that we should not extrapolate from the past into the future. The pre-war period was no guide to the last thirty years of the century since the raising of the school-leaving age in 1972 brought an abrupt equalization in the class chances of staying on until sixteen. However, while cautious agnosticism may be highly scholarly, attempts to predict future trends in school-leaving may not be wholly foolish if we have a sensible theory on which to base them. At any rate, I propose to try.

The theory which I have in mind is a development of the 'pool of talent' concept that has been current for many years. To begin with, most teachers and probably most parents believe that a certain minimum level of measured intelligence is required if a child is to have a reasonable chance of O level, A level or their pre-war equivalents of School Certificate and Higher School Certificate. It does not matter whether these beliefs are sound or not; the crucial thing is that they are believed and acted upon. Now since A level is the main qualification available at the end of the sixth form, we can assume that those below the minimum level will be strongly discouraged from continuing with their studies after O level. Given the differing class distributions of measured intelligence, the pool of able children believed capable of attaining A level will accordingly vary in three classes. If we were to say, for example, that the minimum IQ required was 113, then the assumptions we used earlier when constructing the meritocratic model would indicate that 38 per cent of the service class, 21 per cent of the intermediate class, and 14 per cent of the working class reached this minimum requirement. These figures then represent the size of the 'pool of talent' believed in each class. It follows from this that, *given the present examination structure and current beliefs about educability*, 38 per cent, 21 per cent and 14 per cent give the upper limits to the growth in the numbers from the three social classes staying on to take A level. When these figures are reached, the pools of talent will be exhausted or, to put it a different way, the effective demand for A level courses from the three classes will be satiated.

However, while these figures may give the eventual satiation levels, the evidence suggests that they will not be reached by straight-line growth paths. Indeed, straight-line growth is extremely rare and perhaps non-existent. Instead, there are plenty of examples that, where there is a finite stock of resources of a definite upper limit to demand (as in the case of oil reserves or the demand for television sets), growth tends to follow an elongated S-shape (called a logistic curve) rather than a straight line. That is to say, growth starts rather slowly, then speeds up, and finally tails away as the resources or the demand is gradually exhausted.

This kind of growth path enables us both to make sense of the complex past trends in school-leaving differentials and to make some sensible predictions about the future. The overall picture is given in Diagram 2. The diagram shows three logistic curves, one for each class, the service class having the highest satiation level and starting off on their journey to satiation first. The earlier start of the service class on their journey means that, in the early stages of expansion, they are the ones who get the lion's share, both absolutely and relatively; it is only later on when the service class is approaching satiation that the other classes gain substantial benefits from expansion.

It can be seen now that the section between lines A and B on Diagram 2

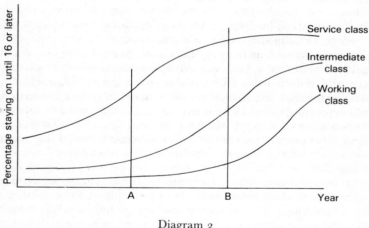

Diagram 2

gives an accurate summary of the trends detailed in Table 6. Thus Table 6 showed that the proportion of service-class boys staying on until sixteen started at a high level, grew rapidly for a time, but then levelled off after the war; conversely, the proportion from the working class hardly grew before the war but then started to move ahead rapidly in the post-war years. The section of Diagram 2 to the right of line B shows what would have happened if there had been no change in the minimum school-leaving age. There would have been a continuing plateau in service-class attendance but rapid growth among the intermediate and working classes before they too levelled off.

Similarly, we would expect the pattern traced by the three logistic curves of Diagram 2 to give an accurate picture of past and future trends in the numbers staying on until eighteen, assuming always that there is no change in the examination structure. The estimates we were able to make in *Origins and Destinations* suggested that the service class had already reached their satiation level – at 38 per cent. It was from this figure that we made the estimate of 113 as the minimum IQ level required for A level, and from this in turn that the eventual satiation levels of 21 per cent and 14 per cent for the intermediate and working classes were derived.

If these three estimates of the class satiation levels are correct, the class differential in attendance in the final year of the sixth form would eventually be reduced from its present 6:1 to 3:1. However, it is important to recognize that this reduction would only occur if expansion in the numbers staying on at school were allowed to take place. The crucial point, if we are correct in our theory, is that the service class has already taken up all the places in the sixth form that it wants; any further expansion must therefore be to the benefit of the other two classes. Doubtless, the intermediate class will be the next to receive the major benefits of expansion, and the working class will as usual bring up the rear.

What, then, are the prospects for meritocracy and class inequalities? What lessons are to be drawn from the educational experience of the last forty years? Perhaps the main one is that there are no short cuts to social justice. Reforms such as the 1944 Education Act did little to bring about equality or meritocracy, but a sustained programme of building Grammar schools did reduce class differentials, and a sustained programme of expanding the sixth forms could do the same again. It does, however, seem to be a depressing fact of life that any reforms of this kind will only benefit the subordinate classes once the dominant one has taken all it wants, and the risk, of course, is that once the service-class demand for Grammar schools or sixth forms is met, the political pressures for further expansion will diminish.

None of this means that more dramatic social reforms which directly benefited the working class could not in principle be achieved, but such reforms would have important costs and it is doubtful whether these costs would always be acceptable in contemporary democratic Britain. For example, the fact that selection at eleven plus and for university entrance was more meritocratic than at sixteen plus suggests strongly that the introduction of a formal selection system for entrance to the sixth form in place of our present *laissez faire* approach would increase the extent of meritocracy, albeit not to any great extent. But even if we regarded this as desirable, it is surely doubtful whether it would be politically feasible in modern Britain.

Again, it would be possible in principle to ensure that all classes benefited equally from any reforms by establishing quotas for sixth-form places, but it is certain that any measure which removed the established rights of the service class to keep their children on at school beyond the minimum leaving age would meet with fierce, and probably effective, political opposition. In a democratic society advantaged groups have the political freedom to organize in defence of their privileges; and in many cases they will have the resources to make that defence effective.

Attempts to achieve meritocracy or equality of class chances on the cheap, therefore, are likely either to be circumvented by the advantaged groups in society (as with the 1944 Education Act) or successfully opposed by them. A more expensive alternative, and one with more hope of success, is that of expansion. If the logic of our logistic curves is sound, expansion would eventually lead to a reduction in class differentials although in the earlier stages the already advantaged groups might get the lion's share of the benefits. Expansion has the further advantage, too, that it will not so obviously antagonize powerful groups who see their interests threatened. It has long been the hope of liberal and social democratic reformers in Britain that a policy of expansion and growth would assist the more deprived groups without actually taking anything away from, and thus antagonizing, the advantaged. Everyone can be made better off and so everyone can be kept happy.

This sounds almost too good to be true, and it probably is. While it is doubtless correct that the fiercest opposition will arise against cuts that make people *absolutely* worse off, it is far from clear that the service class will stand idly by if they see their traditional *relative* advantages eroded. As the working-class boys stay on in larger numbers to take, say, A level, so the service class may attempt to secure new advantages at university. This may thus lead to what has been called a process of 'credentialization'. That is, a process of continual growth in the educational levels required for entry into high-status jobs. As the differentials close at one level, the service class move on to a higher level in order to stay one jump ahead, and what was once a school-leaver's job now becomes upgraded and becomes the preserve of the graduate.

This is a depressing story, but let me try to end on a more optimistic note. Education not only provides a route to the qualifications and credentials needed for good jobs but is also a cultural experience which shapes the attitudes and values of its inmates. A schooling, therefore, which provided a *common* cultural experience for all pupils alike would produce a more homogeneous student body who might be less divided than their parents' generation. Education is one of the more important channels for the transmission and creation of culture, and one of *Origins and Destinations* most optimistic findings was that on the schools' ability to produce new 'cultural capital'. (See *Origins and Destinations*, chapters 5 and 8.)

Tawney wrote that, 'A special system of schools, reserved for children whose parents have larger bank accounts than their neighbours, exists in no other country on the same scale as in England. It is at once an educational monstrosity and a grave national misfortune. It is educationally vicious, since to mix with companions from homes of different types is an important part of the education of the young. It is socially disastrous, for it does more than any other single cause, except capitalism itself, to perpetuate the division of the nation into classes of which one is almost unintelligible to the other' (Tawney 1931; p. 145). Tawney's attack was on the private sector of education, but the same points could be made about the tripartite system, about streaming (a 'tripartite system in miniature'), or indeed about sixth forms and universities. To have one type of education for one class of pupils – be it private education, Grammar-school education, O and A level education, or University education – and another type for children from less favoured backgrounds – state education, Secondary Modern education, the CSE examination, or worse still early leaving without any definite skills – is still today educationally vicious and socially disastrous. The goal to be aimed at is simplicity itself: a long and shared schooling with a common curriculum that makes sense to the whole range of pupils. At some point no doubt the demands of the economy will insist that differentiated vocational training be given, but there is no evidence that such differentiation is more effective for being started earlier.

Acknowledgments

I am very grateful to David Hargreaves and John Ridge for the help they have given me in the preparation of this paper.

Notes

1 We have defined selective schools as Technical, Grammar, Direct Grant and both HMC and non-HMC Independent schools.
2 In analysis of variance terms, the within-group sum of squares is greater than the between-group sum of squares.
3 Strictly speaking we should not try to relate cohorts to generations. There will be wide variation in the birth years of the parents of a given cohort, parents of large families will be over-represented, and childless adults unrepresented.

Bibliography

DOUGLAS, J. W. B. (1964) *The Home and the School*. London: McGibbon and Kee.
FLOUD, J. E., HALSEY, A. H. and MARTIN, F. M. (1956) *Social Class and Educational Opportunity*. London: Heinemann.
GOLDTHORPE, J. H. and LLEWELLYN, C. (1977) 'Class mobility in modern Britain: three theses examined'. *Sociology*, Vol. 11, No. 2.
GOLDTHORPE, J. H. (1980) *Social Mobility and Class Structure*. Oxford: Clarendon Press.
GRAY, J. L. and MOSHINSKY, P. (1938) 'Ability and opportunity in English education', in HOGBEN, L. (ed), *Political Arithmetic*. London: Allen and Unwin.

HALSEY, A. H., HEATH, A. F. and RIDGE, J. M. (1980) *Origins and Destinations: Family, Class and Education in Modern Britain.* Oxford: Clarendon Press.

KALTON, G. (1966) *The Public Schools: A Factual Survey.* London: Longmans.

LINDSAY, K. (1926) *Social Progress and Educational Waste: Being a Study of the 'Free Place' and Scholarship Systems.* London: Routledge.

PEAKER, W. (1971) *The Plowden Children Four Years On.* Slough: National Foundation for Educational Research.

TAWNEY, R. H. (1931) *Equality.* London: Allen and Unwin.

3.4 Social class, ability and opportunity in the comprehensive school

Julienne Ford

[...] Support for comprehensive reorganization of secondary education, while not homogenous, is fairly general and such reorganization is the expressed policy of the political party which forms the present government.[1] Yet there has been very little research into the effects of comprehensive schools,[2] and even less into the question as to the extent to which they can be expected to produce the 'Fairer Society', an expectation which is arguably the basic rationale behind this reorganization.

In order to examine this question empirically it is first necessary to clarify the precise theory on which the hypothesis *Comprehensive schools will tend to produce the 'Fairer Society'* is based. At this point the discussion turns from popular attitudes about comprehensive schools to the published literature on the subject. For there is, of course, no reason to suppose that 'the-man-in-the-street' has explicitly formulated ideas about the relationship between education and 'equality', although aspects of the more academic discussion on the matter may filter into his consciousness through the media of opinion leaders.[3]

If one turns to the published work of the advocates of comprehensive schools, any hope of discovering this theory is, however, soon disappointed. The connection between comprehensive education and the 'Fairer Society' is nowhere made clear, in fact it is often taken to be self-evident, and the connection is considered to be so obvious that no explanation is required. Thus, for example, Armstrong and Young in their Fabian pamphlet[4] assume that comprehensive schools will produce a better society, and merely discuss the various alternatives within the broad comprehensive ideal. Floud and Halsey also advocate comprehensive reorganization, with the proviso that this would produce the desired results 'only if the spirit as well as the form of English secondary education were changed,'[5] yet their reasoning is entirely based on criticism of the tripartite system.

However, while I have not found a complete theory of the effects of comprehensive schooling in any single work, it is possible to build up a sort of *ideal type* theory from the suggestions in the various sources. Such a theory, of course, will never conform completely to the views of any one author, but it should be a reasonable representation of the general line of thought which is current.

The key to the theoretical link between the tripartite system and the 'Unfair Society' seems to lie in the idea of early selection. Few critics reject

Source: FORD, J. (1969) *Social Class and the Comprehensive School*. London: Routledge and Kegan Paul, pp. 8–12 and 32–41.

selection *per se* however, their objections are specifically to *early* and relatively final differentiation on the basis of measured intelligence. Taylor, for example, argues that

if we no longer possess a criterion that will legitimize early selection, allocation and the subsequent differentiation attendant upon them, then it becomes morally imperative to shift the basis of allocation procedures from performance in intelligence and attainment tests and response to primary schooling to a more flexible procedure operating within secondary and post-secondary education, where the range of choices available is such as to make it easier for child, parent and teacher to match interest and attainments and a suitable type of course.[6]

This rejection of early selection is very often accompanied by a rejection of traditional forms of streaming as bases for grouping within the new comprehensive schools. Many writers advocate, and some schools operate, methods of breaking up the school on horizontal lines, not in any way related to academic performance, such as house systems. For it is clear that a rigid system of streaming in comprehensive schools amounts to tripartite differentation with the sole exception that grammar, technical and secondary modern schools are housed in one building. Nevertheless completely unstreamed comprehensive schools are rare and it does seem to be government policy to pursue the comprehensive ideal to its logical conclusion.[7] Thus Crosland has said, 'Both common sense and American experience suggest that (unstreaming) would lead to a really serious levelling down of standards and a quite excessive handicap to the clever child. Division into streams according to ability, remains essential,' and in a footnote he adds, 'some (enthusiasts) their heads perhaps a little turned by too much sociology, even insist on classes being not known by numbers but by their teachers' names lest any mark at all of superior or inferior status be conferred. This is simply egalitarianism run mad!'[8] Where unstreaming does not accompany comprehensive organization the principle of abolition of early selection is often claimed to be protected by the fact that mobility between streams within one school is easier than mobility between schools.

Having identified the major variable in the theory which our ideal-type advocate of comprehensives might put forward, it is now necessary to spell out the remaining intervening variables and the relationships between them. The actual arrangement of propositions in a theory is, of course, a creative business, very much a personal, even artistic endeavour. Two theorists approaching the same problem from similar perspectives could never produce the same theory, just as two painters from the same school could not, without collaboration, paint substantially similar portraits of one woman. Thus the deductive scheme suggested below, while inspired by the arguments which can be found in literature, does not spring directly from those arguments. It is, like all ideal types, an imaginative reconstruction, a product of selective emphasis and exaggeration.

The theory

Proposition One   Early selection of children into groups with differentia educational and occupational prospects

  (i)   prevents the fullest development of talent,
 (ii)   inhibits equality of educational opportunity for those with equa talent,
(iii)   prematurely confines children's occupational horizons,
 (iv)   segregates potential occupational 'successes' from 'failures', henc echoing and reinforcing the system of stratification in the wide society.

Proposition Two   Where conditions (iii) and (iv) occur children's percep tions of the structure and meaning of stratification tend to take the form o rigid dichotomous models.

Proposition Three   Where (iii) and (iv) do not occur children's perception of the structure and meaning of stratification tend to take the form o flexible hierarchic models.

Proposition Four   Under a tripartite system of secondary education early selection of children into groups with differential educational and occu pational prospects is present.

Proposition Five   Under a comprehensive system of secondary educatior early selection does not occur to such a great extent.

Proposition Six   Movement from a tripartite to a comprehensive organiza tion of secondary education will therefore cause

(*a*)   a greater development of talent,
(*b*)   a greater equality of opportunity for those with equal talent,
(*c*)   a widening of children's occupational horizons,
(*d*)   a relative decline in the social interaction in school which takes place within the boundaries of anticipated occupational strata, and a relative increase in interaction across such strata.

Proposition Seven   Conditions (*c*) and (*d*) will produce a tendency to greater frequency of flexible hierarchic models of stratification over rigid dichotomous models.

None of these propositions is inherently untestable; however, I will be concerned with testing only propositions six and seven, as any refutation of these would be sufficient to throw doubt upon the whole theory. Naturally the theory would be even more fundamentally questioned if the fifth proposition were to prove false. While this has not been specifically tested there is sufficient evidence available to give strong grounds for *suspecting* it to be false. Studies of the determinants of educational success in primary schools[9] suggest that academic successes and failures are largely selected long before the stage of entry to secondary school, and it ight be argued that, for this reason, reform of secondary education is relevant. However for present purposes it will be assumed that there is ss early selection under comprehensive educational schemes.[...]

Returning to the sixth and final propositions we see that these two atements suggest five hypotheses:

Comprehensive schools will produce a greater development of talent than tripartite schools.

Comprehensive schools will provide greater equality of opportunity for those with equal talent.

The occupational horizons of children in comprehensive schools will be widened relative to those of children in tripartite schools.

Comprehensive school children will show less tendency to mix only with children of their own social type than will tripartite school children.

Comprehensive school children will tend to have views of the class system as a flexible hierarchy, while tripartite school children will tend to see this as a rigid dichotomy.

[Editors' Note: In the original book, Ford discusses evidence concerning ll five hypotheses. We reprint below only Chapter 3, which considers the econd hypothesis.]

f we cannot, at present, draw any firm conclusions about the extent to vhich comprehensive schools are *productive* of talent, we can at least xamine the extent to which they provide increased equality of oppor-unity for individuals with equal talent potential or 'ability'. For the most ommon criticism of the tripartite system is that, while purporting to effect election on the basis of ability (operationally defined as IQ) it does not in act do so accurately.

Despite the conclusion of Floud, *et al.*, in 1956 that, if measured intelli-ence was taken as a criterion, then the social class distribution of gram-nar school places was equitable,[10] Douglas has more recently shown that problem of social class bias in selection still does exist. The working-class upil must typically have a slightly higher IQ than the middle-class one in rder to stand the same chance of selection for grammar school, simply ecause working-class areas tend to have smaller proportions of grammar chool places than their IQ distributions would justify.[11] It is widely elieved that comprehensive reorganization will go some way towards meliorating this situation, that the extent of 'wastage of talent' or uneducated capacity'[12] will be reduced and that, in fact, '*Comprehensive chools will provide greater equality of opportunity for those with equal talent.*'

Now in order to test this and the remaining three hypotheses a sample of upils in comprehensive and tripartite schools was required. A number of considerations affected the selection of this sample. In the first place, in order for any generalizations to be valid it was necessary to find a comprehensive school which was both typical of the majority of comprehensive schools in England today, and which had been established long enough for the majority of its pupils to have been attending that school for the whole of their secondary education. In addition to these basic criteria it was considered essential that this school be relatively 'uncreamed' drawing almost all the secondary age pupils in the catchment area. For while the *typical* comprehensive school today *is* creamed of the top levels of ability by neighbouring grammar schools, the theory that we are examining concerns the effects of large scale comprehensive reorganization. It is therefore desirable to simulate as far as possible the conditions which will obtain when (as seems likely) the whole of the public sector of secondary education is reorganized in this way. In this respect, then, the criterion of typicality was abandoned in order to do justice to the ideals of the comprehensivists who rightly claim that where creaming occurs the basic principle of comprehensivization – a common education for all[13] – is lost.

The problem thus became one of locating a well-established relatively uncreamed comprehensive school of more or less average size which also embraced three characteristics typical of English comprehensives: some system of horizontal organization on the basis of ability groupings (streams), some system of vertical organization unrelated to ability (houses), and co-education. '*Cherry Dale*' *Comprehensive* was just such a school.

Cherry Dale school stands on a relatively isolated housing estate somewhere in the inner London area. Built to serve the children from the estate, it is certainly a neighbourhood school,[14] for only 1 or 2 per cent from every year's production of eleven-year-olds 'go away' to school. The neighbourhood, like most neighbourhoods in urban England, does tend to be socially homogeneous – the majority of the children come from backgrounds which can be described as working-class – however a sufficient proportion of middle-class children attend the school to allow comparisons to be made.[15]

Cherry Dale is in its physical appearance typical of modern comprehensives. The buildings are light and colourful, there are sports facilities, a swimming pool, a 'flat' where girls practise domestic science, and all kinds of facilities for scientific, technical and art education. But it is also typical in its academic organization. The school is organized both into academic streams or teaching groups on the basis of ability and into the mixed ability groupings called houses and house-tutor groups. This organization is more fully discussed in Chapter 5 [not reprinted here], but it is important at this stage to note that in Cherry Dale, as in most comprehensives the actual teaching takes place in academic streams. There are, in effect seven of these teaching groups in each year group, the first two ('A'$_1$ and 'A'$_2$) being 'grammar streams', the next two ('B'$_1$ and 'B'$_2$) covering the upper-middle ability range and the lower streams ('C'$_1$ and 'C'$_2$) being mainly practical in orientation; the final stream ('D') is a remedial group.[16]

Having selected a suitable comprehensive school, the problem of choosing tripartite schools for purposes of comparison was precisely delimited. For, in order to control as many confounding variables as possible, it was necessary to find two schools which closely 'matched' Cherry Dale in relevant respects. *'Gammer Wiggins' Grammar School* and *'South Moleberry' Secondary Modern* were therefore selected as suitable coeducational tripartite schools in similar working-class areas of inner London.[17]

The sample comprised the complete fourth years of these three schools:[18] 320 fourteen- to fifteen-year old boys and girls.[19] Questionnaires[20] were administered to the children in their form groups (or, in the case of Cherry Dale School, their academic streams), in an ordinary classroom during lesson time, and were completed under supervision. In this way the problem of bias from non-response was virtually eliminated, for all the children present returned a questionnaire and it was possible to ensure that practically all of these were completed fully.

The most obvious way of testing the hypothesis on this sample is by analysis of the interaction of social class and measured intelligence as determinants of academic attainment in the three schools. For we know that, under the traditional system of secondary education, the impact of social class on educational attainment is greater than can be explained by the covariation of class and IQ.[21] In other words, under the tripartite system opportunities for those with equal ability (defined as IQ) are not equal and the inequalities are related to social class. If the hypothesis were correct, then we would expect IQ to be a greater determinant, and social class a lesser determinant of educational attainment in comprehensive than in tripartite schools.

Now a number of writers have suggested that, where comprehensive schools employ some system of academic streaming (as most of them do) this may not be the case.[22] Thus, on the basis of a study of about eight hundred comprehensive schoolchildren, Holly concluded that 'Streaming by ability within the comprehensive school does not seem ... to result in producing a new élite based on attainment or intelligence quotients: it seems merely to preserve the traditional class basis of educational selection.'[23] Yet the comprehensive enthusiast might well reply that, since no one would maintain that comprehensive schools eliminate class bias in educational attainment completely, the more interesting question is whether such schools are *relatively* more effective in this respect.[24]

Some light can be thrown on this question by examination of the social class and IQ composition of the fourth year streams in the three schools considered here.

Social class was determined by responses to the simple question 'What is your father's job?', accompanied by the verbal instruction 'Imagine that you are explaining to a new friend what your father does, try to give as much information as you can.' The information given was in almost all cases sufficient to enable responses to be classified according to occupational prestige.[25] Of course father's occupation as reported by a child is not the best possible measure of social class. A more precise classification could be produced from an *index* including assessments of income, life styles and the education of both parents as well as occupational prestige. But occupational prestige is certainly the best single *indicator*. For its use is based on the reasonably sociological assumption that, since the work role is such a time-consuming one, it is in terms of this that people evaluate one another.[26] Furthermore, owing to the necessity to control several variables simultaneously in the following analysis, the social class variable has simply been dichotomized. And several studies have shown that the most socially significant and meaningful social class classification is a simple non-manual/manual division.[27]

The sample was also dichotomized according to IQ scores.[28] Since such scores are artificially created to represent comparable deviations from a norm of 100, those children with scores up to and including 100 were classified as of 'low IQ', and those with scores of 101 or more were classified as of 'high IQ'. However, as there were no children in the grammar school with scores of 100 or less, in order to assess the relationship between IQ and streaming in this school, the pupils were dichotomized at the median point. Thus for this group 'low IQ' refers to scores between 101 and 120, while 'high IQ' refers to scores of 121 or more. Table 1 shows the relationship between social class, IQ and stream for the three schools.

Table 1   Social Class and IQ Composition of Streams in the Three Schools

School	Stream	Middle Class† High I.Q.* %	Middle Class† Low I.Q. %	Working Class High I.Q. %	Working Class Low I.Q. %	N = (100 %)
Grammar	'A'	84	7	7	3	30
	'B'	60	20	20	0	25
	'C'	41	26	22	11	27
	'D'	20	0	47	33	15
Comprehensive	'A's	33	8	59	0	39
	'B's	4	9	56	31	46
	'C's	8	6	29	56	48
	'D'	0	10	10	79	19
Secondary Modern	'A'	31	7	52	12	29
	'B'	11	22	44	22	18
	'C'	0	8	25	67	24

* That is 120+ for grammar school or 100+ for comprehensive and secondary modern schools.

† That is non-manual paternal occupation.

It can be seen from the table that in all three schools *both* social class and IQ are related to stream. However our interest is primarily in the extent to which the *relative* importance of social class and IQ as determinants of stream differs between the three schools. For this reason Table 2 has been derived from the above figures.

Table 2 shows the strength of the relationships between social class and selection for the 'A' stream *when IQ is held constant*. Only children with 'high' IQs are considered and the extent to which social class affects the chances of these children to be placed in the top streams of their schools is analysed. Thus, for example, 46 per cent of the middle-class children in the grammar school with 'high' IQs are placed in the 'A' stream, while only 10 per cent of the working-class children in the same ability range achieve this placement: a difference which is statistically significant. In the comprehensive school the relationship between social class and placement in the 'A' stream is still statistically significant for the 'high' IQ group, however in the secondary modern school, when IQ is controlled in this manner the relationship between stream and social class is reduced to insignificance.[29]

Table 2 'High' IQs Only: Social Class and 'A' Stream Placement in the Three Schools

School	Middle Class % placed in 'A' stream	Working Class % placed in 'A' stream	$p = *$
Grammar	46	10	.01
Comprehensive	68	35	.01
Secondary Modern	82	52	n.s.

* 'A' stream compared with all the other streams in a 2×2 chi-squared test of significance.

The results of this comparison, then, give no support to the hypothesis. Indeed they tend to confirm the suspicions of Holly and others that selection on the basis of streaming in the comprehensive school, like selection under the tripartite system, tends to underline class differentials in educational opportunity. For in the comprehensive school, as in the grammar school there appears to be a relationship between social class and 'A' stream placement over and above that which can be explained by the well-known correlation between social class and measured IQ.[30] In other words, at the same ability level the middle-class child stands a greater chance of placement in the 'grammar' streams of a comprehensive school than the working-class child, a situation in one respect not substantially different from that which exists under the tripartite system.

Now it might be objected that to show that a class bias in stream placement exists in the comprehensive school is not necessarily to demonstrate that there are inequalities in educational attainment which relate to social class. For just possibly those children who have been placed in the lower streams of the comprehensive school will achieve the same eventual educational levels as those in the 'A' stream: stream might bear little relationship to level of education reached.

A good index of the extent to which this is the case can be derived by examination of the leaving intentions of the children experiencing the various forms of education. For, if a substantial proportion of those in the lower streams of the comprehensive school intend to stay on at school to follow fifth and sixth form courses, then one could argue that the class bias in streaming has little consequence for actual educational attainment. If, on the other hand, children in the lower streams of the comprehensive school resemble those in the secondary modern in their living intentions then clearly streaming has an impact on level of educational attainment and the class bias in streaming is certainly important. In Table 3, therefore, the leaving intentions of children in the three schools are compared.

Table 3   Leaving Intentions by School, Comprehensive Stream and Social Class

School	Social Class	% leaving in 4th year	% leaving in 5th year	% leaving in 6–8th year	N = (100 %)
Grammar	*Middle Class*	0	10	90	68
	Working Class	0	28	72	29
Comprehensive	*Middle Class*	0	50	50	16
'A' streams	*Working Class*	0	87	13	23
Comprehensive	*Middle Class*	20	60	20	15
'B–D' streams	*Working Class*	40	56	4	98
Secondary	*Middle Class*	32	47	21	19
Modern	*Working Class*	40	52	8	52

It can be seen from the table that streaming within the comprehensive school has a definite impact on leaving intentions, for all of the 'A' stream children intend to stay at least into the fifth form, while 13 per cent of the middle class and 40 per cent of the working-class children in the lower streams intend leaving in the fourth year and therefore have no hope of sitting for GCE examinations. This is, of course, hardly surprising. For the 'A' streams have been following five year courses specifically designed to terminate in GCE, and, while many of those in the 'B' and 'C' streams will sit CSE examinations none of those in the 'D' stream are expected to gain any formal qualifications at all. Streaming within a comprehensive school is thus an important determinant of educational attainment and for this reason the class inequalities in stream placement shown in Tables 1 and 2 are important.

Another interesting feature of Table 3 is the comparison of the comprehensive 'A' stream and the grammar school children. For the former represent the highest ability group in the comprehensive, children who might well have gone to a grammar school under the tripartite system, yet only 28 per cent of them intend staying into the sixth form. This compares with 85 per cent of grammar school children intending to stay at least one year in the sixth form – a difference which is highly significant ($X^2 = 40.2$, $d.f. = 1$, $p = .001$). This differential holds both for the working-class children ($X^2 = 18.09$, $d.f. = 1$, $p = .001$), and for the middle class ($X^2 = 14.39$, $d.f. = 1$, $p = .001$).

This raises in an acute form the question of 'wastage of ability' which was examined in the *Early Leaving Report*. For the table shows not only that 'home background influences the use which a boy or girl will make of a grammar school education'[31] (18 per cent more middle than working-class children staying on into the sixth form), but also that this same effect of home background can be observed in the comprehensive 'A' streams. For half the middle-class 'A' stream children in the sample and only 13 per cent of the working-class ones intended to stay beyond the fifth. Indeed it seems from these figures that this 'wastage' is even greater in the comprehensive than in the grammar school.

In order to investigate this alarming possibility it is necessary to compare the leaving intentions of those working-class children who are 'able' enough to profit from sixth form courses under the two systems. For this purpose 'able' children were arbitrarily defined as those with an IQ score of 111 or more – approximately the average level for grammar school pupils.[32] The number of such children in the secondary modern school and comprehensive 'B' to 'D' streams was, of course, too small to be considered.

Table 4   Working Class Children with IQ scores of 111 or more: Leaving Intentions by Type of Schooling

	Leaving in 5th Year %	Staying into Sixth Form %	N = (100 %)
Grammar School	31	69	23
Comprehensive 'A' stream	84	16	19

$(X^2 = 10.98, d.f. = 1, p = .01)$.

The evidence from the three schools, then, far from revealing a greater equality of opportunity for the comprehensive school pupil, shows a persistence of class bias in educational attainment under the comprehensive system. Indeed there is some indication that 'wastage of ability' among bright working-class pupils may be occurring on an even larger scale in Cherry Dale comprehensive school than in Gammer Wiggins grammar school.[33]

For where comprehensive school children are taught in ability groups or streams as nearly all of them are,[34] the 'self-fulfilling prophecy' characteristic of the tripartite system is still very much in evidence. 'Ability' is itself related to social class, but middle-class children get an even larger share of the cake than their ability distribution would justify. The middle-class child is more likely than the working-class child to find himself in the 'grammar' stream at the comprehensive school, even where the two children are similar in ability. And even those working-class children who do succeed in obtaining 'A' stream placement are four times more likely than their middle-class counterparts to 'waste' that opportunity by leaving school without a sixth form education. Thus while, as we have seen in Chapter 2 [of the original book], there is little evidence on the question of whether comprehensive reorganization of secondary education will promote a greater *development* of talent, there is some serious doubt whether it will decrease inequalities of opportunity for those with equal talent.

In short there is little evidence from this study of three schools that comprehensive education as it is practised at the present will modify the characteristic association between social class and educational attainment. Indeed one could argue that it can hardly be expected to do so. For, as C. Arnold Anderson has said, 'In order for schooling to change a status system schooling must be a variable.'[35] In other words, for the relationship between social class and educational success to be destroyed it would not be sufficient to give every child the *same* chance. Working-class children, disadvantaged by their cultural background and inferior physical environs, would need to be given not the same but superior educational opportunities. Yet in the typical comprehensive school the average working-class child starts off with the same handicaps that would have lengthened the odds against his success under the old system. And the outcome of the race appears to be no less predictable.

Notes and References

1 Of course this does not mean that comprehensive reorganization had not got under way before the election of a Labour government. For the progress made up to 1963, see PEDLEY, R. (1963) *The Comprehensive School*. Harmondsworth: Penguin Books.

2 Most of the research available had taken the form of impressionistic surveys such as MILLER, T. W. G. (1961) *Values in the Comprehensive School*. Edinburgh: Oliver and Boyd; and CURRIE, K. (1962) 'A Study of the English Comprehensive System with particular reference to the educational, social and cultural effects of single sex and co-educational types of school', Ph.D. (Ed.) thesis, University of London.

3 See KATZ, ELIHU and LAZARSFELD, PAUL F. (1955) *Personal Influence*. Encino, Calif.: Glencoe.

4 ARMSTRONG, MICHAEL and YOUNG, MICHAEL (1964) *New Look at Comprehensives*, Fabian Research series 237.

5 See FLOUD, JEAN and HALSEY, A. H. (1961) 'Social Class, Intelligence Tests, and Selection for Secondary Schools', in HALSEY, A. H. *et. al.* (eds)

Education, Economy and Society. Glencoe, Ill. (later New York): Free Press, p. 89.

6 TAYLOR, WILLIAM (1967) 'Family, School and Society', in CRAFT, MAURICE et. al. *Linking Home and School.* London: Longmans, p. 233.

7 In the LCC publication *London Comprehensive Schools* (1961) we read, 'None of the schools bases its organization upon the impractical assumption that teaching groups covering the whole range of ability are suitable or desirable' (p. 32).

8 CROSLAND, C. A. R. (1963) *The Future of Socialism.* London: Cape, p. 202.

9 See for just a few examples BERNSTEIN, BASIL (1961) 'Social Class and Linguistic Development: A theory of social learning', in HALSEY et. al., op. cit., pp. 288–314; DOUGLAS, J. W. B. (1964) *The Home and the School.* London: MacGibbon and Kee, pp. 60–5 and 159–62; JACKSON, BRIAN (1964) *Streaming: An education system in miniature.* London: Routledge and Kegan Paul.

10 FLOUD, JEAN E., HALSEY, A. H. and MARTIN, F. M. (1956) *Social Class and Educational Opportunity.* London: Heinemann.

11 DOUGLAS, J. W. B. (1964) *The Home and the School.* London: MacGibbon and Kee.

12 The notions of talent wastage and uneducated capacity are employed in the Crowther Report (1959) *15 to 18.* London: HMSO; and the Robbins Report (1963) *Higher Education.* London: HMSO.

13 'A Comprehensive school is not merely unselective: it is a school which caters for all levels of ability apart from handicapped pupils needing special education. The term is hardly justified unless there are in fact within it sufficient numbers of pupils in all parts of the ability range to call for and justify proper provision for them': (1967) *London Comprehensive School 1966.* London: ILEA, p. 17, para. 23.

14 The notion that comprehensive schools are neighbourhood schools pervades many of the official publications but is discussed most fully in PEDLEY, ROBIN, (1963) *The Comprehensive School.* Harmondsworth: Penguin Books, especially Chapter 5.

15 Approximately a quarter of the pupils *in the sample* from Cherry Dale school were middle class and there is no reason to believe that this differs from the proportion for the school as a whole. There is some evidence that LEA areas may become *more* socially homogeneous, [...] so to this extent it is not unrealistic to examine a comprehensive school in a relatively homogeneous catchment area.

16 Of course the streams were not *actually named* in such an overtly hierarchical way. The picture has also been oversimplified in that the 'D' stream did comprise two small separate groups. But, as these were equal in status and were often grouped together for time-tabling and other purposes (for example they responded to the questionnaire as one group) they will be treated throughout as a single stream.

17 The tripartite schools were chosen from areas more or less similar to that of the comprehensive school with regard to social class composition and general neighbourhood environment. In this way it was hoped to minimize the confounding influence of 'neighbourhood context' on educational attainment, aspirations and attitudes. For the classic discussion of the importance of this variable see ROGOFF, NATALIE (1961) 'Local Social Structure and Educational Selection', in HALSEY, A. H. et. al. (eds) *Education, Economy and Society.* Glencoe, Ill.: Free Press, pp. 243–4. And, for a study of the importance of neighbourhood context in the case of English comprehensive schools, see

EGGLESTON, S. JOHN (1965) 'How Comprehensive is the Leicestershi Plan?', *New Society*, 23 March 1965.

18 Excluding, of course, those who were absent from school on the day t questionnaire was administered.

19 The fourth year was selected as this was the oldest group which could studied before the sample became biased by leavers. Any study of the educ tional and occupational plans and expectations of such a biased sample woul have been highly misleading, c.f. TURNER, RALPH, 1964 *The Social Context Ambition*. Braintree: Chandler.

20 See Appendix II [of the original book].

21 For good summaries of this position see LAWTON, DENIS (1968) *Social Clas Language and Education*. London: Routledge and Kegan Paul, chapter 1; an LITTLE, A. and WESTERGAARD, J. (1964) 'The trend of Class Differentia in Educational Opportunity', *British Journal of Sociology*, XVI (4), pp. 301–15

22 For example, YOUNG, MICHAEL and ARMSTRONG, MICHAEL (1965) 'Th Flexible School', *Where*, Supplement 5, especially p. 4.

23 HOLLY, D. N. (1965) 'Profiting from a Comprehensive School: Class, sex an ability', *British Journal of Sociology*, XVI (4), p. 157.

24 This point is also made by GIDDENS, A. and HOLLOWAY, S. W. F. (1965 'Profiting from a Comprehensive School: A critical comment', *British Journal Sociology*, XVI (4), pp. 351–3.

25 This is the Hall-Jones scale. In those cases where the information wa insufficient or where the father was dead or had deserted the family (about per cent in all) classification was on the basis of mother's occupation. Th open-ended format was used in preference to a pre-coded schedule as it ha been shown that the extent of misunderstanding of the latter is greater than th likelihood of coding bias in the former. See COLFAX, J. DAVID and ALLEN IRVING L. (1967) 'Pre-coded versus Openended Items and Children' Reports of Father's Occupation', *Sociology of Education*, XL (1), pp. 96–8.

26 For a fuller discussion of this notion see Chapter 4 [of the original book].

27 PETER M. BLAU developed a measure of occupational prestige according t the amount of bias in judgments of respondents from different social clas backgrounds, and found that the break between manual and non-manua occupations was the most important predictor of such bias. BLAU, PETER M (1957) 'Occupational Bias and Mobility', *American Sociological Review*., XXII pp. 392–9. F. M. MARTIN similarly found that when a matrix was constructe between Hall-Jones categories and subjective social class categories the *mos* difference between any transition from one grade to the next on the Hall-Jone scale which appeared on the subjective dimension occurred in the transitior from manual to non-manual. See GLASS, C. V. (1954) (ed.) *Social Mobility ir Britain*. London: Routledge and Kegan Paul, pp. 51–75. A more recent review of the English situation also led to the conclusion that 'The two-class formula- tion is much more than an analytical simplification of those who have studied class. It is a simplification which has a profound hold on the perceptions of class found in British society.' See KAHAN, MICHAEL, *et al.* (1966) 'On the Analytical Division of Social Class', *British Journal of Sociology*, XVII (2), p. 124.

28 The scores were obtained from school records.

29 Obviously tables showing class chances of 'A' stream placement for children o relatively low IQ or of, say, 'D' stream placement for those of relatively high or low IQ can also be calculated from Table 1. However these have not been

presented as the strong correlations between the three variables render the numbers involved in such tabulations too small to be meaningful.

30 I say 'appears to be' because in order to make a categorical statement to this effect it would be necessary to produce partial correlations which would indicate the extent and direction of the relationships between the three variables *over their whole range*. The analysis here presented is necessarily crude because the numbers involved preclude anything but dichotomization.

The lack of a statistically significant relationship between class and stream in the secondary modern school may also be explicable by the small numbers involved. For this reason no attempt at *ex post facto* explanation of this has been attempted.

31 CENTRAL ADVISORY COUNCIL FOR EDUCATION (1954) *Early Leaving*. A Report. London: HMSO, p. 19.

32 See FLOUD, JEAN, and HALSEY, A. H., 'Social Class, Intelligence Tests, and Selection for Secondary Schools', in HALSEY, A. H., *et al.* (1961) (eds.) *Education, Economy and Society*. Glencoe, Ill.: Free Press, pp. 212–13.

33 This finding conflicts with that of Miller. He found that, in response to the more evaluative question 'Do you want to leave school as soon as possible?', 83 per cent of grammar, 93 per cent of 'comprehensive grammar ('A') stream, 72 per cent of comprehensive modern' (lower streams) and 57 per cent of modern school children answered in the negative. See MILLER, T. W. G. (1961) *Values in the Comprehensive School*. Edinburgh: Oliver and Boyd.

34 Pedley noted in 1963 that 'Out of 102 comprehensive schools recently questioned on this subject, 88 "stream" the children on entry, 11 during or at the end of the first year. The remaining three do so after two years.' Op. cit. p. 88.

35 'A Sceptical Note on Education and Mobility' in HALSEY, *et al.* (1961) op cit: p. 252.

3.5 IQ in the US class structure

Samuel Bowles and Herbert Gintis

The IQ controversy

The argument that differences in genetic endowments are of central an increasing importance in the stratification systems of advanced technolog ical societies has been advanced, in similar forms, by a number of conten porary researchers.[1] At the heart of this argument lies the venerable thesi that IQ, as measured by tests such as the Stanford-Binet, is largel inherited via genetic transmission, rather than moulded throug environmental influences.*

This thesis bears a short elucidation. That IQ is highly heritable i merely to say that individuals with similar genes will exhibit similar IQ: *independent* of differences in the social environments they might experienc during their mental development. The main support of the genetic schoo is several studies of individuals with precisely the same genes (identica twins) raised in different environments (i.e., separated at birth and rearec in families with different social statuses). Their IQs tend to be fairly similar.[2] In addition, there are studies of individuals with no commor genes (unrelated individuals) raised in the same environment (e.g., the same family) as well as studies of individuals with varying genetic similarities (e.g., fraternal twins, siblings, fathers and sons, aunts and nieces) and varying environments (e.g., siblings raised apart, cousins raised in their respective homes). The difference in IQs for these groups is roughly conformable to the genetic inheritance model suggested by the identical twin and unrelated individual studies.[3]

As Eysenck suggests, while geneticists will quibble over the exact magnitude of heritability of IQ nearly all will agree heritability exists and is significant.[4] Environmentalists, while emphasizing the paucity and unrepresentativeness of the data, have presented rather weak evidence for their own position and have made little dent in the genetic position.[5] Unable to attack the central proposition of the genetic school, environmentalists have emphasized that it bears no important social implications. They have claimed that, although raised in the context of the economic and educational deprivation of Blacks in the United States, the genetic theory says nothing about the 'necessary' degree of racial inequal-

---

*By IQ we mean – here and throughout this essay – those cognitive capacities that are measured on IQ tests. We have avoided the use of the word 'intelligence' as in its common usage it ordinarily connotes a broader range of capacities.

Source: *Social Policy*, Vol. 3, Nos 4 and 5, November/December 1972, January/ February 1973, pp. 66–78.

ity or the limits of compensatory education. First, environmentalists deny that there is any evidence that the IQ difference between Blacks and whites (amounting to about fifteen IQ points) is genetic in origin and second, they deny that any estimate of heritability tells us much about the capacity of 'enriched environments' to lessen IQ differentials, either within or between racial groups. [...]

The vigour of reaction in face of Jensen's argument indicates the liberals' agreement that IQ is a basic social determinant (at least ideally) of occupational status and intergenerational mobility. In Jensen's words, 'psychologists' concept of the "intelligence demands" of an occupation ... is very much like the general public's concept of the prestige of "social standing" of an occupation, and both are closely related to an independent measure of ... occupational status.'[6] Jensen continues, quoting O. D. Duncan: '... "intelligence" ... is not essentially different from that of achievement or status in the occupational sphere ... what we now *mean* by intelligence is something like the probability of acceptable performance (given the opportunity) in occupations varying in social status.'[7] Moreover, Jensen argues that the purported trend towards intelligence's being an increasing requirement for occupational status will continue.[8] [....]

Jensen *et al.* cannot be accused of employing an overly complicated social theory. Jensen's reason for the 'inevitable' association of status and intelligence is that society 'rewards talent and merit', and Herrnstein adds that society recognizes 'the importance and scarcity of intellectual ability'.[9] Moreover, the association of intelligence and social class is due to the 'screening process',[10] via education and occupation, whereby each generation is further refined into social strata on the basis of IQ. [...] Herrnstein celebrates the genetic school's crowning achievement by turning liberal social policy directly against itself, noting that the heritability of intelligence and hence the increasing pervasiveness of social stratification will increase, the more 'progressive' our social policies: 'the growth of a virtually hereditary meritocracy will arise out of the successful realization of contemporary political and social goals ... as the environment becomes more favourable for the development of intelligence, its heritability will increase. ...'[11] Similarly, the more we break down discriminatory and ascriptive criteria for hiring, the stronger will become the link between IQ and occupational success, and the development of modern technology can only quicken the process.[12]

Few will be surprised that such statements are made by the 'conservative' genetic school. But why, amid a spirited liberal counterattack in which the minutest details of the genetic hypothesis are contested and scathingly criticized, is the validity of the genetic school's description of the social function of intelligence blandly accepted? The widespread agreement among participants in the debate that IQ is an important determinant of economic success can hardly be explained by compelling empirical evidence adduced in support of the position. Quite the contrary.

As we will show in the next section, the available data point strongly to the unimportance of IQ in getting ahead economically. [...] we shall argue that the actual function of IQ testing and its associated ideology is that of legitimizing the stratification system, rather than generating it. The treatment of IQ in many strands of liberal sociology and economics merely reflects its actual function in social life: the legitimization and rationalization of the existing social relations of production.

The importance of IQ

The most immediate support for the IQ theory of social stratification – which we will call IQism – flows from the strong association of IQ and economic success. This is illustrated in Table 1, which exhibits the probability of achieving any particular decile in the economic success distribution for an individual whose adult IQ lies in a specified decile.*

Table 1*   Probability of Attainment of Different Levels of Economic Success for Individuals of Differing Levels of Adult IQ, by Deciles

		Adult IQ by deciles									
y	*x*	*10*	*9*	*8*	*7*	*6*	*5*	*4*	*3*	*2*	*1*
10		30.9	19.8	14.4	10.9	8.2	6.1	4.4	3.0	1.7	0.6
9		19.2	16.9	14.5	12.4	10.5	8.7	7.0	5.4	3.6	1.7
8		13.8	14.5	13.7	12.6	11.4	10.1	8.7	7.1	5.3	2.8
7		10.3	12.4	12.6	12.3	11.7	11.0	10.0	8.7	7.0	4.1
6		7.7	10.4	11.4	11.7	11.8	11.5	11.0	10.1	8.7	5.7
5		5.7	8.7	10.1	11.0	11.5	11.8	11.7	11.4	10.4	7.7
4		4.1	7.0	8.7	10.0	11.0	11.7	12.3	12.6	12.4	10.3
3		2.8	5.3	7.1	8.7	10.1	11.4	12.6	13.7	14.5	13.8
2		1.7	3.6	5.4	7.0	8.7	10.5	12.4	14.5	16.9	19.2
1		0.6	1.7	3.0	4.4	6.1	8.2	10.9	14.4	19.8	30.9

Economic Success by Deciles (row label, left margin)

*Table 1 corresponds to a correlation coefficient r = .52.
Example of use: For an individual in the 85th percentile in Adult IQ (x = 9), the probability of attaining between the 20th and 30th percentile in Economic Success is 5.3 per cent (the entry in column 9, row 3).

The data [...] refer to 'non-Negro' males, aged 25 to 34, from nonfarm background in the experienced labour force. We have chosen this population because it represents the dominant labour force and the group into

*In Table 1, as throughout this paper, 'adult IQ' is measured by scores on a form of the Armed Forces Qualification Test. [...] Economic success is measured throughout as the average of an individual's income and the social prestige of his occupation as measured on the Duncan occupational status index. See DUNCAN 'Properties and Characteristics of the Socio-economic Index.'[7]

which minority groups and women would have to integrate to realize the liberal ideal of equal opportunity, and hence to whose statistical associations these groups would become subject. [...] The quality of the data preclude any claims to absolute precision in our estimation. Yet our main propositions remain supported, even making allowance for substantive degrees of error. [...]

The interpretation of Table 1 is straightforward. The entries in the table are calculated directly from the simple correlation coefficient between our variables Adult IQ and Economic Success. In addition to reporting the correlation coefficient, we have described these data in tabular form as in Table 1 to illustrate the meaning of the correlation coefficient in terms of the differing probability of economic success for people at various positions in the distribution of IQs. We cannot stress too strongly that while the correlation coefficients in this and later tables are estimated from the indicated data, the entries in the table represent nothing more than a simple translation of their correlations, using assumptions that – though virtually universally employed in this kind of research – substantially simplify the complexity of the actual data. Now, turning to the table, we can see, for example, that a correlation between these two variables of .52 implies that an individual whose adult IQ lies in the top 10 per cent of the population has a probability of 30.9 per cent of ending up in the top tenth of the population in economic success, and a probability of 0.6 per cent of ending up in the bottom tenth. Since an individual chosen at random will have a probability of 10 per cent of ending up in any decile of economic success, we can conclude that being in the top decile in IQ renders an individual (white male) 3.09 times as likely to be in the top economic success decile, and .06 times as likely to end up in the bottom, as would be predicted by chance. Each of the remaining entries in Table 1 can be interpreted correspondingly.

Yet Tables 2 and 3, which exhibit the corresponding probabilities of economic success given number of years of schooling and level of socioeconomic background,* show that this statistical support is surely misleading: even stronger associations appear between years of schooling and economic success, as well as between social background and economic success. For example, being in the top decile in years of schooling renders an individual 3.76 times as likely to be at the top of the economic heap, and .01 times as likely to be at the bottom, while the corresponding ratios are 3.26 and .04 for social background. It is thus quite possible to draw from aggregate statistics, equally cogently, both an 'educational attainment theory' of social stratification and a 'socioeconomic background' theory. Clearly there are logical errors in all such facile inferences.

---

*In Table 3, as throughout this paper, socioeconomic background is measured as a weighted sum of parental income, father's occupational status, and father's income, where the weights are chosen so as to produce the maximum multiple correlation with economic success.

Table 2* Probability of Attainment of Different Levels of Economic Success ⟨ Individuals of Different Levels of Education, by Deciles

y	x	10	9	8	7	6	5	4	3	2	1
10		37.6	22.3	14.6	9.8	6.6	4.3	2.6	4.4	0.6	0.
9		20.9	19.5	16.2	13.1	10.3	7.9	5.7	3.8	2.1	0.
8		13.5	16.1	15.3	13.8	12.0	10.1	8.0	5.9	3.7	1.
7		9.1	13.0	13.8	13.6	12.8	11.6	10.0	8.0	5.6	2.
6		6.1	10.2	12.0	12.8	12.9	12.5	11.6	10.1	7.8	4.0
5		4.0	7.8	10.1	11.6	12.5	12.9	12.8	12.0	10.2	6.
4		2.5	5.6	8.0	10.0	11.6	12.8	13.6	13.8	13.0	9.
3		1.4	3.7	5.9	8.0	10.1	12.0	13.8	15.3	16.1	13.
2		0.6	2.1	3.8	5.7	7.9	10.3	13.1	16.2	19.5	20.
1		0.1	0.6	1.4	2.6	4.3	6.6	9.8	14.6	22.3	37.

Economic Success by Deciles (row axis); *Years of schooling by deciles* (column heading)

*Table 2 corresponds to a correlation coefficient r = .63.

Example of use: For an individual in the 85th percentile in Education (x = 9), the probabili of attaining between the 20th and 30th percentiles in Economic Success (y = 3) is 3.7 per cer (the entry in column 9, row 3).

Table 3 * Probability of Attainment of Different Levels of Economic Success f Individuals of Differing Levels of Social Class Background

y	x	10	9	8	7	6	5	4	3	2	1
10		32.6	20.4	14.5	10.7	7.8	5.7	3.9	2.5	1.4	0.4
9		19.7	17.5	14.9	12.6	10.5	8.5	6.7	5.0	3.2	1.3
8		13.8	14.9	14.1	12.9	11.6	10.1	8.6	6.9	4.9	2.4
7		10.0	12.5	12.9	12.6	12.0	11.1	10.0	8.5	6.7	3.7
6		7.3	10.4	11.5	12.0	12.0	11.7	11.1	10.1	8.5	5.3
5		5.3	8.5	10.1	11.1	11.7	12.0	12.0	11.5	10.4	7.3
4		3.7	6.7	8.5	10.0	11.1	12.0	12.6	12.9	12.5	10.0
3		2.4	4.9	6.9	8.6	10.1	11.6	12.9	14.1	14.9	13.8
2		1.3	3.2	5.0	6.7	8.5	10.5	12.6	14.9	17.5	19.7
1		0.4	1.4	2.5	3.9	5.7	7.8	10.7	14.5	20.4	32.6

Economic Success by Deciles (row axis); *Social class background by deciles* (column heading)

*Table 3 corresponds to a correlation coefficient r = .55.

Example of use: For an individual in the 85th percentile in Social Class (x = 9), the probability of attaining between the 20th and the 30th percentile in Economic Succes (y = 3) is 4.9 per cent (the entry in column 9, row 3).

Of course, the IQ proponent will argue that there is no real problem here: the association of social class background and economic success follows from the importance of IQ to economic success, and the fact tha individuals of higher class background have higher IQ. Similarly one may argue that the association of education and economic success follows from the fact that education simply picks out and develops the talents o itelligent individuals. The problem is that equally cogent arguments can e given for the primacy of either education or social class, and the orresponding subordinateness of the others. The above figures are qually compatible with all three interpretations.

In this section we shall show that all three factors (IQ, social class ackground, and education) contribute independently to economic success, but that IQ is by far the least important. Specifically we will emonstrate the truth of the following three propositions, which constiute the empirical basis of our thesis concerning the unimportance of IQ in enerating the class structure.

First, although higher IQs and economic success tend to go together, higher IQs are ot an important cause of economic success. The statistical association between dult IQ and economic success, while substantial, derives largely from the ommon association of both of these variables with social class background and level of schooling. Thus to appraise the economic importance f IQ, we must focus attention on family and school.

Second, although higher levels of schooling and economic success likewise tend o go together, the intellectual abilities developed or certified in school make little ausal contribution to getting ahead economically. Thus only a minor ortion of the substantial statistical association between schooling and conomic success can be accounted for by the schools' role in producing or screening cognitive skills. The predominant economic unction of schools must therefore involve the accreditation of ndividuals, as well as the production and selection of personality raits and other personal attributes rewarded by the economic system.)ur third proposition asserts a parallel result with respect to the effect f social class background.

Third, the fact that economic success tends to run in the family arises almost ompletely independently from any genetic inheritance of IQ. Thus, while one's conomic status tends to resemble that of one's parents, only a minor ortion of this association can be attributed to social class differences in hildhood IQ, and a virtually negligible portion to social class differences n genetic endowments, even accepting the Jensen estimates of heritabiity. Thus a perfect equalization of IQs across social classes would reduce he intergenerational transmission of economic status by a negligible mount. We conclude that a family's position in the class structure is eproduced primarily by mechanisms operating independently of the nheritance, production, and certification of intellectual skills.

Our statistical technique for the demonstration of these propositions will be that of linear regression analysis. This technique allows us to derive numerical estimates of the independent contribution of each of the separate but correlated influences (social class background, childhood Q, years of schooling, adult IQ) on economic success, by answering the question: what is the magnitude of the association between any one of these influences among individuals who are equal on some or all the others? Equivalently it answers the question: what are the probabilities of attaining particular deciles in economic success among individuals who are in the same decile in some or all of the above influences but one, and in varying deciles in this one variable alone?

Table 4* Differential Probabilities of Attaining Economic Success for Individuals of Equal Levels of Education and Social Class Background, but Differing Levels of Adult IQ

		Adult IQ by deciles									
y	*x*	*10*	*9*	*8*	*7*	*6*	*5*	*4*	*3*	*2*	*1*
Economic Success by Deciles 10		14.1	12.3	11.4	10.7	10.1	9.6	9.0	8.5	7.8	6.6
9		12.4	11.4	10.9	10.5	10.2	9.8	9.5	9.1	8.6	7.7
8		11.4	10.9	10.6	10.4	10.2	9.9	9.7	9.4	9.1	8.4
7		10.7	10.5	10.4	10.3	10.1	10.0	9.9	9.7	9.5	9.0
6		10.1	10.2	10.2	10.1	10.1	10.1	10.0	9.9	9.8	9.5
5		9.5	9.8	9.9	10.0	10.1	10.1	10.1	10.2	10.2	10.1
4		9.0	9.5	9.7	9.9	10.0	10.1	10.3	10.4	10.5	10.7
3		8.4	9.1	9.4	9.7	9.9	10.2	10.4	10.6	10.9	11.4
2		7.7	8.6	9.1	9.5	9.8	10.2	10.5	10.9	11.4	12.4
1		6.6	7.8	8.5	9.0	9.6	10.1	10.7	11.4	12.3	14.1

*Table 4 corresponds to a standardized regression coefficient ß = .13.
Example of use: Suppose two individuals have the same levels of Education and Social Class Background, but one is in the 85th percentile in Adult IQ (x = 9), while the other is in the 15th decile in Adult IQ (x = 2). Then the first individual is 10.9/9.1 = 1.2 times as likely as the second to attain the 8th decile in Economic Success (column 9, row 8, divided by column 2, row 8).

The IQ argument is based on the assumption that social background and education are related to economic success *because* they are associated with higher adult cognitive skills. Table 4 shows this to be essentially incorrect. This table, by exhibiting the relation between adult IQ and economic success among individuals with the same social class background and level of schooling, shows that the IQ-economic success association exhibited in Table 1 is largely a by-product of these more basic social influences. That is, for a given level of social background and schooling, differences in adult IQ add very little to our ability to predict eventual economic success. Thus, for example, an individual with an average number of years of schooling and an average socioeconomic family background, but with a level of cognitive skill to place him in the top decile of the IQ distribution, has a probability of 14.1 per cent of attaining the highest economic success decile. This figure may be compared with 10 per cent, the analogous probability for an individual with average levels of IQ as well as schooling and social background. Our first proposition – that the relation between IQ and economic success is not causal, but rather operates largely through the effects of the correlated variables, years of schooling and social class background – is thus strongly supported.* We are thus led to focus directly on the role of social class background and schooling in promoting economic success.

Turning first to schooling, the argument of the IQ proponents is that the strong association between level of schooling and economic success exhibited in Table 2 is due to the fact that economic success depends on cognitive capacities, and schooling both selects individuals with high intellectual ability for further training and then develops this ability into concrete adult cognitive skills. Table 5 shows this view to be false. This table exhibits the effect of schooling on chances for economic success, for individuals who have the same adult IQ. Comparing Table 5 with Table 2, we see that cognitive differences account for a negligible part of schooling's influence on economic success: individuals with similar levels of adult IQ but differing levels of schooling have substantially different chances of economic success. Indeed the similarity of Tables 2 and 5 demonstrates the validity of our second proposition – that schooling affects chances of economic success predominantly by the noncognitive traits which it generates, or on the basis of which it selects individuals for higher education.[13]

Table 5* Differential Probabilities of Attaining Economic Success for Individuals of Equal Adult IQ but Differing Levels of Education

		Years of schooling by deciles									
y	x	10	9	8	7	6	5	4	3	2	1
10		33.2	20.6	14.6	10.6	7.7	5.5	3.8	2.4	1.3	0.4
9		19.9	17.8	15.1	12.7	10.5	8.5	6.6	4.8	3.1	1.2
8		13.8	15.0	14.2	13.0	11.6	10.1	8.5	6.8	4.8	2.3
7		9.9	12.6	13.0	12.7	12.1	11.2	10.0	8.5	6.6	3.5
6		7.2	10.4	11.6	12.1	12.1	11.8	11.2	10.1	8.4	5.1
5		5.1	8.4	10.1	11.2	11.8	12.1	12.1	11.6	10.4	7.2
4		3.5	6.6	8.5	10.0	11.2	12.1	12.7	13.0	12.6	9.9
3		2.3	4.8	6.8	8.5	10.1	11.6	13.0	14.2	15.0	13.8
2		1.2	3.1	4.8	6.6	8.5	10.5	12.7	15.1	17.8	19.9
1		0.4	1.3	2.4	3.8	5.5	7.7	10.6	14.6	20.6	33.2

*Table 5 corresponds to a standardized regression coefficient ß = .56.

Example of use: Suppose two individuals have the same Adult IQ, but one is in the 9th decile in Level of Education (x = 9), while the other is in the 2nd decile (x = 2). Then the first individual is 15.0/4.8 = 3.12 times as likely as the second to attain the 8th decile in Economic Success (column 9, row 8, divided by column 2 row 8).

* This is not to say that IQ is never an important criteria of success. We do not contend that extremely low or high IQs are irrelevant to economic failure or success. Nor do we deny that for some individuals or for some jobs, cognitive skills are economically important. Rather, we assert that for the vast majority of workers and jobs, selection, assessed job adequacy, and promotion are based on attributes other than IQ.

The next step in our argument is to show that the relationship between social background and economic success operates almost entirely independently of individual differences in IQ. Whereas Table 3 exhibits the total effect of social class on an individual's economic success, Table 6 exhibits the same effect among individuals with the same childhood IQ. Clearly these tables are nearly identical. That is, even were all social class differences in IQ eliminated, a similar pattern of social class intergenerational immobility would result.[14] Our third proposition is thus supported: the intergenerational transmission of social and economic status operates primarily via noncognitive mechanisms, despite the fact that the school system rewards higher IQ – an attribute significantly associated with higher social class background.

Table 6* Differential Probabilities of Attaining Economic Success for Individuals of Equal Early IQ but Differing Levels of Social Class Background

		Social class background by deciles									
y	x	10	9	8	7	6	5	4	3	2	1
10		27.7	18.5	14.1	11.1	8.8	6.9	5.3	3.9	2.5	1.1
9		18.2	15.8	13.8	12.1	10.5	9.0	7.6	6.1	4.5	2.4
8		13.7	13.8	13.0	12.1	11.1	10.1	8.9	7.6	6.1	3.7
7		10.7	12.0	12.1	11.8	11.3	10.7	9.9	8.9	7.5	5.0
6		8.4	10.5	11.1	11.3	11.3	11.1	10.7	10.0	9.0	6.6
5		6.6	9.0	10.0	10.7	11.1	11.3	11.3	11.1	10.5	8.4
4		5.0	7.5	8.9	9.9	10.7	11.3	11.8	12.1	12.0	10.7
3		3.7	6.1	7.6	8.9	10.1	11.1	12.1	13.0	13.8	13.7
2		2.4	4.5	6.1	7.6	9.0	10.5	12.1	13.8	15.8	18.2
1		1.1	2.5	3.9	5.3	6.9	8.8	11.1	14.1	18.5	27.7

(left axis label) Economic Success by Deciles

*Table 6 corresponds to a standardized regression coefficient $\beta = .46$.
Example of use: Suppose two individuals have the same Childhood IQ, but one is in the 9th decile in Social Background, while the other is in the 2nd decile. Then the first is $18.5/2.5 = 7.4$ times as likely as the second to attain the top decile in Economic Success (column 9, row 10, divided by column 2, row 10).

The unimportance of the specifically genetic mechanism operating via IQ in the intergenerational reproduction of economic inequality is even more striking. Table 7 exhibits the degree of association between social class background and economic success that can be attributed to the genetic inheritance of IQ alone. This table assumes that all direct influences of socio-economic background upon economic success have been eliminated, and that the noncognitive components of schooling's contribution to economic success are eliminated as well (the perfect meritocracy based on intellectual ability). On the other hand, it assumes Jensen's estimate for the degree of heritability of IQ. A glance at Table 7 shows that the resulting level of intergenerational inequality in this highly hypothetical example would be negligible.

Table 7* The Genetic Component of Intergenerational Status Transmission, Assuming the Jensen Heritability Coefficient, and Assuming Education Operates Via Cognitive Mechanisms Alone

y	x	10	9	8	7	6	5	4	3	2	1
							Social class background by deciles				
10		10.6	10.3	10.2	10.1	10.0	10.0	9.9	9.8	9.7	9.4
9		10.4	10.2	10.1	10.1	10.0	10.0	9.9	9.9	9.8	9.6
8		10.2	10.1	10.1	10.1	10.0	10.0	9.9	9.9	9.9	9.8
7		10.1	10.1	10.1	10.0	10.0	10.0	10.0	9.9	9.9	9.9
6		10.0	10.0	10.0	10.0	10.0	10.0	10.0	10.0	10.0	10.0
5		10.0	10.0	10.0	10.0	10.0	10.0	10.0	10.0	10.0	10.0
4		9.9	9.9	9.9	10.0	10.0	10.0	10.1	10.1	10.1	10.1
3		9.8	9.9	9.9	9.9	10.0	10.0	10.1	10.1	10.1	10.2
2		9.6	9.8	9.9	9.9	10.0	10.0	10.1	10.1	10.2	10.4
1		9.4	9.7	9.8	9.9	10.0	10.0	10.1	10.2	10.3	10.6

*Table 7 corresponds to .02 standard deviations difference in Economic Success per standard deviation difference in Social Class Background, in a causal model assuming Social Class Background affects Early IQ only via genetic transmission, and assuming Economic Success is directly affected only by cognitive variables.

Example of use: For an individual in the 85th percentile in Social Class Background (x = 9), the probability of attaining between the 20th and 30th percentiles in Economic Success (y = 3), assuming only genetic and cognitive mechanisms, is 10.1 per cent (the entry in column 9, row 8).

The unimportance of IQ in explaining the relation between social class background and economic success, and the unimportance of cognitive achievement in explaining the contribution of schooling to economic success, together with our previously derived observation that most of the association between IQ and economic success can be accounted for by the common association of these variables with education and social class, support our major assertion: IQ is not an important intrinsic criterion for economic success. Our data thus hardly lend credence to Duncan's assertion that 'intelligence ... is not essentially different from that of achievement or status in the occupational sphere',[15] nor to Jensen's belief in the 'inevitable' association of status and intelligence, based on society's 'rewarding talent and merit',[16] nor to Herrnstein's dismal prognostication of a 'virtually hereditary meritocracy' as the fruit of successful liberal reform in an advanced industrial society.[17]

IQ and the legitimation of the hierarchical division of labour

A preview

We have disputed the view that IQ is an important causal antecedent of economic success. Yet IQ clearly plays an important role in the US stratification system. In this section we shall argue that the set of beliefs surrounding IQ betrays its true function – that of legitimating the social institutions underpinning the stratification system itself.

Were the IQ ideology correct, understanding the ramifications of cognitive differences would require our focusing on the technical relations of production in an advanced technological economy. Its failure, however, bids us scrutinize a different aspect of production – its social relations. By the 'social relations of production' we mean the system of rights and responsibilities, duties and rewards, that governs the interaction of all individuals involved in organized productive activity.[18] In the following section we shall argue that the social relations of production determine the major attributes of the US stratification system.[19] Here, however, we shall confine ourselves to the proposition that the IQ ideology is a major factor in legitimating these social relations in the consciousness of workers.

The social relations of production in different societies are quite diverse; they lay the basis for such divergent stratification systems as communal-reciprocity, caste, feudal serf, slave, community-collective, and wage labour of capitalist and state socialist varieties. In advanced capitalist society the stratification system is based on what we term the hierarchical division of labour, characterized by power and control emanating from the top downwards through a finely gradated bureaucratic order.[20] The distribution of economic reward and social privilege in the United States is an expression of the hierarchical division of labour within the enterprise.

In this section, then, we shall show that the IQ ideology serves to legitimate the hierarchica! division of labour. [...]

The need for legitimacy

If one takes for granted the basic economic organization of society, its members need only be equipped with adequate cognitive and operational skills to fulfil work requirements, and provided with a reward structure motivating individuals to acquire and supply these skills. US capitalism accomplishes the first of these requirements through family, school, and on-the-job training, and the second through a wage structure patterned after the job hierarchy.

But the social relations of production cannot be taken for granted. The bedrock of the capitalist economy is the legally sanctioned power of the directors of an enterprise to organize production, to determine the rules that regulate workers' productive activities, and to hire and fire accordingly, with only moderate restriction by workers' organizations and government regulations. But this power cannot be taken for granted, and can be exercised forcefully against violent opposition only sporadically. [...] Where the assent of the less favoured cannot be secured by power alone, it must be part of a total process whereby the existing structure of work roles and their allocation among individuals are seen as ethically acceptable and even technically necessary.

In some social systems the norms that govern the economic system are quite similar to those governing other major social spheres. Thus in feudal society the authority of the lord of the manor is not essentially different from that of the political monarch, the church hierarchy, or the family patriarch, and the ideology of 'natural estates' suffuses all social activity. No special normative order is required for the economic system. But in capitalist society, to make the hierarchical division of labour appear just is no easy task, for the totalitarian organization of the enterprise clashes sharply with the ideals of equality, democracy, and participation that pervade the political and legal spheres. Thus the economic enterprise as a political dictatorship and a social caste system requires special legitimation, and the mechanisms used to place individuals in unequal (and unequally rewarding) positions require special justification. [...]

The thrust of legitimation: IQ, technocracy, and meritocracy

We may isolate several related aspects of the social relations of production that are legitimized in part by the IQ ideology. To begin there are the overall characteristics of work in advanced US capitalism: bureaucratic organization, hierarchical lines of authority, job fragmentation, and unequal reward. It is highly essential that the individual accept, and indeed come to see as natural, these undemocratic and unequal aspects of the workaday world.

Moreover, the mode of allocating individuals to these various positions in US capitalism is characterized by intense competition in the educational system followed by individual assessment and choice by employers. Here again the major problem is that this 'allocation mechanism' must appear egalitarian in process and just in outcome, parallel to the formal principle of 'equality of all before the law' in a democratic juridical system based on freedom of contract.

While these two areas refer to the legitimation of capitalism as a social system, they have their counterpart in the individual's personal life. Thus, just as individuals must come to accept the overall social relations of production, workers must respect the authority and competence of their own 'superiors' to direct their activities, and justify their own authority (however extensive) over others. Similarly, just as the overall system of role allocation must be legitimized, so individuals must assent to the justness of their own personal position, and the mechanisms through which this position has been attained. That workers be resigned to their position in production is perhaps adequate; that they be reconciled is even preferable.

The contribution of IQ-ism to the legitimation of these social relations is based on a view of society that asserts the efficiency and technological necessity of modern industrial organization, and is buttressed by evidence of the similarity of production and work in such otherwise divergent social systems as the United States and the Soviet Union. In this view large-scale production is a requirement of advanced technology, and the hierarchical division of labour is the only effective means of coordinating the highly complex and interdependent parts of the large-scale productive system. [...] In the words of Talcott Parsons: 'Bureaucracy ... is the most effective large-scale administrative organization that man has invented, and there is no direct substitute for it.'[21]

The hallmark of the 'technocratic perspective' is its reduction of a complex web of social relations in production to a few rules of technological efficacy – whence its easy integration with the similarly technocratic view of social stratification inherent in the IQ ideology. In this view the hierarchical division of labour arises from its natural superiority in the coordination of collective activity and in the nurturing of expertise in the control of complex production processes. In order to motivate the most able individuals to undertake the necessary training and preparation for high level occupational roles, salaries and status must be closely associated with one's level in the work hierarchy. Thus Davis and Moore, in their highly influential 'functional theory of stratification', locate the 'determinants of differential reward' in 'differential functional importance' and 'differential scarcity of personnel'. 'Social inequality,' they conclude, 'is thus an unconsciously evolved device by which societies insure that the most important positions are conscientiously filled by the most qualified persons.'[22] [...]

This perspective, technocratic in its justification of the hierarchical division of labour, leads smoothly to a meritocratic view of the process of matching individuals to jobs. An efficient and impersonal bureaucracy assesses the individual purely in terms of his or her expected contribution to production. The main determinants of an individual's expected job fitness are seen as those [...] capacities relevant to the worker's technical ability to do the job. The technocratic view of production and the meritocratic view of job allocation yield an important corollary, to which we will later return. Namely, there is always a strong tendency in an efficient industrial order to abjure caste, class, sex, colour, and ethnic origins in occupational placement. This tendency will be particularly strong in a capitalist economy, where competitive pressures constrain employers to hire on the basis of strict efficiency criteria.[23]

The technocratic view of production, along with the meritocratic view of hiring, provides the strongest form of legitimation of work organization and social stratification in capitalist society. Not only is the notion that the hierarchical division of labour is 'technically necessary' (albeit politically totalitarian) strongly reinforced, but also the view that job allocation is just and egalitarian (albeit severely unequal) is ultimately justified as objective, efficient, and necessary. Moreover, the individual's reconciliation with his or her own position in the hierarchy of production appears all but complete; the legitimacy of the authority of superiors no less than that of the individual's own objective position flows not from social contrivance but from Science and Reason.

That this view does not strain the credulity of well-paid intellectuals is perhaps not surprising.[24] Nor would the technocratic/meritocratic perspective be of much use in legitimizing the hierarchical division of labour were its adherents to be counted only among the university élite and the technical and professional experts. But such is not the case. Despite the extensive evidence that IQ is not an important determinant of individual occupational achievement, [. . .] and despite the fact that few occupations place cognitive requirements on job entry, the crucial importance of IQ in personal success has captured the public mind. Numerous attitude surveys exhibit this fact. In a national sample of high school students, for example, 'intelligence' ranks second only to 'good health' in importance as a desirable personal attribute.[25] Similarly a large majority chose 'intelligence' along with 'hard work' as the most important requirements of success in life. [. . .]

This popular acceptance, we shall argue, is due to the unique role of the educational system.

Education and legitimation

To understand the widespread acceptance of the view that economic success is predicated on intellectual achievement we must look beyond the workplace, for the IQ ideology does not conform to most workers' everyday experience on the job. Rather, the strength of this view derives in large measure from the interaction between schooling, cognitive achievement, and economic success. IQ-ism legitimates the hierarchical division of labour not directly, but primarily through its relationship with the educational system.

We can summarize the relationship as follows. First, the distribution of rewards by the school is seen as being based on objectively measured cognitive achievement, and is therefore fair. Second, schools are seen as being primarily oriented towards the production of cognitive skills. Third, higher levels of schooling are seen as a major, perhaps the strongest, determinant of economic success, and quite reasonably so, given the strong association of these two variables exhibited in Table 2. It is concluded, thus, that high IQs are acquired in a fair and open competition in school and in addition are a major determinant of success. The conclusion is based on the belief that the relationship between level of schooling and degree of economic success derives largely from the contribution of school to an individual's cognitive skills. Given the organization and stated objectives of schools it is easy to see how people would come to accept this belief. We have shown in Tables 2 and 5 that it is largely without empirical support.

The linking of intelligence to economic success indirectly via the educational system strengthens rather than weakens the legitimation process. First, the day-to-day contact of parents and children with the competitive, cognitively oriented school environment, with clear connections to the economy, buttresses in a very immediate and concrete way the technocratic perspective on economic organization, to a degree that a sporadic and impersonal testing process divorced from the school environment could not aspire. Second, by rendering the outcome (educational attainment) dependent not only on ability but also on motivation, drive to achieve, perseverance, and sacrifice, the status allocation mechanism acquired heightened legitimacy. Moreover, personal attributes are tested and developed over a long period of time, thus enhancing the apparent objectivity and achievement orientation of the stratification system. Third, by gradually 'cooling out' individuals at different educational levels, the student's aspirations are relatively painlessly brought into line with his probable occupational status. By the time most students terminate schooling they have validated for themselves their inability or unwillingness to be a success at the next highest level. Through competition, success, and defeat in the classroom, the individual is reconciled to his or her social position.[26] [...]

The credentialist and IQ ideology upon which the 'meritocratic' legitimation mechanisms depend is already under attack. Blacks reject the racism implicit in much of the recent work on IQ; they are not mystified by the elaborate empirical substantiation of the geneticist position, nor by the assertions of meritocracy by functionalist sociologists. Their daily experience gives them insights that seem to have escaped many social scientists. Likewise women – indeed many poor people of both sexes – know that their exclusion from jobs is not based on any deficiency of educational credentials.

We have here attempted to speed up the process of demystification by showing that the purportedly 'scientific' empirical basis of credentialism and IQ-ism is false. In addition, we have attempted to facilitate linkages between these groups and workers' movements within the dominant white male labour force, by showing that the *same* mechanisms are used to divide strata against one another so as to maintain the inferior status of 'minority' groups.

The assault on economic inequality and hierarchical control of work appears likely to intensify. Along with other social strains endemic to advanced capitalism, the growing tension between people's needs for self-realization in work and the needs of capitalists and managers for secure top-down control of economic activity opens up the possibility of powerful social movements dedicated to the elimination of the hierarchical division of labour. We hope our paper will contribute to this outcome.

Notes

1. JENSEN, 'How Much Can We Boost IQ', CARL BEREITER, 'The Future of Individual Differences', *Harvard Educational Review*, Reprint Series no. 2, 1969, pp. 162–170; HERRNSTEIN, 'IQ'; EYSENCK, *The IQ Argument*.

2. ARTHUR R. JENSEN, 'Estimation of the Limits of Heritability of Traits by Comparison of Monozygotic and Dizygotic Twins', *Proceedings of the National Academy of Science*, 58 (1967): 149–157.

3. JENSEN, 'How Much Can We Boost IQ'; CHRISTOPHER JENCKS et al., *Inequality: A Reassessment of the Effects of Family and Schooling in America* (New York; Basic Books, 1972).

4. EYSENCK, *The IQ Argument*, p. 9.

5. JEROME S. KAGAN, 'Inadequate Evidence and Illogical Conclusions', *Harvard Educational Review*, Reprint Series no. 2, 1969, pp. 126–134; HUNT, J. MCV. 'Has Compensatory Education Failed? Has It Been Attempted?' *Harvard Educational Review*, Reprint Series no. 2, 1969, pp. 130–152.

6. JENSEN, 'Estimation of the Limits of Heritability', p. 14.

7. OTIS DUDLEY DUNCAN, 'Properties and Characteristics of the Socioeconomic Index', in ALBERT J. REISS, ed., *Occupations and Social Status* (New York; Free Press, 1961), p. 142.

8. JENSEN, 'Estimation of the Limits of Heritability', p. 19.

9. HERRNSTEIN, 'IQ', p. 51.

10. JENSEN, 'How Much Can We Boost IQ', p. 75.

11. Ibid. HERRNSTEIN, 'IQ', p. 63.

12. Ibid.

13. For a more extensive treatment of this point, using data from nine independent samples, see GINTIS, 'Education and the Characteristics of Worker Productivity'.

14. For a more extensive demonstration of this proposition, see BOWLES, 'The Genetic Inheritance of IQ'.

15. DUNCAN, 'Properties and Characteristics of the Socioeconomic Index'.

16. JENSEN, 'Estimation of the Limits of Heritability', p. 73.

17. HERRNSTEIN, 'IQ', p. 63.

18. For an explication of the social relations of production, see ANDRE GORZ, 'Capitalist Relations of Production and the Socially Necessary Labour Force', in Arthur Lothstein, ed., *All We Are Saying . . .* (New York: G. P. Putnam's, 1970), and HERBERT GINTIS, 'Power and Alienation', in James Weaver, ed., *Readings in Political Economy* (Boston: Allyn and Bacon, forthcoming).

19. See BOWLES, 'Unequal Education and the Reproduction of the Social Division of Labor', *Review of Radical Political Economy*, 3 (Fall–Winter 1971); BOWLES, 'Contradictions in U.S. Higher Education', in JAMES WEAVER, ed., *Readings in Political Economy* (Boston: Allyn and Bacon, forthcoming), for an explanation of the connection

between the social relations of production and the stratification system.

20. On the origins and functions of the hierarchical division of labour, see STEPHEN MARGLIN, 'What Do Bosses Do?' unpublished manuscript, Department of Economics, Harvard University, 1971; RICHARD C. EDWARDS, 'Alienation and Inequality: Capitalist Relations of Production in a Bureaucratic Enterprise', Ph.D. diss., Harvard University, July 1972; Max Weber, *From Max Weber: Essays in Sociology* (New York: Oxford University Press, 1946); CHESTER I. BARNARD, *The Functions of the Executive* (Cambridge: Harvard University Press, 1938). A similar hierarchy in production occurs in state socialist countries.

21. TALCOTT PARSONS, 'Evolutionary Universals in Society', *American Sociological Review*, 29, no. 3 (June 1964); 507.

22. K. DAVIS and W. E. MOORE, 'Some Principles of Stratification', in R. BENDIX and S. M. LIPSET, eds., *Class, Status and Power* (New York: Free Press, 1966).

23. For a statement of this position, see MILTON FRIEDMAN, *Capitalism and Freedom* (Chicago: University of Chicago Press, 1962).

24. JENSEN reports that a panel of 'experts' determined that higher status jobs 'require' higher IQ. See JENSEN, 'How Much Can We Boost IQ.'

25. BRIM, O. G. et. al., *American Beliefs and Attitudes about Intelligence* (New York: Russell Sage Foundation, 1969).

26. See BURTON R. CLARK, 'The "Cooling Out" Function in Higher Education," *American Journal of Sociology*, 65, no. 6 (May 1960), PAUL LAUTER and FLORENCE HOWE, 'The Schools are Rigged for Failure', *New York Review of Books*, 20 June 1970.

3.6 The great training robbery

Eli Ginzberg

During the past decade, much of the effort of our Conservation Project has been focused, not on the disadvantaged, but on the educated and the talented. From these studies we concluded that, while education often provides access to better jobs and better incomes, it offers no guarantee of either. Our investigations also called attention to difficulties that may arise for both the employee and the employer if a man's work requires far less performance than his educational level and his potential would permit. We had earlier concluded that too little education is a disadvantage; apparently, the proposition must be entertained that under certain conditions too much education also can create difficulty.

The studies referred to above were person-centred. They sought to illuminate various aspects of group behaviour by analysing the characteristics and performance of groups. In addition, during the past several years the Conservation Project has carried on a series of investigations [...] the thrust of which was to emphasize the extent to which the American economy is being transformed in focus from the production of goods to the production of services, and the ever-larger role of the not-for-profit sector (government and nonprofit institutions); the wide range in the educational and other characteristics of people employed in the service sector; the extent to which new industries are able and willing to tap sources of labour supply irrespective of formal qualifications; the subtle and not-so-subtle competition for jobs between white women and Negroes; the way in which employer practices in hiring, assignment, and promotion help to shape the labour market; and the striking differences between the United States and Western Europe in making room for the disadvantaged, including the poorly educated.

While these several investigations of the Conservation Project were under way, directed towards deepening our understanding of the workings of the labour market so that we would no longer have to rely on a model at once too simple and too rigid, public leaders and academic economists were giving birth to a new ideology. They proclaimed that the key to economic development is liberal expenditures for education, which, by improving the quality of labour, are the heart of productivity increases. From the President down, the leadership proclaimed throughout the land: 'Education pays; stay in school.' The economists calculated to a fraction of a per cent the extent to which education pays.

Professor Berg, by temperament a sceptic, by training a sociologist, and

Source: BERG, I. (1972) *Education and Jobs: The Great Training Robbery*. New York: Praeger Publishers, pp. ix–xvi.

by choice a student of manpower, found the new orthodoxy neith
intellectually compelling nor emotionally satisfying. He therefore set o
to study the relations of education to employment, in part by collectir
new data, in part by critically reviewing the principal empirical studi
that had earlier been concerned with this theme.

Here are some of the important findings that emerge from his stud
Professor Berg begins by stressing the bias inherent in American life ar
thought that makes us look at a malfunctioning of the labour market
terms of the personal failings of workers in search of jobs. What is mo
reasonable than to postulate that if only these workers had more educatic
and training they would not be unemployed or underemployed?

Reasonable, yes – but not necessarily right. Among his incisive analys
is Professor Berg's critique of the conventional wisdom of researchers wh
have elaborated the 'human capital' approach. These academics hav
adduced evidence suggesting that the return on investment in people
greater than the average return on other forms of investment. But Profe
sor Berg correctly cautions that one must not be caught in circula
reasoning. The critical point is not whether men and women who con
plete high school or college are able subsequently to earn more than tho:
who don't, but whether their higher earnings are a reflection of bett
performance as a result of more education or training or of factors othe
than the diplomas and degrees they have acquired.

In Professor Berg's terms, perhaps the key to the puzzle is not wha
education contributes to an individual's productivity but how it helps hir
to get a better-paying job in the first place. He is careful not to challeng
the 'human capital' economists on the narrow ground that their calcula
tions are faulty or that they fail to support their conclusion that 'educatio
pays'; rather, he focuses on the reality that underlies their tenet. To prov
their case, Professor Berg argues, they would have to study education i
relation to the intervening variable of productivity rather than jump ove
it and deal only with income. To bring the point home sharply, I hav
often asked my students at Columbia's Graduate School of Business why
leading company is willing to pay them, when they graduate, $11,000 t
$12,000 annually to sell soap or breakfast foods. Why do large companie
offer such handsome salaries to beginners, even those with MAs? Th
trouble with the argument offered by 'human capital' theorists may b
that it is a rational explanation of behaviour that is largely irrational.

One of the interesting statistical exercises in which Professor Ber
engaged was to recalculate with care the large body of data assembled b
the United States Department of Labour about workers' characteristic
and employers' requirements, to determine the nature and extent c
changes in skills required over time in comparison with changes in th
educational preparation of the American working population. His mos
critical finding is that with the passage of time there has been a tendenc
for a larger group of persons to be in jobs that utilize less education tha
they have. If this is a valid conclusion from the admittedly rough data, i

suggests the need for caution in propagating the nostrum that more education is the answer to the nation's problems.

Educational requirements for employment continue to rise. Employers are convinced that, by raising their demands, they will be more likely to recruit an ambitious, disciplined work force that will be more productive than workers who have terminated their schooling earlier. Professor Berg's principal analyses are directed to this central line. His conclusions fail to support employer practices and convictions. First, he reemphasizes the point made by many students about the wide range in education and other characteristics of workers in the same job category – that is, workers who do the same work and earn the same wages. Next, he finds that in certain areas, such as the selling of insurance, workers with less education but more experience perform better and earn more. This is hardly surprising, since the skill involved is modest and education is irrelevant beyond a qualifying level. Nevertheless, the enthusiasts of education continue to press for higher qualifications without reference to the task to be performed or the environment in which the work is to be carried out.

Many employers seek to justify their high educational demands by reference to the need for promoting workers into higher ranks, where their education *will* be needed. But Professor Berg makes two telling points. In many companies only a small percentage of those who are hired are ever promoted to such positions. Further, the more highly qualified are often no longer in the company when the opportunity for promotion arises. Their frustration with work that does not fully utilize their educational background leads them to seek jobs elsewhere.

Professor Berg demonstrates, by reference to the ways in which schoolteachers receive higher compensation, the illogic of the 'education craze'. Teachers who take additional courses in order to earn salary increments eventually catapult themselves out of the teaching arena, since they finally are 'overeducated' for classroom work.

Among the largest and most revealing bodies of data that Professor Berg selects to review critically are those that he obtained from the armed services and the federal civil service. His findings are unequivocal. In every instance, the data prove overwhelmingly that the crucial determinants of performance are not increased educational achievement but other personality characteristics and environmental conditions.

On the policy front, Professor Berg is cautious and constrained despite his devastating attack on the errors in contemporary thought and action which hold that education is the open sesame to economic wellbeing. Specifically, he argues in favour of upgrading many of the 'overeducated' who now fill positions in the middle ranks into the less crowded upper-level jobs and at the same time upgrading those at the bottom so that they could advance into the middle-level positions. The hard-to-employ could then be fitted into the lower-level jobs. This is directly in line with the recommendations made early in 1968 by the National Manpower Advisory Committee to the Secretaries of Labour and HEW Manpower Programs.

The final implication of Professor Berg's analysis is for policy-makers to focus much more on actions aimed at increasing the demand for labour. If there is a shortfall in demand – and the federal estimate places about 11 million persons in subemployment categories – then indeed, changing the characteristics of working by adding to their schooling cannot be *the* answer.

But trenchant as is Professor Berg's treatment of the conventional wisdom, he has had to leave certain critical issues in suspense. They should, however, be briefly noted.

The question of how enlarged efforts on the educational front are specifically connected to increasing productivity of the economy finds no answer in his book – or in the books of the many economists who have addressed themselves specifically to this issue. No one doubts that a linkage exists, but its nature remains obscure. Will economic expansion best be speeded by reducing the proportion of illiterates, improving graduate training, making certain that women are educated to their full potential, raising the level of vocational education? All these questions suggest more education, but it remains to be demonstrated just how doing more on one or all of these fronts is related to accelerating economic growth.

Another subject that has yet to be confronted sharply and clearly is the relation of education to employment from the vantage point of qualifying rather than optimal considerations. Again, few students would deny that minimal levels of educational achievement have distinct relevance, although the conception of the optimum remains to be delineated.

A third tantalizing subject, with which the author deals in passing, relates to the place of education in selection for the entrance job versus its role as a screening factor for career progression. Failure to consider future positions in initial screening is an error matched only by neglect of the consequences of having a surplus of 'overqualified' persons on the staff, all waiting for advancement.

Other problems that are touched upon but not considered in depth include the relative return on investment in educational effort before and after a man enters employment. In what fields of endeavour is the level of education likely to be of determining importance in performance, and in what fields is it likely to be only indirectly related to output? How can the circularity of current 'rate of return' analyses be broken into so that more meaningful findings can emerge about the relations of education, productivity, and earnings? To what extent is education a surrogate for other qualities that are predictive of a higher level of eventual performance? What are the dangers of gearing wage increments to educational accomplishments?

A book that helps to illuminate a large number of important issues, even while forced to bypass others, provides the reader with rich fare. In addition, Professor Berg has opened up important new questions and has cast serious doubts upon accepted answers to old questions that most

Americans had long believed were beyond discussion. In attacking the hallowed beliefs of statesmen, employers, economists, and educators, he has let in new light where light has long been needed. And he has done so with scholarly acumen, stylistic grace, and a saving sense of humour – qualities all too rare in academe.

3.7 Education and economic equality

Lester C. Thurow

However much they may differ on other matters, the left, the centre, ar
the right all affirm the central importance of education as a means
solving our social problems, especially poverty. [...]

This acceptance of the efficacy of education is itself derived from a beli
in the standard economic theory of the labour market. According to th
theory, the labour market exists to match labour demand with labou
supply. At any given time, the pattern of matching and mismatching give
off various signals: Businesses are 'told' to raise wages or redesign jobs i
skill-shortage sectors, or to lower wages in skill-surplus sector
individuals are 'told' to acquire skills in high-wage sectors and are di
couraged from seeking skills and jobs in sectors where wages are low an
skills are in surplus. Each skill market is 'cleared', in the short run, b
increases or reductions in wages, and by a combination of wage change
skill changes, and production-technique changes over the long run. Th
result, according to the theory, is that each person in the labour marke
is paid at the level of his marginal productivity. If he adds $3,000 t
total economic output, he is paid $3,000; if he adds $8,000, he is pai
$8,000.

This theory posits *wage competition* as the driving force of the labou
market. It assumes that people come into the labour market with
definite, preexisting set of skills (or lack of skills), and that they the
compete against one another on the basis of wages. According to th
theory, education is crucial because it creates the skills which people brin
into the market. This implies that any increase in the educational level c
low-income workers will have three powerful – and beneficial – effect
First, an educational programme that transforms a low-skill person into
high-skill person raises his productivity and therefore his earning
Second, it reduces the total supply of low-skill workers, which leads in tur
to an increase in *their* wages. Third, it increases the supply of high-ski
workers, and this lowers their wages. The net result is that total outpu
rises (because of the increase in productivity among formerly uneducate
workers), the distribution of earnings becomes more equal, and eac
individual is still rewarded according to merit. What could be more ideal?

Empirical studies seemingly have confirmed this theory. The economi
literature on 'human capital' is full of articles that estimate the economi
rate of return for different levels of education; while the results diffe

Source: *The Public Interest*, No. 28, summer 1972, pp. 61–81.
Reprinted with permission of the author from *The Public Interest*, No. 28 (summe
1972), pp. 66–81. Copyright © 1972, *National Affairs, Inc.*

ghtly depending on the data and methods used, most studies find a rate
return on higher education slightly above 10 per cent per year for white
ales. This rate of return, as it happens, is approximately the same as that
investments in 'physical capital' (e.g., new machines). [...]

Yet, despite this seeming confirmation, there is reason to doubt the
lidity of this view of the labour market and the importance of the
onomic role it assigns to education. As we shall see, a large body of
idence indicates that the American labour market is characterized less
wage competition than by *job competition*. That is to say, instead of
ople looking for jobs, there are jobs looking for people – for 'suitable'
ople. In a labour market based on job competition, the function of
ucation is not to confer skill and therefore increased productivity and
gher wages on the worker; it is rather to certify his 'trainability' and to
nfer upon him a certain status by virtue of this certification. Jobs and
gher incomes are then distributed on the basis of this certified status. To
e extent that job competition rather than wage competition prevails in
e American economy, our longstanding beliefs about both the economic
nefits of education and the efficacy of education as a social policy which
akes for greater equality may have to be altered.

efects of 'Wage Competition' theory

'hile it is possible to raise a number of theoretical objections against the
uman capital' calculations which seem to confirm the wage competition
eory, it is more instructive to see if in our actual postwar experience,
isting educational programmes have had the effects that the wage
ompetition theory would predict. In fact, there are a number of import-
t discrepancies. The first arises from the fact that, in the real world, the
stributions of education and IQ are more equal than the distribution of
come, as Figure 1 indicates. The usual explanation for this disparity is
at income is disproportionately affected by the *combination* of education
d intelligence. This would explain the wider *dispersion* of income than of
lucation or intelligence – but it cannot explain the markedly different
apes of the distributions. Clearly, other factors are at work.

A second discrepancy is revealed by the fact that, while the distribution
education has moved in the direction of greater equality over the
ostwar period, the distribution of income has not. [...]

Similarly, a more rapid rate of growth of education should have led to a
ore rapid growth of the economy. In the early 1950s the college-
ucated labour force was growing at a rate of 3 per cent per year. In the
te 1960s it was growing at a 6 per cent rate. Yet there does not seem to be
ny evidence that the rate of growth of productivity of the economy as a
hole has accelerated correspondingly. If anything, the opposite has
appened. Productivity today may be increasing more slowly than its
istoric rate of growth of 2.9 per cent per year. [...]

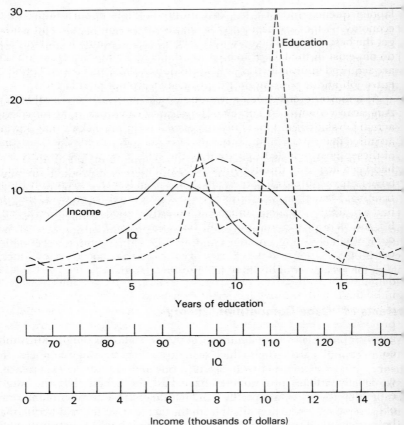

Figure 1 Distribution of income, education, and intelligence (IQ) of males 25 years of age and over in 1965

Sources: Income data from U.S. Bureau of the Census, *Current Population Reports*, Series P–60, no. 51, 'Income in 1965 of Families and Persons in the United States' (1967), p. 34; education data estimated from U.S. Bureau of the Census, *Statistical Abstracts of the United States: 1967*, p. 113; IQ data from David Wechsler, *Wechsler Adult Intelligence Scale Manual* (Psychological Corp., 1955), p. 20.

The 'Job Competition' model

Governmental education and training policies have not had the predicted impact because they have ignored the 'job competition' elements in the labour market. In a labour market based on job competition, an individual's income is determined by: (a) his relative position in the labour queue, and (b) the distribution of job opportunities in the economy. Wages are based on the characteristics of the job, and workers get the best (highest-income) jobs. According to this model, labour skills do not exist in the labour market; on the contrary, most actual job skills are acquired informally through on-the-job training *after* a worker finds an entry job and a position on the associated promotional ladder.

As a matter of fact, such a training process is clearly observable in the American economy. A survey of how American workers acquired their actual job skills found that only 40 per cent were using skills that they had acquired in formal training programmes or in specialized education – and, of these, most reported that some of the skills they were currently using had been acquired through informal on-the-job training. The remaining 60 per cent acquired all of their job skills through such informal on-the-job training. More than two-thirds of the college graduates reported that they had acquired job skills through such informal processes. When asked to list the form of training that had been most helpful in acquiring their current job skills, only 12 per cent listed formal training and specialized education.

Thus the labour market is primarily a market, not for matching the demands for and supplies of different job skills, but for matching trainable individuals with training ladders. *Because most skills are acquired on the job, it is the demand for job skills which creates the supply of job skills.* The operative problem in a job competition economy is to pick and train workers to generate the desired productivity with the least investment in training costs. [...]

[... So] employers rank workers on a continuum from the best potential worker (trainee) to the worst potential worker (trainee) on the basis of estimated potential training costs. (Such costs certainly include the costs of inculcating norms of industrial discipline and good work habits.) But because employers rarely have direct and unambiguous evidence of the specific training costs for specific workers, they end up ranking workers according to their background characteristics – e.g., age, sex, educational attainment, previous skills, and performance on psychological tests. Each of these is used as an indirect measure of the costs necessary to produce some standard of work performance.

Entirely subjective and arbitrary elements may also affect the labour queue. If employers discriminate against blacks, blacks will find themselves lower in the labour market queue than their training costs would warrant. [...]

Jobs and their corresponding training ladders are distributed to individuals in order of their rank, working from those at the top of the queue down to those at the bottom. The best jobs go to the best workers and the worst jobs to the worst workers. Given a need for untrained labour, some workers at the bottom of the queue will receive little or no training on their jobs. In periods of labour scarcity, training will extend farther and farther down the queue as employers are forced to train more costly workers to fill job vacancies. In periods of labour surplus, it is those at the bottom of the labour queue who will be unemployed. [...]

The distribution of job opportunities

The shape of the job distribution (and hence of the income distribution) across which individual labourers will be spread is governed by three sets of factors: (1) the character of technical progress, which generates certain kinds of jobs in certain proportions; (2) the sociology of wage determination – trade unions, traditions of wage differentials, and so on; and (3) the distribution of training costs between employees and employers, which will influence the wage that is associated with each job. The interaction among these factors is exceedingly complicated – and little studied.[1] [...] However, observed changes over the postwar period are in accordance with a job competition model.

If, at the beginning of the postwar period, an observer had been told that the composition of the adult white male labour force was going to change from 47 per cent with a grade school education, 38 per cent with a high school education, and 15 per cent with a college education, to 20 per cent with a grade school education, 51 per cent with a high school education, and 28 per cent with a college education (the actual 1949 to 1969 changes), expectations about the distribution of income would have been very different depending upon whether the observer subscribed to a job competition model or a wage competition model. Assuming there were no offsetting changes on the demand side of the market, the observer subscribing to a wage competition model of the economy would have predicted a substantial equalization of earnings. But the observer subscribing to the job competition model would have predicted something quite different. He would have expected an equalization of income within the most preferred group (college-educated workers), a rise in its incomes relative to other groups, and a decrease relative to the national average. He would have reasoned as follows: As the most preferred group expanded, it would filter down the job distribution into lower-paying jobs. This would lead to a fall in wages relative to the national average. As it moved into a denser portion of the national job (income) distribution, it would, however, experience within-group equalization of income. By taking what had previously been the best high school jobs, college incomes would rise relative to high school incomes.

Such a prediction would have been correct. The proportion of college incomes going to the poorest 25 per cent of white male college-educated workers rose from 6.3 to 9.0 per cent from 1949 to 1969, while the proportion going to the richest 25 per cent fell from 53.9 per cent to 46.0 per cent. While the median income of college-educated workers was rising from 198 per cent to 254 per cent of the median for grade school-educated workers and from 124 per cent to 137 per cent of the median for high school-educated workers, it was falling from 148 per cent to 144 per cent of the national median.

As the least preferred group (those with a grade school education) contracted in size, a job competition observer would have expected it to be moving out of the denser regions of the income distribution and becoming more and more concentrated on the lower tail of the income distribution. Given the shape of the lower tail of the American income distribution, such a movement would have led to falling relative incomes and increasing income equality. In fact, the incomes of grade school labourers have fallen from 50 per cent to 39 per cent of college incomes and from 63 per cent to 54 per cent of high school incomes. The income going to the poorest 25 per cent of all grade school labourers has risen from 2.9 per cent to 6.6 per cent of the group's total, and the income going to the richest 25 per cent has fallen from 53.5 per cent to 49.4 per cent.

Note

1 Further discussion of this matter may be found in THUROW, LESTER C. (1972) 'The American Distribution of Income: A Structural Problem', Committee Print, U.S. Congress Joint Economic Committee.

3.8 The late development effect

Ronald Dore

[...]. Other things being equal (we'll consider what things later), the later development starts (i.e. the later the point in world history that a country starts on a modernization drive):
the more widely education certificates are used for occupational selection:
the faster the rate of qualification inflation; and
the more examination-oriented schooling becomes at the expense of genuine education.

Let us look at each of these in turn.

... the more jobs depend on qualifications

Earlier sections of this book have tried to show how and why educational qualifications counted for more in Japan than in Britain. To be sure, 'late development' is not the only factor. Britain's non-reliance on formal qualifications was extreme, even among early developers, partly, presumably, because Britain has never since Cromwell experienced the sort of modernizing spurt which in Napoleonic France created the Grandes Ecoles, or at least established them in such a position that they soon acquired very important qualifying functions for government and industry. But the 'late development effect' is clear. Certificates undoubtedly counted for more in Sri Lanka in the 1950s than for, say, Japan in the 1910s; more for Kenya in the 1960s than for Sri Lanka in the 1950s. It is easy enough to explain why. Part of it is the later developer's need to catch up fast – by importing knowledge and skills in formal educational packages. The most important part is the general tendency of the late developer to import the *latest* technology from the metropolitan models – social as well as machine technology. And, as a piece of social technology, the device of making even more refined and universal use of educational certificates for job allocation is becoming [...] more and more 'perfected' every year. Thus, Sri Lanka, earlier in the century, followed then current British practice in providing apprenticeship/mid-career-training routes into accountancy and engineering. Kenya, starting later, did not, but instead adopted the degree-entry practices which were just becoming formalized in Britain.

But it is time to look at that 'other things being equal' clause. Some other factors do over-ride the tendencies just described.

Editors' Note: In this paper the author argues for three general propositions concerning the relationships between development and education.
Source: DORE, R. (1976) *The Diploma Disease* (Unwin Educational Books: 32). London, George Allen and Unwin, pp. 72–83.

There are a few odd corners, even in what is conventionally thought of as the developing world, where a man's ability to make his way in the world does depend a good deal less than in most on the educational qualifications he carries. Hong Kong is such – though decreasingly so. It is one of the few places where industrialization has been the product of the same sort of small-scale entrepreneurship as laid the basis for Europe's (especially Britain's) industrialization. Most men's income and status have depended on what they actually know and can do – on their skills and their push and intelligence more than on the pieces of paper they have been able to show potential employers. Hong Kong does not have the same sharp dualistic division between a highly desirable modern sector and an impoverished, despised, traditional sector typical of most developing countries. There is, rather, a steady graduation in enterprise size and modernity and considerable movement along the gradient. [...]

In countries where big organizations – the state or large corporations – have dominated the industrialization/modernization process from the beginning, and where thrusting small-scale entrepreneurs have been lacking, or even positively discouraged by harassing licensing restrictions, the division between the traditional and the modern sector is sharper and the importance of educational qualifications correspondingly greater. Of the total working-age (15 to 59) population of Senegal, about 6 per cent are in jobs secured by social security provisions – modern sector jobs within the purview of the labour inspector. Of these nearly a half are government or public sector enterprise jobs, and of the rest a large proportion in big rationalized French-owned firms which set minimum educational standards for nearly all jobs. In Tanzania the corresponding figures are about 6 per cent in modern sector jobs (in establishments employing more than ten workers) of whom (1970) 58 per cent are in government or in parastatal corporations. A glance at Tanzanian newspaper job advertisements will show how finely graduated correspondence between jobs and educational levels has become. A parastatal printing corporation wants a proof reader: 'Form 6 leaver with good passes in Swahili and English'; a Security Officer: 'at least Standard Seven'; a Costing Clerk Grade II: 'at least Form 2 leavers'. It is not a bad generalization that the almightiness of the certificate varies in direct proportion to the predominance of the state in the development process. Weber made insistence on qualifications part of his classical definition of bureaucracy as an ideal type – and for very good reasons; certificates are objective; governments need, among other things, standards of impersonal judgment which protect them against charges of corrupt favouritism.

The other feature of countries like Senegal or Tanzania is the cliff-like nature of the separation of the modern sector from the traditional one. The twilight zone of what it is now fashionable to call the 'informal sector' – the roadside and empty-lot mechanics who will weld on a Bournville cocoa tin to mend the exhaust pipe of the civil servant's Mercedes, the leather workers making hand-made bags for the tourist trade, the furniture-makers, the men who collect empty Essolube cans from the garages twice a day and have them processed into serviceable oil lamps by sunset – this twilight zone is small in total size, and its tiny enterprises, which are mostly family affairs, offering little wage employment, rarely show much prospect of expanding into modern enterprises, particularly in those African countries where the people who have in the past shown entrepreneurial skills (the Asians in East Africa, the Lebanese in Senegal) are coming under increasingly nationalist restrictions of their activities.

Hence the 'informal sector', the 'transitional zone', is *not* in fact a transitional zone for individuals. It is not a means by which one moves from rural traditionalism into the modern sector by easy stages. Its entrepreneurs have little hope of achieving the life-style or the prestige of the modern-sector managers: its workers are not likely to graduate to more secure, better paid jobs in big firms. They are working in the twilight sector precisely *because* they have failed to get jobs in the modern-sector firm – and their chances of doing so are likely to diminish rather than increase as the new jobs which do become available are snapped up by their educationally better qualified juniors. Where the informal sector is that small and insignificant, then, it does not offer a route up the cliff-face from the traditional to the modern sector. The only way to make that transition is by the cable cars of the educational system. [...]

... the faster the rate of qualification inflation

Qualification inflation results from a faster growth of the school system than of the number of modern-sector job opportunities. Our proposition can therefore be translated either: the later development starts, the slower the rate of creation of modern-sector job opportunities; or, the later development starts, the faster the growth of school enrolments.

The first proposition is unlikely to be true, though there are *some* forces pushing in that direction; the later the timing of industrialization, the more capital-intensive and less labour-intensive it is likely to be, hence the fewer jobs created for any given volume of investment. Two countervailing forces, however, are a probable faster growth in service-sector jobs, particularly government services (because of the greater role of government, see above), and faster overall growth rates. The Japanese economy grew faster in the early stages of industrialization than the British, the Ceylonese than the Japanese, and the Kenyan than the Ceylonese.

It is the second proposition which is the crucial one: school enrolments grow faster – so much faster as to counteract any tendency there *might* be for job opportunities to grow faster too; hence an imbalance which grows at a faster rate in later starters. Compare the figures for our four countries:

Growth in secondary enrolments (% p.a.)

Britain	1864–1893	3%
Japan	1900–1910	8%
Sri Lanka	1950–1960	14%
Kenya	1960–1970	20%

Taunton Commission (1868), Vol. 1, Appx. VI; Bryce Commission (1895), Vol. 1, para. 52 and Vol. IX; Japan: Education (1964); UNESCO (1963, 1971). British figures are for seven sample counties only; endowed and proprietary schools only.

The first reason why this should be so is fairly obvious. It follows from the first of our three propositions. The greater the degree of credentialism, the more the schools are the *only* channel of social mobility; the more complete the absence of any route up the cliff to the modern sector except the educational cable car. Studies of educational aspirations in Malaysia show that there is a smaller proportion of children hoping to press on to the university among the Chinese, who are supposed to be ambitious, persistent and energetic, than among the Malays who are supposed to have rather smaller doses of these qualities. The reason, clearly, is that, for the Malays who dominate the bureaucratized government (and, through government, expatriate big business) sectors of the economy, certificates really count; for the Chinese Malaysians whose opportunities lie in the small business sector, they have less value (Malaysia, 1972).

A second part of the explanation is that the later development starts, the more firmly implanted in the international consensus is the idea (still highly controversial in Britain as late as 1870) that it is a proper, indeed essential function of the state to provide for its citizens' education – and, one might add, to provide schooling and the hope, however fallacious, of escape into the modern sector, is often easier than, say, carrying out a land reform or otherwise redistributing resources in ways that might make life in rural areas more productive and more tolerable.

Thirdly, the later development starts, the worse the dualism is likely to be – the greater the modern-sector/traditional-sector differential in income, power and prestige; the greater the attractions of trying to scale the cliff. Indeed, where population growth, or the initial disequalizing effects of economic growth, have actually worsened living standards in rural areas, there may genuinely be no way out but to try to scale the cliff – push factors not just pull factors, as the students of rural-urban migration say.

Also, fourthly, later developers have better means of communication available; hence the late developer's villages are more integrated into the polity and more subjected to demonstration effect. Tokyo, where all the university graduates were, was a pretty remote place for the vast majority of Japanese villagers in the 1890s; a place on the end of a telegraph line, described in the newspapers which came three days late. A good proportion of Kenya's contemporary villagers have seen Nairobi on a television screen, hear its broadcasts instantaneously on the radio; can join

344 Ronald Dore

their cousins there for the relatively inexpensive price of a bus ride. More people, in other words, know something about life up on the modern-sector plateau and are likely to be susceptible to its attractions.

And they are more likely to see access to that modern sector as feasible as well as desirable because, fifthly, the later development starts, the more the meritocratic ideal of equality of opportunity is entrenched in the international consensus; the more likely, therefore, an integrated school system providing subsidies, scholarships, etc., for poor children to reach the top – given, sixthly, the additional factor that the 'sense of backwardness' is likely to be greater, greater also the urge to catch up, greater the premium placed on efficiency; greater therefore the arguments for meritocracy as a mean of mobilizing all the talents. What these last four factors all combined to produce, therefore is a *greater intensity* of *popular demand* for education, particularly for schooling at the sort of levels at which valid job certificates are thought to be produced. [...]

One [...] variable affecting [the intensity of the pursuit of 'valid job certificates' is] the degree and type of social stratification. In some 'older' societies with long-established status systems, the 'lower orders' have been conditioned for generations to see themselves as 'naturally' condemned to underdog status. If the only primary school available is one which peters out after the third grade, they are not much upset; they do not bewail the foreclosing of chances of mobility they have hardly conceived of. By contrast, in African societies which had little stratification before they were colonized (even in the kingdom of Buganda or the emirates of northern Nigeria there was little elaborated hereditary *cultural* differentiation between the upper and lower strata) the 'modern sector' is equally new to everyone. No particular group is seen as having a preternatural right and everyone is free to compete. One can hardly imagine a Ministry of Education *anywhere* in the modern world setting out, as the Taunton Commission did in Britain in the 1860s (Taunton Commission, 1868, Vol. 1, Appx. 2), to calculate the number of 'upper and middle class school-children' as a means of estimating the requirements for secondary education, though it may be, of course, that the enormous educational advantages which accrue to the children of university-educated parents will lead to sharply entrenched class divisions very rapidly (O'Connell and Beckett, 1975).[1]

The problem is not new in India. Indeed, already at the beginning of the century, the headlong expansion of higher education was sufficiently widely recognized to be a problem that legislative controls were introduced. Nothing better illustrates the marvellous Canute-like hubris of the British Raj than Lord Curzon's confidence that he had settled the problem once and for all. It is worth recalling his words before the legislative council. If he had not acted, he said,

... the rush of immature striplings to our India universities, not to learn but to earn, would have continued till it became an avalanche ultimately bringing the entire educational fabric to the ground – Colleges might have been left to multiply without regard to any criterion either of necessity or merit; the examination curse would have tightened its grip on the rising generation; standards would have sunk lower and lower; the output would have steadily swollen in volume, at the cost of all that education ought to mean; and one day India would have awakened to the fact that she had, for years, been bartering her intellectual heritage for the proverbial mess of pottage. (Quoted in Mazumdar, 1972, p. 6.)[2]

All that, he claimed, he had stopped. Once and for all. In 1904. [...]

... the more schooling equals exam-taking

The mechanisms of this third proposition are obvious. They follow from the last point. If it is to get certificates that people go to school, if it is the need for the desire for certificates rather than knowledge which explains the popular demand for schooling, then the more the schooling process itself is likely to revolve around certification.

Once that process begins it has inbuilt mechanisms that make it self-reinforcing. The more consciously children are sent to school to get certificates and the greater the demand for schooling for that purpose, the greater the number of primary schools geared up to prepare children for secondary entry, the tougher the competition, the more primary schools' and teachers' performance is measured by their proportion of secondary entrance 'successes'. The greater, therefore, the teachers' emphasis on teaching for the examination, sticking to the syllabus, concentrating on learning to remember rather than to understand, showing extra attention to the bright boys who have a chance of making it; in short, demonstrating in all they do, *their* concept of exam results as the be-all and end-all of schooling – and consequently the more the qualification-orientation of the *children* and their parents is reinforced, which in turn reinforces those tendencies in teachers, and so on.

There are three other factors which make the situation worse in later developers. The first is another facet of dualism. Schools themselves belong to the 'modern sector'. Their buildings and furniture are patterned after imported designs if not actually imported. The contracts and modes of payment of teachers follow the conventions of the civil service and the factories, not of traditional rural areas. The rhythms of the school conform to the imported seven-day week, not to the moon phases of local calendars. And, most important of all, the knowledge and attitude content of what they purvey is remote from the context of village experience. In other words, the gap between the culture of the school and the culture of the home is likely to be greater, the more pronounced the dualism of the country's development pattern – which is itself a function of late development. Japanese schoolchildren in the 1890s learned about steam engines which perhaps only one person in their family had ever seen; they learned about Benjamin Franklin, and public libraries. But at least more effort was made to relate them to village life than was done for the children in, say, Jamaica's schools in the 1930s (see V. S. Naipaul's hilarious accoun of the writing of formal compositions on family holidays at the seaside Naipaul, 1961, p. 322).[3] The point is, at any rate, that the more remot school work is from daily experience, the more easily it becomes a mer ritual, a merely instrumentalized means of getting marks.

Because of the tremendous pressure to expand school enrolments o exiguous budgets, schools are poorly equipped. Qualification-orientatio obviously gets worse if there *are* no laboratories and libraries even t provide the opportunity of developing discovery methods of learning, there *are* no alternatives to chalk and talk, memorization and testing.

Finally, in the later developers the birth of a school system and th development of a qualification-based occupational system are likely to b simultaneous. The very concept of 'school' and of formal educatio entered the society in recent times as part of the package of 'modernity brought by the imperialist powers. By contrast, most of the older indus trial countries have formal pedagogical traditions (and some educationa institutes) dating back to pre-industrial times *before* educationa certificates acquired bread-and-butter value – dating back, in othe words, to the time when learning was thought to be about getting *knowledg* or wisdom, to make a man respected or holy or righteous or rich. Thes older traditions still persist in the older countries. They serve to maintai the fiction that education is about moral and intellectual uplift an enrichment. And such fictions *are* important. What men define as real i real in its consequences. The fictions *do* serve as a countervailing force t weaken tendencies towards qualification-orientation, particularly whe they are boldly reasserted by rebellious students demanding the end o examinations, and urging that universities should stop prostituting them selves by subserviently acting as graders of human material for the capital ist system (even if they do falter and fall into confusion when any univer sity teacher offers to take them at their word and abolish all degre *certificates* as well as examinations). In later-developing societies, where a except the very first generation of purely soul-saving mission schools (an even some of those) had selection/credentialling functions, these usefu countervailing fictions, having no roots in any local past, are harder t establish and sustain. The pursuit of certificates can be even more nake and unashamed. [...]

To sum up, in the Third World today the importance of qualifications i greater than in the advanced industrial countries. Educational system are more likely to be geared to qualification-getting, and the consequence for the society and its pattern of development are likely to be even mor deplorable than in our society.

References

1 o'connell, j. and beckett, p. a. (1975) 'Social Characteristics of an Elite-in-formation: The case of Nigeria University students', *British Journal of Sociology,* Vol. 26, No. iii, September 1975.

2 mazumdar, v. (1972) *Education and Social Change.* Simla: Indian Institute for Advanced Study.

3 naipaul, v. s. (1961) *A House for Mr Biswas.* London: Deutsch.

Part Four

Controlling the curriculum

If, as we have argued earlier, debates about standards contain an unavoidable element of social and political controversy, then it follows that curricular policy decisions that affect standards will be always themselves liable to provoke conflict.

In the 1980s, as Shaw points out in his paper, falling rolls in schools (and eventually in the tertiary sector too) will set in motion major changes in the schools, some of which he identifies. These changes will in turn disrupt established expectations and relationships amongst teachers at a time when falling resources are likely to present problems unlike any which most schools have had to face before.

Two general consequences can be confidently predicted to flow from these events. The first is that schools will have to establish and work to a far clearer set of educational priorities than was necessary when expanding schools and growing staff numbers made it easy to advance in several directions at once without undue tensions arising. The second consequence is that, as the need to choose between different aims and aspirations becomes steadily greater, so the divergences in values revealed in the papers in Part One will become the source of potentially greater conflict within school after school. Shaw's contribution then may be read as an attempt to warn us of the kinds of practical contexts within which such conflicts will occur.

On a second level, these changes will also create tensions between different groups who feel they have some right to a say in particular schools concerning what aims should be given priority. Given a national background of rising unemployment and widespread technological and social change, there will be an increasing unwillingness on the part of parents and politicians to leave control of the curriculum solely in the hands of the teachers. In part these stirrings can already be felt as accountability and monitoring become increasingly central (and centralized) concerns.

The paper by House offers, albeit against a different cultural and educational background, some foretaste of one way in which things might go in our own society over the next few years. A reading of his paper against the background provided by those of Barnett, Rowntree, Hall and Bowles and Gintis offers much food for thought.

So, too, in a very different way, do the last two contributions to this collection. Between them White and Sockett offer an analysis of the main dimensions along which the coming debate on curriculum control is likely to be structured – although as always the controversy will no doubt be messier and more confused than systematic philosophical analysis can indicate. Nevertheless, we can reasonably expect that the relative roles of national, local and institutionally based groups will be a major source of argument, as will the respective responsibilities of professionals and lay people. What teachers can reasonably be held accountable for, and how such accountability should be ensured, will also require discussion. It would be nice to believe that ways of making the Department of Education and Science, the government and parents more accountable for their educational responsibilities might also be actively discussed, although this seems somewhat unlikely.

Finally, it is to be hoped that in the rush to get back to basics (and to check that we have done so) we do not omit to ask which things really are basic. If any one message emerges from this collection it is that there are crucial differences of view on this issue and that the conduct of schooling at every level is fundamentally affected by the stance that we take on the matter.

4.1 Managing the curriculum in contraction

Ken Shaw

The end of growth

From the end of the war until the early 1970s educational planning and management were dominated by expectations of expansion. Despite the temporary sag in the demographic curve between the two bulges, the backlog of crowded schools, overlarge classes, shortage of teachers and the aspiration to raise the school leaving age fuelled a psychology of growth which was at its height in the first half of the 'sixties. The experience of an easy job market, the promotions possible in an expanding system, the steady salary advances and increase of resources, new buildings and increasing graduate entry inculcated growth attitudes deeply in successive cohorts of entrants to the teaching profession. Such attitudes have contributed to deep structures of unspoken assumptions and un-analysed expectations which limit vision, hamper planning, and are not easy to change. Kogan (1975) has shown clearly the nature of the highly expansionary view prevalent before 1964 with David Eccles as Minister of Education; there was a high rate of school building, rural reorganization pressed ahead, teacher training was upgraded, and the view that educational investment and economic growth were directly related was unchallenged. Even the Conservatives realized that there was electoral advantage in education legislation. The Robbins Report which foresaw mass tertiary education to follow on from a complete secondary system rounded off this period of confidence and daring. It is not surprising that the golden age of well-financed national curriculum projects had its origins in this era.

But Kogan goes on to document the increasing demand for control and accountability at the political level of educational decision making. There was a loss of optimism which was marked by the student troubles of the late 'sixties and subsequent appearance of graduate unemployment. Finally came economic stringency and the acrimoniously contentious mood of the 'seventies, with its stream of Black Papers, assertions of reading failure, organizational failure, truancy, and finally teacher unemployment. This mood, too, has entered the curriculum scene with a marked 'back-to-basics' swing, calls for more employment-relevant attitudes and content, and emphasis in the 'Great Debate' (Débâcle?) on core subjects. National projects have lost prominence in favour of less costly local initiatives.

Source: RICHARDS, C. (ed) (1977) *Power and the Curriculum: Issues in Curriculum Studies*. Driffield: Nafferton Books, pp. 40–48.

Like the end of empire, the end of growth calls for difficult reappraisals both of practice and attitude. But to translate this national level awareness down to practical policies at the level of the local school is not straightforward. I want to point to some implications for school management and for curriculum which arise from all this, as the changes work down the system, inevitably slowly since schools have a very long production cycle and can generally only make a major adjustment at the beginning of each school year. Just as the curve of declining births is stark and simple at the national level yet cross-cut by many masking variables at the sub-regional and local level, larger patterns in the national system of schools may be severely modified at the level of the particular institution. Nevertheless foresight is a requirement of management, and even if decisions at school level cannot be made simply in the light of national data, the general trends should not be lost to sight.

Constraints: costs and staffing

If one major conclusion can be drawn from empirical studies of curriculum planning in the last decade it is that a view of curriculum restricted to content and method is quite inadequate. To those who have to solve practical problems of innovation in schools such as the introduction of integrated science (e.g. SCISP) or O level courses in former secondary modern schools, it rapidly becomes clear that curriculum, as Goodson (1975) has written, is best seen as a system, an organic whole which embraces organizational structures, staffing, pupil grouping and costs, to say nothing of the arts of decision-making and public relations with governors and parents. Questions of content and method cannot be separated from issues of staff deployment, equitable and effective use of facilities, timetabling, and, in the end, matters of authority at the school level and political choice at LEA level. Before turning to questions of content in detail then, brief consideration of the important constraints (that is, limiting conditions), of costs and staffing is appropriate.

What impact might the prevailing decline in roll numbers be expected to have on the average secondary school? In general the system of capitation grants by which schools are financed, including the scale posts available to the staff, means that resources are closely tied to numbers on roll. The exceptions to this are when LEAs make special grants or are generous with staff because of special curriculum innovations such as primary school French or Nuffield science, or when extra funds are made available during reorganization. When roll numbers drop – the decrease is cumulative as intake numbers fall away – resources must soon be curtailed. Curriculum adjustments have then to be considered. If this did not occur, as Cumming (1971) has shown, costs per pupil would quickly rise to unacceptable levels. With the advent of corporate management systems in local authorities the chief education officer is no longer master in his own house; education is by far the biggest spender amongst the local services and the treasurer is bound to watch costs closely. Now the most obvious fact about school costs is that staffing – salaries and wages – swamps all other costs. Teaching staff costs account for 97 per cent of the costs of teaching an individual subject, 90 per cent of the running costs of the individual school, and even at the level of the LEA they account for 75 per cent of the budget. As recent events have all too clearly shown, the only way that significant savings can be made is by reducing the number of teachers.

As the age of the pupils rises, staffing costs rise disproportionately. At the top of the school there are more staff-intensive options, e.g. half-groups for domestic science and craft; and the salary cost is higher since the staff tend to be more specialist and senior. In the upper part of secondary schools the cost per pupil is three and a half times the cost per primary pupil. Since the school becomes top heavy when intake numbers are falling, costs do not fall proportionately because pupil numbers are concentrated at the high cost end. At first the loss of resources is not very great; but as the large intakes leave and are replaced by smaller ones with fewer points value per head, losses of staff and capitation quickly become significant. Projections of future numbers linked with the points total and differential capitation grants are an absolutely essential framework within which future planning of the curriculum must take place. The information ought to be available to the staff. The consequences of a drop in the points total should not be allowed to creep up unawares. They must be planned for.

With falling rolls capital spending (which affects facilities and thus curriculum possibilities) will come under the most careful scrutiny. There is the danger of providing facilities at high cost which run the risk of being under-used within a few years. At a time when many authorities are likely to take schools out of service (Croydon, one of the few authorities to reveal its plans, is proposing to close eight out of 29 of its secondary schools before 1986) it is unlikely that they will be willing to incur major works in the remainder, and certainly not in those marked down for closure. There are still a substantial number of schools built to secondary modern (or even elementary school) specifications but which despite insufficient laboratories and other specialist facilities are teaching a comprehensive curriculum. In favoured areas such schools have been brought up to at least grammar school standards of provision; but at present, where old schools are retained, updating is bound to be reduced. Modern buildings require more cash for upkeep than older fabric which was built solidly, though inflexibly, to last. All-through purpose-built comprehensives are almost certainly too expensive to consider in a period of population instability.

The government expects to make very considerable savings in the health service as a result of the rapid decline in births. It is certain that the Treasury and local finance officers will expect similar savings in education, particularly in capital spending and the heavy loan charges this generates. More flexible and, in capital costs, cheaper solutions such as the establishment of sixth-form and tertiary colleges are likely. What monies are available are likely to be spent on provision for the sixteen to nineteen age group in Further Education especially in view of the unemployment amongst school leavers; and possibly for similar social reasons, on community schools which may turn out to be the next wave of reform after comprehensive reorganization. The remaining 25 per cent of reorganization schemes still outstanding are likely to be carried out in pinched circumstances. So far as curriculum reforms depend upon buildings and money, they will be more heavily constrained than ever before. Cost, more than lack of awareness or reactionary attitudes, has always been the major brake on innovation. Careful costing of curriculum innovations is an essential practical requirement of school leadership.

Turning now to staffing: because of the high recruitment of young teachers in the past decade the shape of the profession nationally by age cohorts resembles a pyramid; but current recruitment will narrow the base abruptly. As the large recruitment cohorts mature professionally, competition for a declining number of senior posts will become severe. Commuting and housing costs together with job uncertainty have tended to cause staff to stay put; but within schools the reduction in scales from five to four after Houghton has cut down the inducements that can be offered. An ageing and geographically more stagnant profession is less likely to be motivated to innovate, though the increased competition for jobs may act as a counterbalance, particularly if in-service courses, school-based ones especially, develop more freely. The greater proportion of new entrants will be graduates, emphatically single subject specialists in the main. Yet as staff numbers fall in the school there will be a premium on the teacher who can, and is willing, to teach in more than one area. To base a curriculum for the middle years of schooling on single subject specialists is very limiting. Primary school teachers can be redeployed at short notice since in the main they are generalists and substitutable; but the situation becomes critical at the secondary level where an underemployed classics, music, or French specialist is not so easily redeployed, either internally or externally. The central problem as staff numbers decline is that departments will become unbalanced and that some will be hit very hard whilst others are relatively unscathed. The school must try to compensate for this by manipulating options and timetabling; but the extra constraint of keeping specialists decently busy and equalizing the misery will have a distorting effect on curriculum intentions. Careful and longsighted staff recruitment, seeking out staff who can teach two subjects or will accept an integrated approach, and attention to the age structure of the staff so that natural wastage can help with reductions, will be more important than ever.

The relentless logic of costs and provision of a broad and balanced curriculum offering will ultimately force the closure of the least viable schools. When parents know that a school is not full their demand for a place cannot be resisted. The least popular school in an area will lose pupils rapidly in what must become a competitive situation, as is apparent in ILEA primary schools. Then staff reallocations and redundancies will be painful. The temptation to offer trendy curriculum items to retain competitiveness is likely to be strong, at any rate at the secondary stage. Even here, however, and more likely in primary and middle schools, an emphasis on good grounding in the basics, and the demonstrated ability to deliver it, are likely to prove attractive to parents.

Consequences for organization and curriculum pattern

The most obvious implication of contraction in numbers and resources is that the breadth of the curriculum offering must be reduced. The undeniable advantage of size is curriculum variety; a six form entry school can quite simply offer more than a four form entry. The 'bonus' (number of teachers in excess of number of classes) is greater and allows for a wider range of options: classics, Russian, alternative maths and science syllabuses, more crafts and non-examination studies. As numbers decline however, the bonus gets smaller and the size of the teaching groups in the marginal subjects becomes intolerably small. Such subjects can only be maintained with a smaller staff if the size of lower school classes is increased. Inequities in work loads are inevitable in schools, but to extend them in this way when morale is already likely to be drooping will be hard to justify. The precedent of FE regulations which stipulate numbers before a course can begin, and recent national and local announcements about non-viable sixth-form groups, are indications of current awareness of this problem.

But experience has shown that contracting institutions are moved by humanity as well as conservatism; they strive to keep departments going. A kind of inertia works against the re-simplification of differentiated organizational structures which have resulted from growth. The head of department is still in post even if his staff have fallen from four to two. But when the middle management staff, pastoralists and counsellors have been reabsorbed fully into the classroom work force and the part-timers have gone (another loss of flexibility) the next step is departmental reductions and amalgamations. Apart from being high cost (Cumming showed in his sample that classics cost five times as much per pupil as English) the marginal subjects are likely to be taught by one staff member. If he moves the subject may collapse; there is a risk element. This is even more the case for entrepreneurial innovations in curriculum which depend on one enthusiast. A reduced institution cannot take such a risk. So there will be attrition of marginal subjects, second or third language, economics, geology and the like, especially if they are offered elsewhere or at the local sixth-form college. The curriculum pattern will be geared to make the most economic use of reduced staff numbers by teaching full size groups wherever possible.

This is a tacit element in the current concern for the core curriculum. From one point of view the notion of core appeals to progressive ideals, since it treats pupils equally in respect of who gets what, and works against the contemporary tendency to smuggle in streaming by curriculum earlier or later in the school course. But the core curriculum is the cheap curriculum (at any rate in the unsubtle forms of the argument which prevailed in the 'Great Debate') because it is taught to all children in full size groups throughout the school; and it includes those subjects traditionally taught by talk and chalk. What pupils think of core curriculum has not figured much in recent discussions as far as I am aware; probably their views have not been sought at all. Since one of the commonest gambits used to try to reconcile the reluctant RoSLA conscripts to extended schooling has been to vary the curriculum offering, a back-to-basics core would have consequences for order and control which I should like to hear discussed. In any case official opinion has rather belatedly conceded what curriculum planners have long known, namely that cutting down options severely limits the future possibilities open to pupils both academically and vocationally. Cumming's research showed that some schools in his sample with a staff ratio of 20:1 achieved a broader curriculum than others with a more favourable ratio of 16:1. It seems possible at all events that careful planning, wise management and some luck in staff appointments might mean that the worst effects of a simplified and reduced curriculum can be avoided.

In selective schools high cost marginal subjects can be retained more easily because of the very high concentration of academic pupils. In a comprehensive school the situation is very different. A balanced curriculum for the whole ability range is needed; this has helped create the need for more sophisticated management styles, and even collegiate approaches which involve a much wider participation in decision making (Poster 1976). The comprehensive ethos, much neglected in practice, stems from the assumption that the education of all pupils, academic or not, should be of equal worth. To spend capitation disproportionately on a broad curriculum with many option groups for the abler children would not only be an injustice but would reduce the motivation of the less academic children and their teachers. In the early years of secondary schooling mixed ability teaching and measures to individualize learning are often recommended, and sometimes used to avoid streaming and the inequitable distribution of resources. But these methods of teaching are resource-intensive, the initial cost of making the changeover to them is frequently high (mathematics laboratories, resource centres, reprographic aids), and they work best when there are five teachers to four groups. After the change-over, and it includes an organizational changeover too, these methods may cost no more than traditional teaching, though it is easier to do the latter on the cheap; but without cash in hand such innovations will not be attempted. Again, if more innovative learning styles of this sort (Goldsmiths' [College] IDE [Interdisciplinary Enquiry], for example) are to be attempted across the whole ability range, a strong, skilled, well resourced and academically recognized remedial department is essential. Here groups *must* be small and staff-intensive. Thus difficult choices arise: prestigious academic subjects defend the status of the curriculum in the eyes of the middle class parents whose influence cannot be ignored, yet effective remedial departments can service mixed ability teaching and can, it is argued, reduce discipline problems by half. Management, like government, is about choice. During the last ten years schools have increased in size and the pupil/teacher ratio has improved substantially. Both developments provided elbow room for choice and lubricated change. But the trend is now in the other direction and the Taylor Committee wants more public accountability in just these sensitive areas. School leadership is likely to play safe.

Most authorities have sharply reduced their part-time staff. Eventually when numbers drop, some full-time staff will have to be shed. Inducements to persuade older teachers to retire and compulsion to induce less effective teachers to leave the profession have already been mooted. Managerially, the problem is that when staff leave and cannot be replaced because of a reduced establishment, mismatch creeps in between the desirable curriculum and the staff available to teach it. It is always difficult to ask teachers to change their accustomed work even when an allowance can be dangled before them. These will no longer be available. The result is that teaching areas will have to be parcelled out amongst *ad hoc* teams: scientists teaching a little maths, historians a little English and the like. This makes for difficulties in coherent sequencing (Hamilton, 1975) and coordinating progress. Specialist subjects may have to be taught by non-specialists, but perhaps only at the earlier stages, when, however, motivation is won or lost. Commonly as a result of this, less academic children meet more teachers each week than the abler children who tend to get the high ranking specialists. Staff cannot be spared to go on courses for partial reorientation so that less-than-current teaching approaches persist.

In sum, there are two forces at work in practical curriculum planning maintenance and innovation. Maintenance is the task of delivering the services of schooling effectively to the mass of pupils; innovation is the task of keeping up with the times, modernizing and revitalizing the teaching. Even in favourable circumstances maintenance is the dominant activity. Innovation usually waits for a happy conjunction of surplus resources, internal initiative and a strong external stimulus in the form of a problem to be solved. In contraction the maintenance function will be overwhelming and will consume nearly all available energy. Skilled management including procedural management (the arts of dealing with the bureaucracies of contemporary society) is needed even for this. Schools are likely to discover when the heat is on what many colleges of education have recently learned to their cost: few people are concerned to protect them and they lack the social muscle to protect themselves.

I will conclude this section with some comments on the position with respect to the sixteen to nineteen age group. I have argued that sixth form colleges appear to be more economic than all-through comprehensives. They are distinguished as a rule by a more open-access policy, and as a result students there are less homogeneous than in traditional school sixths. The colleges sometimes cater for students who are not repeaters, to whom CSE or O level courses are inappropriate, who take unusual mixtures of O and A level courses, or who only intend to stay for one year. Other students include those with failed aspirations who are improving O levels perhaps with A level aspirations, and there may be A level repeaters. The mix of courses across the arts/science/technology/social sciences boundaries is generally more complex than in schools. This creates embarrassment of priorities because many of these courses cannot easily be doubled up (more than one category of student in the teaching group) and this can lead to small groups which are uneconomic. The situation has been tolerated during the honeymoon period of these new institutions; but a stricter interpretation of costs and viability would fall adversely on precisely those areas in which sixth form colleges have a clear advantage, especially the chance they offer of remotivating youngsters who might otherwise be lost to the educational system. It should never be forgotten that the sixteen to nineteen sector is the only retrieval system in our educational arrangements.

It is the upper socio-economic groups who predominate in the full-time sixteen to nineteen age-group courses; but it has always been an aspiration amongst many educators to attract more of the less favoured groups to stay on. If they succeeded on any significant scale this sector would come under heavy pressure at a time when its resources were least adequate. The colleges should not be much affected by the fall in the birth rate since the groups which supply the bulk of their students have had a low birth rate for most of this century. The problem is to accommodate more students, resulting from a higher staying-on rate, with static resources.

The other aspect of the curriculum offered the sixteen to nineteen age group is the imbalance caused by the predominance of boys in science and girls in arts subjects. In a period of contraction and stringency it is easier to teach the arts subjects in larger groups by traditional methods than science. The closure of colleges of education which offered about 70 per cent of their places to girls has already discriminated against them; disadvantaging arts courses at any stage further adds to this.

Crucial choices made by youngsters aged thirteen to fifteen, where opportunities to take pure sciences or second languages, etc., are effectively rationed, have long consequences. The later outcome is almost invariably discrimination against children of the less affluent social groups and to a lesser extent girls whose choices at the next stage of education are thereby limited. Correction of these distortions in the system is delayed by the pressures of contraction and reduced resources; inequalities are increased.

Balance of power

There are, finally, growing indications that the existing balance of power between local and central government is tilting in favour of the DES. Contraction and stringency with its effects upon teacher employment and the provision of schooling, together with the current concern for account-ability in curriculum matters make for conditions favouring a flow of power to the centre. It is noticeable that the phrasing of earlier DES circulars ('The Minister requests LEAs to submit plans....' 10/65) has hardened ('The Secretary of State looks to LEAs to secure under his control and direction the effective execution of this policy...' 4/74). It may be argued that such semantic matters, if significant, do no more than reflect the sharper political cleavages of the 'seventies. Another pointer, though, arises out of the agitation for reform of local government finances, notably the rates system, which has been reflected in party political policy documents. Obviously, reform would be greatly eased if teachers' salaries became a central responsibility, since they are a large item. If this happened as part of a package deal, the DES and the Treasury would be given a substantial increase in power in the current tight employment situation. Whatever reservations teachers may have about their functions and effects educationally, the LEAs and the examining boards are important buffers between central power and teachers in the spheres of employment and standards. They could be weakened in the one case by central financing, in the other by centrally directed testing programmes.

Professor Simon has recently pointed out (1977) that the Green Paper and the Taylor Report presage an active leadership role for the DES and the inspectorate in the educational as well as the administrative sphere. In contraction we are all more vulnerable to outside pressures. The current review by the DES of local authority curricular arrangements, the increased activity of the inspectorate in this field, the emphasis upon standards, assessment and testing all suggest that the DES is taking a more forward, directive, line. George Tomlinson's 'T' Minister knows nowt about curriculum' has been replaced by 'The Secretary of State cannot abdicate responsibility for curricular matters'. Evidently the management of curriculum in contraction will be as much influenced by this new policy as by economics and demography.

References

CUMMING, C. (1971) *Studies in Educational Costs*. Edinburgh: Scottish Academic Press.

GOODSON, I. (1975) 'The Teachers' Curriculum and the New Reformation'. *Journal of Curriculum Studies*, 7:2.

HAMILTON, D. (1975) 'Handling Innovation in the Classroom' in REID, W. A. and WALKER, D. F. (eds.) *Case Studies in Curriculum Change*. London: Routledge and Kegan Paul.

KOGAN, M. (1975) *Educational Policy Making*. London: Allen and Unwin.

POSTER, C. (1976) *School Decision Making*. London: Heinemann.

SIMON, B. (1977) 'The Green Paper'. *Forum*, 20:1.

4.2 Accountability in the USA

Ernest R. House

A six-week teachers' strike in Detroit. School principals fired because of low test scores in their schools. School districts contracting out parts of their educational programme to industrial corporations. Political infighting in many state capitals. Over the past five years few issues have aroused as much controversy in American education as have those identified under the loose label of 'accountability'. A number of activities are subsumed under the term including, most centrally, programme planning and budgeting, performance-based education, performance contracting, statewide assessment and management by objectives.

The most recent widespread manifestation of accountability in the US education system is the implementation of state-wide testing programmes in more than forty states. The test programmes vary somewhat from state to state, but all are attempting to check on the achievement of the schools and promote public accounting of some kind. In some states the information is simply made public, to have what effects it will. In others sums of money are allocated on the basis of gains in the test scores. In still others accountability legislation requires that all teachers be evaluated by procedures which are more or less loosely defined. For example, California requires teacher evaluation on the basis of student data while Connecticut requires that evaluation procedures be negotiated between local teachers and local district authorities. Other accountability schemes have been tried at the local district level.

A history of the accountability movement has not been written. In its present manifestation it is about five years old but its antecedents extend back many years, some observers calling it 'neo-scientific management'. A major source of impetus has been the programme budgeting and systems analysis movements which have swept through federal and state governments. Much of the original conceptualizing was done by the Rand Corporation under contract with the Department of Defense. A major purpose was to quantify and rationalize such activities as weapons procurement.

When Robert MacNamara was appointed Secretary of Defense by Kennedy, he brought with him a passion for quantification and a group of ardent young enthusiasts determined to apply scientific management techniques to the greatly overblown defense budget. The contest between the ardent apostles of quantification and the generals and admirals, who were more inclined to intuitive decision-making, was often fought in the public media. The techniques were applied with rather mixed results. For

Source: *Cambridge Journal of Education*, Vol. 5, No. 2, Easter Term 1975, Cambridge Institute of Education. Reprinted by kind permission of Professor E. R. House.

example, concepts like 'body count' were used in the Vietnamese War in an attempt to bring the war under analytic control. Conscientious people who had applauded the application of these ideas to the control of the military establishment were appalled that they should be applied to the war.

Whatever the outcomes within the American military establishment, in Lyndon Johnson's administration a deliberate attempt was made to apply these concepts throughout the federal government, especially to social welfare expenditures such as education. The matter was made all the more urgent by the financial drain of the Vietnam War itself. Johnson had chosen to make aid to education a major mark of his Presidency. At first he tried to fund both the war and social programmes simultaneously, but as war costs soared past $25 billions a year on top of the already immense military budget, the American economic machine began to shudder. Cuts would have to come, and they would come, the nation's policy-makers decided, in social welfare programmes.

The extension of scientific management techniques, particularly programme budgeting, assumed new urgency. The Bureau of the Budget – later elevated to the Office of Management and the Budget – assumed unprecedented power. Agency heads were requested to have 'hard data' to support their budget requests. Programme budgeting became universal and social programmes were severely restrained. Federally-sponsored reports began to appear like the Rand Corporation's *How Effective is Schooling?* (1972) which concluded, on the basis of achievement test results, that significant reductions in education aid could be made without deterioration in the quality of education.

In actuality less than 10 per cent of school funds were supplied by the Federal Government. The great bulk of financing came from local and state sources. Between 1960 and 1970 educational expenditure in cities had increased by two-and-a-half times. These increases were achieved in a period of great teacher militancy as teachers became organized into vast professional unions. In combination with other social programmes this put a heavy financial strain on state and local governments. State governments began to search for cost cutting methods and to adopt techniques pioneered at the federal level. In a remarkable concert of action around 1970 most state governors submitted austerity budgets for education as well as for other programmes.

In particular, state education agencies were attracted to the technocratic methods. The tradition of American education has been for local school districts to control education. State education agencies have been limited to an advisory and regulatory function. Quantitative survey methods offered state agencies a handle on local districts which they had not had before. If one believed that numbers could faithfully represent schools and their essence, one could aggregate scores at the state level and make rational decisions about state education.

Also available for service was the huge US testing establishment.

Standardized tests had been used extensively in American life since the first world war. They had been used to sort and select students for training. Seldom had they been used to judge the merit of educational programmes or schools. In fact there was considerable scepticism as to whether they would be valid for such purposes. None the less with a great number of agencies and people trained in testing it was not difficult to apply this expertise to accountability situations. It was perhaps inevitable in this atmosphere that accountability should take on a testing flavour. It is only a slight exaggeration to say that testing was a technology in search of an application.

The social situation was not unprecedented. Victorian England had experienced a similar threefold increase in educational expenditure between 1857 and 1858. During the same period the Crimean War had cost England £78 million (Small, 1972). The Newcastle Report of 1858 recommended that efficiency be increased by granting funds only to schools and children who could demonstrate certain degrees of knowledge. Examinations were developed and payment by results became a fact. Although educationally disastrous according to some observers, the procedure succeeded in drastically reducing governmental expenditure for education.

Another group especially interested in accountability has been private corporations. State Chambers of Commerce have actively lobbied for educational accountability legislation in many states while the US Chamber of Commerce in Washington has produced and disseminated information calling for accountability legislation. Other business groups have responded similarly. In addition, private corporations, some large and some small, have endeavoured to do business with the schools. One of the first accountability thrusts was 'performance contracting'. A corporation would contract with a school district to raise the scores of a segment of its students and would be paid according to results. One of the first contracts was at Texakana, which received bad publicity because it was alleged the company had taught the tests and hence invalidated the results. Because of such publicity, the questioning of the measurement procedures employed, and most of all the inability of companies to raise test scores, performance contracting has not been widely employed.

To the felt urgency of government and business in controlling educational expenditures and the increasing militancy of teachers must be added a third element – the activism of parents. In the American tradition any parent who is dissatisfied with the schools has the opportunity to register his complaint to the elected school board, the school administrators, or the child's teacher. This intrusion is considered well within the parents' rights and school personnel are expected to make a satisfactory response to what is held to be a legitimate demand. In fact it is crucial to an understanding of the American school to appreciate its vulnerability to outside pressures.

In a pluralistic society like the United States there are many demands on the schools, but one of the most outraged and insistent has been the cries of minority groups such as blacks that their children are not receiving an adequate education. Poor test scores, the inability of their children to read, and poor facilities convinces many ghetto parents that the school as an institution is unfeeling and unresponsive to their needs. This is quite a different concern than cutting educational costs. Cutting costs I would call the 'productivity' meaning of accountability. The other meaning signifies how 'responsive' the institution is to its various clientele. Usually the two meanings are not clearly disassociated.

When one calls for accountability, one may have either or both meanings in mind. State agencies are certainly concerned about productivity. Yet many state agencies also see their duty as championing the needs of minority groups by imposing state authority on local schools since these schools are not responsive to the needs of minority children. Accountability becomes a moral obligation and a crusade. A state testing programme that monitors effectiveness and efficiency of operation may also reveal schools doing a poor job and coerce them to do better – or so the argument goes.

A call for school accountability blends an appeal to American pragmatism – making things 'work' – and an appeal to egalitarianism – providing equal life opportunities to those who need them. To this is added the spice of striking out at large and impersonal institutions which seem frustratingly beyond the control of most Americans. Hence the ideas have strong popular appeal. Less altruistically they are advanced by people in government agencies and universities who have the incentive of advancing their own careers and interests and who are in powerful positions to promote these ideas. Accountability is a formidable social movement.

Of course, it may be that the productivity of schools and their responsiveness to their various publics may be antithetically rather than complementarily related to one another. It is not difficult to imagine that quantification techniques employed by a higher level of government on a lower may result in great injustices and a distortion of humane values. The use of 'body counts' in Vietnam is not an entirely mischievous example.

Parents who wish to control education through test scores may find themselves extremely unhappy with what has been done to their child to achieve such scores. I have written extensively in America against some of the most disastrous possibilities inherent in the accountability movement (House, 1973a; House, 1973b). The potential for standardization and dehumanization of schooling is enormous. Yet even I would be extremely reluctant to give up the idea that institutions should be accountable to the publics they serve and in particular to give up the responsiveness of American schools to parents.

As one might expect, social movement which is as virulent as the one I have described has engendered many confrontations. A recent six-week teachers' strike in Detroit was resolved only when the accountability issue was taken off the bargaining table. A few school principals have been fired

ecause their schools have had low test scores. Some teachers have been
iven test items to teach by their school administrators so their schools
vould look good. These events are isolated, however, and generally
ccountability has not yet affected schools at the classroom level.

One of the most highly publicized recent events was one in which I was
nvolved. The State of Michigan has one of the first and most elaborate
ccountability systems of any state. The plan calls for administering
pecially developed objective-referenced tests to all fourth and seventh
raders in the state. A second part of the plan calls for the award of state
noney to schools on the basis of gains in achievement test scores. In the
ast, state test scores have also been made public, published in the
ewspapers, and compared to the scores of other schools. All this has
aused much consternation among school personnel.

The Michigan Education Assocation, which represents about 80,000
Michigan teachers, has been critical but not overtly opposed. In 1973 the
.5 million-member National Education Assocation, the nation's largest
eachers' union, became concerned that the Michigan plan might spread
o other states without an independent assessment of its worth. It commis-
ioned an independent evaluation panel consisting of three evaluators,
ncluding myself. The evaluation was done in 1974 and was highly critical
f the Michigan plan (House, Rivers, Stufflebeam, 1974). Strongly
riticized were the way state goals were derived, the construction of the
ests, the lack of participation by teachers, and numerous technical
ssues.

The Michigan authorities claimed that the 23 objectives in reading and
5 objectives in maths at the fourth grade level represented both a
tatewide consensus of opinion about what should be taught and minimal
performance that every child in Michigan should be able to achieve at that
rade level. The evaluators contended the objectives were neither consen-
ual nor minimal, given their process of derivation. The specially-
onstructed objectives tests based on these objectives were not adequately
validated or field-tested. Teachers were only minimally involved in the
levelopment of both.

Furthermore teachers and schools received little or no help in imple-
nenting the tests and total system. The evaluators labelled the tying of
unding to individual student test scores as 'whimsical' at best. The
publication of such scores by schools has caused dismay and consterna-
ion throughout the state. Finally, the accountability system risked sub-
tituting state objectives and curricula for local ones and posed the threat
of the teacher teaching to the tests rather than to the child. The evaluation
eport concluded by making several specific suggestions as to how some of
hese defects might be remedied.

Upon release of the report with much national publicity, it was in turn
attacked by Michigan authorities (Kearney, Donovan, Fisher, 1974). The
controversy continues today after more than a year. The report has
nfluenced changes in several other state accountability plans which were

in process. Perhaps more dramatic confrontations between teachers
unions and governments lie down the road.

As in any major controversy many basic issues are entangled in th
accountability movement. For example, the American race problem i
involved. The Michigan education agency has been concerned, rightly
think, that ghetto youngsters lag behind in school achievement. The
believe their testing and accountability schemes will alleviate the situa
tion. A further complication is the use of achievement tests. What do th
tests measure? Are they valid and reliable? Should one use criterion
referenced or norm-referenced tests? Should test results be reported to th
general public at all? Are tests fair to minority children?

If the state can prescribe what tests can be used to measure schoo
output, are they not likely to prescribe the curriculum that must b
pursued to achieve good test performance? The idea of a state governmen
rather than local authorities prescribing the curriculum is quite a foreig
idea in the system of local control. Yet where can groups such as minority
parents appeal if local schools are unresponsive to their needs? Part of th
controversy surrounds the issues of how directly each of the fifty stat
governments will control education at the local level. Centralization o
control of education is part of a general trend in American government.

Another control concern is the question of the professional autonomy o
the teachers. Sociologists have sometimes classified American teachers a
semi-professionals. Teachers have made few demands for educationa
policy making, leaving that to administrators and school boards. In th
last few years, they have begun to exert political and policy influence as a
group. How much control over schooling will the teachers have as compared with traditional local authorities or the emerging technocrati
forces represented in the accountability movement?

I would speculate that underlying these dynamics are social forces o
the first magnitude. The mainspring of a technological society lies in th
invention and dispersal of technological innovations which revolutioniz
the means of production. The innovations must be capable of mas
production and the efficiencies achieved by them are almost alway
economies of scale. The pace of technological advance is governed no
only by the invention of new forms but by the ability of the society t
absorb them (House, 1974).

Technological society thus also requires a massive educational estab
lishment to train and retrain masses of people to adjust to the constan
stream of innovation. Yet education itself, conceived as an industry, i
grossly inefficient. More than 80 per cent of the education budget is sunk
in personnel costs – personnel not easily dispensed with nor capable o
being revolutionized by the introduction of new machinery as in a factory
production line. A 'modern' industry would be one which was highly
capital intensive, one in which investment was in machines rather than in
personnel. Machines can be replaced every few years by new ones with
which one can lower costs and improve productivity.

As an anachronistic industry education does not lend itself to such
ϵatment, and productivity is hampered by irreducible and constantly
ϳing costs, particularly in difficult financial times. Accountability is in
ϳrt an attempt to hold down costs by applying efficiency measures. But
is is only a short-range partial solution.

From the perspective of a technological society a long-range solution
ϳuld be to replace people by machines, to make education a capital
ϳensive industry. I would predict strong attempts to do so over the next
ϳw decades. Combined with this will be a greater emphasis on technical
ϳucation, another form of efficiency. Thus the accountability phenome-
ϳn may be seen as the working out of the implicit logic of economy of
ϳale. As the world's most advanced industrial society, the United States
ϳs borne these forces first and perhaps most intensively, but if my
ϳalysis is correct I would expect such forces to emerge before long in
ϳher industrial countries – including Britain.

eferences

ϳUSE, ERNEST R. (1973a) 'The Dominion of Economic Accountability', in
 HOUSE, ERNEST R. (ed.) (1973) *School Evaluation*. Berkeley, Calif.:
 McCutchan.

ϳUSE, ERNEST R. (1973b) 'The Price of Productivity: Who pays?', *Today's
 Education*, Vol. 62, No. 4, September–October 1973.

ϳUSE, ERNEST R. (1974) *The Politics of Educational Innovation*. Berkeley, Calif.:
 McCutchan.

ϳUSE, ERNEST R., RIVERS, WENDELL and STUFFLEBEAM, DANIEL L.
 (1974) 'An Assessment of the Michigan Accountability System', *Phi Delta
 Kappan*, Vol. LV, No. 10, June 1974.

ϳARNEY, PHILIP, DONOVAN, BERNARD and FISHER, THOMAS (1974) 'In
 Defense of Michigan Accountability', *Phi Delta Kappan*, Vol. LVI, No. 1,
 September 1974.

ϳND CORPORATION (1972) *How Effective is Schooling?* Washington, D.C.: Rand
 Corporation, January 1972.

ϳALL, ALAN A. (1972) 'Accountability in Victorian England', *Phi Delta Kappan*,
 Vol. LIII, No. 7, March 1972.

4.3 Teacher accountability and school autonomy

J. P. White

Who should decide what the overall shape of a school's curriculum should
be? Should it be the headmaster alone? Or the staff as a whole? Or
parents? Or pupils? The Schools Council? A Teachers' General Council?
The DES? Parliament? – Or who?

What, first, is the system in Britain? In practice, except for the statutory
inclusion of Religious Education, schools decide their own curricula.
Theoretically, powers are vested in LEAs via governors and managers,
but in fact it is the schools which decide. Here there is a gamut of cases
between the headmaster acting autocratically and a more democratic
system in which all the staff participate.

Many would argue that schools are not in fact as autonomous as they
seem. Secondary school curricula, in particular, are dominated by the
requirements of external examinations, especially from the third or fourth
year onwards.

At this point we must highlight a crucial distinction already referred to
in passing: between (a) the control of syllabus details and (b) the control of
the general framework of the curriculum. It is true that as regards (a)
many schools *are* constrained by pressures from external examinations...
But schools are still largely autonomous as regards (b): they can decide,
for instance, whether to have a common core curriculum, how long it
should last, and what its content should consist of. As we all know, there
are great variations between schools on these points.

How a school decides to organize this general framework can determine
whether it keeps control in its own hands or whether it lets it pass
elsewhere. The more a school approaches a 'cafeteria' curriculum system,
the more the power to decide what the whole curriculum shall be for any
individual pupil passes to that pupil and/or his parents. The more
emphasis, conversely, there is on a common curriculum, the more this
power is retained by the staff of the school.

So much for the factual background. Let us turn back to prescriptive
questions about who should determine curriculum content. Let us in
particular concentrate on the question whether *teachers* (including headteachers) ought to do this.

One familiar view here is that teachers have no right to impose *any*
content on their pupils (either in sense (a) or sense (b)), since any such
imposition would be an interference with a pupil's right to develop in his
own way. This is an extreme libertarian position which underlies a
number of contemporary points of view, from biologically-based growth

Source: *Proceedings of the Philosophy of Education Society of Great Britain*, Vol. X, July
1976, pp. 61–78.

theorists to deschoolers, sociologists of knowledge and the ideologues of Penguin Education.

Now I don't want to enter into a full-scale critique of this position, especially since a main difficulty in it is well known: it rests on the implausible assumption that the pupil is always in a position to know what kind of content is most suitable for him. What is interesting about the position for present purposes is that it challenges the principle of teacher autonomy in matters of content. If teachers are free to organize curricula as they wish, what guarantee is there that they are not swayed in their decisions by preconceptions arising from their social origins, for instance, or from professional traditions, which are at odds with what is good for their pupils? Why, after all, should *teachers* be in any privileged position over content? And if there is no satisfactory answer to this question, then why should not the pupils themselves or the pupils' parents decide content, since it is, after all, the pupils who are most directly affected by whatever decisions are made?

Can this challenge to teacher autonomy be countered? To some extent it can. If it is asked why *teachers* rather than, say, postmen or doctors should make curriculum decisions, the answer may seem pretty obvious: postmen and doctors are not professionally equipped to make these decisions, but teachers are. This seems to me a cogent answer if we are concerned with (a) above, control of syllabus details. Classroom teachers have to marry educational content to the cognitive structures which their pupils already possess. There are all sorts of individual and group differences between pupils in the same age-group in, for instance, what they already know and in what kinds of things will motivate them to learn. Syllabuses have, therefore, to be tailored to meet these differences. On this topic, it is true, teachers *are* professionally equipped to make decisions, whereas postmen and doctors are not. But it does not follow from this that they are better professionally equipped than any other people when it comes to (b), deciding the general framework of the curriculum.

There is one good reason for this. This is that decisions of this sort, when taken together, help to shape the character of society as a whole. Suppose, to take extremes, all teachers agreed to a dualist curriculum framework, whereby, as in Plato or in prewar England, the few get an intellectually oriented curriculum and the many get the opposite. Society would then be likely to consist of a knowledgeable élite and relatively ignorant masses. Or suppose all agreed to put every child through a common curriculum until sixteen: the character of society would be very different. Again, contrast a situation where a 'cafeteria' curriculum was the general rule with one where a Herbartian system was the accepted thing, i.e. one where morality was the end of education, promoted through a common general education in different forms of knowledge and sympathy. While a cafeteria system might help to create a society of self-centred individuals, each intent on doing what he most wanted to do, the Herbartian system might tend to quite the opposite effect. Each of these frameworks is linked to a different conception of a good society. What emerges from this is that teachers cannot make responsible decisions about total curriculum frameworks without considering what kind of society they think is desirable. Granted, not all teachers would ever in fact be in such unanimity as these four extreme examples presuppose. But this does not affect the main point. If a school decides on a certain framework, knowing that other schools are likely to make quite other decisions, in line with quite other conceptions of a good society, then the school is either glad that other schools are making other decisions or it would prefer all other schools to make the same decision as itself. Each of these attitudes embodies a conception of a good society. Even if a school claimed that the content of education was not connected with any such conception, being wholly concerned, say, with the pursuit of theoretical and aesthetic activities for intrinsic reasons, even this policy would have social consequences of which the school should be aware. For one thing, decisions would have to be made about whether this content was for all or only for a few; for another, a society of individuals who held that theoretical and aesthetic pursuits were all important might well be, like Hesse's Castalians, less morally and politically concerned than one in which the education had been of another sort: that the first sort of society is more desirable than the second is itself a value judgment about a good society.

In short, therefore, decisions about curriculum frameworks are inescapably connected with *political* views about the nature of the Good Society. If this is so, then teachers have no professional expertise which justifies leaving these decisions in their hands. If there could be moral experts, then as long as we ensured that there were a sufficient number of these to make curriculum decisions in schools, I might be less alarmed than I am about teacher autonomy in this regard. But I do not believe in the existence of moral experts. Teachers, it seems to me, are not *qua* teachers in any better position than anyone else, postmen and doctors or whoever, to make decisions directly affecting the shape and character of our society.

It is understandable that as this truth, that teachers have no special right to decide curricula, seeps further into the consciousness of those of us professionally or otherwise concerned with education, objections to teacher control of the curriculum should become more and more vocal. This is what I believe has been happening recently. To date the attacks have come largely from the extreme libertarian, or anarchist, wing, proclaiming that power should pass from the tyrant-pedagogues to the people, that is to say to pupils and their parents. Teachers themselves are often the first to respond to such an appeal. Why, after all, should they cling on to powers they cannot in all conscience justify? Hence, perhaps, a partial explanation of the widespread preference for 'cafeteria' curricula. But this is a shortsighted and at bottom irresponsible solution to a problem of conscience. If teachers are in no privileged position to decide whole curricula for any individual, then neither, for the same reasons, are pupils or their parents. Neither, incidentally, are school counsellors, who often find themselves having to help pupils pick their way through the menu of 'cafeteria' curricula, since neither pupils nor their parents can make the decisions required (so far no one else has been dreamed up to whom the counsellors can pass the buck).

Attacks on teacher autonomy come not only from the libertarian wing. Teachers' power over curricula need not only pass downwards, to pupils and parents. It could also pass upwards, to public bodies to which the schools were subordinate.

Elsewhere in Europe it is generally the *state* which lays down the general framework of school curricula. Are there any reasons why it should not do so in Britain as well?

Some might appeal to differing national traditions. But this will not do. Apart from the difficulties of naturalism in arguments from tradition, the claim that Britain has a long-standing tradition of school autonomy simply is not true. Until 1926 the state, in the shape of the Board of Education, laid down curricular frameworks for both elementary schools and teacher training colleges. It continued to do so for secondary schools until 1945; and in further education, as Gerry Fowler's article [not reprinted here] shows, it still keeps its old powers.

Others might say that state control of curricula would be 'totalitarian'. [...] But is there any substance in it? It is true that state control *could* lead to totalitarianism in the sense that all pupils could be indoctrinated in a particular form of state worship, whether Hitlerite or Stalinist. But it *need* not. One of the educational objectives publicly laid down could be to promote a critical appreciation of the principles of democratic government. This would be a far cry from [Orwell's] 1984. In addition, state-controlled curricula exist in many countries which are scarcely models of totalitarianism, like Sweden, for example. As I said, such curricula have also existed and still do exist, to some extent, in Britain.

A third objection might be that there is bound to be disagreement about what the content and objectives of the curriculum should be, so any state control could only reflect the subjective preferences of those who drew it up. This is an argument which needs to be taken very seriously. But it is hardly an argument supporting school autonomy, because, if it is true, then any curriculum which a school has autonomously devised will necessarily reflect merely the subjective preferences of the headmaster or staff. In any case, is it true that there is bound to be disagreement? There may be disagreement about some things but not about others. There is not likely, for instance, to be any disagreement about the inclusion of the three Rs. If the argument breaks down here, it may break down elsewhere: the extent of universal agreement may be greater than critics seem to expect. Lastly, the argument assumes that a prescription could only avoid the taint of subjectivity if there were no disagreement with it. But why so? Not everyone would agree that the earth is round, but that does not mean that there is nothing to choose between this proposition and a flat earth theory on the grounds that both are inescapably subjective.

A fourth objection might be that state control would diminish the quality of teaching: it would tend to become dead and inert, and opportunities for experimentation would decline. Continental experience of state-controlled curricula bears this out. This is why one finds so many European teachers admiring the autonomy their counterparts have in Britain. In assessing this argument it is important to bear in mind the distinction, made earlier, between 'control' sense (a) and 'control' sense (b). The argument is at its strongest when concerned with sense (a). If the State controls syllabus details (as it often does on the continent) teachers will indeed lose their freedom – which I argued above was essential – to devise means of marrying content to individual minds. Experimentation will be impossible and teaching will doubtless suffer. But since the issue under discussion is state control over general curricular frameworks, the argument is irrelevant. There would still be plenty of scope for initiative and experiment. Indeed, since teachers would be working within a clear framework of objectives, it could even be that the quality of teaching, far from declining, actually improved. Teachers, under a state-run system, might have a much better idea of what they were supposed to be doing and where the limits of their responsibilities lay. They could be freed, for one thing, from the anxieties which many of them presently feel about having to make decisions about the ends of education and the Good Society, which they know that they are in no position to make. It is an assumption of this fourth argument that the quality of teaching is high in an autonomous system. But is this assumption well-founded?

These are, then, four initial arguments against state control. As you see, I do not think any one of them will do – at least in the crude forms in which they have been expressed so far. Some of them have, however, more substance to them if we dig a little below the surface to the level of fundamental principles. This I shall do in a moment. First, though, I shall present an argument on the other side, in favour of state control.

This argument is that the educational system as a whole is likely to work more efficiently under state control. There are two ways, at least, in which this might be so. First, longitudinal coordination of courses could be improved. Under the autonomous system, the eleven-year period of compulsory schooling, from five to sixteen, need not be, and very often is not, planned as a whole, since each school makes its own arrangements. The problem is made worse for children moving to a school in a new area. State control could ensure that each child's total curriculum was planned as a whole. It could also, secondly, ensure a match between the schools' requirements and the colleges' or universities' supply of teachers in different content areas. As things are, colleges and University Departments of Education are themselves pretty autonomous in this respect. Of the 6,600 candidates for the London Teachers' Certificate in 1972, 1,123 offered art as a main course, 209 some form of physical science. Do the schools need five times as many teachers with a background in (largely practical) art as in physical science? This *may* be a good balance. But, if so, it is only an accident: it is not the result of deliberate and comprehensive matching.

How cogent are these efficiency arguments? Assuming these two kinds of coordination are desirable, it would have to be shown that either (i) the only way or (ii) the best way of bringing them about would be by state control. (i) would be difficult to establish, since an alternative is conceivable: the different institutions whose work had to be coordinated could autonomously get together for this purpose. A question would then be whether their systems of coordination would not be impossibly unwieldy and unmanageable. If so, coordination originating from a central body rather than from the periphery might well be preferable. I cannot, of course, give a verdict on this point, and it would be inappropriate in a philosophical paper to do so; but it is important to see what *kinds* of argument are relevant here and how much can be built on them. Suppose it *can* be shown that centrally originated coordination is (in some sense) preferable. Does this justify *state* control? Two further conditions would have to be satisfied for it to do so. It would have to be shown, first, that the only or best form of central control was state control; and, secondly, that there are no strong reasons against state control that would outweigh the state's advantage in efficiency. In each case it seems, prima facie, that these conditions cannot be met. There can be central curriculum control which is not *state* control – by an autonomous Teachers' General Council, for instance, whose regulations schools and colleges agreed to accept. And efficiency arguments could never be *sufficient* to justify state control since it would be irrational to agree to *any* form of state control – a Nazi system, for instance – provided only that it was efficient.

These two objections do not destroy the case for state control. In seeking to answer them, we are reminded that the strongest case for it has already been made, implicitly, [...] above. The question: what should be the content of education? is a political one, undivorceable from the question: what is a good society? As such, it must be answered not at the professional, but at the political level. Hence it is not enough to say that if central curriculum control is required, this can be left to a Teachers' General Council; for if an individual teacher is in no privileged position to determine content, then neither is a representative body of teachers. Hence, too, the case for state control cannot merely be based on efficiency, important though this is, but must be substantive as to content: it must, that is, include within it a picture of the good society and its curricular implications.

At this point the deeper difficulties begin. If I cannot conclude an argument in favour of state control without providing a picture of the good society, can any such argument be anything more than an expression of personal preferences? It would be tempting to write into the notion of the 'state', as T. H. Green did when he denied that the Tsar's Russia of his day was a state, that states necessarily promote the common good. Then it might not be difficult to argue that educational content should be left in the hands of the state, but there would clearly be a serious difficulty of application: to whom or what should one entrust the power to decide content? What we ordinarily understand as the apparatus of the state would be no answer, since there is no guarantee that this empirical state is a state in the ideal sense.

A specification of the good society seems inevitable. But is it possible? Martin Hollis has stated [...] that 'if we knew what would count as moral progress, in that we had a blueprint for a good society and knew how to achieve it, then a ruthless educational programme would be warranted.'[1] He argues, however, that we lack such knowledge and hence have no blueprint. He therefore cautions us against radical change in education, arguing that it *may* be the best political strategy to leave the latter to 'men of good sense' who feel their way slowly forward from the *status quo*; but at the same time he is not entirely happy with this suggestion, since he recognizes that 'delay has its effects on the next generation and its price in opportunities foregone'.

Hollis' argument helps us to see the deeper strengths of the objections to state control summarily dismissed [above]. Reliance on traditional forms of curriculum control is recommendable, it may be said, not on the grounds that tradition is always right, but because our tradition (albeit our very recent tradition) has been *of a certain sort*, i.e. one where control has been decentralized. Where we lack the knowledge to introduce a centralized system, it is politically sensible to continue in the old way.

What implications has Hollis' argument for the question whether the schools or the state should determine educational content? He speaks of leaving decisions to men of good sense, 'or at any rate to educationists'. Possibly he would be in favour of school autonomy: it is hard to tell for sure. He in any case faces, in his reliance on 'men of good sense', very much the same kind of problem which Green faced over the 'state'. For if there *were* men on whose good judgment we could rely to let our society slowly evolve in the right direction, it would be sensible for us, perhaps, given that we discounted the problems of dilatoriness, to leave the decisions to them. But how do we identify them, if Hollis is right in claiming that we do not know what would count as moral progress? There is a dilemma here. If we cannot pick out the men of good sense, then we have no reason to believe that leaving decisions about content to the schools will be leaving them to men of good sense: the decision-makers may be leading us not forwards, but backwards, round in circles or up gumtrees. If, however, we *do* know who the men of good sense are, we must have some knowledge of what ought to be done; and if we have, then why could we not seek to ensure that the men of good sense used this knowledge in *central* planning rather than leaving everything to the periphery?

Hollis' argument for decentralized decisions rests on the premise that we do not know what would count as moral progress, in that we lack a blueprint for a good society. Now, if we are *totally* ignorant of what a good society is like, then it is hard to see how *any* central decisions on *any* matter can be justifiable. This path leads quickly to anarchism. But is it true that we are totally ignorant? About many central decisions of the past there is now universal agreement that they helped to promote a good society – the decision no longer to hang sheep-stealers, for instance, or the decision to lay down minimum standards of domestic sanitation. As for educational policy, few would challenge the decision that all children should be legally bound to be educated. This, just as much as the previous examples, rests on a belief about a good society, in this case the belief that a good society is incompatible with widespread ignorance.

It may be objected that this rational agreement about a good society is not likely to get us very far when it comes to making decisions about curricula. We may indeed agree that the state should insist on every child's being educated, but when we go on to determine what we each mean by 'being educated', all kinds of disagreements begin to appear.

There are a number of points to make about this objection. First, it accepts that there can be *some* consensus about a good society. How extensive this is is unspecified. Disagreements, it is claimed, will appear at some point, but where this point is we are not told. The area of agreement, then, might be broader than is commonly imagined. Secondly, disagreements at one level may be compatible with agreements at another. Abortion on demand may be excluded from one person's picture of a good society and included in another's. But both may agree that in a good society everyone ought to be intellectually equipped to reflect on the moral pros and cons of abortion. Similarly, one person's vision of a good society might be dominated by a religious *Weltanschauung* while another's is not. But both may agree that children should not be indoctrinated into any particular ideal of life but that they should all be introduced to as wide a range of ideals as possible. Quite fundamental disputes about the nature of a good society may go together, therefore, with solid agreement about curricular matters. Thirdly, the objection under discussion fails to insist on the objectivity of a point of view. It argues that consensus about a good society is impossible once there is any disagreement. But people can disagree on this for all sorts of reasons. Some people may have fixed ideas about it indoctrinated into them in youth; others' ideas may be easily discounted because they are based on false premises; others' pictures of the good society may be askew because they see it from the standpoint of a sectional interest, and so on. In raising the question of what a good society is like we are assuming that all those whose views on the topic are to be taken into account are seeking an objective answer: they are ignoring, for instance, their present social station; and they are open to rational persuasion, being prepared to give up a point of view if it is shown to be false or ill-grounded.

In the light of these three points I see no grounds for pessimism abou how much objective agreement there can be about a good society. Who knows what agreement there might be if only one got down to the job o assessing it? Certainly there is no *a priori* reason why the pessimist's view must automatically be preferred.

This is not the place to go into a detailed discussion of the nature of a good society, important though this is. Instead, I shall simply indicate two features of such a society which I am confident will be generally accept- able. My purpose is not only to show that curricular consequences of great importance may flow from virtual platitudes of this sort, but also to emphasize the fact that despite the ease with which they can be derived, these curricular consequences are not realized in most English secondary schools today.

(a) The first feature of a good society is that its members are not egoists but have a genuine regard for the wellbeing of others as well as of themselves. There are various ways in which this point would need elaboration in a fuller account. First, one would need to argue the case that no society (regardless of whether it is a good society) is reducible to a collection of atomic individuals. It is an implication of Wittgenstein's 'private language' argument that the notion of a pre-social individual is a nonsense. Any form of individualistic social theory which is based on the atomic assumption is a non-starter: the members of a society must be bound together in some kind of organic unity. This does not, of course, preclude the possibility of some individuals being egoists (whether or not it is possible for *all* to be egoists in the light of the organic nature of society is another question). But egoism is irrational, assuming that the egoist can give no good reasons for generally preferring the promotion of his own wellbeing to that of others. Given, then, that the good society is a univer- sally benevolent community, the next point which would have to be elaborated would be the double universality which is here involved. It would be double because, first, *all* would be benevolent, and, second, because this benevolence would not be restricted to certain classes of individuals, e.g. family, friends, those with whom one has face-to-face relationships, but would include anyone whose wellbeing one was in a position to affect – including one's own. There would be no good reason to restrict one's benevolence in the former way. Since one's sympathies would extend beyond one's face-to-face contacts, one would necessarily be concerned with the wellbeing of others in the community who lived perhaps far away from oneself. One would be concerned that they all had the basic material necessities of life, that they were able to live in peace, that they were not deprived of an education, and so on. In other words, one would necessarily acquire an interest in *political* matters. Members of a good society would see themselves among other things as *citizens* of that society, working together for the common good. (At this point one would need to show how the impossibility of moral experts would necessitate a democratic political organization rather than any other sort.)

I mentioned above the double universality of benevolence. It would need to be explored how far it was, in fact, *trebly* universal. For if a man must be doubly benevolent at some times in his life, why should he be so at some times *only*? Why not at all times? We face the question: is there any purely private sphere in a man's life where he is justified in taking only his own interests into account and ignoring others'? If, as I would be inclined to argue, there is no such sphere, then members of a good society would see themselves *primarily* as citizens: private spheres would be created only within the framework of their public concerns.

All these arguments are deliberately impressionistic and incomplete. But I would hope that, when elaborated, most would be seen as reasonably uncontentious to an objective eye. Some points, especially those in the last paragraph, may seem less uncontentious than others. Even so, if we turn now to a curricular implication of this line of thought, we will see, I think, that even from the most uncontroversial of the claims big consequences follow.

An important aim of education for a good society will be the creation of the citizen. (Whether this is the *most* important aim will depend on the resolution of the problems touched on in the last paragraph but one.) Pupils (not necessarily only schoolchildren: some form of continuation education may also be suitable) will have to have, among other things, considerable understanding of the nature of society in general and of the particular society in which they live. This understanding will have to be both of factual matters of various kinds and of moral values, including democratic principles. Political understanding, then, will become an important feature of the curriculum. Far from being an important, let alone the central, feature in our actual educational system today, it is often peripheral at most. This is one area where state control is necessary to enforce an evidently desirable curriculum ingredient. (It is odd that even in our actual society there is no insistence that all children be politically educated, since, if we seriously want a democratic form of government to continue, a necessary condition is that the citizens of that democracy know something about politics.)

(b) The second feature of a good society that I want to pick out is the importance it attaches to leaving the individual as free as possible to pursue his own concerns within an area of privacy and non-interference. This individualistic ideal is not necessarily linked with atomic individualism and does not sink in the wreck of that theory. It is compatible even with the extreme form of communitarianism mentioned in (a), i.e. with an individual's seeing himself primarily as a citizen and only secondarily as a private person. What it is *not* compatible with is a still more extreme communitarianism in which individuals have to spend *all* their time on cooperative projects with others. There is no good reason that I know why this latter way of life should be mandatory at all. (If each voluntarily decides to dispense with private pursuits, that is another matter.) Since a good society will aim at promoting the wellbeing of individuals and since, as I should want to argue in a fuller account, the individual is to a certain extent the final authority on that in which his wellbeing consists, he must be left as free as possible to develop his own preferred way of life within the framework of his moral, including political, commitments.

To be in a position to know in what his wellbeing may consist the individual will have to have some understanding of the various possible ingredients of that wellbeing – e.g. of all kinds of activities which he may wish to pursue for their own sake, of all kinds of different ways of life, and of the means and hindrances to enjoying any of these. A narrowly specialized education, or an education which did not introduce pupils to whole areas of human endeavour – an education without musical understanding, for instance, or without physical science – would fail to meet this criterion of breadth. Again, as we all know, in our autonomous system there are many pupils, probably the majority, who have not had a broad enough curriculum, especially in the last few years of their schooling when so much could be done. State control would be able to oblige the schools to broaden their curricula and prevent them turning out the tens of thousands of mentally lopsided and mentally stunted individuals which they do at the moment.

It is not the place to go any more fully into the nature of a good society. Some will, no doubt, think I have already gone too far. Whether I have or not, if one is tempted to make the further claim that objectivity on such matters is inconceivable, it is worth stating again that in so far as this constitutes an objection to *state* control of curricula, it also constitutes an objection to *school* control: the headmaster and staff of a school can no more than any central planner be relied on to provide a curriculum consonant with an objective picture of a good society. But if personal preferences must shape their decisions (assuming that they are not blind traditionalists), then why should they be allowed to impose them on generations of pupils?

It may be said that I have conducted this whole debate in too black-and-white a way, as if the only two agencies of control could be the state or the school. But there are other possibilities. I will conclude by a brief discussion of two of them. First, parental control. This could be understood in two ways, as (a) control over the curriculum of the parents' own child, or as (b) control over others' curricula as well. It would be possible, following (b), for a school's curriculum policy to be determined by a committee of parents rather than the headmaster. But protagonists of parental rights in these matters usually have (a) in mind, and it is that that I shall discuss. A demand for parental control (sense (a)) is compatible with and usually goes together with school control. The demand often springs out of a denial that objectivity is possible about a good society. It goes like this. There are, and must be, widely differing views about a good society. Different schools can, and should, encapsulate these different views in the differing kinds of education, including differing kinds of curricula, they provide. Parents should have the power to choose to which kind of school they wish to send their child – a religious school, a school stressing community service, a school with a strong artistic and creative bent, and so on.

This is an increasingly popular argument, especially with [some] Conservative politicians. [. . .] But is it a good one? Why should *parents* have this power? If objectivity is impossible, then what parents choose will be open to the same objection that they are imposing a personal preference on a pupil. I cannot see any feature of the relationship between parents and children which justifies them in this imposition.

Parental control (sense (a)) is sometimes supported on quite other grounds, grounds which presuppose the possibility of some kind of objective determination of the good society. The content of education, it is agreed on this view, is a political matter. But parents, like any other adult, are judged to be qualified in a democracy to make political decisions, e.g. in general or local elections or in referenda. So parents are qualified, among other things, to make decisions about the content of education.

This argument is persuasive to a point, but it can be misleading. It may be true that parents *qua citizens* are in a position to make decisions about content (although, of course, parents are not the *only* citizens). This is to assume that they are looking at the education of children, including their own, from the point of view of the good of the community as well as (or including) the good of the children themselves. The argument is only valid if one writes in such a point of view into the notion of 'citizen': it is less impressive if it is said that parents are qualified to make political decisions simply because they have the right to vote, even if they vote in their own interests or in other sectional interests. The argument can be misleading because it may seem to support parental control as this is normally understood. On this conception a parent is fully justified in favouring a curriculum which will enable his child to 'get on', to open the door to a well-paid job and a comfortable life. Here the parent's vision can be limited to the interests of his child as the parent conceives them. He is not obliged, as he is *qua* citizen, to look at the matter from a wider, community-oriented, point of view. If this wider point of view is important – and it is a premise of the present argument that it is – then we have a powerful argument *against* parental control: if parents are left to determine their children's curricula, what guarantee is there that they will not be directed in their judgment by purely selfish considerations?

Political control of education cannot, therefore, be eroded into parental control. But does it necessarily imply *state* control? A second alternative to the state *v.* school control dichotomy might be that *local* government, not central, should control curricula. In one way, it might be said, that is in fact the *status quo*. Local authorities rarely, if ever, interfere with schools over curriculum policy, but technically they are in charge. But I am not here concerned with this technical point. The question is, rather: if content is a political matter, why should not *local* authorities work out a curriculum policy for all schools in their jurisdiction to follow? Why must it be the state?

There is an assumption in all this that the state excludes local government. 'State' is made equivalent to 'central government'. I do not know how such an assumption would be justified and will leave it to its adherents to do so. But let us take it that the argument is over whether the curriculum should be directed centrally or locally. How should this be decided? One consideration is the following. If one argues for local control, one must show that there are local factors which might justifiably influence the shape of school curricula. In the nineteenth century, I believe, seaports like Portsmouth were allowed to include nautical subjects in the curricula of their elementary schools. Whether or not such a franchise is justifiable would depend on whether curricula in their vocational aspects should be tailored to suit particular industries as distinct from giving pupils the basic equipment for *any* vocation. In a geographically mobile society such as our own there is more reason for favouring the second alternative than in the Britain of a century ago. In any case, whatever good reason might be adduced for giving local authorities curricular franchises of this sort, this still would not show that the *overall framework* of school curricula should be left in their hands. If there is no reason why this overall framework should differ from child to child, there is every reason why it should be worked out centrally. How it is implemented in detail may well be a matter for the periphery not the centre. *That* domestic refuse should be collected may be a matter for central legislation; *how* it is done in detail is often best left to local authorities, since they are on the spot and so in the best position to decide. How curricula are implemented in detail is similarly a matter for the periphery. I express this point in this clumsy way because in the case of curricula 'the periphery', for reasons already given, are the *teachers*, not the local authorities. We have still no argument to support control by the latter. This is not to say that local authorities may not, simply because they are on the spot, ensure that their schools do keep to the curriculum framework laid down by the centre. They may well have such a monitoring role. But it has not been shown that they have any right to *determine* curriculum content.

If there is to be central control, what does this imply? This remains to be worked out. What it does *not* imply, I am sure, is that the framework of school curricula is to be decided by central politicians *alone*. Much of the work may be done by others, perhaps not least educationists. Whether this results in legislation, or a combination of legislation and non-mandatory guidelines as in Sweden, is also as yet undetermined. But whoever does the work must be doing it under the direction and control of the political authorities.

References

1 HOLLIS, M. (1971) 'The Pen and the Purse', *Proceedings of the Philosophy of Education Society*, Vol. V, No. 2, July 1971.

4.4 Teacher accountability

Hugh Sockett

[...] Since the war public expenditure on education has risen dramatically in real terms. This disposition of national resources may not meet the full-blooded commitment to equality of opportunity that Halsey[1] demands, but it does suggest a determination to pursue educational quality with a wider distribution of resources. That period of expansion is over. Results have not matched expectations; so, much exiguous and ill-informed comment is popularly heard on standards of literacy, comprehensive education, student mores and the proliferation of Higher Education provision. Postgraduate education, it is claimed, should be geared not to student whim and professorial fancy but to the needs of industry.[2] The problems are significant even if the comment is banal. Their constant reiteration in times of economic retrenchment will doubtless contribute to the issue of teacher accountability coming to the top of the national educational agenda.

Few would deny that teachers should be accountable. That is an empty assertion, however, unless the form, extent and character of their accountability is clearly adumbrated. The form of teacher accountability most widely known is that currently in vogue in the USA, and it is against this 'utilitarian' model that an alternative may be developed. In this paper, I will first indicate the important accountability questions, dealing briskly with the problem of meaning within which I will note a significant distinction between accountability based on the achievement of specified *results* and accountability based on *principles* governing practice. Second, I will set out briefly the 'utilitarian' model with its results base and indicate its more crippling deficiencies. In the third section I will make a fresh start, suggesting that a 'professional' model of teacher accountability based on principles enshrined in a professional code of practice is worth consideration. This I will attempt to explain and justify in terms of four main features. Finally I will indicate some implications of the model for the teaching profession. [...]

I The meaning of accountability

The purpose of a system of accountability is to maintain and improve the quality of educational provision and, where possible, to provide information to show that this is being done. *Inter alia* discussion of teacher accountability raises initially the following questions: To whom should a

Source: *Proceedings of the Philosophy of Education Society of Great Britain*, Vol. X, July 1976, pp. 34–55.

teacher be accountable, for what, and how do proposals for accountability find practical implementation? Answers will both contain and imply perspectives on the character and purpose of schools, of teachers, and the proper relationships between schools, teachers, parents and others who are party to the educational enterprise. Such implications will be manifest throughout the paper. Yet answers to these questions also presuppose some clarity about the meaning of accountability.

[...] One distinction is of importance which, in terms of the differing conceptions of moral responsibility with which we are familiar, is unsurprising. It is this. An agent may accept accountability for specified results which issue from the exercise of his skill, results which, say, find an ultimate reality on the balance sheet. Alternatively an agent may accept accountability in terms of adherence to standards, to action-guiding principles embedded in a professional code of practice. Law and Medicine may be obvious examples. Thus accountability systems may be distinct in terms of either

(a) the accountability of the agent to providers as beneficiaries of the agent's skills in handling resources, as measured by *results*, or
(b) the accountability of an agent, not to providers or beneficiaries alone, but to client-beneficiaries *and* to professional peers charged with the maintenance of *standards* embodied in codes of practice.

The centrality of either conception within a particular system of accountability does not *ipso facto* exclude the other. Results may well be informative in determining whether principles have been adhered to: after all, the patient did die. Sharp practice in commerce may well be frowned upon by provider-beneficiaries who nevertheless want the best results. We may note, *en passant*, one additional implication within the differing systems which springs from the delineation of these conceptions of accountability. A results-based conception allows the development of institutional hierarchies of accountability: the buck can always be passed. In the system based on adherence to standards, as in moral responsibility, the buck always stops here.

It remains a matter for choice and argument as to which basis is adopted and how, within a particular system, the relationships between the two is erected. My guess is that, in teaching, we have seen ourselves accountable in terms of a results-based model such that, while we do talk of professional standards or professional ethics, we are talking of a rather narrow area of 'misconduct'. Our 'standards' of professional performance in the classroom are our achievements. I would not seek to deny that a teacher should not aim for results in terms of what a learner masters. Rather, as I hope to show, firm adherence to a results-based model of accountability can lead to crippling consequences. It is thus appropriate to examine what a model based on standards in terms of adherence to principles would look like and how we might seek to develop it. The best example of the dangers of extending the results-based model can be seen in some current practices in the USA.[3] This 'utilitarian' model I will now briefly describe and criticize.

II The 'utilitarian' model of teacher accountability

Since the behavioural objectives model of curriculum planning-and-evaluation got a dusty reception from teachers in the USA, its proponents have used political machinery to enforce it in the schools. The behavioural objective, in its pure form, states what the learner is to do having engaged in a learning experience. Its clarity ensures wide audiences. It must be measurable. When incorporated within an *accountability* system, its held advantages are its adherence to good managerial policy, the facility with which public validity can be given to schooling practices and the consequent effective use of resources.

Where accountability springs from this base, the teacher is *accountable* to the public as *tax-paying providers*, through appropriate bodies acting on its behalf. There is concern, of course, with the rights of minority groups, but these are conceived as not getting their share of *public* resources. Educational administrators become the auditors. The teacher is thus *not* accountable to the citizentry *qua* parent, or employer, or to his professional peers: he is certainly not accountable to non-taxable infants. Children and parents become customers. The central focus of the system is on 'results obtained for resources used'.[4] The crudity of the model may be softened in part by overlapping roles, e.g. taxpayers are sometimes parents, but the fundamental conception of the system entails public benefit. Children go to school and are taught what they are taught for public purposes.

The teacher is *accountable* for the achievement of pre-specified performances by children he teaches, performances which embody the desired objectives. Such a purpose is defined in contract: the teacher is 'contracting to perform a service ... according to agreed-upon terms, within an established time-period and with a stipulated use of resources and performance standards'.[5] 'Performance-contracting' has come to have a specific connotation in the USA where commercial enterprises contract to produce specified learning outcomes in certain school districts: but the centrality of accountability for the performance of learners pertains generally throughout the model.

Three additional features complete this model in outline. First, children's performances are assessed against the pre-determined objectives through tests administered by teachers, but not, of course, designed by them. Second, considerable publicity may be given to test-results, just as companies publish the results of the year's trading. Third, there is a firm link between these results and the provision of resources. Improved test-scores may merit bonus payments for teachers, or increased provision for the school. Added to the notion of redress is that of incentive.

'Accountability,' writes Lessinger, 'suggests penalties and rewards: accountability without redress or incentive is mere rhetoric.'[6]

[. . .] Among the galaxy of inadequacies [in the model] I would pick out the following:

(a) The model assumes that measuring a child's performance is a fair and valid way of evaluating a teacher's skills. This assumption may be supported by asserting that it is only his skill in improving test-scores that matters, but at the price of ignoring such factors as the child's emotional and physical state, his background experience, his attitudes to the tests, and so on. Once these factors are admitted, which I would be inclined to do, the efficacy of the system becomes less plausible. [. . .]

(b) There is therefore a severe problem in assessing whether the total model works, in its own terms, 'as a way of improving educational quality and proving that this is being done'. If as a legislator I accept the view of quality, I cannot but accept the system. If on the other hand I wonder whether, say, the investment it requires might be better spent on in-service education of teachers, then I must be using criteria in *that* judgment which the model denies.

(c) One can speculate about the social effects of the model, though there is some evidence to hand.[7] Bureaucratic demands on teachers escalate through the administration of testing: the drop in teacher morale in classrooms is accompanied by an increasing militancy among teacher unions. More importantly, however, the 'public' orientation of the model denies a child's and a parent's right to *privacy* in regard to a child's educational performance. That social effects have not been assessed is because the model is in liege to a myth, nicely assailed by Solzhenitzyn in *The First Circle*, namely that 'there are no poor pupils, only bad teachers'.[8]

(d) Pincoffs[9] has elegantly demonstrated the weaknesses of the model where schools are thought of as providing an education. Educational goals, he suggests, consist in the development of excellence. Excellences are indeterminate dispositions, i.e. a disposition which does not consist in my reaching or acting in the same or similar ways when certain sorts of circumstances are present. Wittiness, modesty, prudence and love of animals he gives as examples. These cannot be defined prespecifically in behavioural terms: thus neither excellences nor educational goals can be so defined. That being so, if the goals are educational, the model cannot be practised successfully. Indeed, the establishment of determinate dispositions as the ends of education, accompanied by the practices I have outlined, may lead to 'practices which are far from producing intellectual excellences and excellences of character'.

(e) Since the viability of objectives is determined by their measurability, the objectives of schooling are determined by the measuring techniques we currently have to hand. Determination of objectives is placed largely in the hands of psychometrists whose sophistication in developing attainment criteria in matters of knowledge is not widely acclaimed for its epistemological quality. If x cannot be measured, you can't try to teach it.

(f) The model is politically unacceptable. For the democrat, perhaps the major issue is the reconciliation of private wants with the public interest. From that issue spring three distinct problems for the educator–democrat. First, he must seek to develop a child's wants and expectations, diverse as they may be, within a moral framework. Second, he must promote an understanding of what is publicly desirable and what it is to consider matters through the eye of the public interest. Third, he must promote understanding and skill in the delicate matter of weighing up such conflicting claims morally and prudentially. Now, in one very general sense, such a conception of the educator's task could be conceived as being to the benefit of the 'public'. Yet the model seems to impose on the teacher a much tighter conception of 'public benefit' with the result that he would be obliged to determine the learning outcomes in terms of that narrow conception. Necessarily, therefore, his teaching task, if conceived in the way I have elaborated it here, would be highly restricted.

For these and other reasons, the 'utilitarian' model of teacher accountability simply will not do. A fresh start is needed, and it could be that a model based on adherence to principles would be more appropriate.

III Towards a 'professional' model of teacher accountability

The 'professional' model would be distinguished from the 'utilitarian' model in four major ways:

First, accountability would be *for* adherence to principles of practice rather than *for* results embodied in pupil performances;

Second, accountability would be rendered *to* diverse constituencies rather than *to* the agglomerate constituency of the public alone;

Third, the teacher would be regarded as an autonomous professional, not as a social technician, within the bureaucratic framework of a public education system and a school;

Fourth, the *evaluation* through measurement of pupil performances (the '*how*' of accountability) would be replaced by a conception of evaluation as providing information for constituents allied to a system of redress through a professional body.

In this section I propose to explain and justify each of these features.

(a) Accountability for what?

We can only be accountable for what is within our control. In this section I will argue that there are strong limitations on what is within our control as teachers in terms of pupils' performances, limitations which render the results-base ineffectual. I will then go on to indicate the possibilities of a model based on principles of practice.

(i) The limits of a teacher's control over learning outcomes

Three things are noticeably *within* a teacher's control: First, the way in which he adheres to standards of professional conduct *vis-à-vis* pupils and colleagues, e.g. his neglect of pupil A in favour of pupil B, his failure to pull his weight in a cooperative curriculum enterprise; second, the extent to which he takes steps to inform his own understanding of his work, the extent to which he seeks insight and the extent to which he brings the insight to bear on what he does; third, the *conditions* he establishes and the *opportunities* he creates for children to learn.

However his control over what children in fact achieve through learning is limited in three ways. First, there are empirical or quasi-empirical constraints. Second, there are logical and conceptual limits derived, I will argue, from the concept of learning. Third, there are moral and educational constraints.

The teacher, it has been suggested, cannot control a wide range of factors which affect a child's learning. More significantly, however, a teacher cannot set upper limits, as it were, on what children in fact learn while they are under his tutelage. Over and above, or besides, the things he wants them to learn, they may well learn other things: how to opt out of lessons while remaining physically present, how to deal with bad-tempered adults, or, like Oakeshott, 'grace, economy and style'.[10] Where undesired learnings are spotted, a teacher may take preventive action. But it is in fact, and perhaps in principle, difficult to see how any learning situation could be controlled such that a boundary could be erected around what is being learnt. The obvious character of this observation is given insufficient recognition. Teachers are blamed for the arts-science imbalance in Higher Education: schools are blamed for Johnny's truancy or Susan's suicide. That they share a responsibility is unexceptionable; that such things are within a teacher's control is quite implausible.

Second, and more philosophically interesting, is the possibility of logical and conceptual limits on a teacher's control of the results pupils achieve through learning. This is particularly important to notice where it is the pupil's knowledge achievements that are under consideration.

To believe *p*, where *p* is true, logically entails among other things that the believer assent to the truth of *p*. Authentic assent is voluntarily given: given under duress, we can never be sure that it is assent to the truth of *p* rather than simply collapse under pressure. Where a pupil is learning true beliefs, *his* achievement is marked by *his* giving his assent to *p*. To regard his giving assent as someone else's achievement is to deny the voluntariness of his assent. (This logical point may be also framed as a moral objection: to regard his assent as someone else's achievement is to devalue truth.)

Unfortunately, educational thought has been bedevilled by a

portmanteau account of learning such that it is now a piece of educational folk-lore to assert that any change in behaviour not brought about by maturation or physio-chemical change is a case of learning. The result is conceptual confusion: for we have to scrape around for words to make the distinctions we need which are locked in the compartments of the portmanteau. We must just kick the baggage out. People have come to hold the beliefs they hold, and they have come to behave in the ways in which they behave, in many different ways: through development, conditioning, hypnosis, exposure to propaganda, through learning and so on. The teacher's interest is in changes brought about through a person *learning* and perhaps also through development. You can get people to acquire beliefs or behave as you want in all sorts of ways: through learning is simply one of them.

It is surely quite unintelligible for us to speak of a person just 'learning' without citing what it is he is learning. Moreover, when he is learning *x*, a person is not doing two things, i.e. learning *and* doing *x*. Rather he is doing *x*, *qua* learner, what he will eventually do, *qua* master. Furthermore, the description we give of *x* is of immense importance: for first it contains a description of the discriminable features of *x* to which the learner must pay attention if he is to *learn*, and second, within *x* are the norms and standards whereby we (and he) judge whether he has learnt and is now a master. Of course it doesn't matter a logical jot whether he is aware of these features or the norms if he is just being got to acquire *x* in ways other than by learning. His assent to a belief, and his awareness however dim that he has reached the standard, *when* that is acquired through learning is *the* signal of his achievement. It is his very own. So the view that this is the teacher's achievement arises from the view of learning as any old form of behaviour-modification. The teacher can control 'learning' perhaps in *that* sense. Certainly, teachers do see children's examination performances as their own glories or failures. Embedded in classroom expectations too are pressures for assent, not under any aspect of truth, but because there is a syllabus to be covered, there's only five minutes to the bell, or a variety of other forms of institutional duress.

This is, of course, a very strong claim: it is further influenced by the fact that knowledge-achievements rather than, say, skills have been taken as the object of teaching and learning. Nevertheless, it may point us towards a much closer consideration of the teacher's task as establishing *conditions* and *opportunities* for learning, still within a conception of teaching as a goal-directed activity. It certainly indicates that, in considering the results of a teaching–learning transaction, it is not to the teacher's achievements *only* that we must attend.

For thirdly, there is something *educationally* inapropos about the view that the child's achievements in learning are the teacher's, for precisely part of the teacher's task, *qua* educator, is to get children to accept responsibility for their own learning, *not* to give their assent to beliefs without due consideration of evidence, to exercise autonomy and judgment, not under a teacher's control.

If therefore we shift our conception of the way in which the teacher is accountable away from an emphasis on the results of learning and towards the quality (and thus the standards) of the conditions and opportunities the teacher established, we have a very different basis for an account-ability system. Of course, our judgment about whether a teacher reaches those standards may well be influenced by the results, e.g. the pupils have learnt nothing. Yet if the point of a system of accountability is to improve the teaching enterprise, a system which focuses on the quality of the procedures judged in terms of professional standards may well prove much more appropriate than a results-based conception. Articulating the standards clearly would enable us to ensure that we, as teachers, live up to them.

(ii) Accountability for principles of practice
Peters[11] has indicated the importance of principles of procedure through his discussion of the aims of the educator and the distinction he makes between 'matter' and 'manner'. From a different perspective Parker and Rubin[12] have attacked the notion of the content of a curriculum as a product and have spoken of content as process: how children learn x is part of what they are learning. Many of the central aims which we have as educators must also guide our practice. From such aims, seen as principles of procedure we may be able to develop a code of practice which would take us from the formality of the principles to the substantive detail of a code.

Among educational ends of the highest importance are a concern for truth and rationality, objectivity and open-mindedness, i.e. the personal and intellectual qualities of the educated man. If we see these as ends we may ask: How do we teach them? How do we get children to learn them? What means can we take to these ends? Now that question, 'What means do we use?', is not much, if anything, of an *empirical* question. For two reasons: first, if we value these ends, as we must, then we must have them guide our own thought and conduct inside and outside the classroom. Such values, in other words, must be instantiated in our own practice. Second, if to acquire such propensities and dispositions through *learning* demands paying attention to their discriminable features, then a teacher must make those features a part of what and how he teaches, part of the ends and the means. It is thus a conceptual point that we teach children to be impartial by ourselves being impartial. Indeed it is difficult to see how a child could ever become impartial without having his attention drawn to the relevant features of experience which make being impartial what it is.

The major source for our principles of practice as teachers therefore derive from the ends we have as educators. An educator must be con-cerned for the truth, be prepared to entertain counter-arguments, search for reasons and so on. This is not simply a technique in teaching which might be dropped if found to be unsatisfactory: it governs educational practice. If we set out these major principles, we can then examine in detail our classroom practice, the appropriateness of the mixture of our teaching acts and practices in the light of these principles. A familiar problem, for example, is that some uses of questioning children in classrooms leads to children not seeking the truth, or attempting to articulate their own point of view, but *guessing* at the answer they think the teacher wants. Observation of classrooms may still be in its infancy: but it has shown considerable promise as a source for elaborating a code of professional practice *vis-à-vis* the practice of teaching.

(b) Accountability to whom?

The teacher ought to be accountable to a range of constituencies and within them different constituents. Parents and children may be seen as homogeneous constituencies: but merely to say that is to invite an immediate riposte on the importances of considering the individuals within those constituencies. The agglomerate constituency of the public may be seen under different descriptions, not merely as taxpaying beneficiaries demanding results for resources. Professional colleagues, colleges, universities, providing authorities and employers each may be seen as the teacher's constituencies. It is simply facile to wish away this plurality of interest in a democracy: a system of accountability must respect it.

It may be thought that the notion of a 'constituency' is misleading here: for, to be sure, they are not *voters*. The point is, however, that education is properly a matter for public concern and that concern will no doubt be manifest within different perspectives or pressure-groups. The curriculum and its content is equally and properly a matter of public concern. Recently there has been talk of the curriculum as a 'negotiated covenant' between the parties concerned. The point of using the term 'constituency' is to draw attention to the double-sided aspect of accountability: that is the drawing-up of the contract and the obligation to deliver an account. However, we need not suppose that education is palpably desirable to many constituents, nor that particular curricula have perspicuous worth. Constituents (like voters) have to be wooed. They also have a right to full explanation and justification of the curricula mounted in schools, and no doubt their opinions will influence the decisions of curriculum-makers.

(c) The teacher as an accountable autonomous professional

Within the confines of this paper it is difficult to do justice to the complexity of issues that will be raised. (Perhaps inevitably the paper reads more like a tract or an agenda.) With the despatch of the 'utilitarian' model, however, there goes the implied notion of the teacher as a social technician, or as Musgrove and Taylor[13] put it, the teacher as an 'expert in means', the parent on their view being the 'expert in ends'. Means, as I have indicated, may also be ends: their conception of the teacher thus becomes largely incoherent. In this section I want first to notice some of the problems of the professional in a bureaucracy. Second, I will simply stake the claim for taking the teacher as an autonomous professional as the base, allowing that limitations have to be explored and justified.

(i) The professional in a bureaucracy

Schein[14] lists the characteristics of a profession as: based on a specialized body of knowledge, requiring a prolonged education; making judgments on the basis of general principles; providing a service for clients; itself as a body defining the criteria of membership; recognizing only members of the profession as entitled to judge a member's actions. Different professions may or may not meet the characteristics viewed as criteria: but they are not claimed to be necessary and sufficient conditions.

Deschoolers apart, we have to regard teaching in publicly maintained schools as set within a bureaucratic system at the macro level of the system and the micro system of the school. A bureaucracy I am taking to be 'the institutional expression of rational authority': there we will find clearly defined rules establishing the boundaries of an office-holder's authority. Delineation of the boundaries cannot in general be totally unambiguous: but in teaching there is little attempt to delimit them, even formally. The contemporary conception of the teacher oscillates between regarding him as an employee and as a professional.[15] *Qua* employee, his work is set within the hierarchical structure of the system and the school; it is judged by many who are not his professional peers (at least under one description), but who have rights to make such judgments. The teacher does not choose his clients: he does not determine numbers of entry to the profession (though his unions are consulted): he has some say in selection. On the other hand, his work is based on specialized skills and knowledge (though we may think *that* somewhat exiguous); he requires a prolonged education, and he is not inappropriately seen as providing a service.

Such a difference of perspective – the teacher as employee and the teacher as professional – suggests a considerable *tension* between the two. As we look around, that tension is paramountly clear, although many of the system's afficionados are themselves unclear about their role. HMIs, surely the most promising candidates by history and convention for bureaucratic officers, have engaged in a shift of role from inspector to adviser and friend, though there are signs of an imminent reversion to type. Some Headmasters, by convention powerful executives, seek to democratize decision-making in schools as opposed to simply delegating it. The public furore over dismissals of Headmasters celebrates the tension. Vice-Chancellors and Polytechnic Directors too are not without their difficulties. Put at its most simple and most common, one can meet with teachers who both expect classroom autonomy *and* expect to be told what to do. The trouble is that the rationale for a professional in a bureaucratic system has not been worked out. Offered here are some preliminary thoughts.

(ii) Academic freedom and the autonomous professional
[...] If we assume that we are after the development of a child's rational autonomy when we educate him, we are seeking to maximize his ability as a chooser. That end is to be acquired by learning. It is not clear how that could be conducted by teachers whose autonomy *vis-à-vis* subject-matter was severely constrained. Now such autonomy is not to be confused with arbitrary whim unrestrained by demands for reason and judgment. Defensible rational judgments made by autonomous professionals will be (and are) made within a corpus of understanding shared by particular groups of professionals. The presumption, however, must lie on the side of autonomy. Maximizing it may be a long business: central control may well stifle it, whatever enlightened form it takes. So you may make the teacher accountable by trying to control what he may teach and how he teaches through legislation, and you may back that up with sanctions, redress and incentives. If you want to improve him as an educator, you had best seek to improve his understanding: maybe you too will learn something reciprocally by doing just that.

(d) Accountability – how?

It has been briefly indicated, by characterizing differing clientele as constituents, that public explanation and justification is important. Currently teachers see their accountability in the form of school reports or examination results. Much bureaucratic accountability is secret: why should not an HMI report on a school be published? Teachers can terrify children, bore them to death, physically and mentally assault them with impunity and without redress: in some quarters the boot is on the pupil's foot. Kogan[16] has recently complained that Education has not been put within the purview of the Local Government Ombudsman. So there is a case for the profession to put its house in order. It may indeed be forced to do that as systems of parental choice of secondary schools develop and push schools into the market place. With a declining birth-rate and a superfluity of teachers, the pressures on the profession will increase. Competition has already arrived within Higher Education, of course. It will be appropriate therefore for the profession to devise its own procedures for teacher accountability.

The 'professional' model, given the features already outlined, would find practical implementation in two complementary ways. First the profession should constitute a form of government, with public cooperation, which would take the style and authority of a craftsman's guild, having responsibility for the maintenance of a professional code of practice and supervision of standards of entry to the profession. Within the system care should be taken to establish easy access for all who seek redress. Such a form could only with difficulty, I believe, be grafted on to the current purposes of teachers' unions whose functions are importantly different. Preferably such a government would recognize no status differential *qua* teacher between the University teacher and, say, the Infant teacher.

Second, that body should establish, in conjunction with its constituencies, modes of evaluation of the work of the profession which, in Macdonald's[17] terms are 'democratic' rather than 'bureaucratic'. The 'bureaucratic' evaluator reports to his superiors, employers or backers: the 'democratic' evaluator reports to an informed citizenry who have a 'right to know'. It is on this second notion of evaluation that I wish to expand briefly in the remainder of this part of the paper.

One problem for the 'utilitarian' model, is as Williams[18] has pointed out, that it has to take people's preferences, as translated by legislative and bureaucratic psychometrics into educational ends, as what the public *actually* prefer, not what they *might* prefer if they were more informed, for example, by having some idea of what things would be like if these collective or individual preferences (or various alternatives) came off. So we find in LEAs where there is a parental choice scheme operating that parents rarely choose on *educational* grounds, for these have to be clearly articulated.[19] A second major problem for utilitarian conceptions of welfare economics is that they resort to notions of quantifiability of utility when considering the disposition of resources: deciding between 'mending broken arms and looking after the elderly' means taking criteria of measurement like 'number of working days lost'.[20]

Evaluation as measurement of performance by pupils in the utilitarian model suffers both these weaknesses. Alternative preferences are not developed or exposed for rational choice, nor is any strategy for developing the range of choice built in to the system. Equally, crude notions of public benefit become the measure of choice between objectives and 'alternative delivery systems'. What evaluation of schools, teachers and educational programmes must seek to do is to provide information which not only can be understood but which widens the basis on which judgments can be made and preferences expressed. The constituencies to which the teacher is accountable deserve no less. The production of such information, of course, meets problems of objectivity on a massive scale. Macdonald and Walker have suggested that, if we take an objectivity paradigm drawn from, say, History or Anthropology, the presentation of a set of profiles or reports fosters objectivity through explicit contrasting perspectives. Macdonald describes the notion of 'democratic' evaluation thus:

Democratic evaluation is an information service to the whole community about the characteristics of an educational programme. Sponsorship of the evaluation study does not in itself confer a special claim upon this service. The democratic evaluator recognizes value pluralism and seeks to represent a range of interests in his issue formulation. The basic value is an informed citizenry, and the evaluator is a broker in exchanges of information between groups who want knowledge of each other. His techniques of data-gathering and presentation must be accessible to non-specialist audiences. His main activity is the collection of definitions of, and reactions to, the programme. He offers confidentiality to informants and gives them control over his use of the information they provide. The report is non-recommendatory and the evaluator has no concept of information misuse.... The criterion of success is the range of audiences served. The report aspires to 'best-seller' status. The key concepts of democratic evaluation are 'confidentiality', 'negotiation' and 'accessibility'. The key justificatory concept is the right to know.[21]

It cannot be claimed that such an approach to evaluation has been perfected, or that it does not confront severe difficulties in the ethics and methodology of case-study, as well as in the presentation of information – some of which may well include measurement results. At this stage in the development of the idea, we should not be surprised at that. What it offers, however, are two possibilities critical to the professional model. First, it suggests a style in which judgments can be made in a systematic way about a teacher's adherence in his practice to a professional code. Second, in its celebration of the 'right to know', it develops the possibility of an increasingly informed conversation between the teacher and the constituencies to which he is accountable.

IV Building the 'professional' model of teacher accountability

If these foundations seem promising, the development of the model upon them will be a lengthy enterprise. Indeed, it will be a continuing development as our understanding of teaching increases. The major implications seem to be:

First, the profession should seek to establish self-government not in any protective spirit but because it can *only* then produce a system of accountability consonant with educational purposes.

Second, the profession should begin to work out a statement of principle on academic freedom.

Third, from such a statement it can begin to devise codes of practice, particularly in the following areas:

  (i) classroom conduct and relationships with pupils,
 (ii) professional conduct in staffrooms and within the hierarchical structure of schools,
(iii) relationships with parents,
 (iv) the implications of self-government in the relationship between schools which are in competition.

Such tasks might be attempted without waiting for legislation on self-government.

Fourth, the statement of principle and the codes of practice would be publicized and they must be accessible to a lay public. They must incorporate possibilities for redress and sanctions, and in cooperation with employers, the development of appropriate procedures for that purpose. [...]

Fifth, the profession should seek to examine the administration of schooling, to disentangle as far as is possible the administrative duties which promotion brings from the lack of rewards good teaching brings. For the craft of teaching is rewarded by promotion away from the craft. Like hospitals, schools might profit from lay administration. In this and other ways the lines between the bureaucratic and the professional aspects of teaching would be more clearly drawn.

Finally, the development of these codes of practice and the appropriate modes of evaluation will depend largely on the development of theoretical work from contributing disciplines in educational theory, particularly in matters of classroom conduct.

Such a programme leaves a number of issues untouched: e.g. exactly who counts as a professional peer? Should the school or the teacher be made accountable? Yet what seems to me of paramount importance is that the issue of teacher accountability should not be conducted within the paradigm of the sterile and redundant form that I have dubbed 'utilitarian', even if imported from elsewhere. We should not be confident that such a model is a non-exportable cultural artefact: indeed, marrying well-tried modes of eleven-plus selection to a revamped Revised Code would not be dissimilar to the 'utilitarian' model. I have attempted in this paper to outline an alternative conception which is, intentionally, crude and subject to considerable modification. We badly need to construct alternative conceptions: badly, because crass versions of teacher accountability could well destroy the educational enterprise we are in business to promote. Philosophers of education should themselves be called to account if no viable alternative appears on the agenda.

Notes and References

1 (1972) *Educational Priority, EPA Problems and Politics*, Vol. 1. London: HMSO.
2 HOUSE OF COMMONS EXPENDITURE COMMITTEE (1974) *Third Report: Post-graduate Education*, Vol. 1. London: HMSO.
3 HOUSE, ERNEST R., RIVERS, W. and STUFFLEBEAM, D. L. 'An Assessment of the Michigan Accountability System', *Phi Delta Kappan*, Vol. LV, No. 10.
4 See LESSINGER, L. M. (1971) 'Accountability for Results: A basic challenge for America's schools', in LESSINGER, L. M. and TYLER, R. W. (eds) (1971) *Accountability in Education*. Washington, Ohio: Charles A. Jones, p. 28.
5 Lessinger, op. cit., p. 29.
6 Op. cit., p. 29.

7 See House, Rivers and Stufflebeam, op. cit.

8 SOLZHENITZYN, A. (1970) *The First Circle*. London: Collins Fontana, p. 38.

9 PINCOFFS, E. L. (1973) 'Educational Accountability', *Studies in Philosophy and Education*, Vol. VIII, No. 2, Fall 1973.

10 OAKESHOTT, M. (1967) 'Learning and Teaching', in PETERS, R. S. (ed.) (1967) *The Concept of Education*. London: Routledge and Kegan Paul.

11 PETERS, R. S. (1959) 'Must an Educator have an Aim?', in *Authority, Responsibility and Education*. London: Allen and Unwin; (1963) *Education as Initiation*, Inaugural Lecture. London: Athlone Press.

12 PARKER, J. A. and RUBIN, L. J. (1966) *Process as Content: Curriculum design and the application of knowledge*. Chicago, Ill.: Rand McNally.

13 MUSGROVE, F. and TAYLOR, P. H. (1969) *Society and the Teacher's Role*. London: Routledge and Kegan Paul.

14 SCHEIN, E. H. (1974) *Professional Education: Some new directions*, Carnegie Commission on Higher Education. New York: McGraw-Hill.

15 This problem was pointed out to me by Rex Gibson.

16 KOGAN, M. (1975) *School Curriculum and Public Accountability*. Address to Third Standing Conference on Curriculum Studies, University of East Anglia, April 1975. Although my approach to the problem is markedly different from Kogan, I heard his paper at a time when my own thoughts were beginning to take shape. As a result, my ideas have been much influenced by him.

17 MACDONALD, B. (1975) 'Evaluation and the Control of Education', in *Safari: Innovation, Evaluation, Research and the Problem of Control: Some interim papers*. Safari Project, CARE, University of East Anglia.

18 See Williams' contribution (particularly pages 135–47) to SMART, J. J. C. and WILLIAMS, B. (1973) *Utilitarianism, For and Against*. London: Cambridge University Press.

19 'Under parental choice the unpopular school has to accept second or third choice, if not numerically fewer pupils where spare capacity exists. Losing out on quantity means a slower growth rate, a lower unit total score, fewer points for above-scale posts and for ancillary staff; hardly attractive to teachers. And losing out on first choices means more than losing the nice feeling that parents believe in you: it usually means you get less than the going proportion of above-average pupils, and a school thus impoverished will find it harder to attract staff, slower to establish a sixth form, and above all lack the enhancing effect of abler pupils in raising expectations (particularly noticeable in mixed-ability work). This effect occurs because when a school is over-subscribed, the off-loaded pupils are those whose parents have produced little or no reason for their choice. In Hertfordshire, parents are advised, "You may wish to seek the advice of the Head of your child's Primary School", and this can only be helpful to the choice procedure. Further, "your wishes and the reasons for your preferences will be important factors taken into account in offering a secondary school place. You should therefore indicate the reasons for your choice, e.g. preference for a denominational school, preference for a single-sex or mixed school, family connexions with a particular school, other educational and medical reasons". Essential and admirable though the "reasons" procedure is, it favours parents (apart from those who have only to write "sister already at school") who can put some sort of case down on paper.' – Extract from HOLT, MAURICE, 'Curriculum Innovation and Community Restraints in a Comprehensive School'. Section paper read at Third Standing Conference in Curriculum Studies, University of East Anglia, 1975.

20 Kogan's examples, op. cit.
21 MACDONALD, B., op. cit., pp. 14–15. See also paper by WALKER, ROB (1975) 'The Conduct of Educational Case Study', same volume.

Index

Acknowledgments

The editors and publisher wish to thank the following for permission to reprint copyright material in this book:

Routledge and Kegan Paul Ltd for 'What is an educational process?' by R. S. Peters from *The Concept of Education* edited by him, also for 'Strategies, decisions and control: interaction in a middle school classroom' by Andy Hargreaves from *Teacher Decision-making in the Classroom* edited by J. Eggleston, for 'The myth of subject choice' by Peter Woods from *British Journal of Sociology*, Vol. 27, No. 2, June 1976, for 'Further education in the 1970s' by Leonard M. Cantor and I. F. Roberts from their book *Further Education Today*, and for 'Social class, ability and opportunity in the comprehensive school' by Julienne Ford from her book *Social Class and the Comprehensive School;* Mr Anthony Crosland and David Higham Associates for an extract from Mr Crosland's book *Socialism Now and Other Essays* published by Jonathan Cape Ltd; Mr Angus Maude for his paper on 'The egalitarian threat' from *Fight for Education: A Black Paper* published by the Critical Quarterly Society; United Nations Educational, Scientific and Cultural Organization for the article 'Education: domestication or liberation?' by Paulo Freire from *Prospects*, Vol. II, No. 2, 1972; Professor Brian Simon and the Philosophy of Education Society of Great Britain for the article 'Problems in contemporary educational theory: a Marxist approach' from *Journal of Philosophy of Education*, Vol. 12, 1978; Mr Correlli Barnett and David Higham Associates for the paper 'Technology, education and industrial and economic strength' from *Journal of the Royal Society of Arts*, No. 5271, Vol. CXXVII, February 1979; Psychology Today Magazine and Ziff-Davis Publishing Company for 'The child as moral philosopher' by Lawrence Kohlberg from *Psychology Today*, September 1968; Macmillan Publishers Ltd, London and Basingstoke, for the extract 'Social anxiety' by Stuart Hall from *Policing the Crisis* by S. Hall, R. Critcher, A. Jefferson, J. Clarke and B. Roberts; Croom Helm Ltd for 'Violence, indiscipline and truancy' by Nigel Wright from his book *Progress in Education;* Professor W. J. Campbell and the Editors of the *Journal of Educational Administration* for the article 'School size: its influence on pupils' from *Journal of Educational Administration*, III, 1, May 1965; Nafferton Books: Studies in Education Ltd for a passage called 'Power and the paracurriculum' by D. Hargreaves from *Power and the Curriculum: Issues in Curriculum Studies* edited by C. Richards, and for a passage called 'Managing the curriculum in contraction' by Ken Shaw from the same book; the Estate of the late Mrs Frieda Lawrence Ravagli and Laurence Pollinger Ltd for an extract from *The Rainbow* by D. H. Lawrence originally published by William Heinemann Ltd; Open Books Ltd for a passage from *Teaching Styles and Pupil Progress* by Neville Bennett; Professor Banesh Hoffmann for the passage called 'A little learning is a dangerous thing: true or false?' from his book *The Tyranny of Testing;* Harper and Row Ltd for a passage called 'The side-effects of assessment' by Derek Rowntree from his book *Assessing Students: How shall we know them?;* Mrs Naomi E. S. McIntosh and her co-authors for the passage called 'Access for whom?' from *Access to Higher Education in England and Wales* by Naomi E. S. McIntosh, Alan Woodley and Moira Griffiths published by The Open University; The Open University for 'Class and meritocracy in British education' by Anthony Heath; Professor Samuel Bowles and Professor Herbert Gintis for the paper 'IQ in the US class structure' contributed to *Social Policy*, Vol. 3, Nos. 4 and 5; Professor Lester C. Thurow and *The Public Interest* for the paper